Advance Praise for

The Parallel Curriculum, Second Edition

"**Q**uality curriculum design requires far more than assigning specific content and skills to grade levels and subjects. *The Parallel Curriculum* provides a comprehensive design model based on four parallel ways of thinking about content in relation to students:

▸ *The Core Curriculum* guides learners to an understanding of the essential nature (content, concepts, principles, and skills) of a discipline.

▸ *The Curriculum of Connections* guides students in the use of common concepts, principles, generalizations and skills to encourage the transfer of knowledge and understanding within, among, and across disciplines, cultures, times, and places.

▸ *The Curriculum of Practice* guides learners in applying the concepts, principles, and methodologies of a discipline as they grow toward expertise.

▸ *The Curriculum of Identity* guides learners in coming to understand their own strengths, preferences, values, and commitment as they reflect on their own development in different fields of study.

"What makes *The Parallel Curriculum* unique in the field of curriculum design is its insistence on the development of conceptual understanding in relation to disciplinary content; and a focus on the abilities, interests, and learning preferences of each student.

"*The Parallel Curriculum* helps us raise the bar further by overlaying the idea of 'ascending intellectual demand.' This edition extends the previous discussion of ascending intellectual demand and provides clear examples from core subject areas to guide educators with their own planning.

"Ascending intellectual demand (AID) articulates the changes that characterize a learner in different incremental stages as they progress from novice to expert. A child can be approaching the expert level in one subject or skill area, yet be a novice level in another area. Ascending intellectual demand is a powerful tool for aiding teachers in providing the optimal level of challenge in curriculum and instruction to meet the emerging needs and abilities of students as they progress from one level to the next in their journey from novice to expert. AID encourages teachers to focus on each student as a learner, how they are changing as learners, and what they need at each stage in their learning journey.

"Quality teaching and learning are complex processes requiring an interplay of relationships, and a passion for intellectual and personal growth and development. *The Parallel Curriculum* provides a path for educators to move form novice toward expert. The clarity of discussion supported by specific examples from classrooms make the model usable for teachers at all levels. As we take the parallel curriculum into practice we will definitely feel more intelligent, more professional, and more effective. And our students will discover themselves as autonomous, self-confident learners."

H. Lynn Erickson
Educational Consultant, Author
Mill Creek, WA

"Five years ago I had the opportunity to open a new middle school. My coordinators and I searched far and wide for an instructional model that *truly* had the potential to teach all students critical thinking and complex problem solving at a high level and *truly* raise student achievement. We wanted our students to succeed *because* of our curriculum, not *in spite of* it. When we found the Parallel Curriculum Model (PCM), we knew we needed to look no further. For teachers, the process of planning and thinking about their content area through the lens of PCM not only strengthens their knowledge and pedagogy, but also, in many cases, helps them rediscover a passion for their discipline based on their own deeper, more connected understanding of it. PCM fundamentally changes the way they think about and teach their subject matter. For students, the depth of investigation and powerful connections made within PCM help them to learn in a real world manner. They think critically and deeply at a level I have never before witnessed, and they quickly come to appreciate the interconnected nature of knowledge and academic study. The questions they ask and the discussion they have are truly stunning. As a principal and instructional leader, PCM has taught me far more about effective instruction and powerful unit and lesson design than anything else I have experienced in 20 years of classroom and administrative experience. PCM is powerful for everyone involved in it. I cannot imagine doing anything else."

Dr. Tony Poole
Principal, Sky Vista Middle School
Aurora, CO

The Parallel Curriculum

A Design to Develop Learner Potential and Challenge Advanced Learners

Carol Ann Tomlinson
Sandra N. Kaplan
Joseph S. Renzulli
Jeanne H. Purcell
Jann H. Leppien
Deborah E. Burns
Cindy A. Strickland
Marcia B. Imbeau

SECOND EDITION

A JOINT PUBLICATION

For information:

Corwin Press
A SAGE Company
2455 Teller Road
Thousand Oaks, CA 91320
www.corwinpress.com

SAGE Pvt. Ltd.
B 1/I 1 Mohan Cooperative Industrial Area
Mathura Road, New Delhi 110 044
India

SAGE Ltd.
1 Oliver's Yard
55 City Road
London EC1Y 1SP
United Kingdom

SAGE Asia-Pacific Pte. Ltd.
33 Pekin Street #02-01
Far East Square
Singapore 048763

Printed in the United States of America

Library of Congress Cataloging-in-Publication Data

The parallel curriculum: a design to develop learner potential and challenge advanced learners/Carol Ann Tomlinson . . . [et al.]: a joint publication with the National Association for Gifted Children. — 2nd ed.
        p. cm.
Includes bibliographical references and index.
ISBN 978-1-4129-6130-1 (cloth) — ISBN 978-1-4129-6131-8 (pbk.)
    1. Gifted children—Education—Curricula. 2. Curriculum planning. I. Tomlinson, Carol A. II. Title.

LC3993.2.P34 2009
371.95'3—dc22   2008030598

This book is printed on acid-free paper.

08   09   10   11   12   10   9   8   7   6   5   4   3   2   1

Acquisitions Editor:	David Chao
Editorial Assistant:	Brynn Saito
Production Editor:	Veronica Stapleton
Copy Editor:	Gretchen Treadwell
Typesetter:	C&M Digitals (P) Ltd.
Proofreader:	Dennis W. Webb
Indexer:	Sheila Bodell
Cover Designer:	Rose Storey
Graphic Designer:	Brian Bello

Contents

Preface to the Second Edition

Nearly ten years ago, the idea that became the Parallel Curriculum Model—or PCM as we have come to call it— had its genesis in a series of conversations between Sandy Kaplan and me. Those elongated conversations, held alternately on the West Coast and East Coast, remain some of the most engaging and challenging of my life. Over the period of a year, Sandy and I sketched out the premise and framework for the Parallel Curriculum Model.

Over the following two years, we expanded the discussion to include colleagues, associates, classroom teachers, and graduate students from across the U.S., inviting them to review and respond to the model. The model benefitted greatly from their counsel.

Ultimately, Jeanne Purcell, Deb Burns, and Jann Leppien signed on to help us "put meat on the bones" of the PCM framework, and became our partners in writing the first edition of *The Parallel Curriculum*.

In time, about a score of noted educators reviewed the draft manuscript. A number of those individuals represented major educational professional groups. Again, they sharpened our thinking and enhanced our work.

The first edition of *The Parallel Curriculum Model* was published in 2002.

Many of the educators who had a hand in originally developing The Parallel Curriculum Model have a background in the education of gifted learners. The Parallel Curriculum Model was initially created with those learners in mind. Those of us who have worked extensively with such students understood that these students are often ill-served by curriculum and instruction aimed at a ceiling of expectations far lower than the one that they can and should reach. For that reason, it was of interest for us to create a contemporary curriculum model that could help teachers extend the considerable intellectual reach of the most able students in our schools. Many of our conversations, and much of the PCM planning, centered around this first understanding.

We also understood a second truth, however. There is no single profile for a highly able or gifted student. There are bright kids whose ability is so overt that no one can miss it. There are kids who are both highly able and learning disabled. There are bright kids who are just learning to speak English, who come from low-income backgrounds, whose performance is muted by issues of gender or race. There are convergently bright kids—and divergently bright ones. There are bright kids who can't wait to go to school each morning, and bright kids who are deeply alienated from school. This second understanding spawned other conversations for us as we tried to ensure that whatever model we developed provided ample room and support for high performing students and for students with the potential to perform well academically, but who do not do so for a stunningly wide variety of reasons.

It is also the case, however, that all of us who authored the first edition have worked with a broad range of students during our educational careers—students of all ages, in many subjects, and a very broad array of learning strengths and needs. We are all champions of better schools and classrooms for kids, and we understand that most students spend too much time working with curriculum and instruction that is "flat" and uninspiring. This third understanding led us, from the beginning, to other conversations and the agreement that virtually all students should work with the kind of curriculum and instruction reflected in PCM.

Said somewhat differently, all of us believe that our schools and the students in those schools would fare much better if educators created curriculum and instruction from the belief that virtually all students would benefit from the very highest quality of curriculum, and then provided a support system to enable most students to work successfully with such curriculum.

In the six years between the first and second edition, all three discussions have continued and expanded.

We have been joined in various PCM writing endeavors by Cindy Strickland, Marcia B. Imbeau, and Kathy Glass. The members of a PhD curriculum seminar at the University of Virginia's Curry School of Education conducted a semester-long, very detailed analysis of our first edition and possible revisions. Professors and students from many colleges and universities have used PCM to study curriculum and to create it. Schools and school districts, both public and private, both in the U.S. and abroad, have adopted PCM as a curriculum model. Once again, our work has been strengthened and our conversations extended by these partnerships.

We hope this second edition of *The Parallel Curriculum* does justice to the interest, time, and investment of many, many people. This new edition does reflect the three ongoing and intertwined conversations that have now spanned a decade. You'll find here a model that makes at least three assumptions. First, it is very important for advanced learners to work with curriculum and instruction designed to serve as a catalyst for their continued advancement as thinkers and learners. Second, to ensure persistently escalating challenge for advanced learners, curriculum developers and teachers must have an understanding of what advanced challenge looks like and a mechanism for consistently incorporating such challenge in curriculum. Third, at a given time, all students are somewhere on a continuum from novice to expert in the various disciplines. The vast majority of those students would benefit from working with rich curriculum designed to engage them with important ideas, enhance their capacity as thinkers, and invite them to address authentic problems as contributing adults do.

Look inside some schools. In many, a limited use of complex multifaceted curriculum will reflect a tacit belief that only a few students are really smart, and they were born that way. In a few schools, broad use of complex, multifaceted curriculum will reflect a tacit belief that many students can be smart if nurtured and supported toward that end. *The Parallel Curriculum* authors are convinced that outcomes for schools and students are predicted by the will of educators to teach far more students as though they were highly capable, and the skill of these educators to do so. We hope the second edition will contribute to both that will and skill.

Carol Ann Tomlinson (2008)

Acknowledgments

The authors, in a variety of ways, have created, nurtured, and refined the vision for the PCM. We signed on for the journey and have benefited from shared conversations, occasional debates, editing, presenting, and teaching around the model.

An unanticipated bonus for all of us has been the work of educators who have taken our work and implemented it into classrooms, schools, and universities. They have, in turn, sent us units, invited us to watch, allowed us to do research, and made suggestions.

Two representatives of this group appear in the second edition. Kelly Hedrick and Jenny Sue Flannigan encountered earlier ideas about the PCM concept of "ascending intellectual demand" and saw the possibility of extending these ideas in ways that could make them more accessible and practical for teachers. The final chapter in this book is largely the result of several years of thought and work on their part. We are grateful for their voluntary partnership, and our work is more potent because of their insights.

It is, of course, our hope that many others will be energized by this new edition of *The Parallel Curriculum* and that they, too, will extend and refine its ideas.

About the Authors

Carol Ann Tomlinson is the William Clay Parrish, Jr. Professor of Educational Leadership, Foundations, and Policy at the University of Virginia's Curry School of Education and Department Chair of Leadership, Foundations, and Policy. Prior to joining the University of Virginia's faculty, she was a classroom teacher for twenty-one years, working at the primary, middle, and high school levels. During that time, she also administered district programs for struggling and advanced learners and she was recognized as Virginia's Teacher of the Year in 1974. Presently, at the University of Virginia, Carol's work focuses largely on curriculum and differentiated instruction. She was named Outstanding Professor at Curry in 2004 and won an All-University Teaching Award in 2008.

Carol is author of over 200 books, book chapters, articles, and professional development materials—many of them on differentiated instruction. Among the books she has authored or coauthored are *How to Differentiate Instruction in Mixed Ability Classrooms, The Differentiated Classroom: Responding to the Needs of All Learners, Fulfilling the Promise of the Differentiated Classroom,* and three *Differentiation in Practice* books for grades K–5, 5–9, and 9–12. Additionally, she coauthored, with Jay McTighe, *Integrating Differentiated Instruction* and *Understanding by Design: Connecting Content and Kids.* Most recently, she coauthored, with Kay Brimijoin and Lane Narvaez, *The Differentiated School: Making Revolutionary Changes in Teaching and Learning.* For the National Middle School Association, she is coauthor with Kristina Doubet of *Smart in the Middle Grades.* On an ongoing basis, Carol works throughout the country and abroad with educators who want to make their schools and classrooms increasingly responsive to academically diverse learners.

Sandra N. Kaplan has been a teacher and administrator of gifted programs in an urban school district in California. Currently, she is Clinical Professor in Learning and Instruction at the University of Southern California's Rossier School of Education. She has authored articles and books on the nature and scope of differentiated curriculum for gifted students. Her primary area of concern is modifying the core and differentiated curriculum to meet the needs of inner-city, gifted learners.

Sandra is a past president of the California Association for the Gifted (CAG) and the National Association for Gifted Children (NAGC). She has been nationally recognized for her contributions to gifted education.

Joseph S. Renzulli is Professor of Educational Psychology at the University of Connecticut, where he also serves as Director of the National Research Center on the Gifted and Talented. His research has focused on the identification and development of creativity and giftedness in young people and on organizational models and curricular strategies for total school improvement. A focus of his work has been on applying the strategies of gifted education to the improvement of learning for all students.

Joseph is a Fellow in the American Psychological Association and was a consultant to the White House Task Force on Education of the Gifted and Talented. From 1968–1969, he was designated a Board of Trustees Distinguished Professor at the University of Connecticut. Although he has obtained more than $20 million in research grants, he lists as his proudest professional accomplishments the UConn Mentor Connection program for gifted young students and the summer Confratute program at the University of Connecticut, which began in 1978 and has served thousands of teachers and administrators from around the world.

Jeanne H. Purcell provides leadership for Advanced Placement and gifted and talented education at the Connecticut State Department of Education. Prior to her work at the State Department of Education, she was an administrator for Rocky Hill Public Schools, where she was a K–8 curriculum coordinator and conducted a three-year staff development initiative on curriculum differentiation; a program specialist with the National Research Center on the Gifted and Talented, where she worked collaboratively with other researchers on national issues related to the achievement of high-achieving young people; and a staff developer for school districts across the country and Canada. She was an English teacher, Grades 7–12, for eighteen years in Connecticut school districts.

Jeanne is the author of five books and has published many articles that have appeared in *Educational Leadership*, *Educational and Psychological Measurement*, *National Association of Secondary School Principals' Bulletin*, *Our Children: The National PTA Magazine*, *Gifted Child Quarterly*, *Parenting for High Potential*, and *Journal for the Education of the Gifted*. Her special interests include curriculum and instruction, with a particular interest in differentiation for all learners.

Jann H. Leppien served as a gifted and talented coordinator in Montana prior to attending the University of Connecticut, where she earned her doctorate in gifted education and worked as a research assistant at the National Research Center for the Gifted and Talented. She is past president of the Montana Association for Gifted and Talented Education and has been a teacher for 31 years—spending 14 of those years working as a classroom teacher, enrichment specialist, and coordinator of the Schoolwide Enrichment Model in Montana. Currently, she is an associate professor in the School of Education at the University of Great Falls in Montana. She teaches graduate and undergraduate courses in gifted education, educational research, curriculum, and assessment as well as creativity and methods courses in social studies. Her research interests include teacher collaboration, curriculum design, underachievement, and planning instruction for advanced learners. She also works as a consultant to teachers in the field of gifted education and curriculum design. Jann is coauthor of *The Multiple Menu Model: A Practical Guide for Developing Differentiated Curriculum* and *The Parallel Curriculum: A Design to Develop High Potential and Challenge High-Abiility Students*. She is active in the National Association for Gifted Children (NAGC), serving as a board member and newsletter editor of the Curriculum Division, and is a board member of the Association for the Education of Gifted Underachieving Students.

Deborah E. Burns's work with differentiation began with her undergraduate education at Michigan State University. After graduating in 1973, Deb applied that training to a remedial K-8 reading and math curriculum for Title I learners in a rural school in Michigan. She received her master's degree in Reading Supervision from Ashland University in 1978 and continued work as a middle school reading specialist and an intermediate agency administrator for gifted education. Deb later received her doctoral degree in Educational Psychology from the University of Connecticut in 1987. For fifteen years, she taught courses in curriculum, instruction, thinking skills, differentiation, and talent development. During that time she also conducted research; wrote books, chapters, and articles about differentiation; and served as a professional development consultant and as a program evaluator in school districts nationwide.

Deb currently is currently the K–8 Curriculum Coordinator for the Cheshire (CT) Public Schools and teaches part-time for Quinnipiac University. With Deb's guidance, Cheshire teachers and administrators have been working on their differentiation initiative for several years. They are in their seventh year of implementing a differentiated reading curriculum and in their third year of practice with a differentiated writing curriculum. Preassessment, small group learning, and standards-based lessons and student work are crucial elements of this work. Their current focus resolves around math differentiation and the needs of special education students and high achieving learners. Deb has two children, eighteen and twenty-two, and lives in Berlin, Connecticut.

Cindy A. Strickland has been a teacher for twenty-five years and has worked with students of all ages, from kindergarteners to graduate students. A member of the Association for Supervision and Curriculum Development (ASCD) Differentiation Faculty Cadre, Cindy works closely with Carol Ann Tomlinson and has coauthored several books and articles with her. In the past eight years, Cindy's consulting work has taken her to forty-six states, five provinces, and three continents where she has provided workshops on topics relating to differentiation, the Parallel Curriculum Model (PCM), and gifted education.

Cindy's publications include *The Parallel Curriculum Model in the Classroom: Applications Across the Content Areas, Multimedia Kit for the Parallel Curriculum* (a finalist for the 2006 Association of Educational Publishers (AEP) Distinguished Achievement Award), and *In Search of the Dream: Designing Schools and Classrooms That Work for High Potential Students From Diverse Cultural Backgrounds*. Publications in differentiation include *Tools for High Quality Differentiated Instruction: An ASCD Toolkit, Differentiation in Practice: A Resource Guide for Differentiating Curriculum, Grades 9–12*, a unit in the book *Differentiation in Practice: A Resource Guide for Differentiating Curriculum, Grades 5–9*, and the ASCD online course Success with Differentiation. She is currently working on an ASCD Action Tool on differentiated staff development.

Marcia B. Imbeau is Associate Professor at the University of Arkansas, Fayetteville, where she teaches graduate courses in gifted education and elementary education. She is actively involved with University/Public School Partnerships and teaches in a local elementary school as a university liaison. Her professional experience includes serving as a field researcher for the National Research Center on the Gifted and Talented, elementary teaching in the regular classroom, teaching in programs for the gifted, and coordinating university-based and Saturday programs for advanced learners. Marcia has been a board member for the National Association for Gifted Children and has served as a Governor At-Large for the Council for Exceptional Children—The Association for the Gifted Division. She is a past president of Arkansans for Gifted and Talented Education, a state organization that supports appropriate instructional services for all students.

Marcia's publications include "Designing a Professional Development Plan," appearing in J. H. Purcell and R. D. Eckert's *Designing Services and Programs for High-Ability Learners: A Guidebook for Gifted Education;* and she is coauthor with B. C. Gartin, N. L. Murdick, and D. E. Perner of *How to Use Differentiated Instruction With Students With Disabilities in the General Education Classroom as a Service Publication for the Council for Exceptional Children*. Additionally, Marcia is a member of the ASCD's Differentiated Instruction Cadre, which provides support and training to schools interested in improving their efforts to meet the academically diverse learning needs of their students.

For those who came before us and had the insights on which we build,
For those who taught us with artistry that revealed to us curriculum as a language for
the mind and heart,
For those who have stood beside us and encouraged us,
For those who have translated what we have envisioned into classroom practice,
All of us are debtors to all of you.

The Rationale and
Guiding Principles for an
Evolving Conception of Curriculum

A Word to New Parallel Curriculum Model Readers About This Chapter

There are few professions in which practitioners must make as many decisions as teachers do, or in which practitioners must make decisions as rapidly as teachers must. Teaching is a decision-driven profession. *The Parallel Curriculum*'s authors believe strongly that educators need to build an increasingly stronger rationale for the curriculum they develop or teach. Educators are more confident and more competent when they are grounded in the theory and research that relates to curriculum and instruction. Simply put, they make better decisions when the decisions are well-informed. For that reason, we have elected to begin this book with a brief exploration of the underpinnings of the Parallel Curriculum Model, or PCM.

We also understand, however, that readers new to the model may prefer to learn first about the model itself and to learn about how the theory undergirds it once the model is clearer in the reader's mind. Therefore, while we hope all users of PCM will come to understand and draw upon the model's rich heritage, we invite new readers to decide whether to begin an exploration of the model by first studying its root system—or to defer that exploration for a later time. In other words, you may begin your study of PCM with this background chapter, or with Chapter 2, which introduces the Parallel Curriculum Model itself.

Reasons for Another Curriculum Model

The quest for learning and the desire to create are essential human behaviors. These behaviors are also the key goals of our profession. As teachers, we understand that it is our responsibility to help young people understand the past so that they might invent a better future.

The same is true about the curriculum model presented within the covers of this book. The authors of this book spent several years asking and attempting to answer their own vexing questions about teaching, learning, and curriculum. As a study group, we examined the structure of knowledge, the characteristics of today's students, research-based instructional strategies, the demands of the future, and our existing structures for writing and implementing curriculum.

Our reading, writing, and conversations resulted in a shared vision for an evolved concept for curriculum. This vision redefines curriculum not as a static set of facts, details, and skills that we expect all students to learn and remember, but instead as a dynamic design process that allows all learners to make powerful and varied connections between their own prior knowledge, interests, and experiences and the essential concepts, principles, skills, habits, and applications within a discipline.

Unlike traditional curriculum models, the Parallel Curriculum Model suggests that the entry point for curriculum decisions should be our knowledge of our learners' characteristics—their strengths, needs, interests, questions, goals, perspectives, and prior experiences. It is our shared belief that high-quality curriculum can honor the essential understandings within a subject area and yet be implemented through a teaching and learning framework that can be modified and adjusted to better meet small groups of learners' essential characteristics and profiles. Used in this manner, curriculum builds a bridge between students' characteristics and the essential content knowledge; curriculum becomes a bridge over which all learners want to cross and need to feel safe and supported in doing so.

A reasonable question prior to an examination of the model of curriculum development proposed in this book is "Why do we need to think differently about curriculum than we have in the past?" Why do we need another model to guide development of curriculum? We suggest at least three reasons that seem compelling to us. We invite readers to add to the list.

1. Our students have different characteristics than they did in the past.

Over the past few decades, both our society and the characteristics of young learners have changed dramatically. Today's society is much more technology-driven, information saturated, faster paced, global, multicultural, consumer-oriented, and pluralistic in its viewpoints and ideas. As such, society demands a greater capacity to adapt to change than was the case in past generations. It also requires workers to be more specialized and more adaptable.

It is not surprising, then, that in order to thrive in such a society, our young people need to be more connected to a wider network of ideas, experiences, people, and support systems than in earlier times. And, it is also not surprising that young people are more demanding and powerful consumers of education than they have been traditionally. They are often open and frank about their need for a relevant, practical, authentic, challenging, and personally rewarding school experience. There is a need for a concept of curriculum to meet these demands.

While we believe there are constant elements in effective curriculum and instruction (described in later sections of the book), we also believe effective curriculum must be proactively responsive to the learner and his or her world. An appreciation of contemporary learners, their world, and the need to maximize the capacity of each learner led us to make conclusions about curriculum design that guided our work.

All curricula are based on such belief systems. The authors suggest that their belief system (that curriculum should respond to the characteristics and needs of the learner) should be collaboratively discussed and analyzed prior to adoption or implementation of PCM. The authors' underlying assumptions follow:

▶ Curriculum should guide students in mastering key information, ideas, and the fundamental skills of the disciplines.

▶ Curriculum should help students grapple with complex and ambiguous issues and problems.

▶ Curriculum should guide students in progressing from novice toward expert levels of performance in various subject areas.

▶ Curriculum should provide students opportunities for original, creative, and practical work in the disciplines.

▶ Curriculum should help students encounter, accept, and embrace challenge.

▶ Curriculum should help students uncover, recognize, and apply the significant and essential concepts and principles in each subject area that explain the structure and workings of the discipline, human behavior, and our physical world.

▶ Curriculum should help students develop a sense of themselves as well as of their possibilities in the world in which they live.

▶ Curriculum should be compelling and satisfying enough to encourage students to persist despite frustration and understand the importance of effort and collaboration.

2. Changing views of intelligence should influence curriculum development.

Building on the work of predecessors such as Alfred Binet (1916), psychologists like Robert Sternberg (1985), Howard Gardner (1993), and Carol Dweck (1999, 2006) have made convincing cases asserting that we should understand intelligence more broadly and flexibly than we have in the past. A careful review of their work teaches us that intelligence is more fluid and less fixed than we might have once imagined. Environment and opportunity can absolutely affect one's intellectual capacity. In addition, intelligence is developmental, and its development differs among individuals. Therefore, educators should be prepared for variability in the development of intelligence in children and be ready to support a range of developmental stages and needs in a single learning environment. We have also learned that rather than the existence of one kind of "intelligence," there are "intelligences," and they are evident in the full range of human endeavors. Therefore, we must understand that intelligence is expressed somewhat differently in different cultures and microcultures.

If the assumptions mentioned above are accurate, as psychologists have believed and demonstrated for the better part of a century, then as educators, we are remiss if we ignore our responsibility to nurture and develop any of those intelligences in our students. Education ought to be about providing environments and opportunities to maximize individual capacity. Therefore, educators should be aware of varied intelligences, and subsequently design learning opportunities that honor diverse perspectives and develop multiple aspects of intelligence.

These beliefs about human intelligence lead us to make at least four key conclusions regarding curriculum design. These conclusions guided our work in developing the Parallel Curriculum Model. First, because environment and opportunity affect intelligence, curriculum for virtually all learners should be rich in opportunities for learners to explore and expand a wide range of intelligences and abilities. That is, we should not restrict the highest quality curriculum and instruction to a few students whom we have decided are "smart," while assuming that other students cannot succeed with—and would not benefit from—such learning experiences. Second, we should design curriculum in ways that both identify and develop high capacity in the broadest possible range of intelligences and learners. Third, curriculum should be flexible enough to address variability in how talent develops over time in a broad range of learners, intelligences, and talent areas. Fourth, curriculum should plan for development of intelligences in ways that are valid for an intelligence area and the domains in which it is expressed.

3. Evolving curriculum should honor the leaders of the past by drawing on their work to build the future.

From the earliest days, pioneering educators have challenged the status quo of teaching and learning in an attempt to ensure appropriate learning opportunities for their learners. In that vein, we offer three assertions related to our work with the Parallel Curriculum Model. First, roots of the past will be clearly evident in curriculum models of the future. Second, curriculum models for the future will differ from the past in ways that are very clear. Third, if the model we propose here has utility in the near term, the time will come when its role will be to join the root system of the past and invite other educators to challenge its assumptions in order to push forward the thinking of the field.

Theoretical and Research-Based Underpinnings of the Parallel Curriculum Model

The Parallel Curriculum Model provides direction for the development of lessons and curriculum units that vary in significant ways from much traditional curriculum. In this era of accountability, it seems appropriate that the authors of *The Parallel Curriculum Model* provide compelling research and a theoretical base for recommendations that depart from the status quo. This section of the chapter provides that link.

The Parallel Curriculum Model extends the ideas of respected educational theorists and researchers such as Bandura (1977), Bruner (1960), Csikszentmihalyi (1990), Dewey (1938), Dweck (1996), Gardner (1993), Glasser (1969), Piaget (1928, 1955), Sternberg (1985, 2006), Taba (1962), and Vygotsky (1962, 1978). Delineating their theoretical principles and assumptions as they relate to PCM's qualitatively differentiated curriculum is beyond the scope and intent of this book, although readers are referred to the citations listed in the Reference section. However, the following section of this chapter does list the essential principles from these theorists' work that are most closely aligned with the foundation of the Parallel Curriculum Model.

1. Effective curriculum respects the unique characteristics of the learner.

A general principle of education is that curriculum should address and thus respect individual learner characteristics. The work of Dewey, Glasser, Piaget, and Vygotsky referenced above is based upon this tested assumption.

We can characterize the traits of all learners into five categories: cognitive abilities, academic skills and knowledge, social and emotional needs and characteristics, interests, and learning preferences. Our student population reflects a range of abilities, characteristics, and potentials in these five categories. This fact provides a rationale for adjusting the breadth, depth, level, and complexity of content, materials, tasks, and student products. While all students have or can develop a broad range of abilities and interests, they often come to our classrooms with vastly different experiences and levels of prior knowledge in the subject areas we teach. Additionally, in regard to learning preferences, some students learn more effectively with more or less structure or in different environments. Inductive and deductive learning preferences also vary among students.

Evidently, then, an inescapable truth is that learners' characteristics vary. Their abilities may be strong in one area or many. Their interests may be few or many, durable or transitory. The learning preferences they exhibit are influenced by factors such as gender, culture, and general development. Further, their capacities may be blatantly evident or camouflaged. For those reasons, it is essential to stress the fact that no single curriculum can adequately address the needs of all learners. For this reason, the Parallel Curriculum Model provides four unique entry points and an approach to developing appropriate challenge for individual learners that honor the prior knowledge, preferences, readiness levels, interests, and experiences of students.

Even a curriculum that appears to adhere to the essential principles of curriculum design as outlined by Tyler (1949), Taba (1962), Bruner (1960, 1966), and their contemporaries needs to be modified for the abilities, interests, and learning preferences of individual students. That type of curriculum will develop student potential to differing degrees, on varying timetables. Curriculum designed to be a catalyst for developing capacity in young people must be flexible enough to provide students with appropriate challenge and support at all points in their evolution as learners.

2. Theories of knowledge should inform our selection of curriculum content.

There are an untold number of books written about theories of knowledge. Various authors have posed several organizational systems for classifying knowledge and studying it in a systematic manner. Curriculum developers can use one or more of these theories of knowledge as a foundation for selecting and organizing content in any given field. Any one of these systems might serve as an underlying framework for a particular approach to curriculum development. We chose the three-part framework designed by William James.

Levels of Knowing

The American psychologist and philosopher William James (1885) suggested a theory of knowledge based on three levels of knowing. These levels are knowledge-of, knowledge-about (also referred to as knowledge-that), and knowledge-how. Before describing these levels, it is important to note that each of the three levels—and especially the second and third levels—exists on a continuum from the simple to the complex. It is the responsibility of the curriculum developer to determine the degree of complexity within each level that might be appropriate for a given age group, readiness level, and individual. In the final analysis, it is the curriculum developer's understanding of the content field and instructional techniques, plus an understanding of human development, that will guide effective decision making with regard to the level of knowledge that might serve as appropriate content for a particular unit taught to a particular group and to individuals within that group.

Knowledge-Of

This level of knowledge supports entry or awareness level knowing. It involves remembering, recalling, and recognizing but does not include more complex sorts of thinking. Because there is certain information that students must simply "know" about any area of study, most curriculum development begins with the knowledge-of level. It is likely that most teachers feel comfortable with the facts and basic data of a topic, but determining which information is essential and which is less so is not always easy. At any rate, unless curriculum planning moves quickly beyond this lower level of knowing, students are unlikely to become engaged in the topic or to find what they learn to be useful or memorable.

Knowledge-About

Knowledge-about involves a more advanced level of understanding than merely remembering or recalling information. It builds upon remembering or recalling and includes more advanced levels of knowing like comparing, analyzing, inferring, finding relationships, and explaining. Being able to explain something might also involve the ability to demonstrate it. At this level, basic "knowing" evolves into "understanding" and is much more durable, relevant, and powerful for the learner than is accumulation of information alone.

It is at the knowledge-about level that learners begin to deal with the key concepts, principles, and skills of a discipline. In order to move from acquaintance with facts to practical comfort in a field, students need to understand the key concepts that organize the discipline, essential principles that govern the concepts, and ways in which professionals in the field see linkages among ideas and examples.

As teachers, many of us are uncertain of the key concepts, principles, and skills of the disciplines we teach. It is of great importance that we invest the time needed to discover these conceptual frameworks and teach through them. Among sources to help teachers develop comfort with conceptual underpinnings of the various disciplines are college textbooks, educational standards documents (the Compendium on the www.mcrel.org Web site) developed by national professional groups, and books on conceptual teaching such as *Concept-Based Curriculum and Instruction for the Thinking Classroom* by H. Lynn Erickson (2006).

Knowledge-How

This level of knowing deals mainly with the application of tools and strategies to create solutions and new knowledge. At this level, the student is transformed from lesson learner or consumer of knowledge to problem solver and knowledge producer. Obviously, the more advanced knowledge-about information an individual has, the more likely he or she is to be able to generate new ideas, procedures, and solutions. Scholars view knowledge-how as the highest level of involvement in a field. This level represents the kind of work that researchers, writers, and artists do to make new contributions to their field. It also relates directly to the demands of the information production era that we are in currently.

While the majority of young learners do not reshape subject areas, they can, nonetheless, replicate, simulate, and begin to work like professionals. This type of authentic work is a part of the progression from novice to expert and should be central in curriculum design. It is also a chief factor in student motivation, effort, and task commitment. Over time, teachers who use curriculum that asks students to use knowledge-how become comfortable creating tasks that help students learn to work like historians (or artists, or mathematicians, etc.).

3. Curriculum should support escalating levels of student involvement in the discipline.

James's three levels of knowing are similar to Alfred North Whitehead's (1929) concepts of romance, technical proficiency, and generalization. According to Whitehead, we first develop an interest in or romance with a particular field. Many learners want to know about a variety of topics and fields as they progress in their education (interest), and may, for a time, involve themselves in one or more of those areas (romance).

Some people follow up this romance by pursuing a field to the point of becoming a proficient practitioner. Most professionals within a field reach their maximum involvement at this level. However, there are some persons who go on to the generalization level, adding new information and contributing new knowledge and products to their field. This third level is, in many respects, consistent with one of the major goals of programs that support talent development.

A theory of curriculum with the goal of developing each child's potential should place a premium on powerful, authentic knowledge and the application of authentic methodology to problem areas within various content domains. Instructional techniques should emphasize complex thinking skills, less structured teaching strategies, and a concern for controversial issues, values, and beliefs. Curriculum should also reflect content selection that maximizes the transfer of knowledge, understanding, and skill. The accelerated rate at which knowledge is currently expanding accentuates the value of this principle and reinforces the PCM principle that the vast majority of students should have access to curriculum and instruction that enable them to find increasing success in a complex world.

4. Curriculum should be based on the enduring knowledge in each field.

All of the fields of human understanding rest on a foundation of enduring knowledge. This foundation consists of the key concepts, basic principles, and methodologies of a field. This foundation is the "engine" that drives the field forward to the acquisition of new knowledge and supports students' understanding. Although concepts, principles, and methods do change slowly over extended periods of time, they represent enduring knowledge as opposed to transitory topics or information.

Concepts, principles, and methods should be viewed as tools that help the learner understand any and all selected topics of a content field. For example, understanding the concept of reliability is central to the study of testing, and therefore is an example of an enduring idea in that field. The specific reliability of any given test, however, is more transitory because it changes over time. It is that kind of information that we can always "look up."

5. Topics for study should represent the essential concepts, principles, and processes within a discipline.

One of the biggest issues in curriculum theory is determining what teachers should teach. Most curriculum experts concur that curriculum should focus students on the knowledge, skills, and understanding that best represent the essential structure of the discipline. In any given field, there is an almost endless amount of information on which teachers and students could focus, and it becomes the task of the curriculum developer to determine what knowledge is of most worth.

Philip Phenix (1964) suggests that educators focus on what he calls "representative topics." These topics emerge from the content of a field and are highly representative of numerous, similar topics that are found in that field. For example, a study of the cell as a system with interdependent parts paves the way for understanding systems of the body, the body as a system, ecosystems, and so on. This is the case because studying the cell as a system provides learners with knowledge, concepts, principles, and tools that facilitate understanding in a vast number of related topics.

A teacher or curriculum developer realizes that students cannot study all possible information and topics. For this reason, it becomes critical to select study topics that illustrate the essential concepts and principles and thus have connections to other topics in the subject area.

While representative topics are important in the development of high-quality curriculum, another critical feature is the use of process skills. The objectives of process skills include a wide array of competencies that range from comprehension, application, analysis, synthesis, to evaluation. They also incorporate opportunities for students to make inferences, learn inductively and deductively, seek varied perspectives, develop and use empathy, become aware of and regulate one's own thinking, generate and maintain standards of quality in work and thought, and develop persistence (Bloom , Englehart, Furst, Hill, & Krathwhol, 1956; Costa & Kallick, 2000; Marzano, 1992; Wiggins & McTighe, 1998). Process skills allow students to do something with what they know—beyond remembering and retrieving information.

6. Because of the greater transferability of the process objectives than knowledge alone, it is important to use representative topics as vehicles to develop both core knowledge and process skills. Process development is discussed further in Chapter 3. A focus on methods and tools supports active student involvement and motivation to learn.

Each content field includes the methods and techniques that are essential to practitioners and experts in that field. A theory of knowledge that has, as its goal, helping learners experience and appreciate real-world applications for the knowledge they learn in school should also emphasize the appropriate use of methods, tools, and techniques used by experts in and contributors to a field.

Although the use of these skills and methods sometimes requires advanced understanding of a field or sophisticated equipment, young students can learn and apply some of the entry-level methods (Bruner, 1960). Engagement with methodology also helps learners develop a positive attitude toward challenge and empathy for contemporary concerns. A focus on learning and using the methods of a discipline also encourages active learning—an effective way to ignite student interest, curiosity, and participation.

7. A product orientation to a curriculum encourages the authentic application of abstract and sophisticated ideas.

We believe that a curriculum that supports high levels of achievement for all learners considers both concrete and abstract products. These two kinds of products generally work in harmony.

Concrete products include the specific segments of knowledge students learn, process skills, and student work (e.g., reports, research projects, stories, timelines, dances, editorials, musical compositions, and community service activities). These concrete products are not intended to be ends in themselves. Instead, they are vehicles for the development of various abstract products.

Abstract products include more enduring and transferable outcomes of learning. Examples of abstract products are ideas, strategies, attitudes, beliefs and values, and personal and social development. Abstract products also include aesthetic appreciation, self-efficacy, and movement toward self-actualization. In most cases, achieving the most mature level of abstract products takes many years. However, each curricular experience should contribute to one or a combination of these more enduring goals of curriculum. Taken collectively, the concrete and abstract products represent the overall goals of a theory of curriculum.

8. Effective curriculum is clearly focused, well organized, engaging, and appropriately challenging.

Leaders in education have delineated the best of what we currently know about curriculum and instruction (e.g., Brandt, 1998; Costa & Kallick, 2000; National Research Council, 1999; Schlechty, 1997; Wiggins & McTighe, 1998). These leaders suggest that high-quality curriculum and instruction for all learners:

- have a clear focus on the essential facts, understandings, and skills that professionals in that discipline value most

- provide opportunities for students to develop in-depth understanding

- are organized to ensure that all student tasks are aligned with the goals of in-depth understanding

- are coherent (organized, unified, sensible) to the student

- are mentally and affectively challenging and engaging to the learner

- recognize and support the need of each learner to make sense of ideas and information, reconstructing older understandings with new ones

- are fresh, rich, surprising, and joyful

- provide appropriate choices for learners

- allow for meaningful collaboration

- are focused on products that matter to students

- connect with students' lives and worlds

- seem real, purposeful, and useful

- deal with profound ideas

- call on students to use what they learn in interesting and important ways

- aid students in developing a consciousness of their thinking

- help learners become competent problem solvers

- involve students in setting their learning goals and assessing their progress

- stretch the student

9. Curriculum should support Ascending Intellectual Demand (AID) for diverse learners.

While the vast majority of learners would benefit from curriculum and instruction characterized by the features noted above, it is also the case that learners vary in their cognitive development as well as in interests and preferred learning modes. There is a substantial body of theory and research to suggest that a student will learn best when curriculum and instruction are congruent with a learner's particular needs. Thus, while most, if not all, learners share a common need for high-level, meaning-focused curriculum and instruction, there will be variance in how students will need to encounter and interact with the curriculum if those encounters are to support continuing success as learners.

Vygotsky (e.g., 1962, 1978) helped us understand an individual learns when a teacher presents tasks to the student at a level of difficulty somewhat beyond the learner's capacity to complete the task independently. When a teacher presents tasks in the student's "zone of proximal development" and then scaffolds, coaches, or supports the student in successfully completing the tasks, the student's independence zone ultimately expands. This causes the need for new tasks at a greater level of demand. For advanced learners in a subject area, the implication is that tasks will need to be more complex than would be appropriate for students who are less advanced in their capacities at that time. The opportunity to work with the key concepts, understandings, and skills of the discipline generally does not change across students. What needs to change is the support system that enables a student to work with those things at a level of challenge appropriate to that student's current development.

More recently, brain research (e.g., Howard, 1994; Jensen, 1998) suggests that students learn best when they are neither over challenged nor under challenged but, rather, when tasks are moderately challenging for the individual. When tasks are too difficult for a child, frustration results. When they are too easy, stagnation and apathy result.

In addition, there is ample evidence that a student's motivation and learning improve when curriculum attends to a student's interests (e.g., Amabile, 1983; Collins & Amabile, 1999; Csikszentmihalyi, Rathunde, & Whalen, 1993). Studies also suggest that matching instruction to a student's preferred mode of learning, gender, culture, and intelligence preferences enhances learning (e.g., Delpit, 1995; Dunn & Griggs, 1995; Grigorenko & Sternberg, 1997; Sullivan, 1993).

Our current knowledge about teaching and learning suggests that we should provide virtually all learners with curriculum that asks them to make sense of and apply the seminal ideas and skills of the disciplines. However, we need to adapt that curriculum to the variability among our students. This means curriculum and instruction must be suited for the prior knowledge of the learner, tap into student interests, and be offered in a style and modality effective for each individual. As students become more advanced in their knowledge, understanding, and skills, the challenge level of materials and tasks must escalate. In this book, we call that escalating match between the learner and curriculum Ascending Intellectual Demand.

Simply put, the Parallel Curriculum Model suggests that most, if not all, learners should work consistently with concept-based curriculum, tasks that call for complex thinking, and products that ask students to demonstrate and use what they have learned in meaningful ways. As a student's knowledge and skills become more advanced, task "demand" will escalate to ensure challenge and progress toward expertise. This concept of Ascending Intellectual Demand is discussed in chapters throughout the book—most fully in Chapter 8.

One premise of the Parallel Curriculum Model is that students will develop along a continuum of knowledge and skill, with some students far advanced beyond age expectations, some moderately or slightly advanced, some in the general range of age expectations, and some slightly, moderately, or acutely behind those expectations. A second premise of the model is that by offering each learner the richest possible curriculum and instruction at a level of demand appropriate for the learner—linked to learner interest and mode of learning, and escalating as the learner develops—we assist each learner in developing his or her capacity to the maximum.

10. Attention to student affect can dramatically enhance the power of curriculum to support challenging learning.

In discussing curriculum design, it is easy to focus on content, process, and products that educators will use with students without acknowledging the role of affect in student growth and success. A lesson or unit plan may look elegant on paper but in practice be of little worth if, in the ends, it fails to touch students' affective needs. We believe that an effective teacher continually tries to develop a learning environment, designs curriculum, and uses instructional approaches with the goal of fostering both cognitive growth and affective engagement.

Such teachers are

- reflective about the needs of each student, continually seeking a deeper understanding of both individuals and the group

- responsive in using what they learn about students to craft curriculum and instruction that are better matched to learner needs and interests

- respectful of students' common and distinct cognitive, physical, social, and emotional profiles

Teachers who are students of their students, as well as of their content, seek to ensure that all learners' classroom experiences lead to

- security and the students' sense that the classroom is a safe place to be—the students know that their teacher understands who they are, asks questions that matter to them, allows them to express their ideas, and makes the errors that are an inevitable part of learning and growing

- affirmation—the students' sense that each of them is actively supported by the teacher and their peers in the classroom

▶ validation—the students' belief that each of them has a valuable and valued role in the classroom

▶ affiliation—the students' sense that each of them belongs to and fits in with the group

▶ affinity— each student's sense of kinship and common ground with the group (Mahoney, 1998)

Teachers who work actively to develop learning environments, curriculum, and instruction that honor all aspects of their learners understand the need each learner has to achieve security, affirmation, validation, affiliation, and affinity. These teachers continually guide their students to become more

▶ respectful of their own contributions, needs, ideas, and products as well as of the contributions, needs, ideas, and products of others

▶ responsive in their work and relationships, as well as responsive to their own need for challenge and quality

▶ reflective about what they learn, how their learning affects who they are, what they believe, what they can do, and how their attitudes and behaviors affect the development and options of other people

Teachers who do their best to be reflective, respectful, and responsive support their students in developing these same traits. These teachers constantly assess the impact of environment, curriculum, and instruction on the security, affirmation, validation, affiliation, and affinity of each learner. As a result, these teachers are more likely to make a major impact on the learning and lives of their students than are teachers who undervalue any of these factors.

A particular challenge for teachers is to ensure that students from all cultures and economic backgrounds feel security, affirmation, validation, affiliation, and affinity. Because so many teachers represent the majority culture and a stable economic background, and an increasing number of students represent an array of minority cultures and low-income homes, it is vital that teachers understand and appreciate the backgrounds of all their students. We must make classrooms flexible enough for a variety of learning modes. We also need to ensure that language and economy do not create learning barriers. Including materials, people, and perspectives that represent a range of cultures and helping students learn to value multiple cultures supports this change, as does ensuring that students who lack fundamental learning experiences and skills find support for developing a sturdy framework for learning in their schools and classrooms.

Complex as it is to respond to all learners, doing so is imperative. In no other way can we make learning personal and relevant. It is simply impossible to overstate the interconnectedness between learning and affect in the classroom.

2

An Overview of the
Parallel Curriculum Model

This chapter provides an overview of the Parallel Curriculum Model (PCM). It helps the reader develop an understanding of this curriculum model by

▶ clarifying the strong relationship between PCM, content standards, and enduring knowledge in each discipline

▶ explaining the purpose of the PCM

▶ defining the term "parallel" as it is used within this model

▶ describing the characteristics of each of the curriculum parallels

The Parallel Curriculum Model suggests the possibility of developing appropriately challenging curriculum using one, two, three, or four "parallel" ways of selecting and designing content for a grade level, course, unit of instruction, independent study, or lesson (see Figure 2.1).

The term "parallel" indicates the authors' belief that there are several different perspectives that educators might use to design curriculum. "Parallel" should not be taken to mean that the formats or approaches must remain separate and distinct in planning or in classroom use. A useful analogy is a superhighway in which lanes run parallel to one another, while allowing movement between lanes as vehicles go in a common direction.

As we noted in Chapter 1, the authors believe that curriculum should take its basic form and function from the facts, skills, concepts, and principles that are central to each field of study. The Core Curriculum Parallel reflects the essential nature of a discipline as experts conceive and practice the discipline. It stresses student understanding of the framework, or nature of a discipline, through exploration of the discipline's key information, skills, concepts, and principles.

A second parallel proposed by PCM is called The Curriculum of Connections. This parallel expands on Core Curriculum concepts and principles to help students

The Core or Basic Curriculum	The Curriculum of Connections	The Curriculum of Practice	The Curriculum of Identity
The Core Curriculum is the foundational curriculum that establishes a rich framework of knowledge, understanding, and skills most relevant to the discipline. It is inclusive of and extends state and district expectations. It is the starting point or root system for all of the parallels in this model.	This curriculum is derived from and extends the Core Curriculum. It is designed to help students encounter and interact with the key concepts, principles, and skills in a variety of settings, times, and circumstances.	This curriculum is derived from and extends the Core Curriculum. Its purpose is to help students function with increasing skill and confidence in a discipline as professionals would function. It exists for the purpose of promoting students' expertise as practitioners of the discipline.	This curriculum is derived from and extends the Core Curriculum. It is designed to help students see themselves in relation to the discipline both now and with possibilities for the future; understand the discipline more fully by connecting it with their lives and experiences; increase awareness of their preferences, strengths, interests, and need for growth; and think about themselves as stewards of the discipline who may contribute to it and/or through it. The Curriculum of Identity uses curriculum as a catalyst for self-definition and self-understanding, with the belief that by looking outward to the discipline, students can find a means of looking inward.
The Core or Basic Curriculum:	The Curriculum of Connections is designed to help students think about and apply key concepts, principles, and skills:	The Curriculum of Practice asks students to:	The Curriculum of Identity asks students to:
• Is built on key facts, concepts, principles, and skills essential to discipline	• In a range of instances throughout the discipline	• Understand the nature of the discipline in a real-world application manner	• Reflect on their skills and interests as they relate to the discipline
• Is coherent in its organization	• Across disciplines	• Define and assume a role as a means of studying the discipline	• Understand ways in which their interests might be useful to the discipline and ways in which the discipline might serve as a means for helping them develop their skills and interests
• Is purposefully focused and organized to achieve essential outcomes	• Across time and time periods	• Understand the impact of this discipline on other disciplines and other disciplines in this discipline	
• Promotes understanding rather than rote learning	• Across locations	• Become a disciplinary problem solver rather than being a problem solver using the subject matter of the discipline	
• Is taught in a meaningful context	• Across cultures		
• Causes students to grapple with ideas and questions, using both critical and creative thinking	• Across times, locations, and cultures	• Understand and use the discipline as a means of looking at and making sense of the world	
• Is mentally and affectively engaging and satisfying to learners	• Through varied perspectives	• Develop a means of escaping the rut of certainty about knowledge	
• Results in evidence of worthwhile student production	• As impacted by various conditions (social, economic, technological political, etc.)		
	• Through the eyes of various people who affected and are affected by the ideas		
	• By examining links between concepts and development of the disciplines		

The Core or Basic Curriculum	The Curriculum of Connections	The Curriculum of Practice	The Curriculum of Identity
		• Comprehend the daily lives of workers or professionals in the discipline: working conditions, hierarchical structures, fiscal aspects of the work, peer, or collegial dynamics • Define and understand the implications of internal and external politics that impact the discipline • Value and engage in the intellectual struggle of the discipline • Function as a producer in the discipline • Function as a scholar in the discipline	• Develop awareness of their modes of working as they relate to the modes of operation characteristic of the discipline • Reflect on the impact of the discipline in the world, and self in the discipline • Think about the impact of the discipline on the lives of others in the wider world • Take intellectual samplings of the discipline for the purpose of experiencing self in relation to the discipline • Examine the ethics and philosophy characteristic of the discipline and their implications • Project themselves into the discipline • Develop self in the context of the discipline and through interaction with the subject matter • Develop a sense of both pride and humility related to both self and the discipline

Figure 2.1 The Parallel Curriculum: A Model for Curriculum Planning

understand how core concepts and principles in any discipline are connected to numerous other topics, time periods, issues, problems, events, cultures, and places. For example, the concept of evolution in biology has a strong connection to the concept of change in history. Studying history from the perspective of evolution brings a new point of view to the forefront, a way of thinking that fosters dialogue, deeper understanding, and a sense of relationships that were not likely apparent before.

As its name implies, the Connections Parallel guides students to make connections within or across disciplines, topics, times, events, and people by looking at how they are linked through concepts and principles. Within the Curriculum of Connections students make connections, analogies, metaphors, and comparisons to deepen, broaden, and strengthen their understanding of key concepts and principles.

A third parallel in PCM is called the Curriculum of Practice. In this parallel, students use underlying concepts and principles to experience and understand ways in which practitioners and scholars use and apply discipline-based ideas and skills to real-world questions, problems, issues, and needs. Student use of authentic strategies, tools, and procedures is central to the Curriculum of Practice. In the Curriculum of Practice, students increase their understanding through action, problem solving, product development, research, and investigation. In other words, they use the key concepts, principles, and skills to function much like experts would.

The fourth and final parallel proposed by PCM is The Curriculum of Identity. Curriculum developed for this parallel guides students to understand their own strengths, preferences, values, and commitment by reflecting on their own development, interests, and goals in a field of study. Here, students use key concepts, principles, and skills to reflect on the disciplines and/or the work of experts in the discipline as a means of understanding both the discipline and themselves more fully.

The Parallel Curriculum Model assumes that teachers may create appropriately challenging curriculum by using any one parallel (at appropriate and ascending levels of intellectual demand) or a combination of the parallels as a framework for thinking about and planning curriculum. We hope this book will aid teachers in developing a solid understanding of the four parallels and of the concept of Ascending Intellectual Demand so that they are ultimately comfortable creating curriculum that integrates all of the parallels in rich, authentic, and appropriately challenging ways.

A Look at the Four Curriculum Parallels

Before taking a closer look at the four approaches to curriculum that the Parallel Curriculum Model proposes, it is important to explain three underlying assumptions. These include the following ideas.

▶ Curriculum and instruction for all learners must be flexible enough to address the broad range of needs within a grade level. Our growing awareness of the diversity of students' prior knowledge, styles, and interests means that we also recognize that there can be no "standard" curriculum that will develop all students' potential. In other words, no single approach is adequate for all learners. Any model of curriculum development that seeks to serve the broad population of learners has to promote flexibility to match curriculum to learner.

▶ Teachers who develop high-quality curriculum for diverse learners must be comfortable with their role as planners and decision makers. Such teachers will also develop a growing understanding of their subject areas and the characteristics of high-quality curriculum.

▶ Using these underlying beliefs, the model provides useful guidelines for thinking about what and how we teach a broad range of learners. It is not a recipe. The parallel curricula described in the model can be used in any order, singly or in combination. Drawing on the flexibility of the model allows curriculum designers to generate learning experiences that are genuinely responsive to learner readiness and interest.

We invite teachers and other educators to think about the Parallel Curriculum Model, try it out, critique it, and, ultimately, add to it and reshape it. We begin with an introduction to the model's four parallels. Later chapters will provide specific guidance in applying the parallels to curriculum design.

The Core Curriculum

The Nature of Effective Core Curriculum

The Core Curriculum Parallel is a starting point for rich, authentic curricula. Core Curriculum is based on the foundational knowledge, concepts, and principles of a subject area. The purpose of Core Curriculum is to ensure that students develop a framework of understandings that prepares them for a journey toward proficiency—and potentially, expertise—in a subject area or discipline. National, state, and/or district learning goals for students should be evident in Core Curriculum.

Among the driving questions posed by the Core Curriculum are the following questions, which the authors believe will be explicitly answered as students engage with authentic, meaning-rich curriculum.

▶ What does this information mean?

▶ Why does this information matter?

▶ How is this information organized to help people understand and use it better?

▶ What are the most important ideas and skills in this topic?

▶ How can I use these ideas and skills?

The Core Curriculum

▶ is built on key facts, concepts, principles, and skills essential to the discipline

▶ is well-organized

▶ is purposefully focused to achieve clear outcomes

▸ promotes understanding rather than rote learning

▸ is taught in a context meaningful to the students and appropriate to the nature of the discipline

▸ causes students to grapple with ideas and questions, using both critical and creative thinking

▸ is mentally and affectively engaging and satisfying to learners

▸ results in evidence of worthwhile student production

Our best understanding of teaching and learning suggests that virtually all students should work with a Core Curriculum that has these characteristics. However, when students demonstrate foundational and experiential gaps or advanced knowledge of particular facets of the Core Curriculum, those students will need to work at varied levels of challenge (or of intellectual demand) and with different support systems in order to grow and learn.

Ascending Intellectual Demand and the Core Curriculum

Ascending Intellectual Demand (AID) is always relative to the need of a particular learner. In relation to the Core Curriculum, varied levels of challenge (or at varied levels of AID) can be achieved in many ways, among them the following:

▸ Using more basic or advanced reading, resources, and research materials

▸ Adjusting the pace of teaching and learning to match the need of the student

▸ Working at greater or less demanding levels of depth, breadth, complexity, and/or abstractness

▸ Applying ideas and skills to familiar or unfamiliar contexts that are similar or dissimilar from the ideas and examples explored in class

▸ Designing tasks that are more open-ended or more concrete in nature—tasks that expect greater independence or provide more scaffolding

▸ Developing trait rubrics for tasks and/or products that articulate levels of quality that include a novice to expert continuum

▸ Encouraging collaborations between students and adult experts in an area of shared interest

▸ Designing work that requires student reflection about important ideas and information

The Curriculum of Connections

The Nature of the Curriculum of Connections

This parallel is designed to help students discover and learn about the interconnectedness of knowledge. Like the Core Curriculum, the Curriculum of Connections emphasizes the key facts, concepts, principles, and skills of a discipline.

However, rather than using those elements primarily to see how the topic and discipline are organized, the Curriculum of Connections asks students to use the key information, concepts, principles, and skills to make links between—or to compare and contrast—topics, disciplines, time periods, instances, people, and so on. The Curriculum of Connections may also ask students to look at how the concepts, principles, or skills influenced and are influenced by various people, varying perspectives, and/or different conditions (such as economic, political, social, or technological circumstances). The Connections parallel extends the Core Curriculum by inviting students to connect their growing understanding into arenas not directly addressed by the Core Curriculum.

Asking students to explore and describe connections within a discipline builds the depth of their knowledge about a discipline or among its subdisciplines. Asking students to make connections across disciplines, or across places, instances, and people, typically aids them in building breadth of knowledge and in uncovering new relationships among ideas.

Essential concepts from the Core Curriculum guide both intra- and inter-disciplinary Curriculum of Connections studies. For example, looking at the concept of "obsolescence" in fields of social studies such as economics, political science, and archaeology should yield a deeper understanding within a discipline. Looking at the concept of "obsolescence" across architecture, literature, and ecology should yield a broader understanding of the concept. In addition, skills can guide explorations in the Curriculum of Connections. For instance, the skill of "hypothesizing" takes on varied nuances of meaning in different subjects, while also helping students generalize about the skill.

Driving questions within the Curriculum of Connections include the following.

▶ How do the ideas and skills I learned work in other topics?

▶ Where else can I use what I have learned?

▶ How does looking at one thing help me understand another?

▶ How do different settings change or reinforce my earlier understandings?

▶ How do I adjust my way of thinking and working when I encounter new contexts?

▶ Why do different people have different perspectives on the same issue?

▶ How are perspectives shaped by events and circumstances?

▶ Why is it beneficial for me to examine varied perspectives on a problem?

▶ How do I assess the strengths and weaknesses of differing viewpoints?

The Curriculum of Connections helps students

▶ use concepts, principles, and skills to see the interrelatedness of knowledge as experts do

▶ find key ideas in various contexts and examine their similarities and differences

▸ apply skills in varied settings

▸ use ideas from one context to ask questions about other situations

▸ use ideas from multiple settings to create new hypotheses

▸ make analogies between contexts

▸ develop ways to see unfamiliar things using familiar ways

▸ develop an appreciation for multiple perspectives on issues

▸ understand the role of individuals in the changes within an evolution of the discipline

Ascending Intellectual Demand and the Curriculum of Connections

As with the Core Curriculum, we assume that the vast majority of students should be guided by curriculum and instruction when making connections across times, places, subjects, and perspectives. However, since learners' experiences, skills, and understandings of core concepts differ, it is important to consider ascending levels of intellectual demand within the Curriculum of Connections as in the Core Curriculum. Here again, it is necessary to recognize that learners vary across a broad range of aptitudes, interests, prior experiences, affective states, and cognitive abilities.

Most of the strategies for creating AID in the Core Curriculum can also be used to develop AID in the Curriculum of Connections. In addition, more specific approaches such as the following are useful in adjusting the "degree of challenge" of a task or product in ways that reinforce the nature and intent of the Curriculum of Connections:

▸ Applying understandings or skills in situations that are more familiar or less familiar to students

▸ Generating more or less sophisticated criteria, which students use to weigh the validity of various perspectives on a problem or issue

And with varying timetables, and varying degrees of teacher support, peer support, and independence, students are assisted with

▸ developing solutions, proposals, or approaches that bridge differences in perspective and address relevant problems

▸ making predictions about future directions based on patterns from student observations

▸ searching for useful connections among related or seemingly different elements (e.g., music and medicine, or law and geography)

▸ looking for patterns of interaction in different areas of connection (e.g., ways in which geography, economics, politics, and technology tend to affect one another)

▸ looking at the world through a perspective similar to or unlike the student's own (e.g., how an age-mate from a similar culture reacts to the student's house, slang, religion, clothing, use of time, music, interactions with adults, plans for the future, and so on)

▸ seeking out and evaluating unstated assumptions that are beneath the surface of decisions, approaches, and so on

▸ developing systems for making connections, achieving balanced perspectives, addressing problems, and so on

▸ making visual analogies among ideas

The Curriculum of Practice

The Nature of the Curriculum of Practice

As is the case with the Core and Connections parallels, the Curriculum of Practice also asks students to focus on and grapple with the essential information, concepts, principles, and skills of a topic or discipline. The Parallel of Practice, however, asks students to use those elements as a practitioner or expert in the discipline would use them. The purpose of the Parallel of Practice, then, is to help students broaden their understandings and skills though applications that mirror those of a professional. The Practice parallel guides students in the journey from novice to expert problem solving and production. In the process, it asks students to engage in the work of professionals and examine the habits, affect, and ethics that permeate their work.

Humans learn through guided experience, and thus human progress is marked by our apprenticeships. In fact, for many students—especially those who respond best to practical and experiential learning—doing is more engaging than passive participation. When the doing takes on the work of the professionals, students are likely to learn far more than through more didactic approaches. The Curriculum of Practice provides an opportunity for students to learn and test the key ideas and skills of the discipline. Their curiosity and taste for complexity are also distilled as they become practitioners in a domain.

At times, the Curriculum of Practice might ask students to function as scholars whose studies lead to an appreciation of the contribution of individuals to the body of knowledge and skills in a subject area. At other times, the Curriculum of Practice might ask students to function as scholars who use (or simulates the use of) the knowledge, skills, and tools in a discipline to develop fuller understandings or contribute new understandings. Students' age and cognitive, academic, and affective development will signal which of the two approaches or combination of approaches is best suited to a particular group of learners.

The Curriculum of Practice promotes proficiency and expertise for young practitioners in a discipline by casting them as disciplinarians.

The Curriculum of Practice asks students to

▸ understand and use authentic application of a discipline's concepts and principles

▸ define and assume the role of practitioners or scholars

▸ use the habits of mind and methods of practitioners or scholars in a discipline

▸ understand the impact of a discipline on other disciplines

▸ become disciplinary problem solvers

▸ understand and use the discipline as a means of looking at the world

▸ comprehend the daily lives of workers or professionals in the discipline

▸ value and engage in the struggles and problems of the discipline

Among the key questions of the Curriculum of Practice are the following.

▸ How do practitioner-scholars organize knowledge and skills in this discipline?

▸ How do practitioners use the discipline's concepts and principles in daily practice?

▸ What are the routine problems in the discipline?

▸ What strategies does a practitioner use to solve routine and nonroutine problems in the discipline?

▸ How does the practitioner know which skills to use under given circumstances?

▸ How does a practitioner sense when approaches and methods are ineffective in a given instance?

▸ What are the methods used by practitioners and contributors in the field to generate new questions, new knowledge, and solve problems?

▸ What are indicators of quality and success in the discipline?

The Curriculum of Practice helps students

▸ learn through experience and in context

▸ expand their experiences in the field, leading to greater comfort, confidence, and identification with the field

▸ develop clarity with using key concepts and principles in the field to understand and address issues and problems

▸ develop awareness of problems in the field

▸ organize their understandings in ways useful for accessing information in the field

▸ recognize key features of various problems in the field

▸ find meaningful patterns of information in the field

▸ distinguish between relevant and less critical information for particular tasks

▸ develop authentic strategies for addressing problems in the field

▸ monitor their own thinking and problem-solving strategies

▸ become acquainted with and ultimately use key tools in the field

▸ become acquainted with and ultimately use professional resources and methods

▸ expand their problem-solving ability in the field

▸ know the indicators of quality in the field

▸ develop and pursue possibilities that the field holds for them as individuals

▸ develop awareness of where practitioners work and how those settings impact both the nature of the work and the practitioner

Ascending Intellectual Demand and the Curriculum of Practice

All students need opportunities to experience what it would be like to be a practitioner, problem solver, and contributor to a variety of fields or disciplines. Many students find school more inviting when they realize that what they are learning is of use to them now and in the future. Often, knowledge is more durable when applied to real situations and problems. Thus, the Curriculum of Practice is of value to virtually all students in schools. As is the case with the other parallels of PCM, the match between a task and a student's readiness and interests will determine appropriate levels of challenge.

As in Core and Connections, Ascending Intellectual Demand in the Curriculum of Practice can be achieved through increased complexity, adjusted pace, degree of independence required, amount of task ambiguity, level of materials, and so on. In addition, Ascending Intellectual Demand in the Curriculum of Practice can be achieved on different timetables and with different support systems to more deeply and fully understand the nature and intent of the Curriculum of Practice. It can be further achieved by asking students who are ready to accomplish the following.

▸ Distinguish between rules of practice that seem relevant in tackling authentic problems in a discipline.

▸ Develop a language of reflection about problems and situations in the field.

▸ Develop personal frameworks of knowledge and understandings related to a field through application.

▸ Test those frameworks of knowledge and understanding through repeated field-based tasks.

▸ Compare standards of quality used by practitioners and contributors in the field to those typically used in school as they relate to problem solving.

▸ Establish goals for their own work based on what they believe to be the next steps in quality for their own growth, and then assess their own work according to those standards.

▸ Share high-quality work with experts in the field for their feedback.

▸ Work with problems that even adult experts find difficult.

▸ Seek understanding and resolution of problems currently posing difficulties to experts in the field.

▸ Develop and use a feedback process as they work on complex problems.

▸ Engage in persistent and prolonged written reflection about their own work and thinking in the field.

▸ Compare and contrast their own approaches to discipline-based dilemmas, issues, or problems with those of experts in the field.

The Curriculum of Identity

The Nature of the Curriculum of Identity

As is the case with Core Curriculum, the Curriculum of Connections, and the Curriculum of Practice, the Curriculum of Identity focuses students on the essential knowledge, concepts, principles, and skills of a discipline. The Parallel of Identity, however, exists to help students think about themselves, their interests, their aspirations, and their opportunities to make a contribution to their world—now and in the future—by examining themselves through the lens of a particular discipline or practitioner of that discipline.

Each discipline has a particular function in helping humans make sense of the world in which they live. Because of the focus of each discipline, that discipline employs ways of thinking and ways of working that are different from all other disciplines. Each discipline looks at issues and problems that are different from the issues and problems of interest to the other disciplines. Thus, each discipline has a unique capacity to shape the world. As a result, practitioners in each discipline work in accordance with the structure and nature of that discipline—as well as in accordance with their own nature and personality.

Curriculum of Identity helps students explore a concept, discipline, and/or practitioners of that discipline in ways that illuminate their own lives. The goal of the Identity Parallel is to help students understand themselves and their possibilities by looking at their own interests, abilities, and preferences in juxtaposition to various concepts, disciplines, and/or practitioners of those disciplines.

This parallel helps students

▶ think about how one's life is shaped by a discipline

▶ understand challenges and conflicts that may exist as one moves through stages of development in a field

▶ identify varied levels of contribution one may make to a field (and to oneself through work in the field)

▶ think about difficulties and successes possible within a field

▶ understand what it means for a person to represent and be represented by a chosen field

Among the driving questions in the Curriculum of Identity are the following.

▶ What do practitioners and contributors in this discipline think about?

▶ To what degree is this familiar, surprising, and/or intriguing to me?

▶ When I am intrigued by an idea, what do I gain from that, what do I give as a result of that, and what difference does it make?

▶ How does thinking about a concept or principle in one or more settings help me understand how that concept or principle might shape my life?

▶ How do people in this discipline think and work?

▶ How do I think and work?

▶ What are the problems and issues on which practitioners and contributors in this discipline spend their lives?

▶ To what degree are these ideas intriguing to me?

▶ What is the range of vocational and avocational possibilities in this discipline?

▶ In which ones can I see myself working?

▶ What difficulties do practitioners and contributors in this discipline encounter?

▶ How do they cope with the difficulties?

▶ How do I think I would cope with these difficulties?

▶ What are the ethical principles at the core of the discipline?

▶ How are those like and unlike my ethics?

▶ Who are the "heroes" in this discipline?

▶ What are the attributes of the "villains"?

▶ What do I learn about myself by studying these attributes?

▶ Who are the "villains" in this discipline?

‣ What do I learn about myself by studying about them?

‣ How do people in this discipline handle ambiguity, uncertainty, persistence, failure, success, collaboration, and compromise?

‣ How do I handle those things?

‣ What has the wisdom in this discipline contributed to the world?

‣ To what degree can I see myself contributing to that wisdom?

‣ How might I shape the discipline over time?

‣ How might it shape me?

An analogy can be made between the Curriculum of Identity and rotations of medical students through various facets of medical practice. In the course of the rotations, two goals are achieved. The medical students come to understand many facets of medical practice more thoroughly. They also come to understand those facets of medicine for which they have particular talent, interest, and passionate commitment. While they develop cognitive preparedness in many facets of medicine, the students also develop an affective awareness of which of the practices is the best fit for them as individuals—a sense of which of the practices can become an extension of themselves and a link between themselves and the wider world.

The Curriculum of Identity is designed to help students see themselves in relation to the discipline both now and with possibilities for the future; understand the discipline more fully by connecting it with their lives and experiences; increase awareness of their preferences, strengths, interests, and need for growth; and think about themselves as stewards of the discipline who may contribute to it and/or through it. The Curriculum of Identity uses the key concepts and principles of a discipline to create curriculum that serves as a catalyst for self-definition and self-understanding, with the belief that by looking closely at the discipline, students can find a means of looking inward.

The Curriculum of Identity asks students to

‣ reflect on their skills and interests as they relate to the discipline

‣ understand ways in which their interests might be useful to the discipline and ways in which the discipline might serve as a means for helping them develop their skills and interests

‣ think about the impact of the discipline on the lives of others in the wider world

‣ examine the ethics and philosophies characteristic of the discipline and their implications

‣ project themselves into a concept, principle, or discipline

‣ develop self in the context of the discipline and through interaction with the subject matter

‣ develop a sense of pride and humility related to both the self and the discipline

The Curriculum of Identity helps students

▶ sample the discipline in order to understand themselves in relation to it

▶ develop an appreciation of the potential of one or more disciplines to help people—including themselves—make sense of their world and live more satisfying and productive lives

▶ reflect on and identify their skills, interests, and talents as they relate to one or more disciplines

▶ understand how they might shape and be shaped by ongoing participation in a discipline

▶ develop a clear sense of what types of lives practitioners and contributors to a discipline lead on a day-to-day, as well as on a long-term, basis

▶ explore the positive and negative impacts of the discipline on the lives of people and circumstances in the world

▶ examine their own interests, ways of thinking, ways of working, values, ethics, philosophy, norms, and definitions of quality by examining those things as reflected in the discipline

▶ understand the excitement that people in a discipline have about ideas, issues, problems, and so on and how those things energize contributors to a discipline

▶ understand the role of self-discipline in practitioners and contributors to the discipline and reflect on their own evolving self-discipline

▶ think about how creativity is visible in the discipline and about their own creativity

▶ develop a sense of pride and a sense of humility related to self and the discipline

Ascending Intellectual Demand and the Curriculum of Identity

All students should have the opportunity to understand how disciplines shape and are shaped by human beings and the world. All students should have opportunities to examine themselves in relation to a discipline to get a clearer sense of their talents, interests, values, and goals. And surely, virtually all students would benefit from consistently working as much as possible like practitioners in a discipline so that schoolwork is connected to real events, problems, skills, ideas, and opportunities.

As in the other PCM parallels, Ascending Intellectual Demand can be achieved in the Curriculum of Identity by matching the degree of task complexity, ambiguity, independence, material difficulty, pace, and so forth with the need of the student. In addition, AID in the Curriculum of Identity can be achieved, on varied timetables and with varied supports, by engaging in experiences such as the following in order to better understand oneself through the lens of a discipline or practitioner of a discipline:

▸ Sharing personal reflections

▸ Making connections to self

▸ Examining multiple points of view

▸ Working with a mentor

▸ Shadowing a professional in the field

▸ Reading biographies of practitioners in the field and making personal comparisons

▸ Examining the characteristics of people who work in the field and making personal comparisons

▸ Making a short- or long-term commitment to the field or one of is problems

▸ Identifying the habits of someone who is passionate about this field

Curriculum Combining the Four Parallels

The parallels in PCM are clearly related. While they can be used separately as a focus of curriculum for an individual, small group, or entire class, it makes good sense to combine the parallels for a curriculum that has great richness and broad reach. Because the Parallel Curriculum Model assumes that the key concepts and principles are foundational for rich curriculum, they are evident in all PCM parallels. The various parallels simply call on students to use the concepts and principles in different ways. Students can productively explore the key concepts and principles, or a topic or discipline, in multiple ways in a single unit. In a unit that combines parallels, the level of intellectual demand should be matched to student need, as is the case in using the parallels individually. One such example follows. In this instance, a teacher combined several PCM parallels to extend the curriculum of a fifth grader with particular interests and strengths in writing and history.

Beth was a fifth grader with strong ability in reading, thinking, and research, as well as a passion for history and historical fiction. She began her work with the concept of "interconnectedness" as it related to the Civil War. In her small town, she discovered a cemetery containing several graves of young women about her age, all of whom died during the Civil War. The question she began pursuing was "In what ways were the lives of young people affected by the Civil War?" She quickly found an interconnection between disease and the Civil War.

Beth used primary documents at the local courthouse to find out about the young people whose graves had captured her attention. In time, she found relatives of the young women still living in her area. Through interviews with these relatives and experts on the Civil War, combined with study of additional primary documents and numerous secondary sources, Beth reconstructed the events that dominated the lives of the young women.

She presented her findings in a formal paper to the local historical society where she received encouragement for her work together with suggestions for the next steps she might take. As her research continued, she translated her findings to a work of historical interest—meeting regularly with professional writers who held scheduled meetings to discuss her work.

Beth's story was published, as was a reflective piece on the journal she'd kept throughout the year. Beth's year-long curriculum reflected key elements of the Core Curriculum, the Curriculum of Connections, the Curriculum of Practice, and the Curriculum of Identity. While the Curriculum of Connections and the Curriculum of Practice took center stage in her year-long efforts, elements of the Core Curriculum served as the catalyst for her work. Her teacher encouraged her to keep a reflective journal as she worked. The teacher provided her with questions for reflection such as those related to the Curriculum of Identity. These questions helped this relatively young student become much more aware of who she was and what she valued through her experience in two fields of study.

Planning Quality Curriculum

Well-designed curriculum systematically addresses required content standards, but does not substitute a list of standards or a textbook for the array of elements necessary to chart a successful course of learning for students. High-quality curriculum is organized to ensure student meaning making. It takes into account the need to tap into student curiosity and motivation. It is tightly aligned to ensure that clearly articulated learning goals feed forward into teaching plans, learning sequences, student work, and assessments. It attends to student development, both at the group and individual level. It incorporates resources that enhance student learning. It contributes to a sense of possibility for each student in the class and to a sense of community for the class as a whole. It strives for student engagement, liveliness, challenge, and support. It provides a path to success for the student who currently lacks content, skills, or work habits, and it provides for the student who is ready to move beyond the prescribed unit parameters.

The Parallel Curriculum Model is a framework for creating well-designed curriculum based on the knowledge, understanding, and skills most relevant to the discipline. This kind of well-designed curriculum benefits school districts, teachers, and schools.

It benefits the school district because it

1. articulates, in writing, a defensible, coherent educational plan

2. promotes consistency of implementation

3. increases the likelihood that all students will benefit from high teacher expectations and high support to achieve them

It benefits students because it

1. supports equality of educational opportunity by including all students as targets of powerful learning

2. supports excellence through increasing levels of intellectual demand

3. elevates thinking (analytical, critical, and creative) by focusing on appropriate learning activities

4. sequences a continuum of learning experiences, preK–12, that leads learners naturally from novice to expert in each discipline; it helps students organize and build knowledge

5. is engaging; it beckons students into a content area through inviting problems, issues, and dilemmas central to a discipline

6. engages students with meaningful products that represent the work of professionals in the discipline

7. makes explicit what constitutes evidence of effectiveness; it clarifies, for students and teachers, a clear set of expectations

It benefits teachers because it

1. extends their ability to design high-quality curriculum and thus enhances their professional capacity

2. promotes the linkage among bodies of knowledge and among parts of a curriculum

3. Elevates the art of lesson planning and decreases teacher reliance on textbooks.

4. establishes educational priorities; it makes teaching and learning more efficient and effective

5. invites professional collaboration in order to enhance curriculum

6. extends their capacity to provide equity of access to excellence for a full range of learners

7. makes planning orderly and effective

Ensuring Fidelity to the Parallel Curriculum Model

It is devilishly easy for educators to "use" a particular model with confidence that their work reflects the intent of the model—and yet also easy to miss the mark. For that reason, it is important to clarify the characteristics of "authentic" PCM. The following attributes will be evident in curriculum developed with the Parallel Curriculum Model as the model is intended to be used.

1. The curriculum is clearly concept based and principle driven with the concepts and principles consistently evident to the students. That is, while the curriculum ensures that students develop knowledge and skills important to be competent in the discipline or topic and to support student success with required content standards or benchmarks, the curriculum has a major focus on using essential concepts and principles to help students understand how the content is organized and how it makes sense.

2. The curriculum reflects the "deep intent" of one or more of the parallels with that intent consistently in the foreground of the unit and of students' work and thought. That is, students regularly seek and pose answers to one or more of a parallel's defining questions (or questions of equivalent depth) in ways that define or shape the unit and the students' work. In later chapters, the defining questions of each parallel are listed and described in greater detail.

3. The curriculum uses all components of the curriculum in ways that give the unit coherence and bring the "deep intent" of the parallel to the forefront of student thought and work. Curriculum components are parts, or elements, of curriculum. They may be conceived simply as (a) clearly articulated goals/objectives/standards, (b) teaching and learning sequences through which students come to "own" that essential content, (c) assessment of student progress toward and beyond proficiency with essential content, and (d) student and teacher reflection on the degree to which teaching and learning "worked" as it should, for whom, and what can be done to further support student success as the year progresses. Curriculum components can also be conceived in a more detailed fashion as including elements such as: (a) content/standards, (b) diagnostic, formative, and summative assessments, (c) introductory activities to set the stage for a unit, (d) teaching strategies, (e) learning activities, (f) grouping strategies, (g) student products, (h), learning resources, (i) extension activities that allow students to explore beyond the boundaries of a unit, (j) modifications or differentiation of instruction to address particular learner needs, (k) lesson and/or unit closure. In either case, each of the elements of the curriculum should be designed to draw student attention—magnet-like—to the concepts, principles, and "deep intent" of the parallel(s). In this book, we have opted to use the second, and more detailed, way to think about curriculum components and will discuss those in detail

in Chapter 3. In either case, effective PCM curriculum will employ all parts or elements of the curriculum to keep students (and the teacher) focused on the nature, purpose, or "deep intent" of the parallel(s) that a curriculum is designed to address.

4. The curriculum uses the principle of Ascending Intellectual Demand to extend student capacity by intensifying the "deep intent" of the parallel and having the student work in increasingly expert-like ways. AID is an approach to differentiation for students' learning needs. It asks teachers to develop awareness of student status with particular content on a continuum from novice to expert and to modify or differentiate instruction to enable students to move from their current comfort levels toward more challenging and more expert-like knowledge, understanding, skill, and ways of thinking and working. The concept of Ascending Intellectual Demand will be discussed in detail in Chapter 8.

Both teachers and their students will grow in competence, confidence, and expertise with essential content to the degree that designers and users of PCM continue to revisit these four elements to ensure that they are reflected in both the written and implemented curriculum.

Looking Ahead in the Book

While we hope you've found the conceptual framework and overview of the model interesting, we know that the key to making PCM useful for educators is carefully explaining its parts in a way that invites classroom application. The remainder of the book has that as its goal. Chapter 3 discusses curriculum components around which educators design and implement curriculum. Chapters 4 through 7 discuss the four parallels of the Parallel Curriculum Model to provide both guidance in applying the model and images of what the model might look like in action. Chapter 8 examines the role of Ascending Intellectual Demand in the Parallel Curriculum Model.

Taken together, the remainder of the book poses answers to the following questions asked by dedicated teachers throughout their careers.

Q: How do I ensure that students really understand what I am teaching them?

A: Teach with concepts and principles in the foreground of teaching and learning.

Q: How can I tap into students' motivation to learn?

A: Use the four parallels of PCM to engage students with learning.

Q: How do I ensure that students stay focused on what matters most in what they study?

A: Ensure that all of the elements of your curriculum retain that focus.

Q: How can I support the success and maximize the growth of each of my students with high-quality curriculum and instruction?

A: Differentiate instruction, including use of Ascending Intellectual Demand.

The chapters are not meant to be recipes or to provide rigid structures for using PCM to create curriculum. In fact, we are convinced that there are no recipes for thoughtful curriculum, and no recipe followers who develop dynamic classrooms. Instead, we offer these chapters as a way to test and extend your thinking about curriculum design—a professional art form as ill suited to paint-by-number approaches as are the fine arts.

3

Thinking About the Elements of Curriculum Design

The Big Picture

This chapter discusses a set of concepts about curriculum and curriculum design. In other words, it is a quick review of (a) key principles of curriculum design and (b) components that may be used for curriculum planning. Its purpose is to serve as a foundation that describes the fundamentals that teachers use and understand to support our teaching and learning. It is important for designing parallel curricula because it helps curriculum designers create comprehensive and coherent curriculum with a framework for stressing the key concepts and principles and "deep intent" that are central to the PCM parallels.

Planning Quality Curriculum

Well-designed curriculum systematically addresses required content standards, but does not substitute a list of standards or a textbook for the array of elements necessary to chart a successful course of learning for students. High-quality curriculum is organized to ensure student meaning-making. It takes into account the need to tap into student curiosity and motivation. It is tightly aligned to ensure that clearly articulated learning goals feed forward into teaching plans, learning sequences, student work, and assessments. Quality curriculum attends to student development, both at the group and individual level. It incorporates resources that enhance student learning. It contributes to a sense of possibility for each student in the class and to a sense of community for the class as a whole. This type of curriculum strives for student engagement, liveliness, challenge, and support. It provides for the student who currently lacks content, skills, or work habits to be successful, and it provides for the student who is ready to move beyond the prescribed unit parameters.

The Parallel Curriculum Model is a framework for creating well-designed curriculum based on the knowledge, understanding, and skills most relevant to the discipline. This kind of well-designed curriculum benefits school districts, teachers, and schools.

It benefits the school district because it

1. articulates, in writing, a defensible, coherent educational plan

2. promotes consistency of implementation

3. increases the likelihood that all students will benefit from high teacher expectations and high support to achieve them

It benefits students because it

1. supports equality of educational opportunity by including all students as targets of powerful learning

2. supports excellence through increasing levels of intellectual demand

3. elevates thinking (analytical, critical, and creative) by focusing on appropriate learning activities

4. sequences a continuum of learning experiences, PreK–12, that leads learners naturally from novice to expert in each discipline; it helps students organize and build knowledge

5. is engaging; it beckons students into a content area through inviting problems, issues, and dilemmas central to a discipline

6. engages students with meaningful products that represent the work of professionals in the discipline

7. makes explicit what constitutes evidence of effectiveness; it clarifies, for students and teachers, a clear set of expectations

It benefits teachers because it

1. extends their ability to design high-quality curriculum and thus enhances their professional capacity

2. promotes the linkage among bodies of knowledge and among parts of a curriculum

3. elevates the art of lesson planning and decreases teacher reliance on textbooks

4. establishes educational priorities; makes teaching and learning more efficient and effective

5. invites professional collaboration in order to enhance curriculum

6. extends their capacity to provide equity of access to excellence for a full range of learners

7. makes planning orderly and effective

Some Key Components of Curriculum Design

In its simplest form, the teaching-learning process involves interactions among three elements. The organization of these elements and interactions can be represented by a triangle (see Figure 3.1). The top of the triangle represents our knowledge about the most important ideas, principles, and information within and across disciplines. The other two points of the figure represent students and teachers. Lines drawn between the three points refer to interactions between the elements.

The line segment between the teacher and the content represents the multiple interactions a teacher might have and decisions that a teacher might make about content knowledge. This includes: (1) a teacher's ongoing acquisition of content knowledge, (2) a teacher's evolving insights about the meaning of the content, and (3) the numerous decisions a teacher makes about the appropriateness of the content for varied learners. The line segment between the teacher and the student represents the array of links a teacher must make with students. This includes gathering information about students' individual learning needs as well as understanding students as members of a group.

In addition, the teacher interacts with students during formative or ongoing assessment, coaching, and questioning and as feedback is provided and received. Students interact with the teacher when they reflect publicly about their learning, demonstrate their understanding during conversations and in assignments, ask their own questions, and respond to the teacher's queries. Student and teacher interactions are vital for learning, assessment, diagnosis, and curriculum differentiation.

Finally, the interactions symbolized by the student-content line segment involve what we think of as learning. This interaction includes such tasks as reading, viewing,

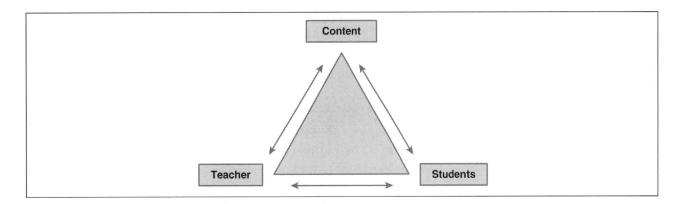

Figure 3.1 Curriculum Interactions

listening, and the processing of new content, concepts, and strategies. A variety of thinking skills are required for the interaction to result in learning. Students must attend and perceive the new content in the learning environment, and they must make a connection between their prior knowledge and this new content. Through observation, conversation, and their own actions, students might compare, contrast, and search for patterns in order to find the similarities and differences between the new content and their existing cognitive scheme. Most important, students make a decision to ignore, accommodate, or assimilate new content into their ever widening bank of personal understandings. Relationships, generalizations, and useful principles are shaped and formed as a result of a successful interaction among students and content. The use of appropriate thinking skills and tasks scaffold their journey through this new learning territory.

The field of education often uses the term "curriculum" or "curriculum and instruction" to refer to the purposeful, proactive organization, sequencing, and managing of these interactions across the three classroom elements: the content, the teacher, and the student. The curriculum, then, is a multifaceted plan that fosters these connections.

Although curriculum writers can make independent decisions about what to teach, how to teach, and when to teach, this sort of independent decision making rarely occurs. In most instances, curriculum is developed only after a lengthy process that involves decisions by teachers, state department of education personnel, content area specialists, and community members about which knowledge is most vital for students to acquire.

Some call this designated body of knowledge and skill the "standards" or the "general" curriculum; others refer to it as the "grade-level expectations" or the "mandated" curriculum. In its most skeletal form, the general curriculum often merely lists the knowledge and skills that students in various grade levels are expected to acquire—perhaps represented in a scope and sequence chart.

This sort of general curriculum document, however, is seldom more than a beginning in the curriculum development process. Typically, the outline, list of standards, or even a textbook provides little more than a list of essential ideas, skills, and information. To assume that curriculum development ends with this document is equivalent to putting either flour, a sack of apples, a couple of cups of sugar, a stick of butter, or a tin of cinnamon on the table and telling diners to enjoy the apple pie. Meaningful curriculum design includes much more than listing raw ingredients!

Comprehensive curriculum plans typically include decisions about components such as content knowledge to be acquired (including, but not limited to, prescribed standards), representative topics, assessments, introduction to a topic or idea, teaching strategies, learning tasks, grouping options, resources, products, extensions, and differentiation strategies. This chapter provides an overview of one approach to designing a meaningful curriculum. It contains: (1) an explanation of some key features of a comprehensive curriculum plan, (2) a description of exemplary characteristics for each of the components, (3) a rationale for developing high-quality curriculum, (4) an example of the curriculum design process in action, and (5) an explanation of the relationship between this curriculum design framework and the four curriculum parallels introduced earlier and described in more detail in subsequent chapters: the Core Curriculum, Curriculum of Connections, Curriculum of Practice, and Curriculum of Identity.

Components of a Comprehensive Curriculum Plan

Through explanations and visuals, this section of the chapter proposes elements likely to be a part of planning high-quality curriculum. These elements represent one perspective on what it means to plan well so students can learn well. There may well be times when a teacher has legitimate reasons not to attend to one or more of the elements we propose here. There are likely to be instances in which teachers would add elements to the ones we've chosen to present.

Further, the curriculum planning process may not always follow a linear process. That is, a teacher may not begin by thinking about content or standards, move directly to thinking about an assessment plan, select an introductory activity, and so on. Early planning may actually begin with assessment data or an idea for a powerful student product that can be used to assess student learning, for example. Our goal in presenting elements of curriculum is not to restrict or prescribe teacher planning but, rather, to prompt reflection on those elements which, when used in concert and with finesse, can strengthen what and how we teach, with the goal of strengthening student learning. In addition to a text explanation of the components, Figure 3.2 lists key components of a comprehensive curriculum, defines them, and suggests some characteristics of exemplars of each component.

Recall again that the goal of this chapter is not to suggest that a curriculum designer must be bound to these components, or that the framework we suggest here is the only way to think about curricular elements. Rather, our goal is to return throughout the book to the reminder that using the various components of curriculum—however you conceive them—is important in keeping the focus on "deep intent" of the PCM parallels in the center of teacher planning and student thinking.

Content (Including Standards)

Content is what we specify students should come to know, understand, and apply as a result of their participation in a lesson, unit of study, or a year in the classroom. Content emerges from a variety of sources. Content may be listed in state or district curriculum documents in the form of learning standards, objectives, benchmark assessments, grade-level expectations, or learner outcomes.

Content decisions also stem from teachers' knowledge of an academic discipline. When we understand a field deeply and richly, we know what matters most! There is no substitute for a teacher's developing expertise in the subject matter he or she teaches.

	Definitions	*Exemplary Characteristics*
Content (Including Standards)	Content is what we want students to know, understand, and do as a result of teaching and learning. These ideas are often written as objectives, grade-level expectations, or as broad K–12 standards statements.	Exemplary content and standards incorporate concepts, enduring understandings, and the processes and skills used within a discipline. Additionally, they provide clarity, power, and authenticity for teachers and students.
Assessments	Assessments are varied tools and techniques that teachers use to determine students' prior knowledge or the extent to which students are learning and applying content goals. Teachers use assessment data to make instructional decisions.	Well-designed assessments are diagnostic, aligned with the learning goals, and provide a high ceiling, as well as a low baseline, to ensure that all students' learning can be measured. They are used before, during, and after instruction. High-quality assessments inform instruction.
Introductory Activities	An introduction sets the stage for a unit. Components may include (1) a focusing question, (2) an assessment to determine students' prior knowledge, interests, and learning preferences, (3) a teaser or "hook" to motivate students, (4) information about the real-world relevance of the goals and unit expectations, (5) information about expectations for students, and (6) consideration of students' interests in or experiences that connect with the unit topic.	A high-quality introduction is likely to include many of these six elements, as well as an advance organizer that provides students with information that they can use to help assess their acquisition of the unit's learning goals. In addition, the representative topic provides not only real-world relevance but also relevance for the age level and student interests.
Teaching Strategies	Teaching strategies are methods teachers use to support student learning. These techniques help teachers introduce, explain, demonstrate, model, coach, guide, transfer, or assess learning.	Beneficial teaching methods are closely aligned to research, learning goals, and learner characteristics. They are varied, promote student involvement, and provide support and feedback.
Learning Activities	A unit's learning activities are those cognitive experiences that help students perceive, process, rehearse, store, and transfer knowledge, understanding, and skills.	Effective learning activities are aligned with the learning goals and efficiently foster cognitive engagement (i.e., analytic, critical, practical, and creative thinking) integrated with the learning goal.
Grouping Strategies	Grouping strategies refer to the varied approaches a teacher can use to arrange students for effective learning in the classroom.	Well-designed grouping strategies are aligned with the learning goals. Effective grouping strategies are varied and change frequently to accommodate students' interests, questions, learning preferences, prior knowledge, learning rate, and zone of proximal development. Group membership may change frequently.

	Definitions	*Exemplary Characteristics*
Resources	Resources are materials that support learning during the teaching and learning activities.	Exemplary resources are varied in format and link closely to the learning goals, students' reading and comprehension levels, and learning preferences.
Products	Products are performances or work samples created by students that provide evidence for student learning. Products can represent daily or short-term student learning, or can provide longer-term, culminating evidence of student knowledge, understanding, and skill. High-quality products often double as assessment tools.	Powerful products are authentic, equitable, respectful, efficient, aligned to standards, and diagnostic.
Extension Activities	Extension activities are preplanned or serendipitous experiences that emerge from learning goals, local events, and students' interests.	Powerful extension activities provide for student choice. They relate in some way to the content/standards, are open ended, are authentic, and generate excitement for and investment in learning.
Differentiation Based on Learner Need (Including AID)	Teachers can enhance learning by optimizing the match between the curriculum and students' unique learning needs. One kind of modification represented in the Parallel Curriculum Model is referred to as "Ascending Intellectual Demand (AID)."	Well-designed differentiation strategies are closely aligned with the learning goals, research, assessment data, students' prior knowledge, cognitive skills, motivation, interests, learning modes, questions, and product preferences.
Lesson and Unit Closure	Lesson and unit closure allows for reflection on the "punch line" of the lesson. What was the point of the lesson? What are students taking away from it? What questions remain? What comes next?	Effective lesson and unit closure help students focus on what matters most. It makes explicit ideas that may have been less clear to students during the unit or lesson.

Figure 3.2 Definitions and Key Components of Comprehensive Curriculum

Currently, standards documents often specify what a grade-level student should learn or be able to do. The quality among standards documents is strongly correlated to the kind of content knowledge valued by the constituency group involved in developing the standards. In general, the most effective standards documents help teachers focus on the lasting, essential, and powerful ideas within that discipline. High-quality standards documents specify the concepts, principles, and skills that give the particular discipline its influence and authenticity. Hilda Taba (1962) made clear the distinctions among different categories of knowledge in her seminal work *Curriculum and Practice* (see Figure 3.3).

When teachers are provided with guidelines for content—whether from standards documents, lists of objectives or benchmarks, texts, or some combination of sources—it's critical for the teacher to determine the degree to which the content

Knowledge Category	Definition and Examples
Fact	A specific detail; verifiable information or data *Example: The capital of New York is Albany.*
Concept	A class of things; a category with common elements *Examples: capital, city, nation*
Principle	A fundamental truth, law, rule, or doctrine that explains the relationship between two or more concepts *Example: Capital cities are often located along major transportation routes. Social, economic, political, and geographic factors influence the location of a capital city.*
Skill	A proficiency, an ability, or a technique; a strategy, a method, or a tool *Example: Locate capital cities using longitude and latitude. Use a map key to identify the symbol for capitals.*
Attitude	A belief, disposition, appreciation, or value *Example: Develop an appreciation for the cultural heritage of capital cities.*
Problem Solving, Transfer, and Application	The ability to use knowledge to address a goal that may not be immediately be understandable *Example: Examination of issues that might arise when a capital needs to be relocated.*

Figure 3.3 Hilda Taba's Knowledge Categories

seems comprehensive (opposed to a disjointed series of facts and skills, for example), coherent (each portion flows from previous portions), authentic (characteristic of content used by a professional in the domain), and relevant (evident in its usefulness to students). When some or all of these characteristics are lacking, it is the teacher's job to supply missing elements in order to improve student learning. To do less is to present students with fragmented learning options that are low on meaning and with information that is difficult to care about, retain, or use.

There is little doubt that content is the most important of the key features of a curriculum plan because it provides teachers with a clear understanding of what students are supposed to learn as a result of their participation in a lesson, unit, or course of study. Without clear content, a curriculum unit dissolves quickly into a collection of disjointed activities unlikely to support meaningful learning. In addition, effective content delineates a learning sequence that fosters the development of ascending levels of understanding and expertise as students progress through the grades.

Assessments

Assessments are tasks assigned to students in order to determine the extent to which they have acquired the knowledge and/or skills embedded within a performance standard or content goal. Assessment tasks provide tangible evidence of student understanding and growth before instruction begins (preassessment or diagnostic assessment), as instruction progresses (formative assessment), and at the end of a segment of instruction (summative assessment).

Preassessment data allow a teacher to know how much and what kind of content students know at the outset of a unit so that the teacher can make appropriate lesson plan adjustments. Little useful learning occurs when a teacher "teaches" something to a student that the student already knows. Likewise, a student generally cannot learn what a teacher teaches if that student has significant gaps in background knowledge, understanding, and/or skill. Used effectively, preassessment eliminates "blind teaching" and encourages teachers to expand beyond one-size-fits-all instruction.

Formative assessment should occur throughout a unit of study. Data from this kind of assessment help teachers know who is mastering ideas and skills and who may need additional assistance to achieve competency with the content goals.

More specifically, summative assessments help teachers understand who has mastered content and skills objectives at a designated "ending point" of instruction. In the classroom, summative assessment at the end of one lesson or unit will often inform a teacher's planning for the next lesson or unit, because—at least in a well-constructed curriculum—the latter flows from the former. Nonetheless, summative assessment also has more of a "high stakes" character than do preassessment or formative assessment. In the classroom, summative assessment may have a major impact on a report card grade. Beyond the individual classroom, summative assessment can affect such decisions as promotion to the next grade, college acceptance, access to special classes or programs, and even judgments about the quality of instruction at a grade level or in a school.

An assessment usually involves the demonstration of a behavior or product that results from the student's interaction with content. The process of assessment is depicted in Figure 3.4.

The following task, designed for use in a three-week high school unit on tragic heroes and the hero quest, illustrates the relationship among the components of an assessment. The task is a culminating (summative) assessment, and the purpose was to determine (a) how much content students had acquired and (b) the extent to which students were able to transfer concepts across genres.

Over the past few weeks we have explored the mythical journeys of heroes such as Jason, Perseus, and Odysseus. We have also examined the pattern of the archetypal quest that was put forth by Joseph Campbell in Hero With a Thousand Faces. *In this book, Campbell describes the major phases of the heroic journey: departure, initiation, and return. Examine three current story plots that contain*

PARTICIPANT + CONTENT + TASK +

COGNITIVE PROCESSING = ASSESSMENT

Figure 3.4 The Assessment Equation

heroes who undertake personal quests. These can be movies, fairy tales, or your own personal journey. In a format of your choice (e.g., short paper, PowerPoint presentation, or brief documentary), explore the similarities and differences among the heroes and plot lines in the three stories that you select.

Using the assessment equation from Figure 3.4, the mythology assessment can be analyzed to reveal its component parts, as shown in Figure 3.5. The student is provided with an assessment task. As a result of his or her involvement with the task, the student is required to think about key content. The student's interaction with the knowledge is the basis for the product. In turn, the teacher uses the product to evaluate the student's understanding of the targeted knowledge.

This same process is also embedded in an assignment. The difference between an assessment and an assignment is that an assessment implies a decision-making function and suggests how a teacher can assist learners and modify instruction.

The key to designing an assessment is aligning the task, the knowledge, and the product format. Teachers must choose cognitive processes and a product format that clearly reveal students' understanding of the knowledge they are to acquire. Part of the alignment difficulty stems from the fact that the knowledge is "hidden" or "disguised" in the product. Teachers need to be confident, for example, that a nutrition poster will reveal a student's knowledge of the food pyramid or that a concept map reflects a student's accurate understanding not only of the major concepts covered in a curriculum lesson or unit but also of the relationships between and among them.

Teachers and students benefit from using a variety of assessment formats. Some possible assessment formats are listed in Figure 3.6. Superior assessments have several attributes. They are reliable, valid, efficient, equitable, seamless, and motivating. Reliable assessments provide a consistent and "stable" reading of a student's knowledge and/or skill acquisition from one occasion to the next—just as a reliable thermometer works in a similar fashion every time it registers 100° Celsius when submerged in boiling water.

Valid assessments measure what they say they measure. Have you ever taken a test that dealt with only a few pages of the textbook and none of the notes? Have you ever created a project for a class when you had no clear sense of what knowledge, insight, or skill it should represent? These were likely not valid assessments because they did not measure the content taught.

Assessments need to be efficient for students and teachers. The effort expended by the student to respond to the task and the effort expended by the teacher to

---

PARTICIPANT (student) + **TASK** (documentary)

+ **CONTENT** (archetypal quest pattern and three current story lines)

+ **COGNITIVE PROCESSING** (finding similarities) = **ASSESSMENT**

Figure 3.5 Applying the Assessment Equation

Sample Assessment Formats		
Oral Questions	Conversations	Recitations
Tests	Essays	Behaviors
Systematic Observations	Portfolios	Performances
Think Alouds	Concept Maps	Lab Reports
Ongoing Records of Progress	Competency Checklists	Auditions
Conferences	Products	Journal Entries

Figure 3.6 Sample Assessment Formats

assess the task, and provide positive and corrective feedback, must balance with the time required for both student and teacher.

Finally, assessments must be equitable, seamless, and motivating. Assessments can be subject to rater bias based on such things as a student's personality or access to state-of-the-art technology. It is, therefore, advisable to use objective rating scales, rubrics, or checklists to evaluate student performances to increase the likelihood of equity in scoring and feedback. Seamless assessments are those that are imperceptibly woven into instruction. They provide teachers with honest "snapshots" of student growth over time. Finally, superior assessments motivate students. They invite and encourage students to explore an area or topic thoughtfully and to work for a high level of quality.

Introductory Activities

Introductory activities are created by the teacher and offered to students in order to acquaint them with a new unit or lesson, its content, and teacher expectations for students' work during the unit. Introductory activities should do more to motivate and orient students than traditional one-sentence introductions such as "Please open your books to page 23."

A comprehensive introduction can actually contain a variety of elements that help engage and motivate learners. First, a focusing question derived from a standard or overarching principle embedded within a unit can promote curiosity in students and help both teachers and students maintain a focus on meaning that is central to the unit. Focusing questions for the unit on tragic heroes might be "What is meant by the phrase 'tragic hero'?" "Who are tragic heroes?" "Is anyone you know a tragic hero?" "What are the common characteristics of their journeys toward self-understanding?"

Second, a "teaser" or "hook" can be highly motivating for students, and may point to the relevance of upcoming content as well. For example, a primary teacher had

"Paul Bunyan" come to her class to talk about how it felt when people exaggerate about you all the time. This brief dramatic monologue absolutely hooked her students on tall tales and established some key understandings for the young learners as well. In another instance, a science teacher introduced the concept of inertia by skillfully pulling the tablecloth off of a table set with flowers and good china. Again, this strategy captured the students' curiosity as it also began to plant the seed for further exploration.

Third, an effective introduction may enable students to attach their own past knowledge, experience, interests, and/or strengths to the new content. Interest checklists, charts that guide students in listing what they already know about a topic and questions they have about the topic, and invitations for students to suggest ways in which they might like to explore the topic or express their learning are just a few ways teachers commonly use introductory activities to help students connect with new content or a new topic.

An effective introduction to a unit may also help students understand the purpose of the unit, the direction it will take, and expectations for high-quality work during the unit. A concept map of ideas in the unit, unit schedule or calendar of events, and presentation or review of rubrics or checklists for quality can assist in these goals.

While there is no formula for introducing content effectively, a powerful introduction can have a very positive impact on learning. For that reason, it's worth a teacher's time to ask the following questions: How will I let students know the content of the unit is going to be worthwhile, interesting, and exciting? How will I orient them to the learning journey we will take together? How do I begin to let them know they can be successful in this study? How can I tap into my students' prior experiences in a way that connects the study to their lives?

Teaching Methods

One of the most important tasks in designing curriculum is the selection of teaching activities, sometimes referred to as methods or pedagogy. A teaching method is a strategy or technique, selected purposefully, that educators use to instruct students or connect them with the content. These strategies forward the learning goals within a curriculum unit and place the teacher in the role of facilitator, trainer, coach, or model of learning.

There are many useful teaching methods, but only a handful of these techniques have been well researched for effectiveness with various age groups and subject areas. A sampling of these is provided in Figure 3.7. The first column in the table identifies a teaching method, and the second provides a succinct definition. The "Benefits" section of the second column includes information about the value that may accrue to students when teachers use the teaching strategy appropriately. Strategies nearer the top of the table are likely to be more teacher centered and require less student inquiry or independence. As the table continues, the strategies become more student centered and require more inference and independence on the

Direct Teaching	Teaching Method	Definition and Benefits
Direct Teaching Direct teaching is a form of instruction in which the teacher provides explicit, clear, and "spelled out" content, explanations, or skills to students.	Lecture	A deductive teaching strategy that consists of a carefully sequenced, illustrated oral presentation of content that is delivered to small or large groups of students. The lecture, or oral presentation, is interspersed with opportunities for reflection, clarification, and sense making.
		Benefits: Efficient acquisition of new content knowledge.
	Drill and Recitation	A teaching strategy that helps students memorize and recall information with accuracy and speed.
		Benefits: Accuracy and speed in student's recall of factual-level information.
	Direct Instruction	A method of teaching that consists of a teacher's systematic explanation of a new concept or skill followed by guided practice under a teacher's guidance.
		Benefits: Efficient and equitable knowledge acquisition.
	Strategy-Based Instruction	A method for teaching a cognitive strategy or procedure; the teacher explains and helps students acquire the strategy, models the strategy, and provides guided practice and feedback to students as they internalize the strategy.
		Benefits: Strategy acquisition; improves students' efficiency and self-efficacy related to skill performance.
	Coaching	A teaching method in which teachers make criterion-referenced observations about a student's performance and provide immediate, specific feedback in order to improve the student's performance.
		Benefits: Proficiency with respect to physical or cognitive skills.
	Concept Attainment	A teaching method teachers use to help students understand the essential attributes of a category or concept. In order to achieve this goal, the teacher systematically leads students through a controlled discussion during which students compare and contrast characteristics of examples and nonexamples of the category or concept.
		Benefits: Acquisition of new categories, concepts, and macroconcepts (e.g., vegetable, adjective, tragic hero, compromise).
	Synectics	A teaching method in which teachers and students share or develop metaphors, similes, and/or analogies that build a bridge between students' prior knowledge or experience and new learning
		Benefits: Acquisition of new knowledge, enhanced creative expression, increased ability to generate creative solutions to problems.
	Demonstration/ Modeling	A teaching method in which the teacher's actions and behaviors serve as an example for students who, in turn, are able to replicate the actions and behaviors in other contexts.
		Benefits: The acquisition of behaviors, skills, and dispositions.

Figure 3.7 *(Continued)*

(Continued)

Teaching Method	Definition and Benefits
Socratic Questioning	An instructional strategy in which the teacher poses a carefully constructed sequence of questions to students in order to help them improve their logical reasoning and critical thinking about their position on an issue; can be used as a technique to bridge students' current level of understanding with new knowledge students need to acquire. (This model is tailored for older students who are middle school and beyond.)
	Benefits: The acquisition of content related to social issues; enhanced ability to think issues through logically.
Visualization	An instructional strategy in which the teacher encourages the students to pretend and imagine; words are not used. Students can be asked to see themselves performing a skill, participating in an event, living at some time in the future, etc.
	Benefits: Encourages literal comprehension, transfer of procedures, reduces anxiety, increases the likelihood of goal attainment.
Role Playing	The involvement of students as participants and observers in a real-world situation.
	Benefits: Growth and understanding as it relates to: content; students' understanding of others' beliefs and values; problem-solving skills.
Cooperative Learning	A teaching activity in which the teacher purposively uses small group interaction to forward new learning and accomplish academic and social tasks.
	Benefits: Collaboration among students; deeper thinking and understanding; enhanced feelings of empathy for others.
Jurisprudence	A teaching strategy in which teachers provide students with the opportunity to collaborate in order to develop cases and persuasive arguments on all sides of an issue, controversy, or decision.
	Benefits: Critical thinking, analysis, evaluation synthesis, oratory, persuasive writing.
Simulation	An inductive teaching method in which students assume roles of people engaged in real-life pursuits.
	Benefits: Increased likelihood that concepts and principles induced from the simulation will be transferred and applied to the real world.
Inquiry-Based Instruction	An inductive teaching strategy in which the teacher poses a task, problem, or intriguing situation and students explore the situation across small changes in the data set and generate insights about the problem and/or solutions.
	Benefits: Increased self-awareness; awareness of different points of view; enhanced curiosity; understanding of concepts and principles; enhanced ability to solve problems.
Problem-Based Learning	An inductive teaching method in which the teacher presents an ill-structured, novel, and/or complex problem for students to investigate and solve collaboratively with teacher guidance and coaching.
	Benefits: Acquisition of new knowledge, concepts, and principles; enhanced problem-solving ability.

Teaching Method	Definition and Benefits
Shadowing Experiences	A teaching strategy employed by a teacher when a student, or small group of students, requires short-term exposure to selected fields or disciplines. A teacher may involve a student for several hours or several days.
	Benefits: Increased ability to use the tools and methodology of the discipline; increased understanding of the life of the practicing professional; a deepening awareness about the fit between a learner's profile and the targeted field or discipline.
Mentorships	A teaching method in which a student spends a period of time under the tutelage of an expert in the field in order to learn the content, methodology, and day-to-day activities of the practicing professional.
	Benefits: Enhanced content area knowledge; increased ability to use the tools and methodology of the discipline; increased understanding of the life of the practicing professional; a deepening awareness about the fit between a learner's profile and the targeted field or discipline.
Independent Study	An instructional strategy in which the teacher encourages individuals or small groups of students to explore self-selected areas related to a curriculum unit.
	Benefits: Enhanced motivation, content area knowledge, and methodological skills.
Independent Investigations	An inductive teaching method in which the teacher provides individual and small groups of students with the opportunity to research and create products and performances under the guidance of a facilitator and/or expert.
	Benefits: Enhanced motivation, content area knowledge, and methodological skills; increased self-efficacy with respect to all aspects of research, creative productivity, and self-directed learning skills.

Indirect Teaching

A form of teaching in which the student take an active role in constructing the content, knowledge, or skills to be acquired

Figure 3.7   Selected Teaching Methods

part of students. Teachers will also have to adjust the level of teacher support, scaffolding, and coaching for various students, depending on factors like complexity of content, student familiarity with the strategy, and student independence in thought and work.

Teacher comfort and competence with each method are valuable, but more valuable is a teacher's ability to match the instructional technique with learning goals and to provide structure, guidance, and support for student success. Within a curriculum unit, teaching methods should be varied, aligned with learning goals and students' learning needs, and promote student engagement and higher order thinking. In addition, these methods promote optimal student learning when they provide for scaffolding, monitoring, adjustment, and feedback.

Learning Activities

Learning activities are tasks designed to develop the knowledge, understanding, and skills specified in the content goals. They should help students perceive, process, rehearse, store, and transfer new information and skill.

Many practitioners equate learning with listening or observing. In these classrooms, children are expected to learn because they read a page, listen to a lecture, or complete an experiment. In actuality, these approaches may help students perceive information, but there is little assurance that students who "fake read" or "fake listen" with these approaches have really "learned."

Learning that results in deep understanding requires activities that call on students to engage thoughtfully with the new information. Analytical, critical, and creative thinking skills require students to "do something" with the new information. When students are required to use and process information, they have to perceive it and manage it mentally. This sort of cognition not only supports learning but also memory retrieval. Cognitive tasks, then, work "double time" for the learner. Some cognitive tasks that can be used as the pivotal elements in learning activities are categorized and defined in Figure 3.8.

As is the case with high-quality teaching methods, high-quality learning activities are aligned with content goals and teaching methods. Moreover, these activities must link to students' prior knowledge and the learning strategies they have already acquired. Finally, learning activities must be efficient for students and their use must fit within the time frame for a curriculum unit.

Grouping Strategies

Grouping strategies enable teachers to arrange students in configurations most likely to enhance the acquisition of content and skills. Teachers can employ a wide range of grouping strategies among which are whole group instruction, cooperative and collaborative groups, flexible small groups, partner checks, book buddies, lab partners, and discussion groups.

At times, it makes most sense for a whole class to work as a unit. At other times, it is wise for students to work alone. Often, it makes sense for small groups of students to work together on part or all of a task. In this latter instance, a flexible teacher will sometimes group students with similar readiness levels, interests, or approaches to learning. On other occasions, however, the teacher will purposefully construct groups in which students bring to the group differing readiness levels, interests, or approaches to learning. Sometimes, the teacher will select student groupings but at other times ask students to decide on group membership. At still other times, the teacher will assign students to groups randomly.

Decisions about grouping should be based on content goals and the needs of students and should include both the directions and support necessary to ensure that students know how to work successfully in the particular grouping. Effective use of varied groupings enables teachers to observe students in a variety of settings and enables students to see themselves in varied contexts, thereby increasing the chance that they will have ongoing opportunities to work in ways that both tap their strengths and help them strengthen areas of weakness.

Thinking Skill	Definition
Analytical Thinking Skills	**Various cognitive processes that deepen understanding of knowledge and skills**
Identifying characteristics	The ability to identify distinct, specific, and relevant details that characterize an object, an event, or a phenomenon
Recognizing attributes	The facility to discern and label general or common features of a set of objects
Making observations	The capability to perceive and select attributes of an object or experience
Discriminating between same and different	The ability to make fine discrimination among objects, ideas, or events
Comparing and contrasting	The facility to see similarities and difference same among objects, events, and people
Categorizing	The ability to group objects or events according to some preconceived classification scheme
Classifying	The capability to extract relevant attributes of a group of objects, people, or phenomena that can be used to sort or organize the same
Ranking, prioritizing, and sequencing	The facility to place objects, events, or phenomena in hierarchical order according to some quantifiable value
Seeing relationships	The ability to see a connection or interaction between two or more objects or phenomena
Finding patterns	The ability to perceive and extract a repeating scheme in objects or phenomena
Determining cause and effect	The ability to see and extract the most powerful reasons or results for a given event or action
Predicting	The ability to see patterns, compare and contrast, identify relationships, determine cause and effect, and anticipate likely events in the future
Making analogies	The ability to identify a relationship between two familiar items or events and similar items and events in order to problem-solve or initiate creative productivity
Critical Thinking Skills	**Various thinking skills that are used to analyze and evaluate data and evidence in order to develop, judge the effectiveness of, or respond to an argument or position**
Inductive thinking	The ability to draw an inferential conclusion based on repeated observations that yield consistent but incomplete data
Deductive thinking	The ability to draw a logical conclusion from premises
Determining benefits and drawbacks	The ability to weight the advantages and disadvantages of a given idea or action
Determining reality and fantasy	The ability to distinguish between that which is fanciful and that which is true or actual
Identifying value statements	The ability to recognize statements that reflect appraisals of worth that cannot be supported through objective means
Identifying points of view	The ability to recognize that individuals and groups may have values and beliefs that influence their perspective on issues

Figure 3.8 *(Continued)*

(Continued)

Thinking Skill	Definition
Determining bias	The ability to ascertain information that is value laden
Identifying fact and opinion	The ability to distinguish between statements that can be proven and statements that reflect personal beliefs or judgments
Judging essential and incidental evidence	The ability to assess information and categorize it into useful and less useful categories
Identifying missing information	The ability to determine essential information that is not given or provided
Judging the accuracy of information	The ability to determine the precision of evidence that is presented
Judging the credibility of a source	The ability to assess whether the given information is believable, valid, and worthy to be considered
Recognizing assumptions	The ability to distinguish between information that is commonly accepted as true and information that is conjecture
Determining the strength of an argument	The ability to extract the reasons for an argument and evaluate the evidence as worthy
Identifying exaggeration	The ability to extract statements that magnify or overstate what is accepted as fact
Executive Processes	**Various cognitive skills that are involved in organizing, synthesizing, generalizing, or applying knowledge**
Summarizing	The ability to reduce a written or oral narrative to its essential components
Metacognition	The ability to consciously monitor, describe, and reflect upon one's thinking
Setting goals	The ability to set desirable outcomes in any situation
Formulating questions	The ability to develop relevant and precise queries related to any endeavor
Developing hypotheses	The ability to use prior observations to develop a possible explanation for an apparent relationship between two variables
Generalizing	The ability to use repeated, controlled, and accurate observations to develop a rule, principle, or formula that explains a number of situations
Problem solving	The ability to describe a problem, identify an ideal outcome, and to select and test possible strategies and solutions
Decision making	The ability to create and use appropriate criteria to select the best alternative in a given situation
Planning	The ability to develop a detailed and sequenced series of actions to achieve an end

Thinking Skill	Definition
Creative Thinking Skills	**Various cognitive skills that are involved in creative production**
Fluency	The ability to generate numerous ideas or alternatives to solve a problem that requires a novel solution
Flexibility	The ability to generate a wide variety of ideas to solve a problem that requires a novel solution
Originality	The ability to generate novel or unique alternatives to solve a problem that requires a novel solution
Elaboration	The ability to create a large number of details that explain a novel solution to a problem
Imagery	The ability to visualize a situation or object and to manipulate various alternatives for solving a problem without benefit of models, props, or physical objects
Using idea/product modification techniques	The ability to use techniques such as substituting, combining, techniques adapting, modifying, making larger or smaller, putting to new uses, eliminating, reversing, or rearranging parts to make a more useful whole
Listing attributes	The ability to identify appropriate improvements to a process or product by systematically considering modifications to the original product's attributes
Brainstorming	The ability to work with others to withhold judgment while identifying varied, innovative, and numerous alternatives for solving a problem
Creative problem solving	Creative problem solving The ability to identify, research, and plan to solve a problem that requires a novel, systematic solution

Figure 3.8   Cognitive Processes That Can Be Used to Design Learning Activities

SOURCE: Burns, D. (1993). *A six-phase model for the explicit teaching of thinking skills.* Storrs, CT: University of Connecticut, National Research Center on the Gifted and Talented.

Resources

A resource is a tool, data set, learning opportunity, or source of information for teachers and students. Resources are used to accomplish the goals within a curriculum, and they can be used by students independently or require teacher interpretation and assistance. Effective resources should provoke thinking and promote clarity of understanding about content goals. Resources are used primarily during the teaching and learning activities but also can be used during assessments, introductions, product development, and extension activities.

Resources can be categorized into two basic types: human and nonhuman. A sample of resources is listed in Figure 3.9. Exemplary resources are varied and closely linked to the learning goals, reading levels, cognitive strengths, and learning needs of the students who will use them.

Resources		
Human	*Nonhuman*	
Content area experts	*Print*	*Nonprint*
Older students	Biographies	Software
Younger students	Poems	Artifacts
Other students in the classroom	Plays	Tools
Parents	Diaries	Inventions
Other teachers of that grade	Magazine articles	Technology
Community members	Journals	Antiques
Teachers from other grade levels	Web	Posters
Other school personnel	College textbooks	Paintings
University personnel	Newspaper	Dioramas
Business personnel	E-mails	Models
Service organization personnel	Nonfiction	Realia
Retired senior citizens	Fiction	Photographs
	Historical fiction	Observations
	Literary analysis	Experiments
	Manuals	Situations
	Maps	Events
	Survey data	Globes
	Tables	Videotapes
	Charts	Exhibits
	Anthologies	Costumes
	Textbooks	Designs
	Historical documents	Music Equipment

Figure 3.9 Resources

Products

A well-designed product or assignment produces tangible evidence of student learning. As such, it is an assessment tool. At the same time, a product is also part of a learning activity. This is the case because most learning activities ask students to make, write, or do something to help process ideas, use skills, and also provide evidence of what has been learned. Thus, products are strongly linked both to learning activities and to assessments. We have elected to include a category called "products" rather than embedding the discussion of products in either learning activities or assessments. This decision reflects a belief in the power of effective student products to motivate learners, distill content, and inform teachers.

Teachers use products to measure student growth over time, to monitor and adjust instruction in order to promote student success, and as a basis for evaluating students. Students use products to communicate their understanding of the learning objectives. Products can be short term—that is, provide evidence of learning over a class period or a few class periods. They can also be longer term—that is, culminating work that brings together knowledge, understanding, and skill from an extended time such as a unit, a grading period, or even a semester or a year. This book addresses both short- and long-term products in the discussion of each of the parallels in the Parallel Curriculum Model.

Products can take many forms: tests, worksheets, journals, performances, problem solving, explanations, or reflections. Exemplary products are closely aligned to content goals, while also authentic, efficient, equitable, and diagnostic. They provide an opportunity for students to link their own interests and talents with content goals or to extend their range of interests and abilities. Good product assignments include very clear expectations for the knowledge and understanding that must be represented in the product, skills that must be used in completing the product, and habits of work that should be used to complete the product. Figure 3.10 provides a variety of student products.

Extension Activities

Extension activities are preplanned or serendipitous experiences that teachers orchestrate for individuals, small groups, or the entire class. These activities expand the basic unit plans and emerge from the unit's content goals as well as student interests. Extension activities can occur at any time during a unit. They may be of short duration (e.g., working with an interactive Web site or listening to a community speaker) or may require more extensive time (e.g., conducting an independent study, participating in a Web quest, or staging a performance). Extension activities may take place in class, at home, or both.

Teachers provide opportunities for extension activities for many reasons. First, extension activities promote the transfer and application of content goals to real-world contexts and problems. Second, they provide an opportunity to blend students'

Advance organizer	Dance	Investment portfolio	Picture book	Skit
Advertisement	Debate	Journal	Picture dictionary	Slide presentation
Animation	Diagram	Lecture	Play	Small-scale model
Annotated bibliography	Diary	Lesson	Podcast	Social action plan
Argument	Dictionary	Letter	Poem	Song
Art work	Diorama	List	Portfolio	Sonnet
Assignment	Display	Log	Poster	Stencil
Audiotape	Dramatic monologue	Magazine article	PowerPoint presentation	Summary
Biography	Drawing	Map	Prediction	Survey
Blog	Economic forecast	Memoir	Protocol	Table or Graph
Blueprint	Editorial	Memoria	Proposal	Terrarium
Board game	Essay	Movie	Puppet	Textbook
Book jacket	Etching	Museum exhibit	Puppet show	Theory
Bulleted list	Experiment	Musical composition	Questions	Think piece
Bulletin board	Fable	Newspaper	Radio show	Timeline
Compact disc	Fact file	Notes	Reader response	TV documentary
Calendar	Fairy tale	Observation log	Relief map	TV newscast
Campaign	Family tree	Oral history	Reflection	Video game
Census	Filmstrip	Oral report	Research report	Video portfolio
Character sketch	Glossary	Outline	Rule	Vocabulary list
Chart	Graph	Overhead transparency	Science fiction story	Web page
Choral reading	Graphic organizer	Pamphlet	Scrapbook	Web site
Chronology	Greeting card	Pantomime	Sculpture	Worksheet
Collage	Hypothesis	Paragraph	Set design	
Collection	Illustrated story	Pattern	Short story	
Comic strip	Interview	Photo essay	Simulation	
Critique	Invention	Photo journal		

Figure 3.10   Selected Products

interests and areas of expertise with content goals. Third, they can link content goals in one discipline to other disciplines or to other topics within the same discipline. Extension activities also can help students gather ideas for writing, products, or problem solving.

High-quality extension activities have several attributes. They are (a) linked to content goals, (b) open ended, (c) authentic, (d) student centered, (e) guided, and they (f) generate excitement for learning. Extension activities can be one way to address varied learner interests or need for advanced content or language in the classroom. That is, when used to tap into or extend particular interests of learners, extension activities are much like the tenth curriculum element that follows.

Differentiation Based on Learner Need (Including AID)

Teachers can greatly enhance student learning by improving the match between learners' unique characteristics and various curriculum components. Among student characteristics that affect learning are students' interests, their readiness to learn particular content at a particular time, and their preferred modes of learning.

When designing a lesson or unit, teachers should use differentiation strategies that address students' learning profiles, communication strengths and needs, reading levels, English language proficiency, or special education requirements. The most effective and efficient modifications in response to learner need are proactive, or preplanned, rather than reactive (or improvisational) on the part of the teacher. That is, the teacher assesses and observes students to understand as fully as possible their readiness for current curriculum goals, their interests, how they learn best, their sense of self-efficacy, and their motivational patterns. In addition to learning about learners through preassessment tools, teachers can see important differences emerge from learner profiles, class discussions, student products, day-to-day interactions among students, teacher-student conversations, homework, and a range of other daily data sources. Using that information, the teacher is able to develop more than one path to critical learning goals.

Based upon the analysis of preassessment data and other observations, teachers adapt one or several of the components of instruction to accommodate the differences identified as potentially significant in student learning. Among the elements of instruction that can be altered in response to learner need are the following: tiering of learning goals and learning materials, methods of assessment, teaching methods (including opportunities for small group reteaching or small group advanced teaching), learning activities, grouping strategies, products, rubrics, resources, coaching or scaffolding, pacing, working arrangements, and extension activities.

Naturally, not all components of instruction need to be altered at a given point. The goal is to modify those curricular elements that encourage each student to learn as much as possible and as efficiently and effectively as possible.

The concept of Ascending Intellectual Demand (AID) in the Parallel Curriculum Model is one type of differentiation based on learner need. It suggests the importance of a teacher monitoring the sophistication of a student's knowledge, understanding, and skill as it inevitably develops along a continuum from fledgling or novice to expert. As the student shows increased sophistication or complexity in thought and work, the teacher modifies one or more curricular elements in response to student growth—not so much to change the content goals of the curriculum as to increase the intellectual demand in how the student works with the curriculum. This is necessary in order to provide appropriate challenge in accordance with student growth. The goal is for students to work at continual intellectual ascent in response to increased intellectual demand encountered in content, materials, tasks, products, pace, and so on. AID is discussed throughout the book and described in detail in Chapter 8.

Lesson and Unit Closure

The reason for a lesson may seem quite clear to a teacher. The teacher may feel that everything in the lesson points to a key principle or leads to a particular conclusion. Chances are good, however, that students in the class will draw different conclusions about the point of the lesson, develop a range of misconceptions about key ideas, or have little sense of what they should take away from the lesson. An effective lesson closure enables the teacher to focus student attention on what matters most—on how the lesson makes sense and how it relates to the students' knowledge, experiences, and lives.

In addition, if students have worked on varied versions of a task, at varied levels of expertise, in different groups, or with different materials, it is important for them to come together to discuss the important ideas all of them have been pursuing, even if they have done so in different ways. Similarly, effective unit closure helps students create a framework of meaning, bring together pieces of learning into a coherent whole, see themselves in what they have learned, and look ahead to new learning that needs to connect with current learning.

Teachers can accomplish effective closure in a variety of ways: through class discussion, use of graphic organizers, having students first share perspectives in small groups and then with the class as a whole, and by using video analogies, to name just a few. Whatever the strategy the teacher uses to bring closure for lessons or units, it should help students solidify their understanding of how their studies make sense, how the ideas and skills can be used, and why they matter. Effective lesson and unit closure ensures that segments of study really "conclude," and not just "quit."

Remodeling a Study Unit Using the Comprehensive Curriculum Framework: One Teacher's Approach

Beginning with this chapter and continuing with subsequent chapters that examine the four parallels of the Parallel Curriculum Model, you will see how "Lydia Janis," a fictionalized fifth grade teacher, uses five approaches to curriculum development to craft the same social studies unit on the Civil War for her students. In this chapter, she uses a "remodeling" approach to revise her original textbook unit. That is, rather than merely following the textbook's directions, she uses the components in the curriculum design process discussed earlier in this chapter to enhance the quality of her unit. As the chapters progress, she will redesign her fifth grade Civil War unit using each of the four parallels in the Parallel Curriculum Model. A note to keep in mind: even though Lydia is a fictionalized teacher, the work presented as hers in the remainder of this book was actually developed by teachers using the thought processes described for each of the five approaches to curriculum design—first, the remodeling approach and then the approaches suggested, respectively, by the Core Curriculum Parallel, the Curriculum of Connections, the Curriculum of Practice, and the Curriculum of Identity.

The "Lydia stories" that appear through the next several chapters are not meant to suggest that every possible curriculum component must be emphasized in every lesson and unit. Nor are they representative of a reasonable level of planning for every lesson in a unit as a teacher begins to design curriculum. Seen at those levels, the illustrations become more aversive than helpful. The point of including the examples and the level of detail they reflect is instead simply to illustrate how various curricular elements can be used to contribute to teaching and learning. Over time, teachers who continue to reflect on and plan for best use of whatever curricular elements they elect to incorporate in their work with curriculum design and implementation will find increasing potential in each of the elements to support student success.

Figure 3.11 reviews the steps that Lydia follows in remodeling her unit from one that simply covers the text to one that is standards-based, more coherent, more likely to help students understand and retain what they encounter, and more inviting to the young learners with whom she works. It is important to note that this fictitious story of Lydia's curriculum work is meant to serve as a concrete example and illustration aligned to the explanation of the curriculum design components that precedes this teaching scenario.

Setting the Course: Aligning Text and Standards

Lydia Janis gathered the student's textbook, teacher's guide, and the notebook containing her state and district's Grade 5 social studies standards and related curriculum guide. She laid them on her dining room table and began her work. First on her list was an examination of the unit's learning standards and objectives.

In Lydia's state, the social studies curriculum incorporates four strands: history, government, economics, and geography. Lydia's state and local objectives were well aligned, eliminating a great deal of time that she might have had to spend aligning those two documents. Lydia's district decided that the fifth grade social studies curriculum would involve the study of early U.S. history. The Grade 5 social studies curriculum committee divided the school year into seven related curriculum units focused on these emphases. These units included the following topics: indigenous people, exploration, colonization, revolution, formation of a new nation, our

Step	Activity
1	Consult national, state, and local curriculum frameworks.
2	Compare textbook objectives with state and local standards to ensure alignment.
3	Design assessments (i.e., pre, ongoing, and post) that embed the targeted knowledge and contain the desired level of understanding.
4	Establish clear learning objectives that address state and local learning goals and consider the learning needs of students.
5	Develop an appropriate set of introductory activities.
6	Select teaching methods that align with the content and students' learning needs.
7	Determine the learning activities and align them with the teaching activities and learning goals.
8	Consider possible grouping formats.
9	Target a variety of student products that align with the learning goals to assess student progress.
10	Identify and locate resources.
11	Consider possible extension activities.
12	Consider differentiating resources, products, content, teaching methods, learning tasks, or grouping strategies based on preassessment data and learner profiles. Provide for Ascending Intellectual Demand when assessment data suggest differences in students' prior knowledge, interests, and strengths.
13	Determine strategies to ensure that students leave their study of the Civil War each day with a sense of what was most important in their work.

Figure 3.11 Lydia's Steps in the Curriculum Remodeling Process

expanding nation, and the Civil War. Each unit varied in length, depending on the number of learning goals to be achieved, but generally lasted from three to five weeks.

After the social studies curriculum committee developed the list of units within each grade level, they worked together to select the learning standards related to each unit. As a result of this decision, Lydia's district developed a curriculum map that contained twenty-five learning standards for Grade 5.

Lydia's first task was to review the curriculum map and the grade-level and unit learning goals in light of what she and her students needed to accomplish in social studies over the course of the year. She realized that she had approximately four weeks to address twelve social studies standards within the context of the Civil War. These standards, taken from *The Connecticut Framework: K–12 Curricular Goals and Standards* (Connecticut State Department of Education, 1998a), included the following.

1. Demonstrate an in-depth understanding of major events and trends in U.S. history (history).

2. Analyze data in order to see persons and events in their historical context; understand causal factors and appreciate change over time (history).

3. Examine current concepts, issues, events, and themes from historical perspectives and identify conflicting ideas from competing narratives or interpretations of historical events (history).

4. Explain reasons for conflict and the ways conflicts have been resolved (history).

5. Explain how economic factors influenced historical events in the United States (history).

6. Display empathy for people who have lived in the past (history).

7. Describe and analyze, using historical data and understandings, the options available to parties involved in contemporary conflicts or decision making (history).

8. Identify and evaluate various perspectives associated with places and regions (geography).

9. Evaluate situations involving conflicts between citizens' rights and propose solutions to these conflicts (government).

10. Use maps, globes, models, graphs, charts, and databases to analyze distributions and patterns (geography).

11. Identify governmental activities that affect the local, state, national, and international economy (economics).

12. Explain how specialization leads to more efficient use of economic resources and economic growth (economics).

Upon reading this list, Lydia concluded that the unit's standards did indeed capture the principles that students should understand about this period in United States history.

Next, Lydia compared the district curriculum guide with the teacher's guide that accompanied her textbook. She located the two chapters in her textbook devoted to the Civil War and searched for the section that described the learning goals. This section was labeled "Lesson Objectives." She noted fifteen learning objectives for the two chapters.

Lydia spread out the list of textbook objectives next to the list of standards that she located in her district's curriculum guide. She then listed in parentheses beside each textbook objective the number of the standard to which the objective seemed to connect. She wanted to make sure that her textbook addressed each of the standards.

1. Analyze the differences between the North and South (**4**).

2. Describe how some enslaved people fought against slavery (**4**).

3. Identify the difficulties faced by free African Americans (6).

4. Identify leading abolitionists and describe their fight against slavery (1, 8, 9).

5. Explain how the movement for women's rights began (3, 6, 8, 9).

6. Describe the compromises over slavery that temporarily prevented the South's secession (*1*, **4**).

7. Analyze the reasons that the South seceded (**4**).

8. Describe how the Civil War began (*1*, **5**, 12).

9. Compare and contrast the strengths of each side (*1*, 2).

10. Explain how technology changed the way wars were fought (2, 10).

11. Analyze the effect of the Emancipation Proclamation on both the North and the South (3, **4**).

12. Describe how women on both sides supported the war effort (3).

13. Evaluate the effects of the war on the North and South (2).

14. Describe Sherman's march (*1*, 10).

15. Describe Lee's surrender at Appomattox (*1*).

Lydia was not altogether surprised when she discovered that many of her textbook objectives related in some way to the first and fourth standards on her list. Six of her textbook objectives were related to the first standard (indicated in italics in the parentheses), and five were related to the fourth standard (indicated in bold in the parentheses). "That's good," she thought. "Students need to know the major events and trends surrounding the Civil War. They also need to know that the Civil War is really about a conflict."

The other thing that really pleased Lydia was the fact that her textbook appeared to cover all but two of the standards, 7 and 11. "Number 11 is about economics," Lydia thought to herself. "I will talk about the different economies of the North and South when we examine causes of the Civil War." She wasn't sure yet how to incorporate Standard 11. On a sticky note she jotted down, "Remember to help students see how government activities can affect the local, state, and national economy." She put the sticky note in her teacher's edition. "This note will remind me," thought Lydia.

Satisfied that the content of the textbook aligned fairly well with her standards, Lydia turned her attention to the other components of her instruction.

Revising the Teacher's Guide Assessment

When Lydia analyzed the assessment section that accompanied the teacher's guide, she found that the assessments addressed only four of the fifteen objectives for the two textbook chapters. A closer analysis of the student's book revealed that the review section for each lesson was more closely aligned to the objectives but that these review sections went only as far as rephrasing each learning objective as a question for the students to answer. Other options for student assessment were sparse or omitted. One-word or short phrases were the only responses required of students. When a review question seemed to support higher level thinking from students (e.g., "Why did Lincoln announce the Emancipation Proclamation after the Battle of Antietam?"), Lydia discovered that the answer to the question need only be paraphrased from the original text (e.g., "President Lincoln also found a way to inspire his troops. Five days after Antietam, Lincoln issued the Emancipation Proclamation.").

She realized she needed to create her own assessments. Her first decision was to create a pre- and a postassessment that mirrored each other. Using these assessments as bookends before and after instruction, Lydia would be able to measure each student's growth and progress with regard to her content. To assess student growth with respect to the objective "Describe how the Civil War began," Lydia chose a simple, open-ended question. Using a graphic organizer that resembled a flow chart, Lydia asked her students to respond to the following prompt: "Use this diagram and your knowledge of the Civil War to list, in order, the major events and people that led up to the beginning of the Civil War." She created a very simple, five-point rubric, reprinted below in Figure 3.12, to evaluate student responses.

The impact of the change Lydia made in assessment strategies was powerful. Not only was she able to assess changes over time in an individual student's growth in critical knowledge, she had also developed a rubric that could be revised easily to fit a number of different objectives and contexts. Also, the use of the preassessment provided Lydia with important information about students' prior knowledge—information she could use to save valuable time for teaching the remaining units in her textbook.

Lydia was aware that the use of preassessment took some time during the course of a four-week unit. However, she believed the time allocated to preassessment was well spent because it provided previously hidden information about students' prior knowledge and because it created an advance organizer for students by alerting

SOCIAL STUDIES RUBRIC: FLOW CHART OF MAJOR EVENTS LEADING UP TO THE CIVIL WAR

Key Feature	*Novice*	*Competent*	*Informed*	*Highly Informed*	*Expert*
Accuracy	Two or fewer major events noted; 2 or more inaccuracies are evident; formatting is incorrect	At least 3 major events are noted; 2 inaccuracies are evident; the formatting has minor mistakes	At least 4 major events are noted; 1 inaccuracy is evident; formatting is correct	More than 5 major events are noted; minor inaccuracies are evident; formatting is correct	More than 6 major events are noted; no inaccuracies are evident; formatting is correct

Figure 3.12 Rubric to Evaluate Students' Flow Chart

them to the major goals within the unit. Lydia continued to develop open-ended questions and related rubrics for the remaining objectives in the textbook unit, attempting to pull together objectives when feasible to help herself and students see connections among them. She was pleased with her progress thus far.

Planning the Introduction to the Unit

The teacher's guide provided suggestions for introducing the unit, including: showing students early photographs from the mid-1800s, asking them what they already knew about the guarantees of freedom provided by the U.S. Constitution, talking about bugles and what they symbolize, discussing quotations from the Emancipation Proclamation, and thinking about the similarities and differences in the lives of farmers, soldiers, merchants, slaves, and slaveholders. Lydia recognized that many of these ideas were potentially powerful, but there were too many of them, and they were too splintered and discrete. Looking in the textbook chapters for introductory activities that would capture her students' interest, she decided to use the photographs in the text. She would ask students to scan the photographs for interesting and familiar elements. Students would then participate in small group discussions guided by questions Lydia provided to help them begin to focus on unit objectives.

To create a more motivating introduction to the unit for her students, Lydia created three additional introductory activities. She visited her school library and borrowed a copy of *The Boy's War: Confederate and Union Soldiers Talk About the Civil War* (Murphy, 1990). She would use this book as a motivational tool and as part of her daily read-aloud to her students. As she read, she would ask students to sketch scenes, events, characters, and impressions from the book in order to improve their mental images of the historical period.

Next, Lydia printed a list of learning goals and expectations for the four-week unit to share with her students. She knew it was important that students understand what was expected of them from the very beginning of the unit in order to increase their ownership in learning. She would use this list as her advance organizer for the unit. Then, Lydia would preassess students' knowledge using the assessment questions and rubrics described in the previous section. Prior to the preassessment, Lydia planned to explain what a preassessment was, why she was administering one, and what she hoped to learn from their early responses to her questions.

Determining Teaching Methods and Learning Activities

Lydia wanted to be sure her teaching activities would introduce, explain, scaffold, organize, and demonstrate new knowledge and skills as well as engage students with the new material. In essence, she would be a bridge builder between learners and the new knowledge they needed to acquire. Good teachers, she knew, challenge learners to think their way through new content, but good teachers never present insurmountable obstacles to the acquisition of knowledge and skills.

When Lydia reviewed the teaching activities in her textbook, she realized that, for the most part, students were expected to acquire new knowledge by independent reading, with only a few clarifying questions posed by the teacher or the textbook every two to three pages. Although the textbook provided a great deal of information for elementary teachers who may not have majored in the social sciences, there was little support for the learner who may be unfamiliar with the content or the structure of textbook learning. There were few focusing questions, little use of headings, and no use of boldface to mark new vocabulary or concepts.

There seemed to be little role for the teacher in forwarding the learning of her or his students. Was Lydia's only job to maintain classroom discipline and on-task behavior, assign pages to be read each day, and ask the questions printed in the side margins of the teacher's manual? How were students to cope with the new knowledge that was so tersely presented in the textbook? Lydia made a decision not unlike those she had made before. She had to provide the scaffolding that the textbook lacked in order to help her students understand the new content they were to acquire.

She would use the writing in the student's textbook to inform her own knowledge base, but instead of expecting her students to absorb the new content by themselves, she would create a structure to help them analyze the text's content. Lydia chose focusing questions, strategy-based teaching, graphic organizers, and cooperative learning as teaching methods to provide this structure. She would also incorporate teaching methods to help novice textbook readers develop effective techniques for reading nonfiction.

First, she created focusing questions for each major section in the two textbook chapters. Then, she identified the kind of analytic thinking needed to process the text's information and answer the focusing questions. Third, she developed a skill strategy to help her students learn how to use this analytic thinking skill. Fourth, she created a graphic organizer that required the use of this analytic thinking skill to answer the focusing question. For example, to help students acquire knowledge about the major differences between the North and the South, Lydia created two related focusing questions:

1. What were the differences between the economies of the North and the South prior to the Civil War?

2. How did these differences contribute to the start of the Civil War?

Next, Lydia located the four pages in the students' textbook that explained differences between the North and the South prior to the Civil War. To help students identify the related factors, she realized her students must use two thinking skills: (a) comparing and contrasting and (b) finding the main idea. She created two skill strategies and two graphic organizers similar to those shown in Figures 3.13 through 3.16.

Lydia knew these graphic organizers were aligned with the major thinking skills needed to understand the factual textbook content and would support students' knowledge acquisition. Students would work with these graphic organizers in small

1. Identify the purpose for comparing and contrasting.

2. Identify the objects, elements, persons, or events to be compared and contrasted.

3. Identify the attributes of each object, element, person, or event that relates to the purpose of the comparing and contrasting.

4. Note the relevant information.

5. Develop a related graphic organizer.

6. Identify a trend or pattern across the attributes or items.

7. Draw conclusions based on the evidence as it relates to the purpose for comparing and contrasting.

Figure 3.13   Skill Strategy for Comparing and Contrasting

Purpose: Compare and Contrast the Economies of the North and the South		
Factors	*North*	*South*
Workers	Worked in factories	Farmhands, slaves
Workplaces	Factories	Plantations
Resources	Coal, wood, iron, machines	Slaves, land, cotton, farms
Products	Ships, cloth, machines, guns, trains	Cotton
Profit	More money, more people	More land, more slaves
Conclusion: Slaves in the South worked on plantations. Free people in the North worked at lots of different factory jobs. These differences made people in the North and South feel differently about issues.		

Figure 3.14   Graphic Organizer to Support Student Comparing and Contrasting

1. Identify the purpose for finding the main idea.

2. Identify passages related to this purpose.

3. Read the passage and identify relevant details related to the purpose.

4. Determine commonalties among the details.

5. Restate the commonalties as an overarching statement.

6. Connect the identified main idea to the original purpose.

Figure 3.15   Skill Strategy for Finding the Main Idea

groups, scaffolded by each other and Lydia's strategy-based teaching, coaching, feedback, and questions regarding their work. The small groups would also dissect and analyze textbook passages as they developed answers to the questions focused on literal comprehension.

Although these changes promoted greater student understanding, they were by no means the only teaching strategies Lydia used during the course of the unit. She also developed brief oral

Purpose: To discover what key factors led to the Civil War and how these factors are connected.

Main Idea: Four different factors led to the Civil War. These factors made Northerners and Southerners dislike and mistrust one another. They couldn't find a solution.

	Factors	Supporting Details
#1	Two very different economies	
#2	Views about states' rights	
#3	Missouri Compromise	
#4	Slavery	

Figure 3.16 Graphic Organizer to Support Finding the Main Idea

presentations and taught specific strategies for improving students' reading of nonfiction and their literal comprehension skills.

The development of the focusing questions, skill strategies, and graphic organizers required two hours of additional time. Lydia quickly realized, however, that her time had been well spent. Now that she had these skills strategies and graphic organizers, she could use them in numerous other units and subject areas whenever students needed to analyze information in order to acquire new knowledge.

During this phase of textbook analysis and remodeling, Lydia also analyzed the learning activities embedded in the unit. After she reviewed the textbook learning objectives, she searched the related student pages to identify the means by which students were to acquire this new knowledge. She recalled that there were only two ways for students to acquire new information—either they read the textbook or they listened to the teacher's explanations and presentations. Further, she remembered that the text activities only called for the cognitive processes of recall and paraphrasing on the part of her students.

Lydia knew that this kind of learning was short lived. Knowledge that was memorized and paraphrased rarely entered a student's long-term memory. Not content with these results, Lydia was glad she had remodeled the teaching methods to support students' analytic thinking instead of restricting her focus to rote learning. To help her students come to a deep understanding of new knowledge, to retain, retrieve, and transfer new knowledge, she had to require students to use literal comprehension skills and analytic thinking. She couldn't assume her students already knew how to use these skills, and the textbook didn't teach them how. Instead, she decided to create and teach skill strategies that explained how expert readers and thinkers find the main idea, compare and contrast, note details, sequence ideas, and draw conclusions.

The graphic organizers she had created to support her teaching activities would be useful aids to scaffold students' literal comprehension and analytic thinking with the textbook content. She realized her revisions would contribute greatly to her students' evolving abilities to read nonfiction material in a variety of content areas.

To find time in the unit to complete these important activities, Lydia had to delete some of the textbook activities with less potential to help students make meaning of the events they were studying. These activities included learning the lyrics to "Battle Hymn of the Republic" and "Dixie," making a paper quilt containing Civil War themes, and creating a bulletin board of famous quotations from the Civil War.

Finding Resources for the Unit

Lydia spent time looking over the list of resources provided in the teacher's edition. They included photographs of log cabins, slaves, cotton fields, and famous people such as Fredrick Douglass, Sojourner Truth, Jefferson Davis, Harriet Tubman, and Abraham Lincoln; excerpts from primary source documents; and portions of newspaper articles and speeches. Songs, paintings, and political cartoons were also available to students via the teacher's guide. One of the strongest sections of her teacher's book was the bibliography that contained lists of historical fiction and nonfiction related to the war.

Lydia was confused about the number and variety of resources presented in her teacher's edition. The quantity of resources seemed overwhelming, and many of them did not seem a match for the factual objectives the book specified for the unit. For example, some of the resources were appealing, but they seemed to pull her away from her learning goals. It was interesting to her that the resources suggested in the book somehow seemed richer than the textbook content and objectives. She didn't want to change the unit objectives to match the resources unless she more fully understood the connections. Next summer, she decided, she'd revisit this issue and try to align the potential of the resources with the unit objectives. For now, she would be content to focus on and assess the original objectives along with her students' growth in reading nonfiction, literal comprehension, and analytic thinking. She continued to use the student edition of the textbook as a major resource.

Lydia supplemented the textbook with a list of learning objectives that she rewrote in students' language. She also made lists of focusing questions for each section of the text, created skill strategies for key skills, developed graphic organizers to support understanding and applying the skills, and duplicated these for distribution to students at appropriate times. She also purchased colored sticky notes and a large supply of colored highlighters. Finally, she duplicated some important textbook sections. She would use these copies along with the sticky notes and highlighter pens to help her students learn to note key ideas, supporting details, evidence, main ideas, and conclusions and how to jot down important thoughts and questions as they read.

These resources seemed a good match for both the content and skills goals she had adopted for the unit. Lydia was satisfied that the resources would help her students be more thoughtful about the content of the text and more effective readers and analysts of nonfiction materials.

Developing Products for the Unit

Now Lydia was ready to review the products mentioned in the teacher's guide. Options included short answers to review questions worksheets with short answers, a bulletin board, a scrapbook, quilts, discussions, a debate, short answers to teacher's oral questions, character sketches, letters, editorials, charts and timelines, and a skit. She decided she wanted to select only those products that aligned with her objectives and would not require a great deal of class time.

Lydia thought a combination of short- and long-term products would work well for her students. She had already decided to create a fifteen-item set of open-ended questions for the unit's pre- and postassessment. These questions related well to focusing questions she had developed for each section of the text and for classroom discussions. She decided to continue to use the review at the end of each section of the chapter because these questions also linked closely with the focusing questions and the main ideas in the text. The questions could be answered in writing by individuals or during whole class or small group discussions.

Still sensing a need to move beyond the factual level recall required in these assignments, however, Lydia considered the long list of optional products in her teacher's manual. She knew she couldn't assign all of them, and besides, many of them seemed a poor match for the unit's goals. She selected development of a timeline because it related closely to several of the text objectives. It would also allow her to use some newly acquired software to integrate technology into student learning—a key initiative in her district.

Lydia also decided to use a long-term collaborative project for her students that could serve as a culminating product. If she selected carefully, the product would be useful to her students in synthesizing all the events, people, and perspectives that played a role in the Civil War. She chose a mural that would depict, in chronological order, key issues, events, and people of the time period. Her directions for the mural would guide student thinking as they worked in small groups to complete the product. The directions would need to ensure a clear connection between the learning objectives and precisely what she asked the students to do.

At this point, Lydia Janis had remodeled her unit to make it more coherent, challenging, and aligned with her learning objectives. Her work should now be more effective in helping students understand content and issues related to the Civil War, retain what they study, and develop the skills of effective readers and thinkers.

Differentiating Unit Plans in Response to Learner Needs

Although the vast majority of learners would benefit from the curriculum Lydia has remodeled, it is also the case that her students, as is the case with most groups of learners, vary markedly in their prior knowledge, experiences, readiness to learn, interests, and modes of learning. Thus, while all learners share a common need for quality curriculum, Lydia knew there would be times when she would modify her curriculum plans to accommodate the learning needs of the diverse students in her classroom. She decided to continually monitor students' work and conversations for indications of their needs, and repeatedly invite them to let her know what was working for them and what was not working so well in their classroom.

Strategies that Lydia would use to differentiate her basic unit plans to ensure that learning was a good fit for all of her students include the following:

▶ Conducting reteaching sessions on topics or skills for students who have difficulty mastering them

▶ Providing audiotapes of the chapter along with an outline of the unit for students who have difficulty reading the textbook alone or who are highly auditory learners

▶ Offering a chance for students to work alone or with partners on some tasks

▶ Varying the amount of support she offers to students during various tasks based on their individual needs

▶ Setting up the classroom so that students sometimes have the freedom to choose where to sit, what surfaces to work on, and with which materials they want to work

▶ Maintaining centers on topics of interest to her learners

▶ Supplementing her oral presentations with overhead transparencies, advance organizers, and opportunities for small group discussions of content

Lydia already knew where several of these strategies would be useful. In fact, she realized, she had built several of them into the unit as she had remodeled it.

First, Lydia's plans called for preassessment of her students. This would help her detect various levels of prior knowledge about the Civil War among her students, and she could respond to what she learned at the outset of the unit by varying homework based on learner need and by excusing students already demonstrating mastery from some of the reading and writing tasks.

Second, her teacher-created graphic organizers would help many of Lydia's learners understand how to find main ideas, supporting details, and cause and effect. However, for students who already possessed these skills, she would encourage them to develop their own ways to show their analysis of text and events and to depict examples of cause and effect in their studies.

Third, the class textbook was written at a fifth grade reading level. This would be advantageous for some of her grade-level readers. On the other hand, a few students would need assistance in reading this book. She would use reading squads with those students, enabling them to read aloud, hear others read aloud, hear her read aloud, and use tape-recorded readings. For her more advanced readers, she would select some additional, more complex nonfiction materials about the Civil War to provide challenge.

Lesson and Unit Closure

Through the unit, Lydia used a variety of strategies to help her students focus on the meaning and intent of lessons. Among the strategies she used were the following:

▶ 1-2-2 exit slips on which she asked students to write the one idea they thought was most important in the lesson, two reasons they chose the idea they listed, and two questions they'd like answered about the lesson. After receiving the cards, Lydia reviewed student thinking and began the following class by spotlighting both student understandings and student misunderstandings.

▶ Grand discussion groups in which she first asked students to meet in groups of three to pose an answer to an essential or guiding question related to the lesson. Each discussion group appointed a spokesperson, recorder, and responder. When each group determined their answer to the question, the spokesperson shared it with the group, the recorder wrote it on chart paper or on a projected computer image, and the responder pointed out ways in which their answer concurred with or differed from responses in other groups.

▶ Excerpts from fiction or film on the Civil War or other wars in which characters represent one or more perspectives on the topic students have been studying. After viewing or hearing the excerpts, Lydia posed the question, "How does this example(s) help us see the point of what we've been doing in class today?" She concluded by writing a statement on the board that reflected the "theme" of the day.

Looking Back and Ahead

In her remodeling effort, Lydia Janis has ensured that her fifth grade Civil War unit is richer and better aligned than it would have been if she had moved her students through text material. To revisit an earlier analogy, she resisted the temptation to serve a list of ingredients and call it a meal. Instead, she blended and combined the ingredients to create a meal. She systematically addressed the key components of effective curriculum. Her plans are thoughtful and thorough, although she understands she may modify them again as the unit unfolds—particularly in light of her ongoing assessment of her students' successes and needs. Lydia also knows that even though she is pleased with these new unit plans, her teaching this year will point her toward changes she can make in the unit next year to make it even more effective. She understands that her goal is not to "finish" writing the unit but, rather, to learn more about teaching each time she uses it and to convert what she learns into refined ways of practicing her profession.

Lydia's work to this point is fundamentally sound but not especially sophisticated. As subsequent chapters explore the Parallel Curriculum Model and its four parallel ways of thinking about curriculum design, you'll see Lydia's thinking evolve. You should see several things as you read. First, the fundamental components of curriculum design are evident in all four parallels. The elements of curriculum don't disappear when a new curriculum model appears. Second, you'll see Lydia's curriculum become richer and more compelling as she restructures it using the four parallels of the Parallel Curriculum Model. We hope you'll see the possibilities offered by this new model and its four parallels to develop high potential in a broad range of young learners, including those who are already advanced. It is the premise of this book that educators—as all professionals—must continually look for avenues to make good practice better.

4

The Core Curriculum Parallel

The Comprehensive Curriculum Framework described in Chapter 3 provides a structure for designing a well-aligned and motivating set of teaching and learning activities stemming from clear objectives and carefully aligned assessments. Over time, this framework can support teachers in decreasing reliance on the textbook-driven or activity-oriented curriculum and moving toward one that both incorporates content standards and is cognitively engaging to learners.

The framework itself is flexible enough to support either lesson remodeling or the development of comprehensive curriculum units that supplement existing textbook chapters for students at any grade level and within any subject area. The key components and the accompanying set of best practices provide a set of guidelines that encourage an evolution of the lesson planning and unit development process. In addition, the framework makes provisions for ensuring that both teaching and learning plans are a good fit for the range of students in the classroom.

Yet, in a book that proposes and describes four additional approaches to or frameworks for curriculum design, two questions immediately arise. First, if the Comprehensive Curriculum Framework is a defensible and effective method for delivering high-quality learning experiences, why does this book contain descriptions of four other approaches to curriculum development? Second, what are the differences among these four approaches; do they provide elements that contradict, complement, or supplant the key features of the Comprehensive Curriculum Framework?

In order to provide at least a partial answer to these questions, this chapter has been divided into four sections. The first section presents a rationale for having four approaches to curriculum design rather than adhering consistently to only one approach. In the second section, readers are given a definition of the first curriculum parallel proposed in this book, the Core Curriculum Parallel, and an explanation of its purpose and function. The third section explains procedures for modifying the key curriculum components in order to align them with the goals and intent of the Core Curriculum Parallel and includes an exploration of the nature of Ascending Intellectual Demand within the Core Curriculum Parallel. The fourth section revisits fictionalized teacher Lydia Janis and provides a description of decisions she used when recrafting her curriculum using the goals and intent of the Core Curriculum Parallel.

Why Four Approaches to Curriculum Design? Isn't One Good Enough?

It's difficult to argue with the merits of using components of the Comprehensive Curriculum Framework either for developing exemplary curriculum or for evaluating and improving existing curriculum. The value of designing or selecting clear learning objectives, aligned assessments, motivating introductory experiences, powerful teaching and learning activities, appropriate resources, products, and extension activities, as well as effective closure, is apparent and universal across the writings of our most honored curriculum theorists and researchers. In addition, the features mentioned above, and the accompanying characteristics and indicators of exemplary design, provide ideal criteria to guide the process of curriculum development. Why, then, might it be useful for an educator to have a working knowledge of other curriculum design approaches? Might additional approaches simply generate confusion and decrease the likelihood of successful implementation?

Perhaps the best way to answer these questions is by relating two anecdotes that are familiar to many of us. They serve as windows that allow us a clear perspective on changes in the curriculum development process over time. Have these events ever happened to you? Consider the learning you acquired as a result of these or similar experiences.

Metaphor #1: The Novice-Expert Continuum

You read an interesting book, short story, magazine article, or poem. A few days later, a friend or colleague mentions having read the same piece of writing. The two of you spend the next fifteen minutes discussing the text. As you end the conversation, it occurs to you that you thought you had a sound understanding of that piece of writing before discussing it with your friend, but now you aren't so sure. Your companion mentioned aspects of the writer's style, perspective, and the text's content that you hadn't considered. It occurs to you that the conversation with your friend has deepened what you believed was already a comprehensive understanding of the topic.

That conversation with your friend caused you to see the text in new ways. You know more now because you had an experience that allowed you to reflect, recognize a gap between what was evident and what was assumed, learn, and, as a result, deepen your initial understanding. Sometimes, conversations cause us to see things with new eyes. Sometimes, solitude, analytic thought, time, distance, perspective, a simple question, or the acquisition of additional knowledge causes that change. Whatever the cause, the effect is the same. Our knowledge base and the depth of our understanding can grow and deepen as a result of our thinking and learning experiences. When this happens, we are often intrigued with the possibilities that this new knowledge offers and with the new doors that it opens.

Curriculum writing, like learning, is the result of a dynamic interaction between a person's cognitive faculties, his or her professional experiences with learners and colleagues, and an existing or new body of content knowledge. The lesson plan or unit that we write and implement today with pride may look different to us in a few years. Our students and our teaching circumstances often change and vary throughout our career. Our understanding of our students and of the topics that we teach often deepens as a result of our own professional learning. When this happens, we may experience a sense of dissatisfaction with curriculum that used to be a source of gratification. Like a shoe that no longer fits, we may outgrow what used to be a perfectly comfortable set of lesson plans in search of a larger, more expansive curriculum that permits us to travel farther, under different circumstances, or for diverse purposes.

That reaction is similar to the one many of us have when we unearth a lesson plan or longer piece of curriculum that we wrote years ago and haven't seen since. Our response is often one of surprise, an initial sense of puzzlement when we see our names on something we can't remember writing. We are often amazed at the lack of depth, the missing information, the gaps, or the inconsistencies in a lesson that at one time seemed so right, so complete, and so compelling.

Our own professional growth and hard work become the source of our dissatisfaction and a catalyst for change. Sometimes, a colleague provides an extra push; other times, it's a book, new research, or our students' reactions or comments. Either way, the inevitable happens. As teachers become more experienced, more reflective, and more knowledgeable—as they evolve from novices to veterans—expertise is enhanced. Although experience and tenure do not guarantee the development of expertise, the teacher who values and pursues lifelong learning and professional growth inevitably opens the door to new encounters, perspectives, knowledge, and needs as time passes. This growth process can affect our content knowledge, pedagogical expertise, and changes in priorities with regard to what students need from teachers and what students need to learn. These changes can also cause dissatisfaction with a curriculum framework that, on earlier occasions, seemed exemplary and comprehensive. As we become wiser and more experienced, our view of the curriculum, and of knowledge and the relationship among topics, disciplines, and learners, often expands. When this happens, it is valuable to have other alternatives for thinking about the curriculum. Not only can alternative options satisfy our need to grow professionally, they can, like a stimulating conversation with a thoughtful friend, be a catalyst for that growth.

Metaphor #2: Form Follows Function

Increasing levels of curriculum expertise do not necessarily imply that eventually we should abandon one framework in search of another. Nor does it imply that if we search long enough, we will discover or develop one framework that is far superior to any other. Instead, growth in expertise usually produces a broader, not just a different, perspective. Instead of evaluating different approaches and finding some exemplary and others lacking, growth in curriculum expertise usually results in a more utilitarian view of various curriculum approaches; one is not necessarily better than another. The various approaches simply serve different purposes and address different needs.

This principle about curriculum design, that form follows function, helps explain the reason why this book shares four such approaches or frameworks for use in curriculum design or remodeling. As defined in this book, a model is a format for curriculum design. It is a special configuration of key curriculum components within the Comprehensive Curriculum Framework designed to meet special needs and purposes. It is the unique arrangement and fabrication of these components that results in the development of a curriculum that is singularly tied to the four special purposes inherent in the four different curriculum frameworks or approaches described in this book.

Metaphor #3: Architectural Design

Just as a curriculum is a purposeful design, written by educators to build connections among teachers, learners, and content knowledge, a commercial architect drafts a blueprint for a building design that forges strong connections among service providers, their service, and the community at large. Just as the development of a curriculum requires the use of a framework comprised of interconnected components, an architectural design requires the combined use of a set of architectural components to construct a sound and functional building. Just as the basic framework of a commercial building remains constant while the form of the building varies according to its function, the key curriculum components and framework remain constant while the form and model (i.e., the special configuration) of these components vary according to the function and purpose of the curriculum.

Imagine that the comprehensive curriculum components are comparable to the basic components of a building: the foundation, the sill plate and flooring, the electrical system, the plumbing, the heating and cooling system, trusses, roof, windows, doors, and rooms. Depending on whether commercial architects are designing a hospital, a restaurant, a library, or a fire station, they would vary the configuration, or form, of these basic components to serve the specific needs of the service providers, the clients of these service providers, or the nature of the services. The special configuration of these architectural components may change the number of rooms, the height of the ceilings, the nature of the flooring, or the thickness of the pipes, but the basic architectural components still exist—as they do in all comprehensive curriculum.

Just as the nature and characteristics of these components vary according to the purpose of the building, the basic curriculum components vary according to the purpose of the curriculum. Each of the four curriculum parallels described in this book follows the same basic curriculum design structure and incorporates the use of the key curriculum components. However, just as architectural form follows the function of a building, the choice to use a particular curriculum framework requires a conscious decision based on the needs of the learner and the purpose for which the curriculum is designed.

What Is "Core" in the Core Curriculum Parallel?

Let's begin with a word association. When you hear the word "core," what expressions spring to mind? If you thought of apple core, core of the Earth, or the core of a nuclear reactor, you probably identified the most common associations for this term. In addition, some other synonyms for core are kernel, heart, gist, essence, basic nature, crux, and fundamental.

As these words imply, the Core Curriculum Parallel provides a format and set of procedures that help curriculum developers get to the core, fundamental, or essential knowledge and meaning of a discipline as they teach topics in that discipline. They see a benefit in using the topic studied to help students become proficient not only with information about the topic, but also with the major concepts and principles in the discipline from which the topic is derived.

With this approach, a unit may focus learning on a specific topic, such as radish plants, the Civil War, Romeo and Juliet, or Beethoven, but that focus would not be an end in and of itself. Instead, a study of fast-growing radish plants is used to forge an understanding of the basic concepts, principles, and skills that cut across the study of all plants and across all topics in botany or biology, knowledge that is core to the discipline in which the topic resides. In the case of radish plants, the learning activities may focus attention on the life cycle, food production, or roles of ecosystem members. The topic being studied—in this case, radishes—serves as a representative topic, not a stand-alone subject, to help learners understand the basic structure of a discipline.

As the Comprehensive Curriculum Framework serves to elevate curriculum development by helping teachers move from coverage of sometimes disjointed information and skills to a richer, more coherent curriculum, so the Core Curriculum Parallel should again "lift" curriculum design to a higher level of quality. The Core Curriculum Parallel exists to move curriculum developers from a well-aligned plan for teaching to one that retains alignment while getting at the core knowledge, structure, and purpose of a discipline.

Because of its goal of helping teachers and students come to understand what constitutes the core knowledge, structure, and purpose of a discipline, the Core Curriculum Parallel suggests that teachers and students continue to ask a set of questions likely to help reveal those things (see Figure 4.1). A close study of these questions reveals the "deep intent," or purpose, of Core Curriculum.

These additional questions probe the content more deeply. They help provide answers to the "So what?" and "Who cares?" questions that can plague teachers in a classroom inhabited by restless young minds. More to the point, these questions demand complex thinking, manipulation of ideas, and awareness of patterns—they have real implications for helping students move from novice-level consumers of someone else's information to more sophisticated meaning makers who deal with the fundamental concepts, principles, and skills of a discipline. Simply put, there is no such thing as an expert in a domain who lacks an understanding of the core organization, purpose, and meaning of that domain. If we are serious about helping

- What does this information mean?
- Why does this information matter?
- How is the information organized to help people use it better?
- Why do these ideas make sense?
- What are these ideas and skills for?
- How do these ideas and skills work?
- How can I use these ideas and skills?

Figure 4.1   Focusing Questions of the Core Curriculum Parallel

more students develop their potential—and about helping more high potential learners maximize that potential—we have to teach them in ways that help them systematically develop and strengthen their understanding of the frameworks of meaning and skill that characterize experts in a discipline.

Within the Core Curriculum Parallel, knowledge is selected for teaching and learning based on its ability to cause a series of chain reactions that link learners to the key concepts and principles of the discipline as a whole. Just as the core in a nuclear reactor contains pellets of a special kind of uranium, capable of causing multiple nuclear reactions, the careful selection of specific aspects of knowledge within a curriculum unit can create a critical mass capable of causing its own kind of chain reaction. However, instead of choosing U-235 over U-238 because of its special capacity for splitting atoms, curriculum designers who use the Core Curriculum Parallel choose knowledge that transcends a topic and links learners to the very core of the discipline. Like the free neutrons in U-235 that bombard and split surrounding uranium atoms to release large sums of energy, the careful use of specific knowledge categories provides a powerful source of energy. The energy inherent in a deep understanding of concepts, principles, and methodological skills can promote a chain reaction that enables students to use their knowledge of one topic to understand the overarching structure of an entire discipline.

What Is the Purpose of the Core Curriculum Parallel?

Effective use of the Core Curriculum Parallel benefits teachers and students in at least six noteworthy ways. First, the Core Curriculum Parallel promotes student understanding of the meaning and structure of a discipline. Second, it makes new learning in the same discipline easier and more efficient for students by providing a common framework for thinking about related aspects of a discipline. Third, it directly promotes students' proficiency, skillfulness, independence, and self-efficacy in the discipline and thus promotes movement toward expertise because it equips them with an expert-like way to understand the discipline. Fourth, use of this parallel helps teachers develop their own frameworks of meaning in the areas they teach—a proficiency often lacking at the end of undergraduate and even graduate education. In fact, the extent to which teachers are provided such frameworks by districts or professional groups, or to which teachers develop these frameworks on their own, often predicts the nature and quality of content that teachers present to their students. Fifth, curriculum developed with the approach suggested by the Core Curriculum Parallel meets the demand of employers and universities for individuals who independently use higher-level thinking processes in response to complex materials and problems in a society marked by an explosion of new information. Finally, using the Core Curriculum addresses issues of equity and opportunity to learn for all students, regardless of their age, economic situation, or intellectual development.

The Core Curriculum Framework also relates directly to Jerome Bruner's (1960) concept of a curriculum spiral. As originally defined by Bruner, a spiraled curriculum is one that treats all learners, regardless of age or cognitive readiness, as active inquirers capable of understanding the major concepts, principles, and skills of a discipline, given age-appropriate curriculum. The major concepts, principles, and skills are revisited across grade levels to ensure a deeper understanding of the complexities of these facets of knowledge as a child becomes more intellectually advanced. From Bruner's perspective, the aim of education is to teach the basic structure of academic disciplines in a way that fosters understanding, regardless of the sophistication of the learner: "Good teaching which emphasizes the structure of a subject is probably even more valuable for the less able student than for the gifted one, for it is the former rather than the latter who is most easily thrown off track by poor teaching" (p. 9).

To guide teachers and students in achieving these benefits, the Core Curriculum Parallel directs teachers and other curriculum developers to ensure that the curriculum does the following:

▶ Stems from the key facts, concepts, principles, and skills essential to a discipline and reflects what experts in the discipline find most important, with emphasis on student meaning making

▶ Is coherent in its organization so that it helps students systematically build knowledge, understanding, and skills and organize what they learn in ways that develop students' abilities to remember, make meaning, and use what they know in unfamiliar situations

▶ Is designed to cause students to consistently use high levels of critical and creative thinking, as well as metacognition (thinking about their thinking), to grapple with ideas and problems

▶ Is taught in contexts that are authentic to the discipline and meaningful to students, and in ways that are mentally and affectively inviting to students

▶ Engages students in worthwhile use of the understandings and skills central to the discipline

How Are Key Curriculum Components Reconfigured to Achieve the Goals of the Core Curriculum Parallel?

Core Curriculum is constructed around the elements of the Comprehensive Curriculum Framework discussed in Chapter 3 and moves beyond them to promote a higher level of quality in the curriculum we develop. The next section examines the key curriculum components as they would exist to address the particular purposes of the Core Curriculum Parallel. Brief examples from various grade levels and subject areas illustrate key points. The final section then explores Lydia Janis's second curriculum planning session, this time using the Core Curriculum Parallel to design her Civil War unit.

A practical question emerges: What does it mean to teach according to the nature of the discipline—to use the key facts, concepts, principles, and skills as organizers for curriculum development? We'll propose some answers to that question as we have a second curriculum planning session with Lydia. Interspersed with descriptions of her unit planning using the Core Curriculum Parallel are explanations of how the key components are modified in this second approach to planning the fifth grade Civil War unit. Figure 4.2 serves as an advance organizer for the remainder of the chapter.

The Role of Content (Including Standards) Within the Core Curriculum Parallel

The current standards movement, as conceived by national education organizations within the various content areas, seeks to identify the same kinds of powerful knowledge emphasized within the Core Curriculum Parallel. The best of the subject area standards statements delineate a concise set of facts, concepts, principles, and skills that reveal the structure of a discipline. These standards statements extend the work of Bloom et al. (1956), Bruner (1960, 1966), Phenix (1964), and Taba (1962) by posing the question "What knowledge, understanding, and skill are essential for an adult to have to master this discipline?" Most specialists who worked to develop these standards documents believe that (a) what students learn should be of service to them as adults and (b) standards should make current learning experiences easier to assimilate and retain. The Comprehensive Curriculum Framework supports alignment of textbook goals and state or local standards. On the other hand, educators who use the Core Curriculum Parallel will go a step further. They will move from mere alignment of content with text material to guiding a student's search for meaning in the content. These teachers will look at the content they must teach (and often beyond it) to find the essential facts, concepts, principles, and skills that give substance and meaning to the content—in other words, that make the content useful. Figure 4.3 reviews and illustrates the key categories of knowledge.

Curriculum Components	Modification Technique
Content (Including Standards)	<ul><li>Identify the major disciplines of knowledge in the unit.</li><li>Find the big ideas in each discipline by consulting an expert in the discipline, a national or state standards document, or a college textbook.</li><li>Diagram standards to make a list of essential knowledge, concepts, principles, and skills of the discipline.</li><li>Identify appropriate representative topics.</li><li>Develop or remodel curriculum units to address key concepts, principles, and skills in the discipline through the use of representative topics.</li><li>Expect and foster changes and increasing levels of cognitive sophistication as you and your students become more experienced.</li></ul>
Assessments	<ul><li>Preassess students for prior knowledge of major facts, concepts, principles, and skills within the topic or discipline.</li><li>Develop rubrics that measure students' knowledge of concepts, principles, and skills.</li><li>Consider concept maps as an assessment format.</li><li>Pre- or postassess to determine student growth in major facts, concepts, principles, and skills within the topic or discipline.</li></ul>
Introductory Activities	<ul><li>Provide students with concept maps.</li><li>Develop and share advance organizers that support development of concepts and principles.</li><li>Use focusing questions to help students assess their prior knowledge related to key concepts, principles, and skills.</li><li>Develop initial learning experiences that show students what experts at the frontier of the discipline investigate.</li><li>Provide an introduction that explains how the topic students are studying is representative of the discipline at large.</li></ul>
Teaching Methods	<ul><li>Use inquiry teaching methods with debriefing techniques.</li><li>Develop or provide simulations or role-playing—opportunities that mimic the role of information analyst.</li><li>Use a Concept Attainment Model, coupled with examples and nonexamples, to teach new concept categories.</li><li>Use Wasserman's (1988) Play-Debrief-Replay method during examination of data, tables, examples, observations, or hands-on discovery.</li><li>Use questioning and Socratic techniques to support the examination and classification of data, concept development, and identification of principles and rules.</li><li>Teach inductively, beginning with examples, and foster the rules and principles that explain patterns and relationships.</li></ul>
Learning Activities	<ul><li>Find high school texts and college resources to identify the major concepts, skills, and principles within a field or discipline.</li><li>Have students analyze and talk about examples, information, and data in small groups using a cooperative learning or guided discussion format.</li><li>Have students use raw data, examples, events, and observations to detect patterns and draw conclusions.</li><li>Ask students to suggest and test principles.</li><li>Have students identify patterns and categories.</li><li>Ask students to work as firsthand inquirers and analysts in the discipline.</li><li>Have students focus on analytic skills, problem-solving skills, and skills of the discipline.</li><li>Locate experiments, published simulations, and problem-solving activities that can be used during the unit.</li><li>Provide opportunities for students to note characteristics and attributes, and search for patterns, sequences, and relationships.</li></ul>
Grouping Strategies	<ul><li>Work with large groups of students to overview the goals of the unit, to provide directions, and to share information about the discipline and representative topic.</li><li>Work with large groups of students to facilitate acquisition of essential knowledge.</li><li>Use pairs and small groups of students to support analysis of examples and information as students develop concepts and principles.</li><li>Briefly conference with individual students to assess the degree to which they are able to relate examples and raw data to core concepts and principles.</li></ul>

Figure 4.2 (*Continued*)

(Continued)

Curriculum Components	Modification Technique
	• Observe individual students and provide feedback to support the development of analytic thinking. • Debrief students in large group, using concept maps and diagrams, to ensure that the entire class can connect activities, data, and examples to core concepts and principles.
Resources	• Locate, reproduce, and distribute samples of research studies and investigations in the discipline or field. • Provide biographies of historical and contemporary inquirers, inventors, and researchers in the field. • Provide journals, blank charts, tables, and diagrams so that students can record their data, reflect on their learning experiences, and outline a schema that represents their understanding of the relationships between concepts and principles. • Develop and share a format for developing hypotheses, designing studies, recording data, and formulating conclusions. • Provide students with concept maps and advance organizers that preview the important concepts and principles explored in the unit. • Provide graphic organizers to support cognitive and methodological skill acquisition. • Develop clear directions and expectations for data analysis, observations, field studies, and independent study. • Identify and locate numerous examples related to the concepts addressed in the unit. • Provide access to Inspiration® software to develop concept maps.
Products	• Ask students to create products that reflect their inquiry and analysis work. • Assign concept maps to analyze the acquisition of concepts and principles. • Ask students to make predictions, explain patterns, and demonstrate the relationship between raw data and primary source information and the core concepts and principles in the discipline. • Ask students to demonstrate connections between unit activities and experiences and the concepts and principles in the discipline. Reflective essays, journal entries, charts, diagrams, and collages support this task. • Provide graphic organizers that allow students to communicate their acquisition of concepts, principles, and skills.
Extension Activities	• Be sure that extension activities stem from or relate back to the key concepts and principles that give meaning to the content. • Ask the gifted education specialist or the media and technology specialist to support your search for adult role models of inquiry and research, primary source documents, field study opportunities, and real-world problems that relate to the core knowledge in the unit or discipline. • Ask content area specialists and other teachers who are experts in inquiry-based teaching to team-teach, coach, or provide useful feedback on the progress and success of the lessons.
Differentiation Based on Learner Need (Including AID)	• Increase or decrease your scaffolding to support concept attainment and cognitive processing. • Use deductive or inductive questioning to support and scaffold students' understanding of major concepts and principles. • Provide additional representative topics for comparison to reduce ambiguity or to add additional layers of complexity. • Encourage a continuing commitment to intrinsic motivation and to the world of ideas. • Ask students to examine ramifications, exceptions, or extensions of the basic concepts, principles, and skills. • Provide students with additional raw data to examine. • Use the Parallel's guidelines for Ascending Intellectual Demand in selecting resources and designing learning activities and products.
Lesson and Unit Closure	• Help students reflect on how key concepts and principles apply to what they have learned and the work they have done during the lesson or unit and to relate the concepts and principles to other work they have done during the year or in other learning situations. • Guide students in naming and describing the kinds of skills they have used in their work. • Use journals, small group, or whole class discussions to focus on the Core questions.

Figure 4.2 Using the Key Curriculum Components to Develop a Core Curriculum Unit

Knowledge Category	Definition and Examples
Fact	A specific detail; verifiable information *Examples:* • *The capital of New York is Albany.* • *5 + 7 = 12* • *George Washington was the first president of the United States.*
Concept	A general idea or understanding, a generalized idea of a thing or a class of things; a category or classification *Examples:* • *Biome* • *Government* • *Landscape* • *Fiction* • *Integer*
Principle	A fundamental truth, law, rule, or doctrine that explains the relationship between two or more concepts *Examples:* • *Balance is an important factor in predicting the longevity of a biome.* • *Forms of government allow for varying amounts of individual freedom.* • *An artist's use of light changes the rendering of a landscape.* • *Conflicts arise between protagonists and antagonists.* • *Two positive numbers can be added in either order.*
Skill	Proficiency, an ability or a technique, a strategy, a method, or a tool *Examples:* • *Learning how to grid a plot of ground and make systematic observations* • *Learning how to analyze the plot of a story (e.g., rising and falling action)* • *Learning how to conduct a social action campaign* • *Learning how to compare and contrast* • *Learning how to calculate statistics*
Attitudes	Beliefs, dispositions, appreciations, and values *Examples:* • *An appreciation of the limits of the environment* • *A belief in the critical importance of individual democratic rights* • *An appreciation of the use of light in Impressionist landscapes* • *A positive attitude toward reading* • *Intrinsic motivation for learning about real-world data*
Problem Solving	The ability to transfer and apply acquired knowledge to address a goal *Examples:* • *Identifying the percentage of open land left in a community or state* • *Developing a strategy to increase parent participation in PTA meetings* • *Creating a meaningful format for displaying a data set* • *Creating an original fiction anthology*

Figure 4.3 Categories of Knowledge

The focusing questions of the Core Curriculum Parallel (Figure 4.1) direct us to use the key facts, concepts, principles, and skills of the discipline as anchors for curriculum planning because it is the facts, concepts, principles, and skills that answer the Parallel's driving questions.

There are at least six ways to determine these elements in any segment of curriculum. First, and most desirable, is a district curriculum map that delineates essential facts (vs. a mass of facts of nonequivalent value), skills, overarching concepts, principles, and grade levels at which these elements will be introduced and extended.

Second, in the absence of such local documents, teachers can turn to high-quality standards documents that are often organized conceptually and presented according to key principles and that specify key methodological skills. In some instances, state standards documents achieve clarity and direction. When they do not, teachers can draw upon the high-quality standards developed by national professional organizations or standards documents published by states other than their own.

Third, there are books that provide excellent guidance in understanding what it means to teach conceptually and how to plan curriculum with that mindset. Among very helpful books currently available are *Concept-Based Curriculum and Instruction for the Thinking Classroom* by H. Lynn Erickson (2006) and available from Corwin Press, *The Multiple Menu Model* by Joseph Renzulli and colleagues (Renzulli, Leppien, & Hayes, 2000) and available from Creative Learning Press, and *Understanding by Design* by Grant Wiggins and Jay McTighe (1998) and available through the Association for Supervision and Curriculum Development. A fourth very useful book—and one that provides a teacher's perspective on the task of designing meaning-based curriculum—is *Starting From Scratch* by Steven Levy (1996) and available from Heinemann. Although each of these books differs in its approach to curriculum design, each deals clearly and directly with what it looks like to move beyond even well-planned, information-based or skills-based teaching to meaning-rich teaching that reveals to learners the power and utility of the disciplines.

Fourth, college textbooks are often rich resources for unearthing the key concepts, driving principles, and practitioner skills in a discipline. At this level, texts nearly always move from organization by topic and a coverage orientation to looking at a discipline through the organizational framework of experts. Thus, even a quick survey of the table of contents and headings in chapters in college texts can provide a sturdy starting point for identifying the authentic essentials upon which a topic or discipline is most effectively taught.

A fifth way to identify the elements of the disciplines is collaboration with experts in those disciplines. Community members who are practitioners in a discipline—or even Internet contacts who practice the disciplines at a high level—are not only invaluable in helping teachers understand what really matters in a discipline but are also excellent sources of information on authentic problems and products related to the discipline.

Finally, many teachers simply take the plunge into concept-based teaching by using available text and standards documents, their own knowledge of the subject in question, some common sense, and a bit of tolerance for ambiguity.

When teachers use these methods to locate the key information, concepts, principles, and skills in a discipline, they may discover that the topic of the original curriculum has to be revised to accommodate the concepts, principles, and skills to be incorporated within the unit. For example, in the past, a kindergarten class might have participated in a November social studies unit titled "Thanksgiving Day." As a result of the need to address core elements that give social studies focus, continuity, and purpose, the teacher may now look at the unit as focusing on "Harvest Traditions Around the World" or "The Legacy of Harvest Traditions."

Assessment Strategies and the Core Curriculum Parallel

In Chapter 3, we discussed the characteristics of exemplary assessment. To be effective, assessments must be aligned to the learning goals. Second, they should be honest and accurate measures of students' learning over time. Third, they must provide some kind of performance or product with which to evaluate student learning. These characteristics are as valid for high-quality Core Curriculum assessments as they are for any of the assessments designed for use with the other three curriculum models described in this book. However, the nature of the learning goals within the Core Curriculum Parallel requires special attention to the design of appropriate rubrics and assessment formats.

In curriculum designed with the Core Curriculum Parallel, learning goals will address core concepts, principles, and skills in a discipline or field of study. Therefore, assessments will also focus on student growth related to core concepts, principles, and skills. To design an appropriate rubric to measure growth in concept attainment, the levels within the rubric must attend to ever increasing levels of knowledge acquisition. Care must be taken to ensure that the rubric does not emphasize the quantity or mechanics of the product (e.g., neatness, proper spelling, and number of bibliographic entries) over the quality of the knowledge. An illustration of this approach follows. You will note here a more meaning-oriented rubric than the rubric Lydia developed in Chapter 3 to assess her students' work.

A group of fifth grade students in a science class might be expected to acquire a conceptual understanding of the term "migration." A fitting pre- or postassessment strategy might be to ask students an open-ended question that probes their understanding of the concept. Using a five-level rubric, the depth of student understanding of the concept might be sequenced accordingly (see Figure 4.4).

A rubric such as Figure 4.4 aligns closely with a standard or objective that stresses concept acquisition. It also allows teachers to measure change over time when used during both their pre- and postassessment.

If, on the other hand, the knowledge goal in a Core Curriculum unit addresses the acquisition of a principle or rule, the rubric shown in Figure 4.4 might vary slightly to assess student understanding of unit principles. Figure 4.5 illustrates this variation with a rubric for the science principle "Animals and insects migrate to fulfill basic needs."

In this example, students might be asked to explain the principle orally or in writing. Another option is to provide students with a word bank, consisting of key concepts from the unit, and ask the students to make a concept map or web that explains the connections between the concepts. Related examples and principles may also be included. Figure 4.6 provides a simple example of such a concept map activity.

	Beginning	Developing	Competent	Proficient	Expert
Level of Understanding	The learner communicates the term associated with the abstract concept.	The learner paraphrases the definition of the concept.	The learner provides examples and nonexamples of the concept.	The learner provides key attributes that distinguish the concept category.	The learner links the concept with other related concepts.
Example	Migration	"Migration is movement of living things for a real reason or purpose."	Examples: Butterflies Whales Salmon Nonexamples: When a subdivision is built Fires Accidents	Beneficial Change Large groups Movement Purposeful Causes Effects Universal	"People and animals migrate to improve their chances to meet their needs."

Figure 4.4   A Rubric for Measuring Growth in Concept Attainment

	Beginning	Developing	Competent	Proficient	Expert
Level of Understanding	The learner defines and provides examples of the key concepts within a rule or principle.	The learner identifies a relationship between two or more concepts.	The learner explains the relationship as conditional, if/then, cause/effect, part/whole, etc.	The learner provides novel examples of the principle or rule within a discipline or field of study.	The learner provides novel examples of the principle across disciplines or fields of study.
Example	Butterflies Whales Salmon	"Animals move around to get what they need."	"Animal migration is all about reasons and results."	"We studied whale migration in class but migration happens a lot in biology, for example, with butterflies and even people."	"Migration in animals is like the Westward Movement in history."

Figure 4.5   A Rubric for Measuring the Acquisition of Principles

If the content standards in a Core Curriculum Parallel unit stress the acquisition of a skill, the rubric and assessment strategies in the parallel call for a similar emphasis. An observation, product, or performance might, for example, be used as the assessment technique to determine level of student proficiency with a particular skill. Students in a science unit might be expected to learn how to detect a pattern.

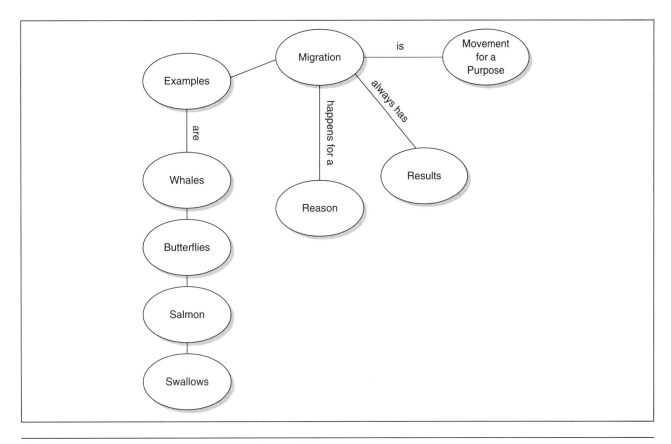

Figure 4.6 An Example of a Concept Map or Web

Their assessment might provide them with a specific set of data from which to work. Students might be asked to compare and contrast the data over time and identify emerging patterns in the data.

In sum, the need for valid and reliable pre- and postassessments is as vital within the Core Curriculum Parallel as it is within any kind of curriculum unit. The format for the assessment, however, varies a bit from the Comprehensive Curriculum Framework example. It varies in order to conform more readily to measuring changes in students' understanding and uses of concepts, principles, and skills that are the keys to helping them answer questions related to how knowledge is organized in the subject, what it means, how people use it, and so on. It's not so difficult, really. It's just a matter of making certain that just as a unit in the Core Curriculum Parallel will be focused to stress essential information, concepts, principles, and skills, so must assessments focus on the framework the unit stresses.

Introductory Activities in the Core Curriculum Parallel

Like all introductions, initial activities in the Core Curriculum should generate excitement and enthusiasm; provide for the preassessment of prior, related student knowledge; orient students to the learning goals; and provide students an opportunity to share previous experiences with the topic. However, in the Core

Curriculum, the introductory activities also function as a vehicle for helping students focus on the concepts, principles, and skills that are central to the Core Curriculum Parallel.

For many students, the role of inductive thinker and analyst, also common in the Core Curriculum, is both new and interesting. Nevertheless, it can also be puzzling and strange. To support student acquisition of this new role, teachers can use introductory activities to explain the kinds of thinking students will perform in order to come to a deep understanding of core knowledge. The teacher needs to assure students that it is perfectly acceptable for them to draw tentative conclusions, revise their thinking, and think out loud. The teacher should explain that it's important for students to think their way to understanding rather than only memorizing or paraphrasing someone else's thinking. Further, the teacher should review her role as a coach and support system for students' thinking, noting that she may answer their questions with a related question to help them focus their own thinking rather than giving them an answer.

Second, teachers of Core Curriculum make a special attempt to use introductory activities as an opportunity to explain to students the relationship between the representative topic they will study, the larger field of study, and the discipline as a whole. For example, as discussed earlier, in a third grade science study of the structure of plants and the function of plant systems, a teacher might use the study of fast-growing radish seeds and plants as the representative topic. During the introductory activities, the teacher displays a large set of five concentric circles that depict the relationship among radish plants, the field of botany, the discipline of biology, and the discipline of science. The teacher and students spend a brief amount of time discussing the relationships among the four terms in order to help students see how the topic they are studying relates to and represents the other three.

Third, teachers can develop a list of key facts, concepts, principles, and skills that the students will learn about during the study. With a concept map or similar diagram, teachers and students can use lines, arrows, and oval shapes to build a map that will depict the relationships among facts, concepts, principles, the representative topic, and the field and/or discipline.

Readers will also recall, from Chapter 3, the importance of focusing questions in introductory activities. These questions help students reflect on their own knowledge related to the Core study. These questions are also useful in monitoring student learning over time, to identify areas of confusion, or to note concepts, principles, or skills that need additional study and support. Further, teachers can use the questions to explore the nature of the concepts, relationships among the concepts, principles, facts, and skills central to the Core study.

As with any high-quality curriculum, the use of guiding questions, concept maps, and advance organizers provides support for students from the early stages of their work. These tools allow students initial opportunities to examine the relationships among the representative topic they are about to study and the overarching concepts, principles, and skills of the discipline at large. The use of new, unusual, and even discrepant information or examples provides intrigue and compels students to attend to unit activities. The use of one can of diet soda and another of regular soda dropped into a 20-gallon aquarium, for example, can provide a powerful introduction to the study of relative density.

Introductory learning activities are often overlooked or underused. The decision to hasten or eliminate these experiences can short-circuit student learning. Assuming a class of students with varied levels of experience with and knowledge about the subject at hand, the quality and comprehensiveness of introductory activities often predicts the degree to which all students can develop rich schemes of thought, analogies, and deep understanding of content. The shared conversations, examples, experiences, and questions posed during introductory activities create a bond among the family of learners. They also provide a shared anchor that the teacher can reference during the remainder of the study to foster acquisition of content.

Revising the Remaining Curriculum Components to Address the Goals of the Core Curriculum Parallel

The Core Curriculum Parallel has two primary goals: to acquaint students with the key information, concepts, principles, and skills of a discipline through the study of representative topics, and to foster this learning by helping students think their way to an understanding of this core knowledge. When students achieve these goals, they are able to answer the parallel's focusing questions (Figure 4.1) and thus demonstrate understanding of the structure and function of the discipline in an authentic way.

To accomplish these goals, changes are required in the learning objectives and teaching and learning methods when planning curriculum with the Core Curriculum Parallel. These changes create a domino effect that also impacts the other curriculum components. The chapter has already discussed changes in content, assessment, and introductory activities. Reconfiguration of the other curricular elements for the Core Curriculum Parallel is discussed in the following sections.

Teaching Methods and the Core Curriculum Parallel

Figure 3.7 in Chapter 3 provides a list of teaching methods arranged along a continuum, with direct teaching activities near the top of the figure and strategies becoming more indirect as the figure continues. There are particular methods at both ends of the continuum that teachers can use to help students acquire core knowledge. Appropriate indirect teaching methods include cooperative or collaborative learning, Socratic questioning, discovery learning, inductive teaching, concept attainment, Play-Debrief-Replay, simulations, and problem solving or problem-based learning. Appropriate direct teaching methods that foster core knowledge acquisition include lecture, deductive teaching, and coaching. The decision to use a direct or an indirect method will hinge on the amount of available instructional time, access to resources at students' independent reading levels, students' proficiency with various analytic thinking skills, and students' prior knowledge in the content area.

For example, a high school English teacher teaching the concept of narrative poetry inductively might decide to use a combination of inductive teaching and modified Socratic questioning. The teacher would ask students to construct their own definition of narrative poetry after reviewing exemplars from the genre. Students might read "Paul Revere's Ride," "Casey at the Bat," "Charge of the Light Brigade," and "The Highwayman" to compare and contrast key characteristics and attributes of narrative poems. Students would then use this information to develop a definition of the concept of narrative poetry. Later, they might also develop a set of principles that explain the significance of narrative poems within a historical setting. The teacher would combine this instructional method with the use of modified Socratic questioning to help students clarify their comparisons—or perhaps to clarify the thinking processes they used to develop the concepts and related principles.

In another setting, a teacher might elect to use a deductive or more direct teaching approach. When teaching deductively, a teacher helps students acquire core concepts and principles by first naming the concept or providing students with the principle. Next, the teacher explains the major attributes and characteristics that distinguish the concept or principle. Finally, the teacher provides students with new information or examples and asks them to find evidence within the examples that transfer the recently acquired concept or principle to the new context.

For example, a ninth grade earth science teacher might want to teach the concept of a spiral galaxy. The teacher would define a galaxy and explain the unique characteristics of a spiral galaxy as one composed of armlike stars that spiral around a center. Next, the teacher gives students several photographs of our galaxy and of the Andromeda galaxy as examples of spiral galaxies. Then, the teacher provides a series of photographs from the galaxy in the constellation Ursa Major and asks students to find characteristics and attributes of a spiral galaxy in this new example. Last, the teacher asks students to explain why the photographs depict a spiral galaxy.

Core Curriculum developers, or teachers, must be mindful of at least one very important caution. Without careful teacher monitoring, questioning, and probing it is far too easy for students to become lost in an array of facts, data, information, and tasks, without focusing on the core concepts and principles behind the information. When this occurs, students may become preoccupied with finding the "right answers" to their teacher's questions and lose focus on the essential questions related to the structure of the discipline, key concepts, and principles. Through skillful use of Wassermann's (1988) Play-Debrief-Replay teaching method, expert Core Curriculum teachers periodically stop students' small group discussions and learning activities, bring the small groups together as a large group, and provide semistructured debriefing discussions designed to elicit patterns across data sets to help students draw conclusions, make hypotheses, and develop rules and principles. In this way, the teacher plays a leadership role in helping students focus on making meaning of what they are studying.

Learning Activities and the Core Curriculum Parallel

To be most effective, Core Curriculum teaching methods must be coupled with learning activities that provide numerous opportunities for students to think analytically and to draw conclusions inductively and deductively. Most of the analytic thinking skills and many of the critical thinking skills listed in Figure 3.8 of Chapter 3 strengthen this connection. Analytic skills worthy of particular emphasis in Core Curriculum units include comparing and contrasting, classifying, finding patterns, making analogies, seeing relationships, and showing cause and effect. Key critical thinking skills are deductive and inductive thinking, and judging essential and incidental evidence; key executive thinking skills are formulating questions, developing hypotheses, summarizing, and generalizing.

Least effective in helping students make meaning of the discipline are activities that require students to memorize or paraphrase new information. Although some of the activities in any unit must call on students to learn or memorize information, in this Parallel, activities that stress meaning making and discovery are in the foreground.

Grouping Strategies and the Core Curriculum Parallel

In order to support the development of concepts and principles, students need to be coached and guided as they attempt to think their way through problems, questions, and investigations. The teacher's role within the Core Curriculum Parallel is one of coach, guide, and facilitator. The successful use of these teaching strategies requires in-depth content knowledge and a strong ability to follow and respond to differences in students' trains of thought and individual reasoning processes. The teacher's job is to help students find the answers and learn new concepts and principles by analyzing new information, identifying patterns and categories, and generating hypotheses, relationships, and principles.

Students who work with Core Curriculum units must process their way through new information. When students experience problems or frustration with this role, teachers must be ready to step in with follow-up questions, hints, or examples that jump-start a stalled cognitive process. They must be able to shed sufficient light on a problem or concept to allow students to see their way through to a solution or generalization. A long-term observation of a teacher implementing a Core Curriculum unit reveals a continual use of open-ended questions, follow-up questions, clarifying questions, and reflective questioning strategies.

In addition, opportunities for students to work in pairs or small groups facilitate the analytic and reflective dialogue among learners that fosters concept attainment, the development of principles and generalizations, and the acquisition of methodological, cognitive, and inquiry skills.

Resources in the Core Curriculum Parallel

It's not hard to imagine that changes in learning goals, as well as in introductory teaching and learning activities, would require concomitant changes in the choice of student and teacher resources. Rather than simply reading a section of the textbook and paraphrasing the author's perspective on causes of the Civil War, students working with the Core Curriculum use factual information, tables, graphs, maps, raw data, examples, events, and observations to detect patterns and draw inferences. Students not only study the conclusions of others, they analyze information and draw inferences on the basis of the analysis.

High school and college texts can provide core knowledge for the teacher about to implement Core Curriculum. Grade-level textbooks can also be used by students for information acquisition. However, learners also need access to tools, primary sources, examples, tables, charts, graphs, evidence, and data. They need to engage in observations, dialogue, and firsthand analysis. Depending on students' age and experience, graphic organizers and templates can provide support for the novice thinker, and frequent debriefing sessions and the use of Socratic questioning can speed the inquiry and discovery process.

Teachers of a Core Curriculum Parallel unit also have special resource needs. Ideas for discovery learning, document analysis, simulations, and problem-based learning experiences don't just pop out of the air. Access to high-quality commercial simulations, such as those published by MESA, Tom Snyder, Foss, GEMS, Interact, and Kendall-Hunt (as well as many other excellent publishers), provids a wealth of ideas. Web-based simulations or journal descriptions of simulations other teachers have designed can be equally helpful. For the teacher who has an interest in curriculum development, there are dozens of books that describe the process for developing and writing such simulations and problem-based learning activities in social studies, science, math, health, and art.

Products in the Core Curriculum Parallel

The choice to use the Core Curriculum Parallel also impacts the nature of student products—both short-term products and longer term, or culminating, products. Concept maps, hypotheses, theories, expository essays, research reports, journal reflections, charts, diagrams, and tables can reflect the thinking of student inquirers and provide a vehicle for learners to share their knowledge about overarching concepts and principles that result from the study of the representative topic as well as their expanding skill as analytic thinkers.

As is the case with other components of a Core Curriculum Parallel unit, the focus of a product in this parallel is helping students come to understand the organization and nature of the discipline, make sense of its organizing framework, and use its key concepts, principles, and skills. Both the product assignments and plans for assessing products should focus on student understanding and application of these fundamental building blocks of meaning.

If students in a Grade 6 statistics unit flip a penny one hundred times to gather probability data, their related, short-term product might be a table of results. More important than the table, however, would be a written explanation of the inductive conclusion they drew about the relationship between the number of data sets observed and the changes in probability. The two products—tables and conclusions—can also be used as a seamless assessment to measure the extent to which students understand basic concepts and principles about probability and sample size.

Whether daily (short-term) or culminating (long-term), products created in Core Curriculum should support development and communication of core knowledge. As such, they must call on students to understand, convey, illustrate, and use the key information, concepts, principles, and skills of the topic.

Extension Activities in the Core Curriculum Parallel

Within the Core Curriculum, extension activities can be used effectively to provide opportunities to learn additional information, examples, concepts, principles, skills, and applications not addressed in the basic Core Curriculum plan. This allows for close alignment of extension opportunities with content goals but still allows students to pursue their particular questions or interests. Figure 4.7 provides examples of extension activities for an eighth grade health unit on the

Subject Area: HEALTH	Grade 8 Concept: VIOLENCE	Disciplines: Psychology, Sociology
Knowledge Categories	Essential Knowledge	Potential Extensions
Facts	• Risk factors associated with violence • Situations that lead to fights	Myths versus facts about the causes and frequency of violence
Concepts	• Victim • Violence • Assailant • Mediation • Resolution • Escalation • Hostility • Free-floating anger	Learn more about: • Confrontation • Negotiation • Gangs • Fight or flight • Instigator • De-escalation • Micro-insults • Risk factors
Principles	• Violence is often perpetrated by people who have had personal contact with the victim • Poverty is more highly correlated with violence than is ethnicity	• The relationship between access to various weapons especially guns is correlated to incidence of violent crimes • Frustration and hopelessness may increase violence
Skills	• Conflict resolution skills • Conflict mediation strategies	• Developing advice for students about how to deal with a bully • Investigating nonviolence in popular music
Applications	• Logging violence on television • Interviewing people about their experiences with violence	• Analyzing violence in popular music • Analyzing domestic violence statistics in your town

Figure 4.7 Illustrations of Extension Activities Aligned With Core Curriculum Goals

concept of violence in which the extension activities closely align with the unit's goals. The figure describes the unit's essential knowledge in five areas of knowledge. The third column of the figure illustrates some ways in which the key categories of knowledge can be extended as student interest evolves. Contemporary textbooks often provide a wealth of suggestions for extension activities in teacher's guides and student texts.

While time constraints make it impossible to do everything that would be interesting and helpful to student learning within a particular segment of study, it is still important to allow students opportunities to pursue relevant, interesting, and motivating knowledge as an extension of their core study. By helping students develop extension activities, investigations, or products that reinforce and extend the key concepts, principles, and skills of the core curriculum, teachers can attend to both student curiosity and content goals.

Differentiation Based on Learner Need
(Including AID) in the Core Curriculum Parallel

It is the contention of this book that concept-based teaching and analytic learning opportunities should not be restricted to a select group of students. The roots of this parallel stem from general education and the fervent wish of scholars and researchers in the disciplines to instill an intrinsic appreciation for the world of ideas in all learners. It is the belief of many experts in the disciplines that the best way to achieve this ideal is through frequent student exposure to a curriculum that addresses the structure of a discipline by having students interact with examples, factual information, evidence, and the analytic and inductive process.

It seems evident that this approach to curriculum is already richer and more substantial than is curriculum designed with predominant emphasis on mastery of facts and skills. The Core Curriculum Parallel, correctly used, results in students wrestling with abstract and complex ideas, working at high levels of thought, and becoming more independent as thinkers and learners. Thus, many students would find the Core Curriculum quite challenging, particularly as they work through the transition from a more teacher-directed and prescriptive classroom.

In most classrooms, in fact, there are students who require teacher support or scaffolding to read texts or supplementary materials, follow directions, find appropriate resources, use time effectively, and so on. For these students to benefit from the Core Curriculum—or the curriculum designed by another approach—teachers must modify materials, provide additional opportunities for direct instruction and hands-on learning, give support in following directions, and so on.

In most classrooms, there are also students whose level of advancement, interest, and capacity in a particular subject suggests a need to delve more deeply into the subject and to work at levels of ascending demand or challenge so that they continue movement toward expertise in that subject. It is this continual movement toward expertise that is addressed in the concept of Ascending Intellectual Demand (AID) presented in this book. This concept will be the focus of sections in the book on modifications based on learner need. This emphasis is not intended to minimize the necessity of modifications required by most students at some points in their schooling, and by some students at most points in their schooling, to ensure growth toward competence in basic understandings and skills. Such approaches to modification of instruction for students who struggle with school have been examined and described effectively in many other publications. A goal of this book is instead to support teachers in understanding how to extend student capacity as it evolves beyond competence. For that reason, the book describes and emphasizes the concept of Ascending Intellectual Demand as a means of guiding teachers who want to know more about extending student capacity beyond general expectations—even in the face of a rich and complex curriculum.

Most human endeavors reflect varying levels of expertise, and scholars have studied and written about the nature of expertise in most of those endeavors. For instance, we quickly get a sense of the difference between a young driver with a learner's permit and a NASCAR racing champion. We see the difference between someone who dons ice skates and takes to the rink for the first time and an Olympic medalist in ice skating. In our own careers, we understand the difference in confidence and competence between a brand-new teacher and one who has polished his or her craft for two decades. It is our contention that we benefit from thinking about our learners along a growth continuum not unlike that of the driver, skater, or teacher.

Figure 4.8 notes some common traits and skills of expertise distilled from examination of experts in a range of fields. This information is helpful because it provides some direction for the sorts of advanced attributes toward which teachers could be guiding their students. The figure should illustrate the fact that rich curricula, such as that suggested by the Core Curriculum Parallel, provide all students better opportunity to progress along a continuum toward expertise than do even well-aligned curricula focused primarily on acquisition of information.

Achieving Ascending Intellectual Demand relies on the growing capacity of the teacher to (a) understand the continuum of developing knowledge, understanding, skills, and attitude in the subject in order to have a sense of where students are in their development as well as to know appropriate next steps in growth for each student and (b) design learning opportunities and environments that continually encourage students to take the next steps in learning and to support them in doing so.

Figure 4.9 proposes some ways in which teachers may prompt advanced students to work at ascending levels of intellectual demand in the Core Curriculum. In addition to these approaches to assisting students to move toward expertise, it is also important for teachers to take into account in their instructional plans both students' interests and their preferred modes of learning. Additional suggestions for teachers to support learners from novice to expert in the core content areas are outlined in Chapter 8.

Traits/Attitudes of the Expert	Skills of the Expert
• High curiosity, reflection, concentration • Understands domain at a deep level • Uses present knowledge to plan for future directions in learning • Raises questions about reasons for and use of knowledge • Spends time to lay foundation, understand contexts and problems • Seeks out multiple resources and knows how to use them • Demonstrates high level of skill that looks effortless • Can mentally represent a problem and its parameters • Transforms content to use in new areas • Reflective, evaluative behavior • Makes great number of connections and more complex connections • Sensitive to task demands when solving problems • Has confidence in ability to solve problems • Examines impact of decisions on self, others, and society • Self-monitoring • Able to step outside personal experience • Insightful • Open-minded • Tolerates risk and uncertainty • Assumes responsibility for own learning • Driven to work hard • Inspires self to work • Disciplined approach to work • Continues to push for improvement • Incorporates struggle and failure in the journey to learn • Chooses to learn from experience • Seeks meaningful practice and critique • Has a commitment to excellence • Leads others to productive accomplishment • Envisions new possibilities	• Organizes knowledge for meaning and accessibility • Maintains an internal organization and has a classification system • Represents problems in a qualitatively deeper way • Transfers content and skills from one context to use in another • Sees differences between typical and novel instances • Has fast, accurate pattern recognition • Reflects on adequacy of own thinking processes • Anticipates sequences in learning • Poses insightful questions about content and problems • Can recount and evaluate events and their impact • Anticipates problems • Uses efficient methods of reflection and problem solving • Uses efficient pattern recognition to apply prior knowledge to new situations • Develops systems and habits for effective, efficient learning • Searches for subtle examples and information • Gleans pertinent information from seemingly extraneous data • Has a heuristic rather than a formulaic approach to solving problems • Works at high level of abstract, analytical, and creative thinking • Works at level of automaticity • Flexibly adapts parameters to facilitate purposes • Engages others in reflective, insightful dialogue • Creates novel products and applications

Figure 4.8 Some Traits and Skills of Experts

- Call on students to use more advanced reading, resource, and research materials.
- Assist students in determining and understanding multiple perspectives on issues and problems.
- Adjust the pace of teaching and learning to account for rapid speed of learning or to permit additional depth of inquiry.
- Develop tasks and products that call on students to work at greater levels of depth, breadth, complexity, or abstraction.
- Have students apply what they are learning to contexts that are unfamiliar or are quite dissimilar from applications explored in class.
- Design tasks and products that are more open-ended or ambiguous in nature and/or that call on students to exercise greater levels of independence in thought and scholarly behavior as learners and producers.
- Develop rubrics for tasks and products that delineate levels of quality that include expert-level indicators.
- Encourage collaborations between students and adult experts in an area of shared interest.
- Design tasks that require continuing student reflection on the significance of ideas and information and cause students to generate new and useful methods and procedures to represent ideas and solutions.
- Include directions and procedures that ask students to establish criteria for high-quality work, assess their progress in working toward those criteria, and seek and use feedback that improves their quality of efforts and methods of working.
- Ask students to reflect on the personal and societal implications of solutions they propose to problems.

Figure 4.9 Some Paths to Ascending Intellectual Demand for Advanced Learners in the Core Curriculum

Lesson and Unit Closure in the Core Curriculum Parallel

As is the case with closure in all four parallels, the purpose of lesson and unit closure in the Core Parallel is to ensure that each student leaves the lesson with the ability to articulate what is most important in the lesson and how such conclusions can be reached. In all parallels, closure activities are important opportunities for "taking stock" and looking ahead for both students and teacher. What distinguishes closure in Core curriculum is the emphasis on two elements: (1) key concepts and principles evident in the lesson or unit and (2) the focusing questions of the Core Parallel. While a teacher may well want to include other aspects in closure activities, it is an emphasis on these two elements that helps students focus on Core meaning—just as an emphasis on these two elements in all other parts of the curriculum ensures that Core curriculum really is Core!

Closure is typically a brief part of a lesson and therefore does not allow for intricate multipart strategies. Using Think-Pair-Share; a quick write followed by group sharing; a teacher-led whole class discussion; or some other straightforward strategy can help strike a balance between summary and student engagement. For example, a teacher might ask students to provide evidence from the day's work that

▶ Confirms a particular principle

▶ Demonstrates where a particular concept or pair of concepts is apparent in what they have just read

▶ Answers a Core focusing question such as how lessons from the past week are coming together to help them make sense of what is going on (in a time period, science topic, math computation, novel, political debate, cultural study, etc.)

Depending on the degree of clarity evidenced in student discussion or writing, it may be wise for the teacher to end with a statement like, "So, we can probably conclude that . . ." or "Two important things you seem to be saying we should investigate further are . . ." or "I hear you saying that the strategy you found most useful in your work today was. . . . because . . ." or "Based on my observations while you were working today, and what several of you have just said, I think tomorrow we should continue to work with . . . in order to improve the quality of your understanding." Such teacher-crafted statements can sharpen language, focus thought, and clarify direction for students. It's also often the case that one day's closure activity can provide an important bridge to introducing the next day's lesson.

Using the Goals of the Core Curriculum Parallel and Key Curricular Elements for Lydia Janis's Civil War Unit

Determining Content

A year has passed since Lydia first revised her fifth grade textbook unit on the Civil War unit to address the components and exemplary characteristics described in the Comprehensive Curriculum Framework. As you recall from Chapter 3, her initial attempts at revision led to improvements in the introductory activities, the development of assessments and rubrics better aligned to the textbook objectives, and the creation of graphic organizers that supported improvements in students' ability to read and comprehend social studies content as presented within the structure of a textbook. When we left Lydia, we learned that she reconciled national and state social studies standards with her textbook objectives by simply "marking off" the standards she believed were addressed in the textbook unit.

Between her last unit revision and this year, Lydia had time to read and learn more about standards and their purposes. She understands their role in ensuring equity and opportunity to learn for all students. She also learned that the developers of the standards documents took special care to identify the major facts, concepts, principles, and skills inherent in each subject area and discipline so that students could spend more time studying the key concepts and principles in any given field. This new knowledge led to some ongoing reflection for Lydia. She realized that the standards documents were indeed identifying what was "core" to each subject area and discipline. She began to wonder to what extent her textbook objectives really addressed the same kinds of powerful knowledge inherent in those standards documents.

Once again, Lydia turned to her teacher's manual and found the page that listed the objectives for the Civil War (see Figure 4.10). Working in the Core Curriculum Parallel, she needed to spend time actually analyzing the kinds of knowledge inherent in each objective statement. To do that, she would identify the content within each objective statement and categorize it as fact, concept, principle, skill, disposition, or application. She used the state standards document (Figure 4.11) for this purpose. Her results are printed in parentheses next to each objective listed in Figure 4.12.

Demonstrate an in-depth understanding of major events and trends in U.S. history (history).

1. Analyze data in order to see persons and events in their historical context; understand causal factors and appreciate change over time (history).

2. Examine current concepts, issues, events, and themes from historical perspectives and identify conflicting ideas from competing narratives or interpretations of historical events (history).

3. Explain reasons for conflict and the ways conflicts have been resolved (history).

4. Explain how economic factors influenced historical events in the United States (history).

5. Display empathy for people who have lived in the past (history).

6. Describe and analyze, using historical data and understandings, the options which are available to parties involved in contemporary conflicts or decision making (history).

7. Identify and evaluate various perspectives associated with places and regions (geography).

8. Evaluate situations involving conflicts between citizen's rights and propose solutions to these conflicts (government).

9. Use maps, globes, models, graphs, charts, and databases to analyze distributions and patterns (geography).

10. Identify governmental activities that affect the local, state, national, and international economy (economics).

11. Explain how specialization leads to more efficient use of economic resources and economic growth (economics).

Figure 4.10 Social Studies Performance Standards From Lydia's Standards Document

Knowledge Category	Definition and Examples
Fact	A specific detail; verifiable information *Examples:* • The capital of New York is Albany. • 5 + 7 = 12 • George Washington was the first president of the United States.
Concept	A general idea or understanding, a generalized idea of a thing or a class of things; a category or classification *Examples:* • Planet • Biome • Capital • Narrative poem • Vowel

Figure 4.11 Categories of Knowledge

Lydia also noted fifteen learning objectives listed within the two chapters of the textbook. Most of the objectives required students only to identify and describe facts. In addition, Lydia was struck by the discreteness of the fifteen objectives. Few principles were provided to help students integrate and transfer the vast amount of historical information about conflict and resolution to other cultures and time periods.

---

1. Analyze the differences between the North and South (fact).

2. Describe how some enslaved people fought against slavery (fact).

3. Identify the difficulties faced by free African Americans (fact).

4. Identify leading abolitionists and describe their fight against slavery (fact).

5. Explain how the movement for women's rights began (fact).

6. Describe the compromises over slavery that temporarily prevented the South's secession (fact).

7. Analyze the reasons that the South seceded (fact).

8. Describe how the Civil War began (fact).

9. Compare and contrast the strengths of each side (fact).

10. Explain how technology changed the way wars were fought (fact/concept/principle?).

11. Analyze the effect of the Emancipation Proclamation on both the North and the South (fact).

12. Describe how women on both sides supported the war effort (fact).

13. Evaluate the effects of the war on the North and South (fact/principle?).

14. Describe Sherman's March (fact).

15. Describe Lee's surrender at Appomattox (fact).

Figure 4.12   Lydia's Textbook Objectives for the Civil War Unit

On the other hand, the state standards document (Figure 4.11) emphasized concepts, principles, dispositions, and skills. Eleven standards from this document had been selected by Lydia's school district for emphasis within the Civil War unit. These standards, taken from *The Framework: K–12 Curricular Goals and Standards* (Connecticut State Department of Education, 1998a), included the goals listed in Figure 4.10.

As she read this list, Lydia concluded that the standards document did capture the key understandings that students should develop about this period in United States history. She then had to make a decision. Which set of goals would dictate student learning: those in the textbook, the standards document, or both? To make this unit meaningful for her students, she decided to reframe the unit around the more powerful standards described in her state document. The students would acquire the factual knowledge about the Civil War embedded in the two textbook chapters. However, this knowledge would be used as a bridge to develop the more long lasting concepts, principles, and skills associated with historical thinking and themes. To do this, she wouldn't have to abandon the text and its lesson plans, but she would have to replace the textbook objectives with standards.

Understanding the Standards

Making a conscious decision to teach a unit of study by addressing core knowledge is the first big step in unit development or lesson remodeling. However, teachers also need an opportunity to come to a deep understanding of the concepts, principles, and skills that provide the structure for a discipline. There are at least three strategies that educators and curriculum developers can use to become more knowledgeable about the concepts and principles.

One strategy for increasing our familiarity with the essential ideas in a discipline involves a simple listing, underlining, or categorizing procedure. Consider the fourth standard in Lydia's state document, reprinted below:

> *Explain reasons for conflict and the ways conflicts have been resolved.*

This standard was designed to describe one vital aspect of the study of history. It represents core knowledge in the field of history. When Lydia examined the standards statement, she carefully underlined and listed the key ideas embedded in the sentence. Her list looked like this:

> ▷ Reasons (methodological skill—cause and effect)
>
> ▷ Conflict (concept)
>
> ▷ Resolution (concept)
>
> ▷ Explanations (principle)

On further analysis, Lydia categorized each of the terms and phrases within each of her standards statements. Figure 4.12 may be helpful in categorizing a phrase or item within one of the six categories of knowledge. In the example above, one possibility might be to categorize "reasons" as a cognitive thinking skill associated with the inquiry process a historian undertakes. In a similar manner, both "conflict" and "resolution" could be categorized as major concepts within the field of history. If one were to identify a relationship between the two concepts, conflict and resolution, and the cognitive process of identifying causes and effects, it might be possible to develop teachable principles such as these:

> 1. All conflicts have causes.
> 2. The key to resolving conflicts is a comprehensive understanding of related causes and effects.

If we extend this process and categorize all of the standards for the Civil War unit listed in Figure 4.12, we create an opportunity that fosters a deeper understanding of the nature of complex, multifaceted standards statements. Figure 4.13 depicts this process for categorizing the twelve standards in Lydia's revised unit.

Standard	Facts	Concepts	Principles	Dispositions	Skills	Application
1	X	X	X		X	
2	X		X	X	X	
3	X	X	X		X	X
4	X	X	X		X	
5	X	X	X	X		
6	X	X	X	X		
7	X	X	X		X	X
8	X	X	X	X		
9	X	X	X		X	X
10	X	X	X		X	
11	X	X	X		X	

Figure 4.13 Categorizing the Knowledge Categories Within Standards Statements

	Beginning	Developing	Competent	Proficient	Expert
Levels of Understanding	The learner can communicate the term associated with the abstract concept.	The learner can paraphrase the definition of the concept.	The learner can provide examples and nonexamples of the concept.	The learner can provide key attributes that distinguish the concept category.	The learner can link the concept with other related concepts.
Example	Civil	"Civil means something to do with the citizens of a place. A civil war is a war fought inside a country and among its citizens."	Examples: • I am a citizen of the United States. • I am not a citizen of Russia. • World War II was not a civil war. • Ireland is having a civil war now.	• Citizens • Members • State • Nation • Law • Rights • Laws • Public • Internal	"People have civil wars when they can't resolve their conflicts or achieve their rights peaceably."

Figure 4.14 A Rubric for Measuring Growth in the Attainment of the Concept "Civil"

Lydia knew that in the past she had concentrated her teaching around the events related to the Civil War. She had addressed these events in chronological fashion, moving from the causes of the Civil War to the events and people involved in the battles and the war. Equipped with new knowledge about the importance of concept-based teaching, Lydia revised the sequence and content of her lesson plans and approached the four-week unit by first having students study the difference among states, a federation, and a nation. Next, she planned to introduce a study of the livelihoods and economies of various people and groups (e.g., factory workers, slaves, factory owners, plantation owners, farmers, women, and children) in the North and the South. She followed this with an examination of slavery: its conditions, roots, and consequences. Next, she planned to have students learn about the various perspectives within the emerging nation about state and civil rights issues. Then, students would examine the concepts and principles related to perspectives, viewpoints, balance, conflicts, compromise, consensus, and resolution by studying specific examples, documents, people, and events in the 1860s. Students would learn about the familiar people and events related to the Civil War but within the larger context of the disciplines of history, geography, economics, and government.

Planning Assessment Strategies

Lydia was comfortable with the use of preassessments, ongoing assessments, and rubrics to measure her students' learning progress. She knew she would have to use similar procedures to measure student learning in this unit. She identified several of the major concepts related to the Civil War (states' rights, conflict, perspective, slavery, federation, nationalism, compromise, consensus, economy) and principles related to the Civil War. She developed a word bank of the concepts and designed a pre- and postassessment that asked students to create a concept map, to provide examples of the concepts in the word bank, to draw lines between related concepts and explain the resulting principle, and to give definitions and examples of each concept. She used rubrics similar to the one reprinted in Figure 4.14 to measure students' conceptual learning over time.

On the other hand, when the knowledge goal in a Core Curriculum unit addressed the acquisition of a principle or rule, Lydia used a rubric similar to the one shown in Figure 4.15. In this example, Lydia's students might be asked to explain, orally or in writing, the principle related to the causes of civil wars. Another option would be to provide students with the same kind of word bank used in the first example and ask them to make a map or web that explains the connections among the concepts.

When the core knowledge was focused on a skill instead of a concept or principle, however, Lydia changed her assessment strategy and used an observation, product, or performance. When the skill was cognitive, her assessment strategy asked students for a written reflection on their cognitive process in work that used the specified kind of thinking, or she used an observable Think Aloud performance. For example, when

	Beginning	*Developing*	*Competent*	*Proficient*	*Expert*
Levels of Understanding	The learner can define and provide examples or a synthesis of the essential information upon which a principle is based.	The learner can identify a topical or temporal relationship among concepts and essential information.	The learner can extend the principle or rule to novel examples within the discipline or field of study.	The learner can articulate a general conceptual relationship as conditional, if/then cause/effect, part/whole, etc.	The learner can extend the principle across disciplines or fields of study.
Example	"The Civil War was a war between the northern and southern states in the United States in the 1860s."	"The Civil War was fought because of disagreements about slavery, economics, and states' rights."	"There have been recent civil wars going on in Yugoslavia, Ireland, and Mexico. They were caused by the some of the same kinds of things that caused our Civil War."	"Civil wars are caused by citizens' inability to find a way to resolve their differences about rights and laws peacefully."	"Empathy, compromise, and consensus can be used to resolve conflicts peacefully because they honor individual perspectives and values."

Figure 4.15 A Rubric for Measuring the Acquisition of Principles and Rules

- Clearly states the claim or argument
- Provides sufficient evidence related to the claim or argument
- Selects credible evidence sources
- Consults multiple sources
- Selects relevant evidence
- Clearly explains all assumptions
- Provides a logical argument
- Refutes alternative claims or arguments

Figure 4.16 Criteria for Judging the Strength of an Argument

Lydia altered her fifth grade Civil War unit to reflect the core knowledge in the discipline of history; she expected her students to use historical thinking skills. Specifically, she might ask them to demonstrate their ability to use multiple evidence sources in order to make a warranted historical claim or argument.

To assess growth in that ability and evaluate the extent to which individual students can create a strong argument, Lydia created a skills-based checklist of criteria similar to the one reprinted in Figure 4.16. Each item on the checklist was rated on a 1–3 or 1–5 scale, so that growth between the preassessment and the postassessment could be easily analyzed.

The need for valid and reliable pre- and postassessments is as vital within the Core Curriculum Parallel as it is within any kind of curriculum unit. The format for the assessment, however, varies in order to conform more readily to measuring changes in students' acquisition of concepts, principles, and cognitive skills within a discipline. Both the assessment strategy and the assessment criteria vary slightly to accommodate this special purpose.

Planning Introductory Activities

Next, Lydia considered how she might alter the introductory activities for the unit to fit the parameters of the Core Curriculum Parallel. She knew she needed to develop several aspects of an introduction that were missing from the original unit. She wanted to preassess her students on their prior knowledge about the facts, concepts, and principles related to the Civil War. She also knew that her students didn't necessarily connect the study of the Civil War with the study of history, geography, economics, or government, so she needed to show them how this topic was related to those important disciplines within the social sciences. She wanted to prepare them for their role as thinkers and analyzers of documents, examples, data, and events. She also wanted them to understand what concepts and principles were all about. Finally, she wanted them to have an opportunity to tell her what they wanted to learn about the Civil War so that she could begin planning related extension activities.

In order to show her students how the Civil War related to the four disciplines of history, government, economics, and geography, Lydia prepared a flow chart. She listed the four disciplines on the chart and under each discipline listed some of the major concepts in each discipline that students would study in order to understand the Civil War. She prepared open-ended discussion questions to generate students' conversations about their interests, their prior experience with these concepts, and the Civil War in particular. She also developed and printed multiple copies of her preassessment. Finally, Lydia visited the Library of Congress (2000) Web site and downloaded several copies of some Mathew Brady photographs of the Civil War. She made her selection carefully because she wanted to choose a small set of photographs that could be used to detect a pattern and a relationship—just the kind of thinking she would expect students to use as they unearthed the concepts, principles, and core knowledge related to this topic. Lydia used these photographs and the accompanying analysis activity as the culmination of her introductory activities.

Selecting Teaching Methods, Learning Activities, Grouping Strategies, Resources, and Products

Because of the need in the Core Curriculum Parallel for students to understand the key concepts and principles of a discipline, Lydia's predominant teaching methods were inductive. She used concept-based teaching, open-ended questioning strategies, coaching, Socratic questioning, and scaffolding to help students analyze information about events, individuals, and settings related to the concepts that she used to structure her four-week unit. As students examined documents, photographs, evidence, and information, she continually posed questions: "What does this mean to you? How is this the same or different from the things we have just studied?

Which pieces of information fit together as a category? Can you give me other examples of this concept? Do you see a pattern emerging? What do you think caused this? What rule or principle can you make now that you have reviewed this information? What do you think will happen next? Why did this happen? Is there more than one reason? Will there be more than one effect? How do you know your answer is right? Can you show me evidence to prove your conclusion is valid? What other information do you need to be sure? Do the other students see it the same way you do? Why or why not?"

During one point in the unit, when students were examining varying perspectives on people's rights compared with the rights of states, she allocated two days for them to recreate the Lincoln–Douglas debates and the Dred Scott decisions. These role-play activities and simulations were followed by small group reflection opportunities and large group debriefing sessions in order to flesh out the related concepts and principles. The students enjoyed the departure from their normal routine and became extremely motivated about finding and citing evidence to "prove" their point of view.

If a visitor to the classroom had been asked to describe Lydia's behavior and role during this unit, he or she would more than likely remark that she "Answered all of the students' questions with more questions" or that she "Gave them information and asked them to think hard about what it really meant." Also the visitor would probably have noticed that Lydia spent the majority of her time giving students something to think about, helping them think their way through it and decide what it meant in the broader scope of history, geography, economics, and government.

However, on occasion, Lydia would also teach deductively, by explaining the nature of a concept and providing information about its key attributes, characteristics, and examples. This was most often the case when students were dealing with factual information, concepts, or skills that were novel or difficult for them to comprehend, such as the concept of suffrage or people's reaction to the Harper's Ferry incident.

If the introductory activities are successful, students should come to an understanding about their role in a Core Curriculum unit. In the case of Lydia's Civil War unit, her students understood that they were going to be given data, tables, charts, graphs, information about events and actions, photographs, and documents, and that they would be expected to work together to develop an understanding of the underlying concepts or principles. The focusing questions Lydia developed and shared during the introduction scaffolded their analysis of video footage they viewed, the Emancipation Proclamation, and additional Mathew Brady photographs. Students reviewed abridged diaries of women, slaves, soldiers, and the newspaper articles of the time. They were on a constant search for concepts, categories, patterns, relationships, causes, effects, and principles. Some of Lydia's focusing questions to support student learning about the concepts and principles that connect the Civil War with the discipline of economics included the following.

> ▷ What are the factors that explain economic conditions?
>
> ▷ How do resources, goods, and services interact?
>
> ▷ How do resources, goods, and services affect wants and needs?
>
> ▷ How do resources, goods, and services affect supply and demand?
>
> ▷ How does supply and demand affect economic well-being?
>
> ▷ What are the special characteristics of Northern economic conditions?
>
> ▷ What were Southern economic conditions?
>
> How did these economic conditions affect the Civil War?

The nature of these focusing questions goes to the very heart of the discipline. They vary greatly from those printed in Lydia's original textbook unit:

> ▷ What was the Fugitive Slave Law?
>
> ▷ How did Frederick Douglass and Harriet Tubman fight against slavery?
>
> ▷ What events help turn the war in favor of the Union?
>
> ▷ Why did Lincoln announce the Emancipation Proclamation after the Battle of Antietam?

The use of Socratic teaching methods, focusing questions, and simulations provided support for the students' analytic inquiry. Lydia's choice of resources and materials provided students with opportunities to examine the relationships among the representative topic they studied, the related evidence and information gleaned from political cartoons, newspaper accounts, diaries, and their textbooks, and the overarching concepts and principles within the related disciplines. The use of large group and small group sessions supported students' analysis and concept attainment through the use of discussions, shared inquiry, Think-Pair-Share activities, and debriefings.

Last, Lydia's use of short-term or daily products such as document analysis worksheets, graphic organizers, concept maps, and reflective journals provided ongoing assessments to help her monitor and adjust her instructional support to ensure students' success with analytic information processing. For example, Lydia planned to have students meet in small groups to analyze perspectives on slavery by reviewing "Cannibals All! Or, Slaves without Masters," written in 1857 by George Fitzhugh (1857), and "My Bondage and My Freedom," written in 1852 by Frederick Douglass (1855). Lydia knew the documents would be tough going for fifth graders. Therefore, she prepared advance organizers that alerted students to unfamiliar terms in the passages. She gave them yellow markers to mark the important phrases, numbered each line of the documents so students could follow them more easily, and provided focusing questions to guide student thinking. These instructional aids fostered students' inquiry and enabled them to use authentic documents from the time period to draw their own conclusions.

Lydia also developed a culminating product for her students to help them focus on the key information, concepts, and principles in the Civil War unit. Students could work alone or in groups of two, three, or four to develop a visual plan for a Civil War quilt. Directions for the quilt product, as well as criteria she and the students would use to support successful work, made it clear that the goal of the product was a demonstration of student understanding of what was important during the time period and why it was important. Specifically, quilt squares had to depict (1) key people and events of the Civil War period, (2) livelihoods, cultures, and economies of various groups in the North and South, (3) roots and consequences of slavery, (4) how varied viewpoints and perspectives led to conflict, (5) how these varied viewpoints were dealt with through conflict resolution and compromise, and (6) other conclusions they had drawn about what is most significant to understand from the Civil War period. These requirements for the culminating product ensured that students would review and focus on both essential information about the time period and key concepts and principles they had studied. To strengthen the focus, and to call on key skills students had developed during the unit, the culminating product assignment also asked them to do some reflective writing to go along with the quilt design. Specifically, each student had to individually interpret the quilt on which they worked by addressing how the quilt depicted the six requirements. They also had to provide evidence that their conclusions were well supported in information they had studied. This process caused them to reflect on their inquiry as they draw on key skills in their unit, including analysis, cause and effect, providing evidence, generalizing, and seeing relationships. The assessment rubrics illustrated in Figures 4.15 through 4.16 provided Lydia with a starting point for developing criteria to determine student growth as reflected in the culminating product.

Choosing Extension Activities

Lydia wanted her extension activities to support students' interests in subtopics and related concepts aligned with the Civil War. Her open-ended questions during the unit's introduction identified students with interests in several topics connected to core information, concepts, principles, skills, and applications related to this Core Curriculum unit. Some students preferred to gather more information about the Battle at Gettysburg because they had traveled there during summer vacations. Other students wanted to read more about Abraham Lincoln and Jefferson Davis because they had seen their statues on vacation trips. One group of students wanted to read more about slavery during the Civil War period—some in novels and others in nonfiction. The majority of students, however, wanted an opportunity to examine more of Brady's photographs or to watch Ken Burns's videos on the Civil War.

Armed with this knowledge, Lydia labeled social studies time on three Thursdays as "Specialty Days." During this time, students developed study questions related to their interests in the Civil War, used library research skills to find information regarding their questions, reviewed the information, developed their findings, and participated in a small group sharing experience. Important in the whole process were Lydia's debriefing questions. She continually asked students to reflect on what they had chosen to study and related it back to the core knowledge, concepts, principles, and skills they had studied together. She also provided guiding questions to help students maintain this focus as they shared their work with one another.

Lydia found that the extension opportunity promoted ownership in the unit among her students. The interest-based investigations also yielded contributions for students to make to the Civil War unit as the extension activities and unit as a whole evolved simultaneously.

Modifying Plans Based on Learner Need (Including AID)

Lydia realized that despite all of her preplanning to improve the quality of the Civil War unit, there were students who would need a modified approach to the unit of study based on their level of sophistication with materials and content. For students with learning difficulties, she chose different print documents, song lyrics, and sections from children's historical fiction to support the analytic reading of students who would have a difficult time using the selections cited above. Some of the students also used the Ken Burns videos on the Civil War to lend further support for understanding text material. In addition, she worked with students needing additional help in small groups and during conferences to scaffold their concept-based learning and analysis of the documents. Finally, students with difficulty in written language had the option of tape-recording the analysis for their culminating products and working with the teacher to prepare for the tape recording.

For her more advanced readers and thinkers, Lydia understood that she would need to guide them to work at a more intense level of intellectual demand in order to ensure their growth and challenge during the unit. For these students, Lydia searched for more sophisticated print documents. She found excerpts from *Uncle Tom's Cabin*, the Emancipation Proclamation, and the Fourteenth Amendment to the Constitution for them to read during related learning activities. However, the most challenging option appeared when she discovered a Civil War–related Supreme Court decision, *Ex parte Milligan*, regarding three men in Indiana who were found guilty by a military court of conspiring with the Confederate States of America to set up a Northwestern Confederacy. Later, they were sentenced to be hanged. Lydia planned to ask her advanced learners and readers to review Lincoln's martial law proclamation in 1862, the arrest and conviction of the three defendants, the Supreme Court appeal and brief, and the Justices' opinions. Students would search for evidence in the brief regarding the suspension of the defendants' civil rights of habeas corpus and the Supreme Court's reversal of the lower court's conviction. She would have the students work with this case when other students needed additional time for readings, reteaching, or guided small group discussions in order to be comfortable with the key information, concepts, principles, and skills that formed the core of the unit.

The advanced students were ready for a real challenge. The complexity of materials and the abstract nature of the concepts behind the ruling would provide that opportunity. Further, this exploration would call on these students to use scholarly behavior, reflect on the significance and societal implications of ideas, examine an issue from multiple perspectives, and link what they are learning in the unit with unfamiliar contexts. With proper support from Lydia and their peers, her advanced students could achieve a deep understanding of the role of the Bill of Rights, the Constitution, and the Supreme Court in ensuring and protecting the civil rights of all citizens. Once again, she would blend information and insights from these students into whole-class discussions on a range of topics.

Lesson and Unit Closure

Lydia continually posed questions throughout her unit to focus students (and herself) on the unit's meaning. She followed that pattern during both lesson and unit closure activities. Sometimes she revisited with her students an important question she had raised during class, asking, for example, "Now that you've spent some time analyzing the Civil War video, what important issues seems to be occurring repeatedly in the conflict between the North and the South?" "Why are these recurring themes?" "What principles that we have discussed before seem to be at work in these tensions?"

One strategy Lydia often used for lesson closure during the unit was a "principle wall" she and her students created. The wall had three columns in which students could place principles they wrote on tag-board strips. Column 1 contained principles students proposed might help reveal how the events of the Civil War played out. Column 2 contained principles that the class ultimately agreed should move from Column 1 because "testing" the proposed principle suggested it was useful in understanding the Civil War. Column 3 contained principles the class ultimately agreed did not "hold up" in their investigation of the war. Often in closure, Lydia would ask her students to consider how a day's work was shaping their thinking about one or more of the principles, and whether a particular principle now seemed to belong in the second or third columns—or whether students had any new principles to propose for Column 1.

For lesson closure on another day, Lydia gave her students envelopes with words on small pieces of index card. They worked in groups of two or three to use the words to build a concept map that reflected their understanding of the Civil War unit. Each group wrote an accompanying paragraph to translate their map into prose. The concept maps were very helpful to Lydia as an ongoing assessment tool.

Sometimes lesson closure for her students simply involved discussing one or two focusing questions for the Core Parallel. Using the questions helped Lydia stay centered on the "deep intent" of the parallel and helped her students do the same. As part of unit closure, Lydia read her students' excerpts from a letter written by a young soldier in World War II. She asked the students in small groups (using a copy of the letter) to suggest concepts and principles they had concluded were important in understanding the Civil War that seemed to be useful in thinking about the letter. Once students shared their ideas with the class, she asked them to reflect on skills they had used in text and video analysis during the unit and to determine which of those skills they used in analyzing the letter from World War II.

She reminded them that principles are useful in multiple settings, and told them she was pleased to see them use skills they had developed in one context to help them think about another.

Looking Back and Ahead

The essence of the Core Curriculum Parallel is well expressed in the words of children's author Margaret Wise Brown, who in 1949 wrote and illustrated a picture book titled *The Important Book*. Each page of the book illustrates a common object such as a daisy or a spoon. Writing follows the pattern of listing several noteworthy traits of the object, then emphasizing the most essential one by ending with the line "But the important thing about _____ is that it _____." That's much like the goal of the Core Curriculum Parallel as it seeks to help students understand the essential nature of what they are studying.

As we attempt to provide students with a comprehensive K–12 curriculum that spans a multitude of topics and subject areas, we must also keep in mind our long-term purposes for teaching and learning. It is vital we remember that amid all of the details, facts, activities, and assignments, the important thing about school is that it provides students with the understandings and skills they can use all of the rest of their lives. Effective use of the Core Curriculum Parallel ensures that students can truly find the forest for the trees.

The Core Curriculum Parallel also sets the stage for meaning in the other three parallels of the Parallel Curriculum Model. The Curriculum of Connections asks students to look at key information, concepts, principles, and skills across contexts. The Curriculum of Practice asks students to think about and use key information, concepts, principles, and skills as a practitioner uses them. The Curriculum of Identity asks students to reflect on ways in which practitioners in a discipline use key information, concepts, principles, and skills to contribute to and learn from their work—and then to reflect as students on what they learn about themselves by comparing themselves with those practitioners. In each instance, the "core" of meaning in the exploration pivots on the essential structure of the content and discipline the student is studying.

5

The Curriculum of
Connections Parallel

One of the first things a visitor to the University of Virginia campus notices is its amazing horticultural beauty and remarkable architecture. A stroll through the center of campus offers a glimpse of history and an opportunity to view learning through the eyes of the university's founder, Thomas Jefferson.

Recently, two of the authors were fortunate to be treated to a historical tour of the center of campus by a caretaker who beamed with pride as he related stories about the design and layout of the campus. A portion of that guided tour is worth relating, for it serves as a fitting segue to our next curriculum parallel, the Curriculum of Connections.

The mall, as it is called, is a long, wide, open expanse of rolling lawn, surrounded on three sides with buildings. On both the east and the west sides of the great lawn sit single, elongated rows of five two-story brick buildings. Connected by walkways and columnar porticos, the two rows of buildings originally housed the classrooms and living quarters of the professors and deans of each of the ten colleges served by the university.

The caretaker explained to us that Jefferson designed the university mall and its buildings as a metaphor to symbolize knowledge and learning. The two rows of buildings represent the two branches of knowledge, the arts and the sciences. The five buildings on each side of the lawn represent the five disciplines within each of the two branches of knowledge. The five buildings to the west of the lawn originally accommodated the five schools of the arts: philosophy, language, literature, the performing arts, and the visual arts. The five buildings to the east of the lawn housed the schools of science: math, earth science, physical science, life science, and the social sciences. Both sets of buildings were joined to the north by the Rotunda, a domed building that served as university offices, meeting rooms, and the library (see Figure 5.1).

What a profound story for an amateur historian to share with two strangers! We left with little doubt that his words would linger with both of us, far into the future.

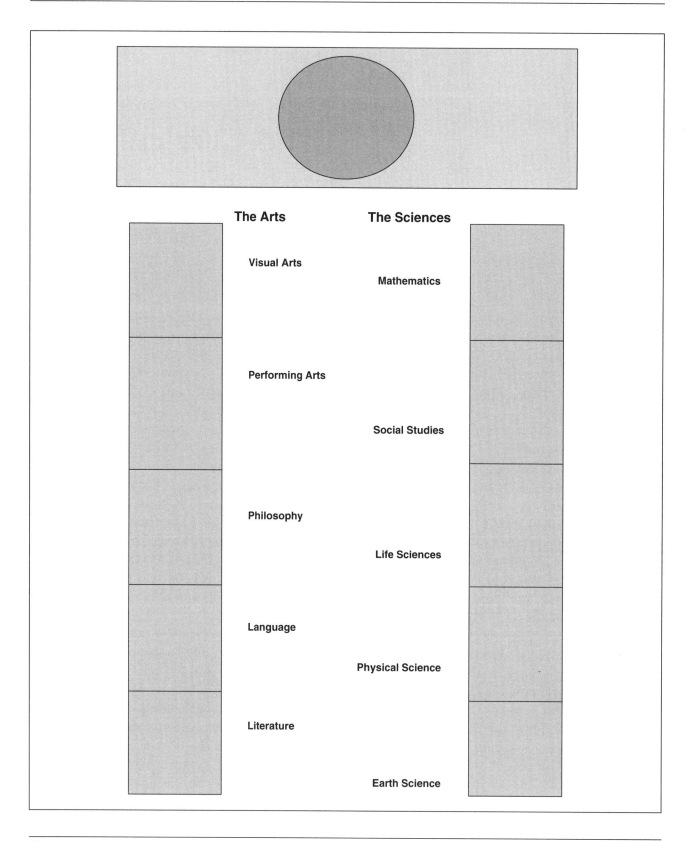

The Arts

Visual Arts

Performing Arts

Philosophy

Language

Literature

The Sciences

Mathematics

Social Studies

Life Sciences

Physical Science

Earth Science

Figure 5.1   The Branches and Fields of Knowledge

Perhaps that was Jefferson's wish as well, to provide a powerful message that inspired young learners and college students to continue to seek wisdom by making connections across disciplines, time, events, and topics for the rest of their lives.

This chapter explains the second in a set of four parallel approaches to curriculum design—the Curriculum of Connections. Like the other three curriculum parallels, The Curriculum of Connections Parallel uses concepts and principles as well as key components of the Comprehensive Curriculum Framework to design powerful and effective learning experiences for students. It strives to improve the impact of curriculum and instruction by helping students see how experts use concepts and principles to make connections between and among bodies of knowledge—and to help students build their own connections. Connections forged within this parallel are, in that way, different from the kinds of connections students make as they participate in the Core Curriculum, the Curriculum of Practice, or the Curriculum of Identity.

This chapter explores those differences and provides descriptions of the various ways in which the key curriculum components can be modified to fit the special functions of the Curriculum of Connections. In addition, the reader will find examples, charts, and tables designed to support the curriculum writing or curriculum remodeling process.

What Is the Curriculum of Connections?

The Curriculum of Connections is a format for designing teaching and learning activities, lesson plans, or curriculum units that use important concepts and principles of a discipline to help learners focus on the discovery of relationships, associations, and ideas across various instances and aspects of knowledge and information. The ability to grasp multiple and layered connections is acquired as a result of a learning and maturation process that gradually yields analogous relationships, thereby enlarging one's perspective, cognition, and awareness.

A learner can discover connections by examining data, facts, and concepts within a topic or discipline. Lessons and units designed around the Curriculum of Connections, however, are more likely to emphasize the search for overarching connections—those that can be developed across events, time, places, topics, principles, and disciplines. The Curriculum of Connections bears a strong resemblance to the Core Curriculum in that it draws on the concepts and principles within a discipline. Nonetheless, the purpose for making connections in this parallel is to identify or use macroconcepts (overarching concepts that connect many disciplines and topics), principles, processes, or dispositions across disciplines and novel problems. The Curriculum of Connections provides opportunities for learning by supporting students as they use analogous or comparative thinking among equivalent classes, relationships, and systems in the same or varied disciplines to discover connections through reflection.

In much the same way that an infant peers into a full-length mirror and initially believes that what appears is a new, enticing, and unusual playmate, the Curriculum of Connections brings together two or more seemingly different, but intriguing, ideas for students to examine. When successful, the analysis and examination of these apparently distinct entities results in a deeper understanding of equivalence through the use of insight and the recognition of symmetry and congruence.

The Curriculum of Connections asks students to take on the role of detective. As students proceed through a lesson or unit of study, they develop or use a set of basic rules about how things look, work, and relate to each other in a specific circumstance or venue. Then, they actively search for the ways in which these same characteristics, concepts, processes, dispositions, rules, and principles apply in new contexts. This deductive search for meaningful connections and analogies helps students achieve deeper understanding and draw conclusions about new and unfamiliar sets of information—and, in fact, about life itself.

Students can identify connections by using previously learned characteristics, concepts, and rules to examine two or more people, events, products, topics, time periods, cultures, or disciplines. The generalizations that result from this search help learners appreciate the fact that we can "see the world in a grain of sand" and that there truly are fewer than "six degrees of separation" between any one topic, person, or event, and other topics or people across time and cultures. The essence of this curriculum parallel is its emphasis on the development of connections: personal, topical, temporal, intradisciplinary, or interdisciplinary.

Focusing Questions in the Curriculum of Connections

Each of the four curriculum parallels structures its format and purposes around the key questions it helps students answer. The Core Curriculum Parallel asks students to consider three overarching questions: What is the structure of this discipline? What are the key concepts and principles in this discipline? How can I develop an understanding of the concepts and principles as a result of studying this topic?

By contrast, the Curriculum of Connections extends these understandings and poses three additional overarching questions: How are the key concepts and principles in this topic or discipline related to the key concepts and principles in other topics or disciplines? How might I use what I already know about the key concepts and principles in a topic or discipline to acquire a deeper understanding of those same concepts and principles in other topics and/or disciplines? How might I use interdisciplinary concepts, themes, and processes to solve novel problems? Figure 5.2 lists "smaller" questions on which students will need to focus in order to formulate answers to the three overarching questions in Curriculum of Connections.

To support the development of a Curriculum of Connections, teachers must pose to themselves three questions: What are the major concepts and principles in the discipline that are related to the topic or unit that is my focal point? What other topics or problems in this discipline or other disciplines address these same concepts and principles? How might I develop a connection between the topic or unit that is my focal point and other topics or problems to encourage a deeper understanding of the concepts and principles that connect them?

What key concepts and principles have I learned?

In what other contexts can I use what I have learned?

How do the ideas and skills I have learned work in other contexts?

How do I use the ideas and skills to develop insights or solve problems?

How do different settings cause me to change or reinforce my earlier understandings?

How do I adjust my way of thinking and working when I encounter new contexts?

How do I know if my adjustments are effective?

How does looking at one thing help me understand another?

Why do different people have different perspectives on the same issue?

How are perspectives shaped by time, place, culture, events, and circumstances?

In what ways is it beneficial for me to examine varied perspectives on a problem or issue?

How do I assess the relative strengths and weaknesses of differing viewpoints?

What connections do I see between what I am studying and my own life and times?

Figure 5.2 Some Focusing Questions for Students in the Curriculum of Connections

The Purpose of a Curriculum of Connections: Why Should a Teacher Emphasize Connections and Relationships?

The Curriculum of Connections emphasizes relationships, patterns, and ideas for several reasons. First, the ability to recognize connections and relationships both broadens and deepens one's understanding of, and appreciation for, the interconnectedness of knowledge. At its most sophisticated level, the ability to see connections allows us to perceive all topics and disciplines as sharing integrated facets or as aggregates sharing common and analogous attributes, purposes, or functions. In turn, an appreciation for such analogous thinking fosters a habitual search and appreciation for the many ways in which units that are parts of classes are part of a system, and that systems share common functions, attributes, and principles. It is this appreciation of universality and timelessness that distinguishes wisdom from content knowledge. With wisdom comes the ability to search for, perceive, and appreciate, for example, the aesthetics of science and the science of pottery.

The acquisition of an integrated perspective was never more apparent than in the words of a graduate student—a carpenter by trade—who returned to college to pursue a second career as a teacher. During his first graduate class, his fellow students, all practicing teachers, became involved in an animated conversation about teaching and learning activities in various subject areas. After listening to them in silence for fifteen minutes, he finally remarked in a quiet but firm voice,

"You teachers really slay me—all this talk about math versus reading, music versus science—everything's a separate subject area to you. You know, when I build a set of stairs for a customer, I never stop and think, 'Now I'm doing science, now I'm doing math, now I'm using psychology.' I just see it all as part of the same thing."

The ability to perceive and search for connections also decreases "nearsightedness" or episodic thinking and the accumulation of isolated, disconnected information and details. In fact, an accumulating body of research suggests that the ability to create connections among concepts, principles, events, and disciplines actually supports increases in long-term memory, enhances retrieval, and develops a "high road" transfer of acquired knowledge to novel and complex situations and ill-structured problem solving.

The ability to see these connections, and a disposition to look for commonalties and connections, actually diminishes a learner's sense of confusion and frustration when confronted with new data or information. Looking for familiar themes and concepts in strange situations also decreases the amount of time needed for a learner to understand new content, improves efficiency and precision, and enhances a learner's self-efficacy for independent learning.

A purposeful search for connections also improves insight and creativity through metaphoric thinking and analogy making. When confronted with a problematic situation, astute connection makers continually ask themselves, "What does this remind me of? How can I connect and use what I already know to solve this problem?"

The "Eureka!" sensation and the feeling of "Aha!" usually follow a lengthy incubation period that revolves around a difficult problem or a confusing situation. A willingness to tolerate the ambiguity that accompanies uncertainty and indecision allows us to search our minds, purposefully or unconsciously, for metaphors, connections, and analogous situations stored in our long-term memories. When discovered and retrieved, these connections and analogies can be generalized, transferred, and applied to a novel problem in order to solve it in an effective and creative manner. A prolonged search for the proper analogy also prevents us from leaping to action or judgment and reduces the likelihood of implementing ineffective solutions or drawing inappropriate conclusions.

Last, and possibly most important, the ability to see connections also supports a person's ability to view ideas or events from multiple perspectives. This, in turn, enhances empathy, open-mindedness, and nonjudgmental thinking while decreasing stereotypical thinking and bias.

The Curriculum of Connections: When Should I Use This Parallel?

Despite the importance of these varied purposes for, and benefits of, the Curriculum of Connections, it is nonetheless the case that no single curriculum approach is appropriate for all situations. It is as ineffective to "force fit" this parallel into every unit of instruction as it is to make it fit the needs of every learner and every teacher in the same way and time. Personal content knowledge, grade-level expectations, the availability of resources, and opportunities to work with teachers from other disciplines predicts the likelihood of deep understanding and efficacy as well as initial implementation and long-term use.

The journey to professional expertise is a long one, and many teachers may discover and apply these connections only after lengthy study and reflection in multiple content areas. We can, however, support the likelihood that more teachers will be able to develop these connections and identify interdisciplinary generalizations and macroconcepts through interdisciplinary collaboration and exposure to advanced content in various disciplines.

Although not every teacher or student may be prepared to find concepts, principles, and universal connections independently, most teachers and students can be supported and coached to enhance their ability to think and reflect in this manner. Separate sections of this chapter illustrate various techniques that can be used by teachers and teachers' coaches to scaffold this kind of thinking for both youngsters and adults.

The Characteristics of the Curriculum Components Within the Curriculum of Connections

If an educator analyzed a Core lesson or a unit designed by using the Comprehensive Curriculum Framework and compared it to a Connections lesson or unit that emphasizes connections and relationships, the key components (i.e., content (including standards), assessments, introductory activities, teaching methods, learning activities, grouping strategies, resources, products, extension activities, differentiation based on learner need, and closure) would be evident in both examples. The characteristics and format of these components would, however, exhibit subtle differences. In the Core example, components of the Comprehensive Curriculum Framework would promote understanding of concepts and principles that help organize the content of the lesson or unit and help that content make sense. In the Connections lesson or unit, by contrast, components of the Comprehensive Curriculum Framework would promote making connections among topics within or across disciplines, times, places, and other contexts. This section describes how key curriculum components can be used to help students make such connections.

Figure 5.3 provides a graphic organizer that lists the key curriculum components as they might appear within the Curriculum of Connections in the left column. Techniques for developing each component are listed in the right column.

Choosing Appropriate Content and Learning Objectives to Support a Curriculum of Connections

Of the key components in the Comprehensive Curriculum Framework, the content and standards component probably changes the most to address the goals of the Curriculum of Connections Parallel. The differences are subtle, however, because an examination of the content objectives and standards would still reveal

(Text continues on p. 126)

Curriculum Components	Reconfiguration Techniques
Content (Including Standards)	• Identify the units or topics assigned to teach. • Identify the discipline(s) with which these topics are associated. • Make a list of the major facts, concepts, principles, dispositions, and skills to be addressed in each unit of study. • Consider the kinds of information students will learn—places, events, people, things, or characteristics. Identify analogous items in other topics, locations, time periods, fields, or disciplines. • Consider the concepts that students will learn in this unit. Identify the use of similar concepts in other topics, fields, or disciplines. • Consider the principles that students will learn in this unit. Identify analogous principles that explain relationships within other topics, fields, or disciplines. • Consider the dispositions that students will address in this unit. Identify analogous dispositions in other situations, career areas, fields, or disciplines. • Consider the skills that students will learn in this unit. Identify analogous skills needed to think, learn, investigate, or produce in other topic areas, fields, or disciplines. • Consider working with colleagues who teach different subject areas to the same students. Discuss how you might connect two or more units of instruction through a focus on common concepts, principles, skills, and dispositions.
Assessments	• Supply students with word banks that list major concepts and ask them to create concept maps that link related concepts and principles in one topic with those in another topic or discipline. • Develop rubrics that address growth in the understanding of macroconcepts, processes, and generalizations across topics and disciplines. • Provide preassessments to identify students' prior experiences with the discipline and the concepts and principles they have attained to date. Build on this knowledge in the upcoming unit through the use of synectics and metaphoric thinking.
Introductory Activities	• Provide students with concept maps. • Develop and share advance organizers that list the major concepts, principles, skills, and dispositions they will acquire in this unit. • Introduce the ideas of macroconcepts, generalizations, and themes. Contrast these terms with concepts, rules, and principles. • Share a familiar Aesop's fable with students or ask them to identify and list common axioms, adages, or proverbs. Ask students to discuss and identify the purpose for proverbs and axioms. Explain that this unit of instruction will have a similar purpose. • Provide students with three parts of an analogy or a portion of a simile. Ask them to complete the missing portions. Discuss why or how they use analogies or similes in their daily lives. • Make a list of the many ways that analogies, metaphors, and similes support new learning, decrease confusion, or enhance problem solving. Explain that the purpose of this unit will be to build the same kinds of bridges and connections for students. • Develop and share focusing questions that bridge two or more concepts, skills, principles, or dispositions across topics and disciplines.

Curriculum Components	Reconfiguration Techniques
	• Introduce the overarching theme, generalization, or macroconcept at the outset of the integrated unit. Remind students that they will continually search for connections between the specifics they are studying in one discipline and these multidisciplinary themes and macroconcepts.
	• Prepare a list of the concepts, skills, principles, and dispositions students will learn during this unit. Next to each, print a symbol of a bridge, connection, umbrella, and so on. Tell students that throughout the integrated unit they will continually search for the words or terms they can use to describe the macroconcepts, dispositions, processes, generalizations, or themes that apply to similar classes or relations across multiple disciplines or topics.
	• Introduce an intriguing problem or puzzle in a topic or discipline distant from the unit or discipline students are about to begin studying. Tell students that careful reflection during the course of this unit should help them discover macroconcepts, themes, generalizations, or analogies that will, in turn, help them solve the cross-discipline puzzle or problem by the end of the unit.
Teaching Strategies	• Use the synectics teaching model to help students build a bridge between the concepts, principles, and dispositions in one unit and analogous concepts, principles, skills, and dispositions in another model.
	• Share or help students create metaphors to build bridges between topics and disciplines.
	• Use Socratic questioning and deductive logic as scaffolds to help students make connections between abstract units, classes, relations, and systems.
	• Provide opportunities for students to work in cooperative groups as they make analogies between topics, events, and disciplines.
	• Use examples and nonexamples within the Concept Attainment Model to help students develop macroconcepts and themes.
	• Improvise on Wassermann's (1988) Play-Debrief-Replay teaching methods. Help students acquire and reflect on learned concepts and principles, and then replay the use of the same concepts and principles with another venue. Follow with another debriefing and reflection opportunity.
	• Use intra- or interdisciplinary problem-solving simulations or scenarios to support the development of macroconcepts.
Learning Activities	• Develop learning activities related to content acquisition that require students to identify connections, acquire macroconcepts, make cross-discipline generalizations, and use themes to solve integrated problems. Involve students in the use of the following thinking skills:
	Comparing and contrasting
	Deductive and inductive thinking
	Making analogies
	Creative problem solving
	Making generalizations
	Hierarchical classification
	Seeing patterns and relationships
	Developing insights
	Systems thinking

Figure 5.3 (*Continued*)

123

(Continued)

Curriculum Components	Reconfiguration Techniques
Resources	• Provide students with concept maps and advance organizers that preview the important concepts and principles explored in the unit. • Find high school texts and college resources to identify the major concepts, skills, and principles within related fields and disciplines. • Provide graphic organizers to support analogy making, creative problem solving, and classification. • Identify and locate numerous interdisciplinary examples related to the concepts, principles, skills, and dispositions being addressed in the unit. • Find photographs, journals, data, primary source documents, newspaper articles, historical accounts, magazine articles, Web sites, paintings, and so on that address the same concept in various disciplines. • Locate an interdisciplinary problem or simulation related to the unit's learning goals. • Provide biographies of historical and contemporary inquirers, inventors, and researchers in various disciplines who used the same concepts or processes.
Products	• Ask students to create graphic displays that explain the patterns they have identified across topics, events, people, or disciplines. • Create an imaginary forum, similar to Steve Allen's old television show *Meeting of the Minds*, in which students take on the role of various historical figures across time as they discuss a contemporary or historical problem or issue (Bourman, 1996). • Assign concept maps to analyze the acquisition of macroconcepts and integrated principles. • Ask students to demonstrate the relationship between the core concepts and principles in one topic, discipline, or event, and those in another field or time period. • Ask students to demonstrate their knowledge of integrated connections through the use of reflective essays, journal entries, charts, diagrams, analogies, and collages. • Provide graphic organizers or double-entry journals that enable students to communicate their acquisition of macroconcepts and generalizations. • Ask students to create a synectics diagram to demonstrate the use of metaphoric thinking to solve an interdisciplinary problem.
Extension Activities	• Ask the gifted education specialist to provide the connections unit to interested students as an extension of the regular course of study. • Ask the technology teacher to help you identify Web-site links to other topics, time periods, or individuals. • Ask the librarian to help you identify biographies of philosophers and books about philosophical thought to share with students. • Team with a teacher of another subject area to provide concurrent integrated units of study that culminate in an interdisciplinary problem-solving activity. • Provide interested students with an opportunity to study philosophy, wisdom, or epistemology. • Team with another content area specialist and identify macroconcepts, themes, dispositions, and interdisciplinary processes that can be incorporated within two or more consecutively taught units of instruction. • Teach students the process of hierarchical classification or systems thinking.

Curriculum Components	Reconfiguration Techniques
	• Teach students how to use the synectics model for making analogies or for problem solving. • Develop a simulated or real-world problem that students can solve by applying the concepts, principles, skills, and dispositions of one field to another topic or discipline. • Provide opportunities for students to interview and visit with artists, researchers, college professors, philosophers, and interdisciplinary problem-solving teams to discuss how they use knowledge in other fields and disciplines in their daily work and problem solving. • Ask content area specialists and other teachers who are experts in the concepts, principles, dispositions, and processes within one field or discipline to co-plan, team teach, coach, or provide useful feedback on the progress and success of the lessons.
Grouping Practices	• Work with large groups of students to overview the goals of the unit, to provide directions, and to share information about macroconcepts, generalizations, and processes. • Use pairs and small groups of students to support pattern finding and the development of macroconcepts and themes. • Briefly conference with individual students to assess the degree to which they are able to relate interdisciplinary examples and real-world problems to core concepts and principles. • Observe individual students and provide feedback to support the development of cognitive skills. • Debrief students in large groups, using maps and diagrams, to ensure that the entire class can connect macroconcepts, generalizations, and processes to core concepts and principles.
Modification Based on Learner Need, Including Ascending Intellectual Demand	• Increase or decrease teacher scaffolding to support the development of macroconcepts, interdisciplinary processes and dispositions, themes, and systems thinking. • Provide additional representative topics for comparison to reduce ambiguity or to add additional layers of complexity. Keep these topics within the same discipline to decrease cognitive difficulty or expand to other disciplines to increase intellectual demand. • Use less obvious topics or disciplines for comparison with students with more sophisticated levels of deductive thinking. Encourage a continuing commitment to intrinsic motivation and to the world of ideas. • Use the Parallel's guidelines for Ascending Intellectual Demand in selecting resources and designing learning activities and products.
Lesson/Unit Closure	• Guide students in reflecting on key concepts and closure principles in one segment of study that can help them achieve understanding in another segment of study. • Ask students to make connections between what they are studying and their own experiences. • Have students propose examples from music, arts, sports, technology, or other interests that seem to operate according to the concepts and principles they are studying in class. • Guide students in thinking about differences in the way particular concepts are used in one context vs. another, or ways in which principles might be reworded slightly to reflect a particular context. • Spotlight key information, vocabulary, and skills from the lesson or unit. • Ask and explore answers to the connections focus question.

Figure 5.3 Using the Key Curriculum Components in the Curriculum of Connections

a concentration on concepts and principles. What would be different is the extent to which the content objectives address concepts and principles that cross topics, events, time periods, and disciplines.

Figure 5.4 demonstrates the nature of the concepts, processes, skills, principles, applications, and dispositions addressed in the Curriculum of Connections. A contrast between this table and a similar discipline-based set of knowledge categories in Figure 4.3, in the Core Curriculum chapter, reveals the integrated and interdisciplinary nature of the knowledge highlighted in the Curriculum of Connections.

Once teachers and curriculum developers come to a clear understanding of the connected nature of knowledge, the search for integrating topics, concepts, and principles begins. During the initial stages of planning, teachers clarify the names of the units or the topics they are assigned to teach in a specific content area. Next, teachers identify the appropriate discipline(s) associated with these topics and the major pieces of information, concepts, principles, dispositions, and skills that need to be addressed in each unit of study. To this point, the planning process for the Curriculum of Connections Parallel closely resembles the development process for the Core Curriculum Parallel.

However, after identifying the essential information, concepts, skills, dispositions, and skills related to a single topic, the teacher continues to search for analogous knowledge, topics, events, or people across time periods, cultures, or disciplines. Figure 5.5 demonstrates one aspect of this kind of thinking, with each listing several concepts related to a given subject area. The last column lists terms commonly referred to as macroconcepts. Macroconcepts are "generic" concepts that are essential to the structure of more than one discipline, although the terms for the concept may be slightly different from one discipline to the next.

The search for analogous concepts in multiple disciplines is evident in the use of the term "immigration" in social studies, "migration" in science, and "influence" in art. A Curriculum of Connections unit that seeks to illustrate and examine the same concept over multiple disciplines might ask students to study the causes and effects of movement, progression, migration, and immigration. For example, by concurrently exploring the movement and migration of people, animals, and art across cultures, geographic regions, biomes, or time periods, students come to a deeper understanding of the impact of movement on change and progress. Once these two macroconcepts are linked together in the students' minds, they can begin to explore the overarching, interdisciplinary generalization that explains the relationship between movement and progress, or movement and change—across time, cultures, and disciplines.

When a teacher decides to create Curriculum of Connections, the search for common concepts across disciplines or topics—macroconcepts—is the first step in the planning process. Figure 5.6 illustrates a teacher's use of a graphic organizer to support the search for discipline-based concepts, related concepts in other disciplines, and macroconcepts. The initial unit in social studies addressed the topic of early 19th-century immigration in the United States. The teacher listed the essential topic-based concepts in the first column. A search for related concepts in other disciplines proved fruitful in art and science but much more forced, artificial, and strained in physical education and the language arts. Rather than trying to make

Knowledge Category	Definition and Examples
Macroconcepts	A general idea or understanding, a generalized idea of a thing or a class of things; a category or classification that extends across disciplines *Examples:* • Form • Function • Systems • Change • Patterns • Conflict • Perspective • Interdependence
Generalizations and Themes	A fundamental theme or generalization to explain the relationship between two or more concepts in two or more disciplines *Examples:* • Form follows function. • Our perspectives are shaped by and shape our experiences. • Change is painful. • Measure twice, cut once. • Parts of systems are interdependent.
Interdisciplinary Processes	Proficiencies, abilities or techniques, strategies, methods, or tools that have multiple, interdisciplinary applications *Examples:* • Identifying patterns • Making deductive inferences • Observing • Making a plan • Solving a problem • Researching and communicating findings
Interdisciplinary Dispositions	Beliefs, dispositions, appreciations, or values that transcend cultures, time, and disciplines *Examples:* • An appreciation for patience • A belief in the critical importance of empathy • An understanding of perspective • A positive attitude toward curiosity • Intrinsic motivation for learning

Figure 5.4 Categories of Knowledge Emphasized in the Curriculum of Connections

Social Studies Concepts	Science Concepts	Art Concepts	Music Concepts
transportation	evaporation	shadow	scales
government	circulation	light	notation
tributary	fertilization	perspective	rhythm
war	temperature	depth	beat
battle	gravity	hue	percussion
treaty	magnetism	tint	woodwind
commerce	energy	composition	harmony
leader	work	texture	echo
services	matter	line	jazz
goods	homeostasis	dimensionality	timbre
resources	sound	symmetry	resonance
culture	waves	portrait	range
immigration	resonance	media	baritone
poverty	plasticity	abstract	projection
navy	scientific	method	gradiant
explorer	evidence	aesthetic	mood
delta	migration	landscape	pitch
caste	tropism	realism	volume
migration	movement	influence	melody
longitude	pressure	balance	conductor
Language Arts	Health and Physical Education Concepts	Math concepts	Interdisciplinary Macroconcepts
vowel	touchdown	multiplication	form
stereotype	goal	sum	function
claim	heatstroke	integer	systems
persuasion	dribble	prime number	structure
hero	drug	ratio	change
conflict	linesman	angles	communities
folktale	cancer	mode	constancy

Language Arts	Health and Physical Education Concepts	Math concepts	Interdisciplinary Macroconcepts
resolution	fluid	denominations	symbolism
poetry	sprint	symbols	relationships
alliteration	fullback	ray	properties
symbols	sunscreen	perimeter	measurement
syllable	referee	correlation	classes
noun	offense	standard	deviation patterns
preposition	antioxidant	central	tendency
personification	warm-up	order of operations	cycles
skim	point guard	graph	variables
point of view	protein	pie chart	factors
cause and effect	emergency	random	criticism
archetype	accident	symmetry	movement
main idea	conditioning	chaos	perspective

Figure 5.5   A Comparison of Discipline-Based Concepts With Interdisciplinary Macroconcepts

Subject Area and Unit Name: Social Studies— Immigration to the United States at the Beginning of the 20th Century							
Social Studies Concepts	Related Math Concepts	Related Science Concepts	Related Language Arts Concepts	Related Music Concepts	Related Art Concepts	Related Physical Education Concepts	Interdisciplinary Macroconcepts
culture		species biome system habitat niche		genre	form	style	FORM
transportation immigration emigration		circulation migration transfer	segues storytelling		school influence	movement	MOVEMENT PROGRESSION CHANGE
resources needs	variables	survival energy	folktales		subject media		
Topic-Based Relationship: Immigrants used various means of transportation to move from their homes and cultures to the United States in order to seek abundant resources and opportunities to improve their living conditions. Discipline-Based Principle: Throughout time, some individuals and subgroups within a culture have used available means of transportation to explore or resettle in other locations and regions in order to find or use new or additional resources or opportunities. Interdisciplinary Generalization or Theme: Living things, human products, and technology adapt, improve, or make progress as a result of movement.							

Figure 5.6   Identifying Macroconcepts

a connection to multiple disciplines just for the sake of making connections, the teacher's initial search for related concepts suggests that social studies, art, and science are indeed the best links for developing macroconcepts and integrated themes or generalizations.

Next, the teacher considers the principle students will learn in this discipline-based unit when they search for relationships among the concepts. This principle is also listed in Figure 5.6. The results of a search for an analogous principle in the social sciences and an interdisciplinary generalization or theme are listed as well.

In a similar fashion, teachers might search for analogous skills, dispositions, or problems across topics, disciplines, events, times, and so forth. Once again, teachers would make a list of the skills, dispositions, or problems within the topic or discipline to be studied. By identifying comparable skills, dispositions, or problems in another topic, discipline, event, time period, etc., teachers would prepare themselves to generate authentic rather than forced or contrived connections for integration.

Remodeling Examples

The strategy just discussed to generate significant connections is often not used. Three more typical strategies to find connected content, concepts, principles, or problems come to mind. They are more common approaches to seeking connections—and less effective in generating connections essential to the nature and purpose of the disciplines. To illustrate, contrast the strategy just discussed with the three scenarios presented next. Determine which of the four techniques have the most promise for making authentic connections across topics, disciplines, cultures, times, events, places, and so on.

Scenario 1: We Read About It

When Michelle first heard about the Curriculum of Connections, she said that she already used that approach to design lessons—she'd just never called it that before. She said that in her district, at the elementary level, they call it thematic teaching, and the high school teachers called it interdisciplinary teaching. Michelle offered an example. "In November, when we're supposed to talk about the pilgrims with the kids during the social studies unit, I saved a lot of time by connecting it all together and choosing a great picture book about Thanksgiving and the pilgrims to read aloud to my kindergartners during circle time. That way it's all related—social studies and reading."

Scenario 2: Webbing It

Margaret added, "I do it a little differently, but I still know what you mean. You see, in my school we're supposed to do social studies and science for a half hour every day. Well, with all the emphasis on reading, writing, and math, there just isn't enough time to pack it all in. So, when I'm about to start a new social studies or science unit I just make a web, with the social studies or science topic in the center. Then, I think about all the activities I could have the kids do to connect the social studies or science unit to the other subject areas. Here's an example of what I mean. It sure saves a lot of time, and the kids love all the activities."

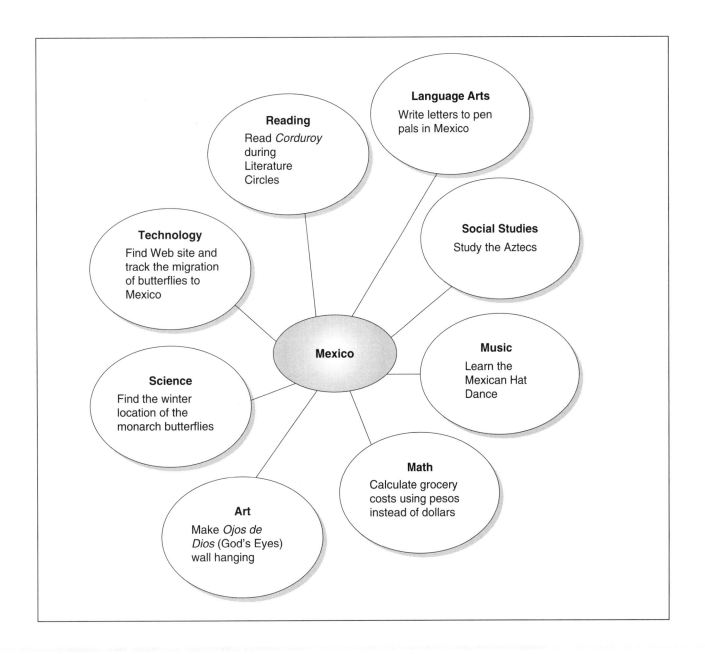

Scenario 3: Integrating Subjects

Montie, a sixth grade teacher, offered another perspective on webbing. "We're departmentalized at the middle school, but our four-member team has a teacher from each of the four major subject areas. We have two periods a day for planning so that we can do just what you're talking about. We make sure that at least a third of our units are integrated with the other three subject areas. We use either science or social studies as the focal point for each of our units. When I'm about to begin a social studies topic, the science, English, and math teachers work with me to find connections to their disciplines. The English teacher finds a book about our social studies topic for the kids to read and discuss. The science teacher finds some biology or earth science topic for the students to study related to the region we're studying in social studies. The math teacher always has the hardest time making the connections. Usually, we find a way to work math in by creating word problems related to our social studies or science content. That way the kids have a sustained and long-term exposure to the topic."

The examples cited above could be used to describe the state of integrated curriculum development in most school districts throughout the country. The concept of integration is appealing to many of us, largely because of the opportunities it seems to afford for collaboration, teaming, and time management. However, structured and collaborative time to research content prior to writing curriculum and time for brainstorming, planning, decision making, and revision is scant. As a result, many integrated curriculum units fall short of hitting their mark with regard to the rigor, power, and meaning that is central and authentic to the disciplines. Until more teachers have greater opportunities to plan collaboratively, to receive and provide constructive criticism on their work, to sample students' work products for the quality of ideas and skills they demonstrate, and to rework lessons and unit plans, the promise of meaningfully integrated curriculum units remains out of reach.

If we were to fine-tune and remodel the "integrated" units cited above, students might still be using picture books as resources, but there would be two or more books that students would use to compare and contrast content, concepts, processes, dispositions, or principles. Pilgrims could be compared to newcomers to a school, neighborhood, or town. Thanksgiving could be contrasted with harvest festivals in Alaska, China, or Egypt. Mexico could be compared with other Central American countries or with California and Texas. The Aztecs could be contrasted with the Mayans or the Incas. The "integrated" middle school science, social studies, and language arts units would all be remodeled to focus on a macroconcept, such as diversity, a theme such as man's continual search for knowledge, or the interdisciplinary skill of observation and perspective. This approach is vastly different from concurrent study of *Grapes of Wrath* in English, the water cycle in science, and the Great Depression in social studies.

Despite the popularity of the three scenarios, there is no unifying macroconcept or generalization that connects all three units. The language arts curriculum focuses on a resource and not a skill, the social studies curriculum focuses on an event and not a concept or principle, and the science curriculum focuses on a system without connecting it to other systems or cause and effect relationships.

Less common, and far more powerful, is the use of the strategies described in this section coupled with a conscious decision to focus the integration of common concepts, principles, dispositions, and skills across topics, time, cultures, and disciplines. To develop a truly powerful and overarching Curriculum of Connections, teachers must first ask the three questions posed at the outset of the chapter: What are the major concepts and principles in the discipline that are related to this topic or unit? What other topics or problems in this discipline address these same concepts and principles? How might I develop a connection between these topics and problems to encourage a deeper understanding of these concepts and principles? Planning the Curriculum of Connections, then, becomes the teacher's journey in answering those questions and then gathering resources and designing tasks and products that will enable learners to make those connections as well.

Summary

Although both the Core Curriculum and the Curriculum of Connections address content knowledge, concepts, skills, and principles, the chief difference between the two parallels is the degree of importance the Curriculum of Connections places on the ability to see relationships. The Curriculum of Connections emphasizes (a) common concepts, principles, and/or skills across topics, individuals, events, cultures, and/or time periods; (b) common concepts, principles, and/or skills across disciplines; (c) the identification of macroconcepts across multiple concepts; and (d) the discovery of generalizations across principles.

Reconfiguring Other Curriculum Components for the Curriculum of Connections

Assessment Strategies in a Curriculum of Connections

In Chapter 4, we discussed the characteristics of exemplary assessment. To be effective, assessments must be aligned to the learning goal. Second, they should be honest and accurate measures of students' learning over time. Third, they must provide some kind of performance or product with which to evaluate student learning. These characteristics are as valid for an assessment used within a Curriculum of Connections unit as they are for any of the assessments designed for use with the other three curriculum models described in this book. However, the nature of the learning goals within the Curriculum of Connections Parallel requires special attention to the design of appropriate rubrics and assessment formats.

A comparison of the assessment components in both models reveals subtle differences in both the rubric design and the assessment strategies. Although best practices for both models support the use of a four- or five-level rubric, rubrics in a Curriculum of Connections unit frequently contain descriptors of greater student expertise as well as criteria related to students' ability to demonstrate knowledge of patterns, principles, and themes across topics, time periods, and disciplines. In turn, the performance assessment must be aligned with this purpose and allow students to communicate growth, over time, in their ability to see larger and broader classifications for facts, concepts, and principles. The use of concept maps, graphic organizers, reflection journals, and dual-entry logs are common formats for assessments that support the analysis of students' understanding of principles and generalizations.

Take, for example, a learning goal that addresses core concepts in a discipline or field of study. To design an appropriate rubric to measure growth in concept attainment, the levels within the rubric must attend to ever-increasing levels of knowledge acquisition. However, within an integrated curriculum unit, the concept being assessed is generally a macroconcept that crosses disciplines, fields, or topics. To ensure a valid assessment, the accompanying rubric must address interdisciplinary connections at the upper levels of the rubric. Figure 5.7 provides an example for the concept of "migration."

As with other rubrics, a student's understanding of a macroconcept could be measured during both preassessment and postassessment. If, on the other hand, the knowledge goal in the unit addresses the acquisition of an interdisciplinary rule or a generalization, the rubric shown in Figure 5.8 might prove useful.

An appropriate assessment for the rubric in Figure 5.8 might ask students to explain the theme or generalization orally or in writing or to provide appropriate examples. As an alternative, students might be asked to analyze teacher-provided examples and develop related hypotheses or generalizations.

	Beginning	*Developing*	*Competent*	*Proficient*	*Expert*
Level of Understanding	The learner can define and provide key attributes that distinguish a concept in a given field or discipline.	The learner can use the concept to categorize and understand new information in the same field or discipline.	The learner can identify commonalities between concepts in one field or topic and concepts in another field or discipline.	The learner can classify and name comparable concepts in two or more fields as macroconcepts.	When confronted with new infomation in another discipline, students attempt to classify the new information using an interdisciplinary macroconcept.
Example	"Migration is the purposeful movement of living things across regions."	"Migration is evident during the 1880s, the early 1900s, the 1930s, and the 1940s in various part of the United States."	"The migration of whales has several things in common with the migration of human beings."	"The concept of beneficial movement is evident in both biology and anthropology."	"The population in our small, rural town experienced a decline in the 2000 census. I wonder if migration is a factor?"

Figure 5.7   A Rubric for Measuring the Attainment of a Macroconcept

	Beginning	*Developing*	*Competent*	*Proficient*	*Expert*
Level of Understanding	The learner can identify and explain a principle or relationship within a topic or field of study.	The learner can provide novel examples of the principle, theme, or generalization across events, topics, field of study, or disciplines.	The learner can use knowledge about principles in various disciplines or topics to develop an interdisciplinary theme or generalization.	The learner searches for interdisciplinary themes or generalizations in unfamiliar information in order to identify analogous or equivalent situations.	The learner searches for interdisciplinary themes or generalizations in unfamiliar information in order to identify analogous or equivalent situations and develop creative solutions to real-world problems.

Figure 5.8   A Rubric for Measuring the Acquisition of an Interdisciplinary Rule, Principle, or Generalization

The need for valid and reliable pre- and postassessments is as vital within the Curriculum of Connections as it is within any kind of curriculum unit. The format for the assessment, however, varies in order to conform more readily to measuring changes in students' acquisition of macroconcepts and generalizations across topics, times, places, and disciplines.

Introductory Activities in a Curriculum of Connections

Students about to participate in a Curriculum of Connections benefit from introductory activities that carefully explain the nature of the unit and teachers' expectations for students' learning. Unless the students clearly understand that their role involves a search for overarching connections, they are likely to get mired in the details and specifics of the cases, events, topics, and people they study and examine during the course of the unit. The use of focusing inquiry, reframed as questions that address the essential nature of knowledge, are extremely useful in helping students understand the focus of the unit.

In a Curriculum of Connections unit, one is unlikely to hear Lydia tell students "During this unit we will be studying the Civil War." Instead, her introductory comments might ask students what they think the word "civil" means, what a war is, and whether or not they think other countries, or other time periods, experienced civil wars. She might ask students about conflicts in their families and ask them to share stories of compromises made because of conflicts between needs and wants, rights and responsibilities. Beginning the curriculum unit with connections to personal conflicts helps students begin the process of developing analogies between what they are about to study and prior experiences in their own lives. Periodic reminders to make connections, modeling the making of connections, use of active teaching and learning strategies, debriefing opportunities, and reflective journals must follow such an introduction to ensure its effectiveness in helping students assume the appropriate role during the remainder of the unit's learning activities.

In addition, introductory activities in this parallel might include preassessments to identify students' skill in making analogies, in comparing and contrasting, and in classifying—essential skills in this parallel. Advance organizers might list the related topics, events, time periods, cultures, people, and/or disciplines students will compare. Further, teachers must be sure to emphasize the relevance of this approach to learning for improving students' abilities to find commonalities across topics, thereby accelerating and deepening the learning process. Finally, it is quite useful to invite students to begin to connect concepts and ideas from the topic or unit of study to their own lives and experiences through the use of shared concepts and principles.

Teaching Methods in a Curriculum of Connections

A third difference between the curricula created using Core and Connections Parallels has to do with the teaching methods selected for lessons. Although both the Core Curriculum and the Curriculum of Connections incorporate varied instructional strategies, coaching, and scaffolding, the strategies used most often in the Curriculum of Connections promote students' ability to perceive, understand, and appreciate the connections across topics, disciplines, and concepts. Among the teaching methods, or strategies, most likely to be used within the Curriculum of Connections are Socratic questioning, synectics, metaphorical thinking, cooperative learning, debriefing, problem-based learning, and inquiry-based teaching.

The essential role for the teacher is that of mediator between the student and the new learning. As such, the teacher builds bridges that enable students to perceive or demonstrate a connection between two different sets of information, two or more concepts, or two or more principles. Using two or more topics, events, pieces of literature, time periods, or disciplines, the teacher scaffolds as students treat knowledge like a set of Russian Petrushka dolls. Under the teacher's guidance, students attempt to "nest" and classify knowledge as they search for overarching connections by noting common features and attributes. It is a search for commonalties not unlike the thinking that goes into playing that old television game show "The $100,000 Pyramid."

Learning Activities in a Curriculum of Connections

Although both the Core Curriculum and the Curriculum of Connections promote students' active learning and cognitive involvement with new knowledge, the Curriculum of Connections tends to rely on students' use of a specific subset of analytic thinking skills to support their ability to make and understand those connections. These analytic thinking skills are listed in Figure 5.9.

If teaching and learning activities begin by providing students with an explanation of a macroconcept or generalization, then students are most likely to use deductive thinking to analyze raw data so as to determine the extent to which

- Making metaphors and analogies
- Comparing and contrasting
- Finding key attributes
- Classifying
- Sequencing
- Noting patterns
- Detecting relationships
- Interpreting
- Inferring
- Drawing conclusions
- Relating
- Identifying part and whole
- Inventing
- Constructing meaning
- Pursuing insight

Figure 5.9 Some Key Process Skills in the Curriculum of Connections

their characteristics fit the concept or theme. If, on the other hand, the teacher shares multiple examples across time periods, topics, events, or disciplines and asks students to form hypotheses or generalizations, then students are most likely to use inductive thinking to reach conclusions regarding the patterns they observe. Regardless of the approach, inductive or deductive, it is the teacher's skilled use of questioning, feedback, and debriefing that cements students' ability to make interdisciplinary connections and perceive overarching relationships.

Resources in a Curriculum of Connections

An analysis of the resources used in a Core Curriculum and a Curriculum of Connections unit also reveals subtle differences. Both models encourage use of primary source documents, varied media, and appropriate reading levels, but the materials in Connections lessons usually include content from more than one author, event, culture, topic, or discipline. A unit that seeks to teach students the common literary elements and devices in a given genre—folktales, for example, would likely include numerous myths, fables, and folktales from various cultures or time periods for students to read and analyze. If, on the other hand, students are searching for connections across disciplines, time periods, or cultures, teachers must have access to print materials that students can read or examine to identify patterns and common attributes. Collaboration with the school media specialist or librarian can be very helpful in supporting teachers' ability to plan for and implement a Curriculum of Connections.

In addition, students are likely to use graphic organizers that support their use of the analytic thinking skills and their search for universal concepts and generalizations. The availability of concept maps, double-entry journals, Venn diagrams, and reader response questions also supports the student's role in the Curriculum of Connections.

Products, Grouping Strategies, and Extension Activities in the Curriculum of Connections

There are few tangible differences in the products, grouping strategies, or extension activities used in a Core Curriculum unit and in a Curriculum of Connections unit. Students who participate in both kinds of units benefit from opportunities to produce open-ended products and assignments that enable them to explain their conclusions, demonstrate their thinking process, share supporting evidence, and reflect on the personal and conceptual connections they forged as they studied the data and information within the unit. Essays, collages, PowerPoint presentations, concept maps, theories, hypotheses, and scholarly treatises are excellent examples of appropriate product formats. As noted at several earlier points in the chapter, the difference between product assignments in a Core Curriculum and Curriculum of Connections is that the former would call on students to identify, apply, and illustrate frameworks of meaning and skill within a particular discipline, whereas the latter calls on students to deal with those frameworks across disciplines, topics, time periods, cultures, and so on.

Small groups and dyads allow students to work collaboratively, provide constructive feedback to each other, and participate in the critical, deductive, and inductive thinking so closely associated with the Curriculum of Connections. Students need opportunities to make hypotheses, argue the merits of their conclusions, listen to others' perspectives, and refine their own thinking. In a well-constructed Curriculum of Connections, the room is a busy place, filled with students engaged in speculation, debate, and a search for corroboration evidence.

Extension activities are a natural in the Curriculum of Connections. Because of the interrelatedness of knowledge, it is simple for a teacher to help students explore key macroconcepts and generalizations in areas of particular interest to students. These sorts of extensions can occur as a result of teacher illustrations in class, through individual or small group tasks, via strategies such as group investigations that invite student selection of topic, and by encouraging students to make connections in culminating products between required topics and concepts and related ones in fields or topics of interest.

While the basic formats of products, grouping strategies, and extension are similar between Core Curriculum and Connections Curriculum, the focus of these elements nonetheless differs in a way that should be familiar by this point. These curricular elements are used in Core Curriculum to help students probe and come to understand how the topic and the discipline in which it is found make sense—how they are organized—by using key concepts and principles. In Curriculum of Connections, by contrast, these same curricular elements are used to help students link ideas and knowledge through exploration and application of concepts and principles.

Differentiation and Ascending Intellectual Demand in the Curriculum of Connections

Informed by ongoing assessment, teachers can support differences among students' readiness levels and prior knowledge or experience through use of tiered assignments, scaffolded questioning, small group instruction, student conferences, and two-way journaling. Carefully crafted sequences of questions and graphic organizers support students who might be easily frustrated with open-ended assignments to identify macroconcepts and overarching themes and generalizations. It may also be useful for students who need extra support in the Curriculum of Connections, at least in the beginning, to interpret and apply teacher-generated analogies, metaphors, and generalizations prior to generating their own.

As students show evidence of advancing understanding and skill in the Curriculum of Connections, teachers can generate tasks with Ascending Intellectual Demand, or challenge, by using the "generic" strategies listed in Chapter 4, Figure 4.9. In addition, Figure 5.10 suggests additional strategies to provide appropriate demand for advanced students moving notably toward expertise in the discipline or topic being studied.

As was the case with the Core Curriculum Parallel, it is our belief that virtually all students should work with connections-making curriculum. It is also our belief that, as students continue to develop along a continuum toward expertise, an effective teacher provides ascending challenge and support for reaching that challenge. This is the case with highly advanced students as much as with students who need support to reach more basic or moderate levels of challenge. Only when there are continually escalating expectations for each student, and a support system for the ascent, do students grow cognitively, in independence, and in self-efficacy as learners.

Lesson and Unit Closure

Lesson and unit closure in the Curriculum of Connections focuses students on the interconnectedness of knowledge from various contexts—and the connections of that knowledge with their own lives and experiences. As is the case with the other PCM parallels, it is helpful to use the focusing questions for the Parallel of Connections in developing lesson and unit closure activities.

Some lesson closure activities in the Curriculum of Connections will necessarily focus on content "assigned" to a unit, subject, or grade level. At those points, teachers would ask students to think, for example, how concepts or principles that they are learning about the Industrial Revolution might relate to the American Revolutionary War. In other lesson closure activities, however, it's useful to expand applications students can make, asking, for example, how principles they are exploring in the Industrial Revolution can be applied to what some people might call a technological revolution in the past quarter century, or to times in their lives that have been marked by great change or upheaval. Curriculum of Connections provides great opportunity to help students see themselves and the broader world, moving past what can seem like compartmentalized and restricted classroom content. Lesson and unit closure are another point in the Curriculum of Connections that invites teachers and students to reach beyond the confines of a textbook or syllabus and to help students see the interconnectedness of many elements in their worlds.

- Increase the unfamiliarity of the context or problem in which understandings or skills are applied.
- Ask students to generate defensible criteria against which they then weigh diverse perspectives on a problem or solution (or use professional criteria for the same purpose).
- Call on students to develop solutions, proposals, or approaches that effectively bridge differences in perspective but still effectively address the problem.
- Ask students to make proposals or predictions for future directions based on student-generated,discipline-related patterns from the past in a particular domain.
- Have students search for legitimate and useful connections among seemingly disparate elements (for example, music and medicine or law and geography).
- Develop tasks or products that seek patterns of interaction among multiple areas (for example, ways in which geography, economics, politics, and technology affect one another).
- Call on students to look at broad swaths of the world through a perspective quite unlike their own (for example, how an age mate from a culture and economy very different from the student's would react to the student's house, slang, religion, clothing, music, relationships with adults, toys or gadgets, plans for the future, and so on).
- Develop tasks and products that seek out unstated assumptions beneath the surface of beliefs, decisions, approaches, or perspectives.
- Ask students to develop systems for making connections, drawing generalizations, achieving balanced perspectives, or addressing problems.
- Design criteria for students' work that call for a higher standard of quality (such as insightful, highly illustrative, highly synthetic, unusually articulate or expressive, and so on) as opposed to a less demanding but still positive standard of quality (such as appropriate, accurate, feasible, informed, defensible, and so on).

Figure 5.10 Some Paths to Achieve Ascending Intellectual Demand for Advanced Learners in the Curriculum of Connections

An Example of the Curriculum of Connections Using Lydia's Civil War Unit

In the past, Lydia Janis developed two related Civil War curriculum units, one that aligned content standards with the components of the Comprehensive Curriculum Framework and one that was adjusted to address the goals of the Core Curriculum Parallel. We now describe her third revision, one that is based on the goals of the Curriculum of Connections Parallel.

Lydia's Focusing Questions for the Curriculum of Connections

What are the major concepts and essential knowledge related to this topic or unit?

What are the comparable macroconcepts in this or other disciplines?

How might I develop a deeper understanding of these concepts within or between disciplines through the study of related topics, events, people, and/or problems?

Content Connections

Lydia began by asking herself some key questions related to the Curriculum of Connections Parallel—questions that would help her focus her curriculum writing.

Key Concepts Related to the Civil War	Topics, Events, Products, and People Related to the Study of the Civil War	Related Concepts From Other Topics, Subjects, or Disciplines	Related Topics, Events, Products, and People From Other Time Periods, Cultures, or Disciplines
Culture Perspective Time Period	Northern States Southern States Slave Culture	Culture Perspective Time Period	Taliban Regime Indian Reservation System Apartheid in South Africa The U.S. in the 1960s U.S. Women's Culture from 1820 to 1920
Labor Resources Goods and Services	Dred Scott Decision Frederick Douglass Factories Plantations Slave Trade Industrialization Slavery	Property Human Rights Civil Rights Immigration Prejudice	Child Labor Unionism Great Migration
Abolitionist Movement Emancipation	Harper's Ferry John Brown Sojourner Truth Harriet Tubman Uncle Tom's Cabin Harriet Beecher Stowe Levi Coffin Lucretia Mott Underground Railroad	Freedom Movements Trends Change Loss	The Suffrage Movement The Civil Rights Movement of the 1960s Women's Rights Movement Peace Movement Native American Movement Americans with Disabilities Movement War on Poverty Green Revolution Nationalism in South Africa
States' Rights Federalism Balance of Power	Secession Confederacy United States Westward Movement Territories	Colonialism Nationalism Balance of Power Independence	Bill of Rights British Colonies Ireland Branches of Government
Conflict Compromise Consensus Civil War/Unrest Resolution	Missouri Compromise Compromise of 1850 Fort Sumter Battle of Gettysburg Antietam Battle of Vicksburg Sherman's March Appomattox	Conflict Compromise Consensus Treaties Civil War/unrest Revolution Revolt Demonstrations	Egypt-Israel Peace Accord Vietnam War Great Plains Wars Bosnia War Irish Conflict Indian Revolution
Leadership	Abraham Lincoln Jefferson Davis General Grant General Lee General Sherman Stonewall Jackson Henry Clay Nat Turner	Change Agents Leadership	Nelson Mandela Martin Luther King, Jr. Elizabeth Cady Stanton Betty Friedan Gloria Steinem Thurgood Marshall Mahatma Ghandi Susan B. Anthony

Figure 5.11   Lydia's Ideas About Possible Connections With the Unit's Key Concepts

To organize her search for the answers to these questions, Lydia developed a chart (see Figure 5.11). In the first column, she listed the major concepts she had used in her work with the Core Curriculum Parallel to revise and reorganize her original textbook unit. In the second column, she listed all the events, people, products, and topics that her students studied in the Core Curriculum unit to address and understand the concepts in the first column. In the third column, she attempted to identify intradisciplinary or interdisciplinary concepts or macroconcepts aligned with the concepts in the first column. In the fourth column, she attempted to identify and list topics, events, people, and products from a variety of time periods, cultures, and disciplines that could be used to illustrate the multitude of connections between these topics and their related concepts and macroconcepts.

When Lydia stopped to analyze the content of the fourth column in her lists, she noticed that most of the connections were to other time periods, people, problems, issues, and cultures. As she intended, the connections came from the four disciplines within the social sciences: history, geography, economics, and government.

Lydia considered related connections in math, science, and the language arts. She could, for example, ask her students to read historical fiction about the Civil War, research leadership in the field of science, or examine conflict and resolution as a component of writer's craft, but those connections felt awkward for her current purposes. Instead, she decided that her decisions regarding the three focusing questions would revolve around connections made within the social sciences. She chose to make intradisciplinary connections among concepts rather than interdisciplinary connections.

Next, she chose five topic-based concepts as key concepts for the unit: slavery, emancipation, industrialization, plantation, and abolition. She then selected eleven intradisciplinary concepts that she believed were crucial to deep understanding: culture, time period, labor, resources, goods and services, prejudice, rights, compromise, consensus, leadership, and civil war. Last, she chose five interdisciplinary macroconcepts as the overarching ideas she wanted to foster in her Curriculum of Connections: perspective, balance, change, loss, and conflict. She recognized that, up to this point, she had made similar decisions when she organized her unit around the goals of the Core Curriculum Parallel. Just as she had done in the Core Curriculum unit, Lydia decided to teach the topic and discipline-based concepts through an examination of the information and evidence about the people, events, products, and topics surrounding the Civil War.

Moreover, with this revision she went a step further. She decided to use a compare and contrast focal point to help students build a bridge between the information and concepts they would learn about the Civil War and related examples of these concepts and principles in other events, people, time periods, and cultures. If she succeeded, she was convinced her students would understand that history truly does repeat itself. They would come to appreciate the fact that the same overarching concepts and principles resurface and help explain the actions of different people in other time periods who also struggled with issues that were explained by perspective, change, balance, loss, and conflict. In addition, she hoped the students would come to value the search for relationships, analogies, and metaphors because the ability to make such connections makes it easier to understand novel problems and unfamiliar situations.

Resources

To implement her dual goal of using macroconcepts and a compare and contrast focal point to foster student learning, Lydia needed to select compatible content for students to examine in other cultures and time periods. Her list of potential compare and contrast topics, events, issues, and people was fairly lengthy (see column 4 of Figure 5.11). She could have her students compare Lincoln to Martin Luther King, Jr. in order to study the concept of leadership. They could compare the Civil War to the more recent conflict in Ireland in order to study perspective, compromise, and conflict. They could compare the abolitionist movement to the suffrage movement to analyze the effects of change, loss, and balance of power. However, she reminded herself that planning time was short and that it might be harder to find materials about some topics than others, especially when she had to take into account the fact that the instructional reading levels of the students in her classroom usually spanned at least four grade levels.

Although it seemed more logical to make assessment decisions after she selected the content for the unit, Lydia realized that in this case she might have to put the cart before the horse and select content that was both relevant and accessible. She also had to be practical. She had to consider the type and number of resources she could locate and the speed with which she could access these materials. Ideally, she would need newspaper articles, diaries, photographs, books, videotapes, and even access to community members who had experienced events connected with the concepts and macroconcepts.

It occurred to her that the search for these materials would progress faster if she had help. A call to the other teachers on her grade-level team, to the media specialist, and to the special education and gifted education teachers garnered more support than she had anticipated. Using the "divide and conquer" approach, the four other teachers who demonstrated enthusiasm for the curriculum revision project conducted a quick search of library databases, publishers' catalogs, the school's book depot, and related Web sites. In a brief time, they had conducted their search and narrowed their choice of topics to those most easily accessible for their Grade 5 students.

The Jackdaws Company sold artifacts related to the women's suffrage movement and the civil rights movement. History Compass published appropriate Grade 5 materials about child labor and the great migration north. Scholastic Book Company published several materials about the civil rights movement in South Africa, its leaders, and cornerstone events. In addition, they discovered six videos in the school and town library about child labor, the great migration, the Vietnam War, South Africa, and the civil rights movement.

While the teachers were searching through catalogs, the media specialist looked for Web sites. She discovered 120 sites about the women's movement, 311 sites about the Vietnam War, 82 sites about child labor, 96 sites about the suffrage movement, 92 sites about the civil rights movement, and 112,613 sites about the Irish conflict! Martin Luther King, Jr. garnered 153 sites, Nelson Mandela had 2,331, Bosnia had 23, and Elizabeth Cady Stanton had 18 sites in her name. Even if only 10 percent of the sites proved useful and appropriate for Grade 5 students, there seemed to be more than enough materials to make connections across three or four events and/or individuals.

Blending Content Decisions and Grouping Strategies

The good news about the wealth of materials and sites gave rise to yet another decision. With all the information available to Lydia and her students, she decided on three topics joined with the key individual associated with each as the focal points for comparisons with the Civil War and its leaders: suffrage and Elizabeth Cady Stanton, apartheid in South Africa and Nelson Mandela, and the civil rights movement of the 1960s and Martin Luther King, Jr. Lydia noticed that she seemed to be jumping around from content to resources to grouping decisions—so much for following a precise sequence for making her curriculum decisions and plans related to the key curriculum components! Lydia then decided that maybe the sequence wasn't quite as important as the quality of the decisions and the alignment of the components.

During the Core Curriculum unit, Lydia had divided her twenty lessons into six segments, each segment addressing one core concept. Her original list included (1) culture, perspective, and time; (2) labor, resources, goods, and services; (3) the abolition movement; (4) states' rights, federalism, and the balance of power; (5) conflict, compromise, consensus, civil war, and resolution; and (6) leadership. Students used information and evidence about people, events, and situations surrounding the Civil War to develop their own explanations for these concepts and related principles.

During her Curriculum of Connections, Lydia decided to maintain the same number of segments with slight changes in conceptual emphasis. Her first, fifth, and sixth focal point would remain the same because these concepts transcended the topic of the Civil War and reflected major understandings in several social science disciplines. Her second conceptual focus would broaden from a concentration on goods, services, labor, and resources to a broader look at property, human rights, civil rights, and prejudice. Her third focal point, abolition and emancipation, would be revised to address freedom, movement, trends, and change. Her fourth conceptual lens, states' rights and federalism, would now broaden to incorporate the macroconcepts of independence, dependence, and balance.

Lydia knew that these time/content decisions had to be directly related to her choices for student groups. Choosing the concepts, macroconcepts, topics, events, time periods, and individuals to foster her Curriculum of Connections was one thing. Finding the time to conduct the study and a way to manage and organize the content and the groups of students was yet another.

After considering and abandoning several ideas, Lydia decided to use a large group setting for her unit introduction, her sharing, and her debriefing sessions. She would use both homogeneous and heterogeneous small groups to conduct evidence and information analysis about the concepts, macroconcepts, the Civil War, key leaders, and the related topics and leaders from other time periods and cultures. Sometimes, the groups would be based on common interests among students and sometimes based on similar or mixed readiness, depending on student needs and availability of resource materials.

Teaching Methods and Learning Activities

Lydia's next two decisions were fairly easy. When considering her role and chosen teaching methods for this unit, she decided to use the same pedagogies she had used in the majority of the Core Curriculum unit: Socratic questioning, concept attainment, inductive teaching, scaffolding, and coaching. The use of simulations and problem-based learning didn't seem appropriate, given the time constraints and the fact that she would have to juggle multiple sets of content.

While her students were examining the evidence she put before them, she would ask them to search for patterns, identify relationships, classify information, and define concepts. They would search evidence inductively in order to build the concepts and define the principles that explained the concepts surrounding the Civil War. When they examined information about individuals and issues across time periods or cultures, such as Nelson Mandela and Jefferson Davis or suffrage and the Civil War, she would support the students' use of compare and contrast strategies, analogy making, and deductive thinking. She knew these skills were particularly appropriate in helping them determine the extent to which the content and principles they created understand the Civil War also worked to explain the events, issues, and conflicts in South Africa and the United States during both countries' civil rights movements and during the women's suffrage movement in America.

Student Products and Assessments

Lydia's decision to structure the Civil War unit around the goals of the Curriculum of Connections would require a substantial amount of teaching and learning time. To save as much time as possible for these valuable activities, Lydia decided to dovetail her selection of students' short-term products with her assessment formats. She would assess students' short-term or daily products (their document analysis worksheets; graphic organizers; Venn diagrams; and persuasive essays comparing two or more events, people, concepts, or issues) to measure growth and development. The rubrics for assessing macroconcepts, generalizations, and themes, detailed in Figures 5.7 and 5.8, would be especially useful. They simply needed to be revised to suit the specific concepts and macroconcepts related to this unit.

In addition, the skill proficiency rubrics Lydia created for the Core Curriculum unit (see Chapter 4) would come in handy as she assessed students' ability to apply learned analytic reasoning skills to novel content and information. Specifically, she would assess students' skill at comparing and contrasting, deductive reasoning, inductive thinking, and making analogies. She would also assess their ability to make warranted claims about observable patterns—claims that were backed up with evidence from the numerous sources they consulted as they became more knowledgeable about people and events of the Civil War, the civil rights movement, South Africa, and suffrage.

Concept maps and compare and contrast charts would be especially useful to measure students' acquisition of declarative knowledge, both specific information about various events, people, and issues and more general knowledge of key concepts, principles, macroconcepts, and themes. Essays and reflective journals might also prove helpful.

For a culminating product, Lydia decided to ask her students to make connections drawing on some of their particular interests. Each student was to examine a leader to help the class understand the struggle for civil rights and that leader's time period. In each instance, students would use a variety of resources to gather information about the person and time they selected. Ultimately, students would show how the person and time period they selected were similar to and different from the Civil War time period and its leaders. They would also need to show how culture, perspective, change, loss, conflict, and conflict resolution were at work in the person's life and time period. Their findings would be compiled in a "Who's Who of Civil Rights" anthology. To support student work, the teacher assumed the role of Editor-in-Chief of the anthology and created an editor's guide for her "staff" to use in preparing their entries to the anthology. In addition to prompting her students to examine the central macroconcepts across contexts, the product would call on them to use key skills of drawing conclusions, comparing and contrasting, detecting relationships, inference, constructing meaning, and pursuing insight.

Introductory Activities

Next, Lydia turned her attention to the introductory activities she would design for this Curriculum of Connections unit. She knew that one of the most important things she could do during the introduction was to reinforce her vision for this unit. Students needed to understand that they were not merely taking on the role of knowledge consumers. They were expected to be analyzers, inductive thinkers, detectives, and metaphoric bridge builders. How to explain that to ten- and eleven-year-olds was another matter!

Lydia's media specialist introduced her to a book by Paul Fleischman (1996) titled *Dateline: Troy.* The author compares the ancient Greek story of Odysseus and his adventures with current-day events and individuals. It was a perfect metaphor for the kind of thinking she wanted students to do in this unit. Previewing the book and the author's purpose during her introductory activities seemed like an ideal way to acquaint students with their role as analogy makers. In addition to this read-aloud, Lydia would also conduct a discussion to probe students' interests in civil rights, South Africa, the Civil War, or women's rights. She could use this information to decide on membership in some of the small group activities.

Lydia knew that in a Curriculum of Connections unit it was unlikely she would tell students "During this unit we will be studying the Civil War." Instead, as pointed out earlier, her introductory comments might ask students what they think the word "civil" means, what a war is, and whether or not they think other countries, or other time periods, experienced civil wars. She decided to ask students about conflicts in their families and ask them to share stories of compromises made because of conflicts between needs and wants, rights and responsibilities. She knew that beginning the curriculum unit with connections to personal conflicts would help her students begin the process of developing analogies between what they were about to study and prior experiences in their own lives.

Extension Activities

In thinking about her students, Lydia recognized real differences in the individual interests of her twenty-four fifth graders. Although she couldn't be positive until she began the unit and had the students in front of her, Lydia made some educated guesses about why and how she might want to extend this Curriculum of Connections unit.

For one thing, she knew she would want to have varied resources, materials, and documents available for the students. She would create a library corner with artifacts and materials. Students would have access to the materials throughout the unit. She would spotlight materials at appropriate times in the unit—sharing with students her own feelings about particular materials. She would also encourage students to work in the library corner when they finished assignments in class and to sign out materials for overnight use at some points. In fact, she might develop a couple of "free choice" homework assignments through which students would have a chance to explore and briefly report on some of the extension materials. Of course, as students raised questions during the Civil War unit, she hoped the materials would be a good source for finding answers.

Lydia would align some learning activities with certain materials she would specially select with students' interests in mind. Not everybody in the room would want to read everything she was beginning to collect. On the other hand, some of her students would probably be fascinated with opportunities to read firsthand Civil War diaries and accounts from big city newspapers like *The Washington Post* and *The New York Times*. Some students would be drawn to biographies or even novels about the Civil War and civil rights struggles in other times and places. Videos and audiocassettes provided other good extension options besides the print sources she was gathering. The Internet, too, would be a source of good information, as well as an attractive vehicle for learning for many of her students.

In addition to linking extension materials to short-term learning activities and products, Lydia would also coordinate the extension opportunities with the culminating anthology product students would develop during the latter stages of the unit. By giving students a chance to learn about a range of civil rights leaders though exploration of extension materials, she would assist students in making informed choices about who to study for the culminating product. The extension materials would also help students begin to gather data for their anthology pieces and reinforce their awareness of the sorts of research materials available.

Lydia also planned to work with her students to find some parents or community members who had personal experiences with civil conflicts in other times or places. In past years, parents who had been a part of our nation's struggle during Vietnam, who had lived through conflicts in the Middle East or Ireland, or who had participated in the struggle for civil rights or women's rights in the United States or elsewhere had talked with her class. Discussions based on presentations such as those would be great for helping her students learn how to connect time, cultures, places, and perspectives using the unit's macroconcepts and skills.

Differentiation Based on Learner Need (Including AID)

In addition to addressing differences in her students' interests, Lydia would also have to address differences in student readiness or learning sophistication. She knew that most of her students could compare and contrast, categorize, sequence, and classify. But several of them had difficulty explaining key features in a relationship, and few of them had experience in making their own analogies. She wanted to make this unit challenging for everyone, without overwhelming any of her students. To accomplish that goal, she knew she might need to pull some students into small groups to share cognitive strategies, offer coaching, and increase scaffolding to improve their likelihood of success with concept development and metaphoric thinking.

Her more advanced thinkers would probably be challenged by the expectation to cross topics, cultures, and time periods, or to compare, contrast, and make analogies. She could ensure that these students had the opportunity to work with disparate context, at least in part, by including in the extension library corner materials about countries and time periods less familiar to the students and about conflicts related to individual rights in fields such as science, technology, and so on.

If the advanced students needed additional challenge, Lydia decided that she could escalate the quality of their thinking through the use of persuasive essays and some mini-lessons on logic and reasoning. Other students might want to use their strong verbal and logical thinking skills to get involved with debates about issues relating to civil rights, prejudice, slavery, and so on. In either case, Lydia would ensure that her directions and criteria for these students' work emphasized complex skills such as artful expression of ideas, well-constructed arguments, and identifying the assumptions of people with varying perspectives on a topic or issue.

Lydia would also meet with students who needed to think at a more expert-like level as they selected and developed their anthology entries. She would reinforce their need to use elegant language and high-quality logic in their work, as they had in their essays and debates. She would also have them include in their anthology entries criteria to weigh diverse perspectives on the issues central to the leader they selected and then to weigh the actions and solutions of the person based on those criteria. She would be able to conduct mini-lessons to support this sort of language, logic, and abstraction in the same way she would conduct mini-lessons to help other learners learn to draw conclusions, infer, or make analogies.

Lesson and Unit Closure

In the Curriculum of Connections, as in other PCM parallels, the goal of closure activities is to encourage student reflection on learning, ensure student clarity about important content, and demonstrate to students that while they may sometimes work in different ways, they are all achieving the knowledge, understanding, and skills that are central to success in the lesson, unit, and discipline. Also as in other parallels, closure activities are typically brief in duration and play a role in ongoing assessment for teacher and students.

What differs in Curriculum of Connections closure in comparison with closure activities in other parallels is the teacher's clear focus on skills, concepts, and principles that link content examples within and across disciplines, times, places, cultures, and so on—and that link content examples with students' own lives and experiences. For example, in one lesson closure, Lydia showed her students two photos—one representing a Civil War scene and another showing a school yard fight. She first asked students to talk about culture, time, and perspective in the first photo, using information from their Civil War study to help them interpret the photo. She then did the same with the photo of the school yard fight. Next, she asked students to hypothesize what elements would be necessary to end each of the conflicts. Ultimately, she presented to them two principles about perspective, conflict, and conflict resolution and asked the students to select which of the two statements best captured their ideas, and told them that as the unit continued, they would have a chance to think further about how culture and perspective can play roles in both conflict and conflict resolution. The whole closure discussion took less than ten minutes.

Lydia's Reflections

Lydia was satisfied that she had considered all of the key curriculum components in making decisions and developing her plan for a Civil War unit that revolved around the Curriculum of Connections. She was struck by the fact that, in the end, she didn't need to follow a specific sequence for her planning. In reality, she often found herself moving from planning one component to another and back to a previously considered component to make revisions and slight alterations. Upon reflection however, she was sure the components were aligned, powerful, and would lead to a much deeper understanding of the content. She knew she was already wiser for the process!

The shift from planning to implementation would be an interesting one. How well could her students think their way through the content? What kind of conceptual explanations would they build? How much help would they need? How motivated would they be to make connections to other "grown-up" topics? Would they gain an appreciation for connection making and analogies? How well would this whole curriculum development process work with younger students, or in other subject areas? What would happen if Lydia had revised only part of her unit to attend to the purposes of the Curriculum of Connections? What if she had used this model with some but not all of her students? These would be interesting questions to contemplate as Lydia reflected on the impact of her new unit on her students and on her own professional growth.

Looking Back and Ahead

The Curriculum of Connections provides teachers and students with opportunity to learn an extremely valuable life skill—the ability to make connections, analogies, and metaphors. No other cognitive skill is as important as metaphoric thinking in supporting a student's ability to analyze new information and data independently. Once acquired, the ability to make connections, see relationships, and "make the strange familiar" empowers students to continue a life's search for connections among all pieces of information, all facets of knowledge, all topics and disciplines, and their own prior knowledge. Prolonged opportunities to make connections, see relationships, and develop inductive and deductive conclusions empower a student to pursue learning, and the search for universality, as a lifelong vocation.

It is also crucial for students to see themselves at work in the various disciplines—to understand that people make contributions to our world every day through their active involvement with the ideas, issues, and skills rooted in the disciplines. The Curriculum of Practice Parallel, discussed next in Chapter 6, retains the focus on the key concepts, principles, and skills of the disciplines and invites students to become practitioners who not only think about important ideas but also apply what they learn to address meaningful problems with concepts and principles as guides for their thinking.

6

The Curriculum
of Practice Parallel

Agroup of sixth grade students in the state of Oregon has just completed a unit on World War II in Mrs. DeFranco's classroom. To bring closure to the unit, she asks them if there are any other questions that they have about this topic. Charles, who is fascinated by this time period, says, "I know the causes of the war, and who the great leaders were, but I still would like to know what was happening in our town during the war." This question causes Sarah to raise her hand and ask, "How was our town affected by the war?" Then Alyssa asks, "How were children our age affected by the war?" Mrs. DeFranco seems a bit surprised by these questions, but the students seem eager to have their questions answered, so she takes the opportunity to ask students to consider the time period and to generate any other questions that seem personally relevant to them. After spending time over a few days generating these inquiries, it appears that the questions require the students to learn a series of new skills that she hadn't thought of using— conducting oral histories and analyzing historical documents. She recognizes that the questions are personally motivating to the students and require them to learn skills that "real" researchers use. Additionally, she has arrived at the conclusion that there are no predetermined answers to these questions and more important, *she doesn't know the answers*! Thus, her journey begins in facilitating research with her students.

As in this example, most students ask questions that seem quite natural, but if examined closely, parallel the questions asked by researchers in various disciplines. These questions might emerge when (1) students personally interact with the content and emotionally become invested in a specific topic, (2) what they have read or experienced does not match their understanding, or (3) intriguing ideas are generated as they try to make connections between and among contexts to extend their understandings. Therefore, throughout all grades, teachers should systematically assist students in developing curiosity, pursuing topics that interest them, identifying intriguing questions, learning the skills used by professionals to answer their questions, developing plans to find out more about those questions, managing time, setting goals and criteria, and presenting new understandings to audiences who can appreciate them.

The Curriculum of Practice emphasizes opportunities for students to learn the skills that professionals use in various disciplines to construct new knowledge in their fields and to extend their understandings about a particular topic or idea. Additionally, the Curriculum of Practice encourages educators to design learning experiences where students apply the methods of the practitioner in a discipline to problems or inquiries that are of importance and interest to them. The Curriculum of Practice, as with the other PCM parallels, focuses on key information, concepts, and principles. This parallel, however, guides students in using the concepts and principles to take part in the journey of researching questions or solving problems as scholars or expert practitioners in the discipline would. To accomplish this, the Curriculum of Practice assists students in learning the skills and methodologies used by professionals in various disciplines. In learning how professionals study their field, what questions they explore, and how they move knowledge forward, it is possible that many students will understand and retain far more content than through more direct but limited approaches to teaching and learning.

In this chapter, a format similar to that of other chapters in the book provides an overview of the Curriculum of Practice. Readers will find (1) a definition of the Curriculum of Practice, (2) a rationale for using this approach to curriculum development, (3) an explanation of key features and exemplary characteristics inherent in this design, (4) an example of this process in action, (5) specific procedures and techniques for adapting the components of the Curriculum of Practice for Ascending Intellectual Demand, and (6) an explanation of the curriculum parallel's relationship to the three other curriculum parallels described in this book.

What Does It Mean to "Practice" in a Curriculum?

Every field of knowledge has a set of key facts, concepts, principles, and skills that help define the discipline. Concepts help us label and make sense of large amounts of information and serve as the vocabulary of a discipline (e.g., interdependence, systems, change, adaptation, and patterns). Unlike facts, which are limited to specific situations, concepts are broad enough to apply to many situations. Some concepts are domain specific, whereas others are more connective in nature. Principles are generally agreed-upon truths that have been arrived at through research and experience. Principles help learners probe the governing ideas of a discipline and help teachers get to the heart of the content. Using principles and concepts at the center of curricular planning is particularly useful because of the potential they hold for organizing large quantities of information in a meaningful way.

In addition to core concepts and principles, every field of knowledge has a set of skills and methodologies that professionals use to (a) answer questions about a particular idea or to solve problems within a discipline, (b) acquire and use information, (c) analyze and organize data, and (d) reach conclusions. These skills, when taught directly to students, can equip them with the tools used by professionals to uncover important ideas in the field, pursue answers to probing questions, and experience firsthand what it is like to be a practicing professional within any field of knowledge. These skills and methodologies define the work or "practice" of the professional and define the mode of inquiry that is used by scholars to figure out correct or reasonable answers to a certain set of questions. This is the type of practice used in lessons or units based on the Curriculum of Practice Parallel. In the Parallel of Practice, students do the discipline rather than simply trying to absorb it.

Skills and methodologies used in various disciplines assist professionals in constructing knowledge that is ever changing. These skills also encourage professionals to be open-minded, skeptical, willing to suspend initial judgments, curious, creative, able to collaborate with others, and persistent in the face of failure. In most cases, the activity and pleasure derived from the experience of finding out is as important as knowing the answer. In science, the inquiry process relies on the skills of asking questions, making observations, setting up experiments, refining and validating hypotheses, and drawing conclusions. Historians use the skills of seeking evidence and determining the authenticity of documents, documenting bias, and a host of other skills to find out about the past. In all disciplines, a certain mode of inquiry directs the learning process and requires scholars to use certain thinking skills, tools, and procedures to systematically answer their questions.

The intent of the Curriculum of Practice is to develop opportunities for students to use the skills and methodologies of a discipline by asking them to function as practicing professionals in a discipline. In some situations, a student will be asked to function as a "scholar"—use the knowledge, skills, and tools to develop a fuller understanding of the domain. At other times the student will be the "expert practitioner"—using the knowledge, skills, and tools of the discipline to produce new knowledge. Figure 6.1 lists focusing questions in the Curriculum of Practice.

In essence, the Core Curriculum begins with students acquiring knowledge of the key facts, concepts, and principles within a discipline and how they are structured to organize the discipline. The Curriculum of Practice extends these understandings by enabling students to "practice" or to learn firsthand how to use the skills and methodologies used by practicing professionals in various disciplines to answer their questions, to probe the meaning of the key ideas of the discipline, and to test their adaptability with those ideas. Therefore, it is important to note that one educator might be able to use the Curriculum of Practice to arrive at the same destination as the teacher who uses the Core Curriculum, or the Curriculum of Practice can be used to extend and deepen an understanding of the principles and concepts as students move from novice to expert production in a discipline. While the two approaches to curriculum development are certainly related, a way of thinking about a key difference in them is that the Curriculum of Practice places in the foreground of consideration the methods and skills used by practicing experts or scholars in a discipline.

- What are the theories that govern the field of knowledge?
- How do practitioners organize their knowledge and skill in this field?
- How do the concepts and principles that form the framework of the discipline get translated into practice by those in this field?
- What are the features of routine problems in the field?
- How does a practitioner know which skills to use in given circumstances?
- What strategies does a practitioner use to solve nonroutine problems in the discipline?
- What tools does a practitioner use in his or her work?
- How does one gain access to and skill in using those tools?
- How does a practitioner sense whether approaches and methods are effective in a given instance?
- What constitutes meaningful evidence versus less significant information in this field or in instances in the field?
- On what basis does a practitioner in the field make educated guesses?
- On what basis does a practitioner in the field draw conclusions?
- What are the methods used by practitioners and contributors in the field to generate new questions, to generate new knowledge, and to solve problems?
- What personality traits support productivity in the field?
- What drives the work of practitioners in the field?
- What are indicators of quality in the field?
- According to what standards does the field measure success?
- What are the ethical issues and standards of the field?

Figure 6.1   Some Focusing Questions in the Curriculum of Practice

Why Does It Matter to Have Students Engage in a Curriculum of Practice?

The importance of teaching students the methodologies used in various fields has been long advocated by researchers. In the later 1800s and early 1900s, John Dewey proposed creating schools around the practice of problem solving through the scientific method. Life and society outside the school were viewed as relevant, and Dewey suggested that curricular experiences should prepare students for their future role as citizens and workers. He suggested that student learning should be shaped by problems they encounter and that their involvement in research and activity would teach them a model or process of problem solving that would be applicable in school and in life (Dewey, 1938).

Upon a closer look at the knowledge level of the "cognitive taxonomy" developed by Benjamin Bloom and his colleagues (1956), there is further evidence of the importance of teaching students the methodologies of a discipline. "Cognitive taxonomy" describes three types of knowledge: (1) knowledge of specifics, (2) knowledge of ways and means of dealing with specifics, and (3) knowledge of the universals and abstractions in a field. The first category deals with the basic elements a learner must know to become acquainted with a field, which centers on knowledge of terminology and knowledge of specific facts—somewhat as a high-quality Comprehensive Curriculum might call on learners to do. The third category focuses on the key concepts and principles of the disciplines—as an effective Core Curriculum or Curriculum of Connections would do. It is the second category in Bloom's thinking that is reflected in the Curriculum of Practice. The second category includes ways of organizing, studying, judging, and critiquing ideas, events, and phenomena in a field and closely approximates the idea behind the Curriculum of Practice. Bloom and his colleagues felt a student should come to understand the modes of inquiry, techniques, and procedures that characterize a particular field and assist the professional in investigating problems.

Research and theories put forth by Jerome Bruner (1960), Phil Phenix (1964), Hilda Taba (1962), Joseph Renzulli (1977), and others are testimony to the importance of students learning how to use the methodologies in various disciplines to construct and apply knowledge. Bruner (1960) explained the importance of being the professional when he stated that "intellectual activity anywhere is the same, whether at the frontier of knowledge or in a third-grade classroom. What a scientist does at his desk or laboratory, what a literary critic does in reading a poem, are of the same order as what anybody else does when he is engaged in like activities—if he is to achieve understanding" (p. 14). Renzulli (1977) has long advocated placing students in the role of the "practicing professional" to pursue problems or questions based on individual or group interests. The goals are to acquire advanced-level understanding of the knowledge and methodology used within particular disciplines, artistic areas of expression, and interdisciplinary studies.

Helpful to educators today is the realization that inherent in every high-quality standards document is careful attention to the modes of inquiry in each discipline. For example, within *National Science Education Standards* (National Academy Press, 1996) is a chapter devoted to "Science as Inquiry" and guidelines for how it should be taught at each grade level. Accordingly, a set of historical thinking skills is outlined in *National Standards for History* (National Center for History in the Schools, 1996). These skills are summarized in Figures 6.2 and 6.3.

Clearly, it benefits society for its members to understand and appreciate how to learn and how to use inquiry skills to solve problems that affect present and future generations. It also benefits teachers and students to focus on such knowledge, understanding, and skill because it

1. provides them with a means for continued learning

2. assists them in knowing how to respond when answers to problems are not immediately apparent

3. teaches them to use data in valid and reliable ways

4. promotes and values the questioning of assumptions

5. expands their fluency and flexibility as problem solvers in the field

6. Organizes their understandings in ways useful for accessing information in the various fields

7. encourages the development of a community of learners

Understandings About Scientific Inquiry and the Abilities Necessary to Do Scientific Inquiry in Grades K–5	*Understandings About Scientific Inquiry and the Abilities Necessary to Do Scientific Inquiry in Grades 6–8*	*Understandings About Scientific Inquiry and the Abilities Necessary to Do Scientific Inquiry in Grades 9–12*
Scientific investigations involve asking and answering a question and comparing the answer with what scientists already know about the world. Ask a question about objects, organisms, and events in the environment.	Different kinds of questions suggest different kinds of scientific investigations. Some investigations involve observing and describing objects, organisms, or events; some involve experiments; some involve seeking more information; some involve discovery of new objects and phenomena; and some involve making models. Identify questions that can be answered through scientific investigations.	Scientists usually inquire about how physical, living, or designed systems function. Conceptual principles and knowledge guide scientific inquiries. Historical and current scientific knowledge influences the design and interpretation of investigations and the evaluation of proposed explanations made by other scientists. Identify questions and concepts that guide scientific investigations.
Scientists use different kinds of investigations depending on the questions they are trying to answer. Types of investigations include describing objects, events, and organisms; classifying them; and doing a fair test (experimenting). Plan and conduct a simple investigation.	Current scientific knowledge and understanding guide scientific investigations. Different scientific domains employ different methods, core theories, and standards to advance scientific knowledge and understandings. Design and conduct a scientific investigation.	Scientists conduct investigations for a wide variety of reasons. For example, they may wish to discover new aspects of the natural world, explain recently observed phenomena, or test the conclusions of prior investigations or the predictions of current theories. Design and conduct scientific investigations.
Simple instruments, such as magnifiers, thermometers, and rulers, provide more information than scientists obtain using only their senses. Employ simple equipment and tools to gather data and extend the senses.	Mathematics is important in all aspects of scientific inquiry. Technology used to gather data enhances accuracy and allows scientists to analyze and quantify results of investigations. Use appropriate tools and techniques to gather, analyze, and interpret data. Use mathematics in all aspects of scientific inquiry.	Scientists rely on technology to enhance the gathering and manipulation of data. New techniques and tools provide new evidence to guide inquiry and new methods to gather data, thereby contributing to the advance of science. The accuracy and precision of the data, and therefore the quality of the exploration, depend on the technology used. Mathematics is essential in scientific inquiry. Mathematical tools and models guide and improve the posing of questions, gathering data, constructing explanations, and communicating results. Use technology and mathematics to improve investigations and communications.
Scientists develop explanations using observations (evidence) and what they already know about the world (scientific knowledge). Good explanations are based on evidence from investigations. Use data to construct a reasonable explanation.	Scientific explanations emphasize evidence, have logically consistent arguments, and use scientific principles, models, and theories. The scientific community accepts and uses such explanations until displaced by better scientific ones. When such displacement occurs, science advances. Develop descriptions, explanations,	Scientific explanations must adhere to criteria such as: a proposed explanation must be logically consistent; it must abide by the rules of evidence; it must be open to questions and possible modification; and it must be based on historical and current scientific knowledge. Formulate and revise scientific explanations and models using logic and evidence. Recognize and analyze alternative explanations and models.

Understandings About Scientific Inquiry and the Abilities Necessary to Do Scientific Inquiry in Grades K–5	Understandings About Scientific Inquiry and the Abilities Necessary to Do Scientific Inquiry in Grades 6–8	Understandings About Scientific Inquiry and the Abilities Necessary to Do Scientific Inquiry in Grades 9–12
	predictions, and models using evidence. Use mathematics in all aspects of scientific inquiry. Recognize and analyze alternative explanations and predictions.	
Students make the results of their investigations public; they describe the investigations in ways that enable others to repeat the investigations. Communicate investigations and explanations.	Science advances through legitimate skepticism. Asking questions and querying other scientists' explanations are part of scientific inquiry. Scientists evaluate the explanations proposed by other scientists by examining evidence, comparing evidence, identifying faulty reasoning, pointing out statements that go beyond the evidence, and suggesting alternative explanations for the same observations. Communicate scientific procedures and explanations.	Results of scientific inquiry—new knowledge and methods—emerge from different types of investigations and public communication among scientists. In communicating and defending the results of scientific inquiry, arguments must be logical and demonstrate connections between natural phenomena, investigations, and the historical body of scientific knowledge. In addition, the methods and procedures that scientists used to obtain evidence must be clearly reported to enhance opportunities for further investigation. Communicate and defend a scientific argument.
Students review and ask questions about the results of other scientists' work. Communicate investigations and explanations.	Scientific investigations sometimes result in new ideas and phenomena for study, generate new methods or procedures or an investigation, or develop new technologies to improve the collection of data. All of these results can lead to new investigations. Communicate scientific procedures and explanations.	

Figure 6.2 Science as Inquiry

SOURCE: Reprinted with permission from *National Science Education Standards* © 1996 by the National Academy of Sciences, Courtesy of the National Academies Press, Washington, DC.

8. expands their learning environments by using professionals in the field and the community at large

9. requires that they learn how to effectively communicate their understandings to others

10. makes learning enjoyable and personally relevant

Scientific investigations sometimes result in new ideas and phenomena for study, generate new methods or procedures or an investigation, or develop new technologies to improve the collection of data. All of these results can lead to new investigations and communicate scientific procedures and explanations.

Type of Thinking Skill	Explanation of the Skills	Student Example
Chronological Thinking Students develop a clear sense of historical time—of when events occurred and in what temporal order—so they can examine relationships among them or explain historical causality.	Distinguish between past, present, and future; identify the temporal structure of a historical narrative or story; establish temporal order in constructing their own narrative stories; measure and calculate calendar time; interpret data presented in timelines; create timelines; and explain change and continuity over time.	Investigate a family history for at least two generations, identifying various members and their connections in order to construct a timeline.
Historical Comprehension Students understand the chronology of events, that events in history reflect stories or narratives that allow us to interpret, reveal conditions, changes, and consequences and explain why things happened as they did.	Identify the author or source of the historical document or narrative; reconstruct the literal meaning of a historical passage; identify the central question(s) the historical narrative addresses and the purpose, perspective, or point of view from which it has been constructed; read historical narrative imaginatively, taking into account the historical context in which the event unfolded (the values, outlook, crises, options, and contingencies of that time and place); and what the narrative reveals of the humanity of the individuals involved (their probable motives, hopes, fears, strengths, and weaknesses); appreciate historical perspectives; draw upon data in historical maps; draw upon the visual and mathematical data presented in graphs; and draw upon the visual data presented in photographs, paintings, cartoons, and architectural drawings in order to clarify, illustrate, or elaborate upon information presented in the historical narrative.	From data gathered through family artifacts, photos, and interviews with older relatives and/or other people who play a significant part in a student's life, draw possible conclusions about roles, jobs, schooling experiences, and other aspects of family life in the recent past. Draw upon a variety of stories, legends, songs, ballads, games, and tall tales in order to describe the environment, lifestyles, beliefs, and struggles of people in various regions of the country.
Historical Analysis and Interpretation Students examine historical situations and raise questions or define problems for themselves; compare differing ideas, interests, perspectives, actions, and institutions represented in these sources; and elaborate upon what they read and see to develop interpretations, explanations, or solutions to the questions they have raised.	Formulate questions to focus their inquiry and analysis; compare and contrast differing sets of ideas, values, personalities, behaviors, and institutions by identifying likenesses and differences; analyze historical fiction on such criteria as the accuracy of the story's historical details and sequence of events and point of view or interpretations presented by the author; distinguish fact and fiction by comparing documentary sources; compare different stories about historical figures, event, or era; analyze illustrations in historical stories for information they reveal and compare to other documents to judge their accuracy; consider multiple perspectives; explain causes in analyzing historical actions, including the importance of the individual in history, the influence of ideas, human interests, and beliefs, and the role of chance, the accidental, and the irrational;	For various cultures represented in the classroom, compare and contrast family life now with family life over time and between various cultures and consider such things as communications, technology, homes, transportation, recreation, school, and cultural traditions. Draw upon data from charts, historical maps, nonfiction and fiction accounts, and interviews in order to describe "through their eyes" the experience of immigrant groups. Include information such as where they came from and why they left, travel experiences, ports of entry and immigration screening, and the opportunities and obstacles they encountered when they arrived in America.

Type of Thinking Skill	Explanation of the Skills	Student Example
	challenge arguments of historical inevitability by giving examples of how different choices could have led to different consequences; and hypothesize the influence of the past, including both the limitations and opportunities made possible by past decisions.	
Historical Research Capabilities Students engage in "doing history" by formulating problems or a set of questions worth pursuing. Students are encouraged to analyze historical documents, records, or a site itself. The historical inquiry is a search in which answers are not known in advance, and finding and interpreting the results is a genuine process of knowledge building.	Formulate historical questions from encounters with historical documents, eye-witness accounts, letters, diaries, artifacts, photos, historical sites, art, architecture, and other records from the past; obtain historical data from a variety of sources; interrogate historical data by determining by whom and when it was created; testing the data source for its credibility, authority, and authenticity and detecting and evaluating bias, distortion, and propaganda; and marshal information of the time and place to construct a story, explanation, or historical narrative.	Examine and formulate questions about early records, diaries, family photographs, artifacts, and architectural drawings obtained through a local newspaper or historical society in order to describe family life in their local community or state long ago.
Historical Issue Analysis and Decision Making Students are asked to consider the historical dilemmas with which people have coped at critical moments in the past and near present. Problems confronting people in historical fiction, fables, legends, and myths, as well as in historical records of the past are usually value-laden. Examining these dilemmas, the choices before the people who confronted them, and the consequences of the decisions they made provides opportunities for children to consider the values and beliefs that have influenced human decisions both for good and for ill.	Identify problems and dilemmas confronting people in historical narratives; analyze the interests, values, and points of view of those involved; identify causes of the problem or dilemma; propose alternative ways of resolving the problem or dilemma and evaluate each in terms of ethical consideration (is it fair? just?), the interest of the people involved, and the likely consequences of each proposal; formulate a position or course of action on an issue by identifying the nature of the problem, analyzing the underlying factors contributing to the problem, and choosing a plausible solution from a choice of carefully evaluated options; identify the solution chosen by characters in the story or in the historical situation; and evaluate the consequences of the actions taken.	Identify a problem in the community's past, analyze the different perspectives of those involved, and evaluate choices people had and the solution they chose.

Figure 6.3   History as Inquiry

SOURCE: National Center for History in the Schools, UCLA. http://nchs.ucla.edu

This section on the Curriculum of Practice has focused on the importance and the benefits of using the Curriculum of Practice to develop comprehensive curriculum. In the next section, we explore how the Curriculum of Practice is designed. Figure 6.4 may serve as an advance organizer for the ideas that follow.

Key Features of the Components of Curriculum in the Curriculum of Practice

When teachers identify the principles and concepts to be explored in a curricular unit, student understanding and involvement can be enhanced by generating a series of essential questions (e.g., Wiggins & McTighe, 1998) that can be used by students to probe the meaning behind these ideas. Essential questions are the questions that touch our hearts and souls and help us to become engaged with knowledge. They are central to our lives and help to define what it means to be human. In the social studies curriculum, essential questions probe the deepest issues confronting us: perspective, identity, revolution and change, leadership, invention, inspiration, culture, honor, integrity, courage, and power. In science, we explore our natural surrounding and its related concepts so that we can protect it for future generations. In literature, we explore ideas such as truth, love, wisdom, myths, and perspective so that we become more human. While some student-generated questions seem simplistic in nature, educators can assist students in probing the meaning behind these ideas in order to bring to light more abstract questions (e.g., Why are wars fought? How much diversity can any nation tolerate? What does it mean to be a citizen? How are relationships sustained? What is meant by friendship?). The Curriculum of Practice helps us probe these meanings in a way that helps us retain childlike wonder and awe in our discoveries.

Content (Including Standards) in the Curriculum of Practice

Educators who are planning a Curriculum of Practice unit must first identify the goals students must achieve within the unit. Depending on the method a teacher selects to direct the inquiry, students must come to understand the role they play in learning and applying certain principles, concepts, and skills within a discipline, since we are asking that they assume the role of producer or scholar in the discipline. These roles may be new or different to the students. Additionally, students need to understand the role that the teacher plays in facilitating the inquiry in order to seek assistance and to understand the types of questions that teachers will be asking them throughout the Curriculum of Practice unit. Sharing these goals with the students establishes the student's role and assists educators in selecting the types of instructional strategies and activities that will facilitate student understanding and accomplish the intended goals.

Curriculum Component	Modification Techniques
Content (Including Standards)	• Consider which methodologies (tools, procedures, and skills) of a specific discipline might assist students in answering their own research questions, probing the meaning of the key ideas of the discipline, and testing the adaptability of those ideas in other contexts. • Determine the types of questions, problems, or discrepant events that will be uncovered by the students as they apply the research methodologies. • Consider how the students will use the information they discover in their investigations to deepen their understanding of key principles and concepts and their relationships. • Determine the type of problem-solving process or modes of inquiry that will be used to solve problems or to investigate questions. • Work with students to generate questions, determine the methodologies and procedures for carrying out the investigation, gather and analyze data, reach conclusions, and determine the implications of the research findings. • Identify which habits of mind are to be developed through the use of this learning experience (e.g., independence, persistence, and dealing with ambiguity). • Consider which ethical issues or problems can be used as subjects for the investigation. • Identify the modes of inquiry that are listed in national standards documents (e.g., National Science Teachers Association [NSTA], National Council of Teachers of Mathematics [NCTM], National Council for the Social Studies [NCSS], and National Council of Teachers of English [NCTE]).
Assessments	• Determine the varying levels of sophistication, expertise, or technical proficiency in the use of methodological skills to assist learners toward continued growth. • Consider how students will demonstrate their understanding in using the methodological skills, how their knowledge has changed over time, and the degree to which they interpret, apply, and transfer the knowledge and skills that they have gained to new contexts. • Determine which products will be used to communicate new understandings and document growth. • Consider a variety of products that can be used to show evidence of understanding of new ideas, new connections, transformations of existing ideas in new contexts, and flexibility in acquiring data. • Provide ample opportunities for students to communicate their findings in a variety of formats. • Observe and note changes in behavior (e.g., persistence, independence, and skepticism) over time.
Introductory Activities	• Use focusing questions, problems, dilemmas, and discrepant events to justify the need for methodological skills. • Identify experts who can assist students in identifying problems, developing technical expertise in the use of inquiry skills, and knowing which tools and procedures to use to best address these problems.
Teaching Methods	• Use a variety of teaching methods to support and scaffold learning. • Develop a repertoire of teaching strategies that are more inductive and more inquiry based in accordance with the goal of developing behaviors used by scholars (e.g., investigative studies, problem-based learning, independent studies, Socratic questioning, small and large group investigations, simulations). • Adjust and match teaching methods to the learners as they demonstrate continued growth in using the tools and procedures of the professional.
Learning Activities	• Make sure that the learning activities are those that provide opportunities for students to use the tools of the professional to acquire new information, enhance learning, and engage in research. • Select activities that target the development of essential principles and concepts or encourage the inquiry process. • Introduce students to the inquiry process or steps to research. • Acquire tools and technologies to advance the level of research that students conduct (e.g., probes and sensors, statistical software, word processor, data collection devices). • Use graphing techniques to analyze data.

Figure 6.4 *(Continued)*

(Continued)

Curriculum Component	Modification Techniques
Grouping Strategies	• Employ a variety of grouping arrangements (flexible, small group, individual, interest-based, across grade levels, multi-aged) based on students' readiness levels, learning styles, skill accomplishment.
Resources	• Locate methodological tools that can be used to collect data. • Identify community experts who can help students learn the skills and methodologies used in various disciplines. • Locate videos, books, artifacts, photographs, artwork, electronic information, community members, experts in the field, primary and secondary source documents, and methodological guides (how-to books) to support student research.
Products	• Determine the variety of products that can be used to provide evidence of increased understanding of the principles and concepts in a particular field, research procedures, and new discoveries made about an area of study. • Select the types of products that are close approximations of the types of products that practicing professionals create in their fields (e.g., gallery displays, documentaries, books, articles, social action plans, compositions, and scientific studies). • Consider the audience that can best provide students with authentic evaluation of their work.
Extension Activities	• Listen carefully for other questions that students raise prior to, during, and after instruction. • Consider community experts who can provide advanced technical assistance to those students who are ready. • Determine other areas in which students want to explore, practice, or apply newly acquired skills of practice.
Differentiation Based on Learner Need, (Including AID)	• Provide opportunities for students to guide their own inquiries. • Devise tasks and products that cause students to develop, through application, personal frameworks of knowledge, understanding, and skill related to the discipline. • Escalate the level of resource materials that are used by the students during their research. • Identify new contexts for transferring and applying knowledge. • Guide students in establishing their own goals for work at what they believe to be the next steps of research. • Escalate the level of analysis for the investigation. • Network students with mentors in the field to advance their knowledge and research skills. • Use the Parallel's guidelines for Ascending Intellectual Demand in selecting resources and designing learning activities and products.
Lesson and Unit Closure	• Help students focus on essential questions, methods used to seek answers to those questions, and the degree to which their methods were fruitful. • Guide students in considering how concepts and principles informed their thinking. • Ask students to reflect on which knowledge they used in their work and how they knew it was (or wasn't) useful in their thinking and problem solving. • Have students compare their experience as practitioners with experiences of experts in the discipline about whom they are learning. • Ask students to reflect on their work and products using expert-level rubrics, standards, or indicators of quality. • Ensure that students use the vocabulary of method, thought, and habits of mind and work that experts would use. • Help students articulate how they approached issues that are complex and/or have ethical implications.

Figure 6.4   The Comprehensive Curriculum Components Illustrated in the Curriculum of Practice Parallel

It is also helpful for teachers to focus on skills students will need during the learning process. These skills will guide teachers in developing an extended set of goals. As a result of engaging in learning activities that help them to probe a discipline at a deeper level of understanding, students will learn how to use and apply the skills (strategies and tools) that practitioners use to solve nonroutine problems or answer their questions, acquire advanced understanding of how the field translates concepts and principles into practice, and learn new applications of the theories that govern the knowledge of a particular field of study. It is also probable that the students will confront the ethical issues and standards of the field.

Finally, when students tackle meaningful problems or employ the methodologies of researchers, they are likely to develop productive dispositions or habits. These "habits of mind" described by Costa and Kallick (2000) reflect attributes of humans who behave intelligently. Although the list of attributes that follows is not meant to be complete, teachers may notice several of these attributes resulting from prolonged engagement with the types of learning experiences offered in the Curriculum of Practice. These attributes of intelligent behavior include the following:

- Persisting
- Managing impulsivity
- Listening to others with understanding and empathy
- Thinking flexibly
- Thinking about our thinking (metacognition)
- Striving for accuracy and precision
- Questioning and posing problems
- Applying past knowledge to new situations
- Thinking and communicating with clarity and precision
- Gathering data through all senses
- Creating, imagining, and innovating
- Responding with wonderment and awe
- Taking responsible risks
- Finding humor
- Thinking interdependently
- Learning continuously

Based on these goals and the focusing questions for the Curriculum of Practice (See Figure 6.1), teachers can develop standards to guide their selection of instructional activities for the Curriculum of Practice.

Students will be able to

1. define, refine, and refocus broad questions or problems within a particular unit of study

2. design, conduct, and execute an investigation by formulating questions and designing a plan for the investigation

3. use appropriate skills, tools, and techniques to gather, analyze, and interpret data

4. develop descriptions, explanations, predictions, and models using evidence gathered

5. communicate findings of the inquiry with an audience

6. illustrate, or extend the understanding of, a principle or concept in a particular unit of study

7. demonstrate dispositions that approximate those of the professional

These standards are quite broad, and a teacher can develop more specific objectives that correlate with the content of a particular unit. For example, a teacher who is working with students to identify the causes of conflicts prior to the start of a unit on the American Revolutionary War might ask students to survey all sixth graders to gather information about the perspective of conflict in the lives of sixth graders. Upon gathering the data, students will analyze them to see what categories emerge. In most cases, the data can be grouped in the following categories: economic, religious, social, and political. These categories can then be used to assist students in organizing the information they will learn about during this unit of study and enable them to make connections between and among other wars that are fought. For this activity, then, the teacher can generate a more specific set of objectives that address the broader ones noted above. For example, some of the objectives for this lesson might include the following.

1. Generate a series of questions that can be used to guide the investigation.

2. Design and conduct a survey that can be used to gather data about the perspectives of sixth graders in regard to conflict.

3. Analyze the survey data to determine the categories they represent.

4. Use the categories to compare factors that influenced conflict in the American Revolutionary War with factors that influence conflict in the sixth graders' lives.

5. Provide evidence of these factors through written and visual examples.

In the end, these objectives combine knowledge, understanding, and skills stated (or implied) in text and standards documents with the goal of the Curriculum of

Practice. With these as a focal point, students develop and use critical knowledge, understanding, and skill while acting as scholars or expert practitioners would.

Assessments in the Curriculum of Practice

In the Curriculum of Practice, students are invited to learn how to construct knowledge by applying the skills, methods and procedures, and strategies of the professional. By engaging in this type of work, students demonstrate important qualities of understanding that can be assessed in a variety of formats (e.g., student reflections, products, observations, performances, or conferences) and by using a rubric that articulates a continuum of expertise—from novice through apprentice to expert. This rubric also allows for the diagnosis and coaching of students' progress along this continuum. In writing these rubrics, an educator may find it helpful to use the four qualities of understanding defined by Mansilla and Gardner (1998): (1) ability to refine, transform, or replace naïve content understandings with more sophisticated levels of understanding; (2) application of research methodologies to build reliable data; (3) ability to recognize the purposes and interests that drive knowledge construction; and (4) level of expertise used in creating performances or products that communicate new understandings. In formulating the assessment portion of a unit that focuses on the Curriculum of Practice, educators can identify a range of instructional techniques that will facilitate student understanding in these four areas and generate learning activities through which understanding can be achieved. This reinforces that tightly forged link in excellent curriculum between content goals, assessment strategies, and instructional techniques.

Introductory Activities and the Curriculum of Practice

Every discipline has a set of skills and research procedures that a scholar or expert practitioner uses to answer questions or study problems and to make contributions to a discipline. The essence of a discipline is not so much the accumulated knowledge and ideas but rather the ongoing struggle and persistence required to find out how these ideas change, adapt, or affect other things. From a disciplinarian's perspective, answers to questions are often elusive and require systematic study. And in this journey, a researcher seldom stops in any particular place for long because questions sometimes lead to answers and invariably lead to other questions.

In the beginning, educators must plan opportunities for introducing students to the dispositions used by scholars in a particular discipline so that they too can understand what it takes to pursue this type of work. Educators can read stories about historians who have uncovered new information relating to a particular topic that has been studied in class, invite guest speakers into the classroom who can be asked to demonstrate particular skills that they use in answering their questions, or view multimedia resources that illustrate strategies practitioners use to solve nonroutine problems in the discipline. The purpose of these introductory activities is to establish a classroom environment that promotes active inquiry in students. Students must feel that their ideas and inquiries are respected, that they are capable of uncovering the answers to their questions and, more important, feel safe in questioning assumptions and being somewhat skeptical of knowledge as it is presented in text resources.

Some educators begin this type of unit with a brainstorming session or through a series of questions designed to activate students' background knowledge and introduce the Curriculum of Practice unit in an accessible manner. Other educators tell effective stories that provide a "hook" to demonstrate the relevance of the topic to the real world or to clarify a misunderstanding through sustained research. Whichever strategy is used, it should serve to plant the seed for further inquiry into a unit of study and clarify the role that students will assume in the unit.

Teaching Methods and the Curriculum of Practice

Within this curricular unit, teaching methods will be varied. Because the primary purpose of the Curriculum of Practice is to help students extend and apply their understandings and skills in a discipline in much the same way as scholars study their field, educators will find themselves moving in and out of instructional techniques that best facilitate their students' understanding and application of the methods. At times, educators will use more direct methods of teaching (e.g., teaching students background information for the unit or teaching students how to conduct interviews with community members). At other points, teachers will need to use more indirect methods of teaching (e.g., facilitating a group discussion about the ways to organize data that students have collected). However, the Curriculum of Practice does place a premium on those teaching methods that are more inductive and more inquiry based in accordance with the goal of developing behaviors used by scholars. Depending on the nature of the skill and the readiness levels of the students, some teaching strategies may better facilitate student understanding. Above all, the methods of teaching should put the learner in the role of a scholar or an inquirer in each subject or discipline area being taught.

Educators not only need to be familiar with using a variety of teaching methods, they must also be knowledgeable about the concepts and principles of a discipline and the characteristic methods of inquiry used in that discipline. Throughout a Curriculum of Practice unit, students will require feedback on the accuracy of their information and suggestions for designing better questions, analyzing data, conducting interviews, and using other data collection methods, as well as methods of acting on problems in a discipline.

Learning Activities and the Curriculum of Practice

When students behave as scholars, they will use, rather than simply acquire, information. The learning activities component of a Curriculum of Practice unit are arranged to provide opportunities for using methodological skills to acquire new information and to use this new information to form products new to the students. First and foremost, the learning activities should engage students in using the research process (the strategies, methods, and procedures) to acquire information. Although these methods may vary across disciplines, they generally involve a series of investigative procedures that include the following:

1. Identifying a problem within a content field

2. Finding and focusing a problem within an area of study

3. Posing research questions or generating hypotheses

4. Gathering information from a variety of sources

5. Locating and constructing appropriate data-gathering instruments

6. Classifying and categorizing data

7. Summarizing and analyzing data

8. Reporting findings through a variety of products

A second type of learning experience that will be provided to the students will focus on the domain-specific skills researchers use in completing the more comprehensive tasks outlined above. For example, students might need to learn a series of how-to skills to carry out their research (e.g., how to set up a scientific experiment by controlling variables, how to develop a survey to gather data, how to analyze historical photographs and documents, how to critique a piece of writing). Collectively, these two types of learning experiences equip students with the know-how of investigative methodology, which moves them closer to the goal of behaving like scholars.

In addition to the skills of problem finding and problem solving, and the more specific skills a researcher uses in the research/problem-solving process, certain creative and analytical thinking skills are also well suited to the goals of the Curriculum of Practice and to helping learners work like scholars or expert practitioners. Figure 6.5 illustrates, with examples, some of the skill categories important for student learning activities in the Curriculum of Practice.

Recall, too, that some learning activities in the Curriculum of Practice might ask students to function as scholars, developing an appreciation for the contribution of individuals to the body of knowledge, skills, tools, and methodologies of a domain. Other activities in the Curriculum of Practice might ask students to function as expert practitioners, actually using the body of knowledge, skills, tools, and methodology of the domain. In this regard, it is important for educators to be mindful of the developmental and readiness levels of their students. In some cases, a student will be ready to assume the role of an expert practitioner, whereas another student will be ready only to simulate the role of an expert practitioner. A student's cognitive and affective development should signal which of the two approaches, or combination of approaches, is best suited to that particular learner at a particular time. Examples of these two types of experiences follow.

Type of Thinking Skills	*Student Examples*
Information-Processing Skills Students locate and collect relevant information to sort, classify, sequence, compare and contrast, and analyze part to whole relationships.	• Ask students to write their addresses. Ask the children to draw a map of their route from home to their classroom and describe their route to a partner. Discuss with the children who lives the farthest away and who lives the nearest. • With the children's help, design and carry out a survey of how children come to school. Help students use the information to draw a graph, which can be computer generated, and analyze the findings. • Have students observe and take photographs in the local community. Using these photographs, students research the history behind the locations. Conduct interviews with local residents to gain historical information about the community.
Reasoning Skills Students provide reasons for opinions and actions, draw inferences and make deductions, use precise language to explain what they think, and make judgments and decisions informed by reasons and/or evidence.	• Using the data collected in the activities listed above, have students design a historical walking tour map of the area. Students will make recommendations of places to see, describe their historical relevance, and add pictures of historical statues or sculptures that merit recognition. • Present these recommendations and the tour guide to an audience, such as a local historical museum.
Inquiry Skills Students ask relevant questions, pose and define problems, plan what to do and ways to research, predict outcomes and anticipate consequences, and test conclusions and improve ideas.	• Arrange for the children to complete a simple traffic survey on the road outside the school. With the children's help, label a wall display of photographs of the road outside the school to show aspects related to traffic (e.g., road signs, road markings). • Ask the children to think about their own road at home and decide whether it is quieter or noisier than the school road. Encourage the children to think up their own questions about traffic around the school. Discuss with the children what makes a "fair" test in a survey (e.g., times, frequency, place). With the children's help, design and carry out a survey of the numbers of cars parked in the street. Ask the children to present the results as a graph, using simple graphing software, and analyze the results. Ask the children to consider questions like: Are the parked cars there all day? Where do people go when they park their cars?
Creative Thinking Skills Students generate and extend ideas, suggest hypotheses, apply imagination, and look for alternative innovative outcomes or solutions.	• Ask the children to identify methods of making an area safe (e.g., bicycle paths, pavements, fencing, "no parking" zones, road signs, pedestrian crossings) and to think about how the school grounds and other streets they know are made safe. • Ask the children to make use of all the evidence they have collected (photographs and survey results) to write a letter to the transportation department at the local council to ask about the possibility of a safety feature (e.g., a pedestrian crossing) being constructed.
Evaluation Skills Students evaluate information; judge the value of what they read, hear, and observe; develop criteria for judging the value of their own and others' work or ideas; and provide reasons for their decision.	• Students will discuss the pros and cons of building a hotel near a small coastal region. • Divide the children into five groups, each assuming one of the following roles: fisherman, local government official, travel company representative, store owner, and local resident. • Students will first work in small groups with peers portraying the same role to develop information and prepare statements that support their viewpoints about building the hotel. • Next, new groupings will be formed, this time composed of one representative from each role group. In these new groups, all participants will listen to, take notes on, and discuss the varying viewpoints on the hotel project. • After students have had a chance to revise their statements, the class will stage a mock public hearing on the hotel project. A vote will be taken to determine the outcome.

Figure 6.5   Critical and Creative Thinking Skills

An Example of Simulating the Role of an Expert Practitioner

The students in Mr. Harper's third grade class are studying the characteristics of organisms and have recently become intrigued by the earthworms they found on the playground after a recent rain shower. After visiting with the science coordinator at the school, Mr. Harper found out that the coordinator could order earthworms, egg cases, and baby earthworms from a biological supply company. This would allow his students to observe adult earthworms, the egg cases, the young earthworms, and some of the animal's characteristics.

While waiting for the earthworms to arrive, Mr. Harper took his students outside and asked the students to make observations of the earthworms in their natural habitat. Then he posed the question, "If we wanted to study how earthworms behave, how would we set up an environment in our classroom that closely resembles the natural setting?" This stimulated the students to gather books from the library to draw plans for a simulated environment that would be arranged in the classroom.

After discussing their plans, the students decided to create a habitat for an earthworm by using a terrarium strategically placed away from direct sunlight. The students covered the sides of the terrarium with black paper, then added soil, leaves, and grass to the habitat. After the other earthworms arrived from the supply company, they were placed in the terrarium.

In the first weeks of instruction, students were asked for many observations that would record how earthworms move, a description and an illustration of what they looked like, and what they thought the earthworms were doing. The students described the earthworm's color and shape; they weighed and measured the earthworm and designed large data charts to record their observations. The focus of their observations was mainly descriptive at this point.

As the unit progressed, students began to generate questions that were recorded on the chart by Mr. Harper. These questions were used to develop several explorations for the students to conduct. One group chose to investigate the life cycle of earthworms. They found several egg cases in the soil, and this led them to books in the library that described the life-cycle process. They were also interested in trying to figure out a way to keep track of the growth of a baby earthworm as it developed over time.

Three other groups of students were trying to investigate the types of environments that earthworms prefer. Mr. Harper suggested that they try different things—light, moisture, and temperature—and then coached them through the process of controlling variables.

A fourth group was trying to decide what the earthworms liked to eat. The students had read about the kinds of food earthworms preferred and were now just beginning to set up experiments to try to determine what the earthworms liked best.

The last group was trying to set up a transparent environment for the earthworms so that they could study what earthworms do in various types of soil.

In this study and inquiry into the life of an earthworm, Mr. Harper's students learned about the basic needs of a particular organism, the basic structures and functions of this organism, its life cycle, and some features of animal behavior. They simulated the role of a scientist by generating questions, planning and conducting experiments, measuring and recording data, identifying patterns in data, and reaching conclusions about some of the basic concepts and principles underlying the life sciences.

An Example of Becoming Expert Practitioners in a Field of Study

Mrs. McQuerry is a middle school teacher who uses every opportunity she can to engage students in problem-based activities that introduce or extend the learning process in meaningful ways. She looks for newspaper and journal articles that highlight important concepts that her students are learning in their curriculum and tries to turn these ideas into problems for her students to solve. She has found that this way of teaching motivates her students and assists them in seeing the relevance of what they are learning to the reality of life. This extends to a project documenting her methods that was published in a book called *Nuclear Legacy* (McQuerry, 2000). This book was written by students from two communities: Richland, Washington, home of the Manhattan Project; and Slavutych, Ukraine, home of the workers at the Chernobyl site. *Nuclear Legacy*, written in English and Ukrainian, is an example of authentic collaboration between cultures that captures a perspective on nuclear culture as seen by the first post–Cold War generation and gives us insight into what may be possible for our global future as nuclear cultures now work together. Student perceptions of the history of their communities and hopes for the future of our world tell the nuclear story from the perspective of those who will inherit its legacy.

This project became a way to help Ukrainian and American students connect what they were learning in school to a real product that would be valuable outside the walls of the classroom. The book includes firsthand accounts by young people of the 1986 Chernobyl nuclear accident and interviews with scientists and engineers who worked on the 1940s' Manhattan Project in the United States. In this book, students of the two countries explore the history, present, and future of their nuclear communities and discuss with fresh voices their hopes for the future.

The study began in a one-semester elective course at Hanford Middle School in Richland, Washington, where students were given an opportunity to pursue a passion while also receiving instruction in the inquiry method of research. This project was one of several conducted by the students. Each student was expected to become an active researcher by writing a project plan, taking and organizing notes, and conducting original research. In this class, Mrs. McQuerry provided guidance to students as they selected projects of interest. Students interacted with practicing professionals and designed projects that required them to use the skills and modes of inquiry that fit particular disciplines. The class culminated with a presentation before a committee of "experts."

In summary, learning experiences arranged by the teacher for the Curriculum of Practice may focus on an inquiry that is student generated or teacher constructed. In all cases, general methodologies, domain-specific skills, and thinking skills are taught to the students and then used by students in their inquiries. The goal in writing this section is to create opportunities for students to be the scientists, sociologists, poets, artists, historians, cartographers, mythologists, and so forth and to apply the skills these professionals use to construct knowledge and to make sense of their experiences. Figure 6.6 summarizes some of the key skills of the Curriculum

Time management
Organization
Decision making
Learning to learn
Quotation
Paraphrasing
Goal setting
Evaluation
Self-motivation
Critique of ideas and processes
Scholarship/scholarliness
Drawing on the known while thinking originally
Determining when to ask questions and what kind
Establishing and maintaining integrity of ideas
Having a vision versus accepting the status quo
Determining when to fight and when to relinquish
Maintaining focus without rigidity
Developing and using skills of collaboration
Developing and using skills of independence
Using specific methods and tools of research
Recognizing problems
Refining problems
Analyzing data
Reporting research findings
Seeking and using feedback

Figure 6.6 Some Key Process Skills in the Curriculum of Practice

of Practice—including examples from habits of mind, the comprehensive skills of research and problem solving, specific skills of disciplines, and thinking skills.

Grouping Strategies in the Curriculum of Practice

Depending on student experience with inquiry-based activities, a teacher can use a variety of grouping practices within the classroom setting. Early on, teachers may feel more comfortable having all students work on one inquiry-based unit as a benchmark teaching unit. Later, small groups and individuals will learn how to establish and conduct their own inquiries. Using this incremental approach, teachers can introduce students to the experience of conducting research rather than assuming students have those skills.

In the Curriculum of Practice, students should learn how to assume the role of the professional, learning how to work independently as well as collaboratively, and to self-regulate their learning behaviors. Skills of independence, collaboration, and self-regulation must be taught. We teach for this by arranging guided independence prior to more complete independence by ensuring that students are taught how to collaborate effectively, by helping students address issues that arise when collaboration efforts are bumpy, and by also helping students set goals for their work and assess their progress according to those goals. Figure 6.7 illustrates one simple format that students can use to support their learning goals. Journals and group planning sheets can also be used to document their progress.

Teachers should use flexible grouping practices throughout the unit. Groupings should be responsive to the students' learning preferences, readiness levels, and cognitive and affective development so that optimum learning can occur. In some cases, a group of students can manage the work on its own with little assistance, whereas other students need structured support and regular guidance from the classroom teacher. At some point in the unit, a teacher will need to work with the whole class to teach a methodological skill (e.g., how to generate open-ended questions for an interview or how to set up a museum-quality exhibit). At other times, some students will be comfortable with a particular skill (e.g., finding Web sites on the Internet or finding the mean of a data set), and others will need additional instruction on that skill. Sometimes teachers will have a reason to assign student groups, and sometimes it is ideal for students to compose group membership. Sometimes students will work more

---

Student Planning Record

Name _____   Date _____

Inquiry _____   Class _____

The tasks I worked on today: **Completed:**

_____   _____

_____   _____

_____   _____

Evaluation:

_____   I completed my goals.

_____   I used my time wisely.

Next time, I plan to:

_____

_____

_____

Materials or resources I'll need:

_____

_____

Figure 6.7 Sample Student Planning Form

effectively alone, and sometimes they might need the support and partnership of peers. In all cases, students should be encouraged to support each other in their work.

Resources in the Curriculum of Practice

Students and teachers use a variety of resources to accomplish the learning goals within a Curriculum of Practice unit. Resources should appeal to a wide range of readers and their interest levels. In gathering resources for an instructional unit, educators should locate books, journals, artifacts, photographs, artwork, electronic information, community members, experts in the field, primary and secondary source documents, and methodological guides (how-to books) used by practicing professionals in a variety of disciplines. Additionally, resources may include the equipment or tools that are used by scholars in the field to conduct their research.

Pictures and slides of students completing inquiry-based projects are helpful when trying to orient students to the role that they will play in the investigation. Children's literature, such as *Tibet: Through the Red Box* (Sís, 1998) or *Starry Messenger: Galileo Galilei* (Sís, 1997), can be used to introduce students to the value of conducting research and the significance of the work that is produced by scholars and experts. Additionally, magazines, such as *Discover*, *Scientific American*, *Nature*, *Scholastic Magazine*, and *Consumer Reports*, can assist educators in finding interesting topics that might be turned into problem-based investigations or ideas that can be used to generate interest that may lead to student-generated projects.

Products in the Curriculum of Practice

Students can create a variety of short-term and long-term products (e.g., journals, student forums, service, performances, problem solutions, explanations, publications, performances, exhibits, and reflections) that will provide evidence of increased student understanding of the application of principles and concepts in a particular field, research procedures, new discoveries made about an area of study, and the implications and significance of their research findings. These products offer an endless array of opportunities for assessing student progress, growth over time, and adjusting student instruction in order to promote student success and technical expertise within a field of study.

While it is appropriate to select the types of products students will create, it is important that the students create products that are close approximations of the types of products that practicing professionals create in their fields. Because students are acting as real inquirers and scholars, their products address real problems and real questions and involve transformations rather than summaries of existing ideas or information. Students should be provided with opportunities to select those products that resemble the work of scholars and that best match where they are as learners.

It is also important to have students present their products to a significant audience. Audiences provide students with an opportunity to share their findings and understandings. Audiences also provide us with direct feedback from others who are interested in our work. These conversations may encourage further research.

The key here is to locate authentic audiences—those who are interested in the students' work, those who might benefit from the results of the students' findings, and those who can provide expert-like evaluations that can assist students in improving upon their knowledge, understanding, ideas, working processes, and skills.

Extension Activities in the Curriculum of Practice

Inquiry-based learning activities might lead to other questions to be studied in other subject-area classes. A teacher can follow up on student-generated ideas by networking with other colleagues to provide places for these ideas to be explored. Activities created for students using the Curriculum of Practice can become interdisciplinary projects that are tied together through principles and concepts.

Further extensions can be designed to have students interact or work with researchers, college professors, or community experts who can provide methodological support and assistance to the students. It is possible for teachers to ask writers, archaeologists, sociologists, biologists, mathematicians, or community members who have specific interests for assistance in creating these units for their students. These professionals can help generate problem-based experiences that might be incorporated into a teacher's unit of study, provide methodological guidance in helping students learn the procedures to conduct research, write books, graphically illustrate important ideas, or even provide the resources and materials that will be needed by the students to conduct their investigations.

While it is possible that these types of learning experiences are new to the students, it is also possible that this type of teaching may be new to the teacher designing or implementing this Curriculum of Practice. Seeking assistance in creating these learning experiences provides an exciting adventure for both the teacher and the students and makes teaching come alive! Seeking assistance often leads to surprising events, as it did for Mrs. Anderson, a fourth grade teacher.

Mrs. Anderson's students had just finished a unit on fables. She had invited Mr. Alvera, a university English professor, to the school to present his research on fables in other countries and how they compare with fables in our own country. In the middle of his presentation, a student named Sam raised his hand and said, "I read one of these fables to my mom and dad and when I asked them what they thought the moral of the story was, they both had a different answer. Why would this be?"

Surprised by this question, Mrs. Anderson turned to Mr. Alvera and asked him if he could respond to Sam's inquiry. After careful reflection, Mr. Alvera responded, "Sam, this is an interesting observation. I don't know if I know the answer to this question."

Sam, being persistent, replied, "Don't you think we should find out?" By this time everyone was interested in the exchange that was taking place between Sam and Mr. Alvera. Mrs. Anderson then turned to Mr. Alvera with a surprised look on her face and stated, "I don't have any idea how we would do this. Do you?"

This conversation continued during recess, with Mr. Alvera suggesting that he thought he could be of assistance in setting up this project for the students. He had some university students that he was working with in a children's literature class, and he agreed to present this idea to them at their next class meeting.

After meeting with the university students and Mrs. Anderson, Mr. Alvera arranged to have his students work with her students to design an experiment that would allow the students in her classroom to investigate the following question: Does gender play a role in how fables are interpreted? He taught the students how to set up the experiment, his students served as assistants in this project to transcribe the interviews the students had conducted with males and females after they read a selected fable out of a book, and Mrs. Anderson learned firsthand what it meant to be flexible and to follow the lead set by questions asked in the classroom. Out of this experience grew many more collaborative projects designed by Mrs. Anderson and other experts in her community.

Differentiation Based on Learner Need, Including Ascending Intellectual Demand

Curricular experiences using the Curriculum of Practice acknowledge that students require a wide variety of assistance, reference materials, and examples to help them reach an understanding of the concepts and principles they are examining or acting on. Teachers who provide learning experiences of this nature share some common characteristics.

▶ They work in a way that mirrors experts in a discipline as they seek answers to questions in order to expand their knowledge and understanding.

▶ They are knowledgeable about their students' interests, cognitive and affective development, physical attributes, motivation, and learning preferences, which helps them to plan and differentiate student learning options.

▶ They orchestrate discourse among their students to create a community of scholars who will learn from each other. Classroom environments are respectful of children's voices and encourage all students to make their learning known.

▶ At all stages of the unit, they match their actions to the particular needs of their students. At times, they will provide additional instruction, modeling, or examples for students to guide their understanding and skill. At other times, they will demand more rigorous grappling by students, deciding when and how to guide learners to new levels of sophistication in their thinking and work.

▶ They know when they don't know, yet are willing to investigate with the students to determine a method for finding out. They recognize that they, too, are becoming more comfortable with understanding how knowledge is constructed so that they can provide experiences that are rich and meaningful to their students.

▶ They recognize that on some days the learning experiences don't go as planned. They are able to revise their plans with their students and begin the process again.

As students become more expert-like, or more expert in their work with a Curriculum of Practice, teachers may need to employ strategies of Ascending

Intellectual Demand in order to ensure continuous intellectual ascent in these students—even in a curriculum as inherently rich and complex as the Curriculum of Practice. As is the case with the Core Curriculum and the Curriculum of Connections, there are some "generic" methods of increasing the challenge level for advanced students. Those are listed in Chapter 4, Figure 4.8. Additional paths to Ascending Intellectual Demand for advanced learners that are particularly relevant to the Curriculum of Practice are provided in Figure 6.8. These generally more complex approaches involve students in working more at an expert level rather than engaging them in work at more foundational levels. Chapter 8 explains the full progression of Ascending Intellectual Demand as it applies to all learners.

Lesson and Unit Closure

As is the case with lesson and unit closure in the previous two PCM parallels, lesson and unit closure focuses on the intent of the particular parallel. In the case of Curriculum of Practice, that means the teacher will use lesson and unit closure activities to help focus students on their work as practitioners in the discipline.

Students will need to review, summarize, and bring clarity to their knowledge of how scholars and expert practitioners in the field work to solve problems and address important issues. Student will also need to understand the sorts of dispositions and work habits reflected in the contributions of experts and the methods these experts use to learn and to extend knowledge in the discipline. They will need to identify how society benefits from contributions of disciplinarians and how experts know whether their work is worthwhile. In addition, students will

---

- Encourage students to distinguish between approaches that seem relevant in tackling authentic problems of the discipline and those that are less relevant.
- Call on students to develop a language of reflection about problems and scenarios in the field.
- Devise tasks and products that cause students to develop, through application, personal frameworks of knowledge, understanding, and skill related to the discipline.
- Have students test those frameworks through repeated field-based tasks and refine them as necessary.
- Have students compare standards of quality used by practitioners, connoisseurs, and critics in the field to standards of quality typically used in school as they relate to problem solving in that field.
- Guide students in establishing their own goals for work at what they believe to be the next steps in quality for their own growth and to assess their own work according to those standards.
- Make it possible for students to submit best-quality exemplars of their own work to experts in a field for expert-level feedback.
- Have students work on problems currently posing difficulties for experts in the discipline.
- Structure products and tasks to require students to engage in persistent, prolonged, written reflection about their own work and thinking in the field, with analysis and critique of those patterns as they evolve.
- Call on students to compare and contrast their own approaches to discipline-based dilemmas, issues, or problems with those of experts in the field.

Figure 6.8 Some Paths to Achieving Ascending Intellectual Demand for Advanced Learners in the Curriculum of Practice Parallel

need to compare and contrast their own expert-like working experiences with those of experts—in terms of essential questions; use of information, concepts and principles, and methods; standards of quality; and outcomes.

Strategies such as comparison and contrast charts, analysis of expert rubrics, use of mini-biographies of experts, and whole class and small group discussions can help the teacher focus students on a review of the vocabulary and methodology of a discipline, as well as its key concepts, principles, skills, and information. Focusing questions for the Parallel of Practice can be very helpful in framing lesson and unit closure activities.

Summary

The components of curriculum that comprise the Curriculum of Practice Parallel are the same as for the other parallels, but the characteristics and emphasis varies somewhat because of the teacher's desire to orchestrate experiences through which students can construct understanding in much the same way a professional constructs understanding. The ability of teachers to develop and guide such a curriculum requires a sophisticated set of judgments about the content, students, learning, and teaching. Creating a network of educators (colleagues, parents, students, and experts in the community) is one way to increase professional sophistication.

An Example of the Curriculum of Practice Using Lydia's Civil War Unit

Once again we revisit Lydia Janis, our fictionalized teacher, and the Civil War unit she's been constructing for her fifth graders. Here she uses the Curriculum of Practice to develop a curriculum that will extend her students' understandings of the time period. Her focus will be on having her students work as practicing historians as they become acquainted with the Civil War. Although her goal is not predominately focused on absorption of facts about the time period, students will nonetheless come away with critical information about the time period as well as with a framework of understanding and a set of authentic skills.

In much the same way that biographies and autobiographies touch our lives, history can reveal compelling stories that explain how individuals lived their lives long ago. Historical accounts share with us the fears, perspectives, and experiences that change people as they live their lives during times of conflict. After reading the examples in this chapter, Lydia decided that she wanted to try writing a unit that allowed students to assume the role of historians who document the lives of individuals who experienced the events during the Civil War. She carefully thought through how the Curriculum of Practice would help her accomplish this goal.

Increasing an Understanding of Historical Research

Prior to identifying goals for students as practitioners, Lydia called the local historical society to see if its staff could assist her in understanding how historians conduct their work and what type of skills and methods of thinking they use. Mrs. Esquith, the Director, helped her understand that historians are dependent on documents and written records that have been left behind and are often contained in special collections, libraries, or the National Archives. By drawing on such a variety of sources, historians are able to develop rich and detailed descriptions about what they are studying. These documents give historians a time perspective, which is essential in understanding and describing what happened in the past. Usually, historians like to interview individuals who have firsthand experience in what is being studied by conducting interviews or using surveys and questionnaires; however, when those people are gone, they use what artifacts they leave behind.

With Mrs. Esquith's help, Lydia was able to understand the role that she wanted her students to play during this unit; she could then begin thinking about the goals of this unit, and she could begin the process of locating some of the resources that the students would use to gather their data.

Identifying the Goals of Content (Including Standards) in the Unit

Lydia next reviewed her district's curriculum framework, the textbook adopted by the school, the National Standards for History, and other curriculum resources. With this, she highlighted the standards that most closely paralleled what she wanted the curriculum unit to address.

First, she knew that she needed to engage students in reading about the time period—to interact with narrative accounts that would provide the students with an understanding of the time period through the eyes of those who lived it. She knew that her students enjoyed reading historical fiction and often remarked that the individuals in the past were courageous, faced difficult hardships, and experienced things that they would never experience in their lifetime. The latter comment was the one that she was most interested in pursuing with the students during this unit. Lydia wondered if she could design an inquiry-based unit that might help students see the relationship between their world and the world during the Civil War.

Second, she wanted to design the unit so that students would deepen their understanding of the time period accurately by using diaries, journals, photographs, and other historical documents that could provide an accurate account of what life was like during the Civil War. By having her students analyze these documents, she would create opportunities for them to identify the various viewpoints of those whom the war affected. Using these documents would help the students compare and contrast the varying points of view, document how the war affected various lives, and realize that lives change in significant ways that help to shape a course of events that eventually affects future generations.

Her third goal was to encourage students to raise questions about their findings and research, to identify new questions that could lead to future research projects, and to create a climate that closely approximates that of historians and sociologists.

She would teach them how to look for evidence, question the evidence, and gather and record data to answer their questions.

From this thinking, Lydia developed a set of understandings, or principles, that would help guide the development of her lessons. These were the ideas that she felt were enduring over time and could help her create learning experiences to assist students in constructing and deepening their own ideas about this time period. Her content/standards goals read as follows:

Students will understand that

▶ as a nation becomes more diverse, so do the perspectives of its members

▶ a person's point of view is influenced by cultural, social, economic, political, and religious factors

▶ differing viewpoints can lead to conflict

▶ conflict can lead to changes in the social, economic, political, or religious order

▶ successful historical research involves answering questions, using reliable and valid sources to answer these questions, analyzing and looking for patterns in the data, and drawing conclusions

From this list, Lydia generated a series of questions that would be added to a list of questions that the students would generate prior to the start of her unit. These questions would guide the students' research and would make the understandings listed above more user friendly and more inquiry based for her fifth grade students.

▷   What was life like for those who lived during the Civil War?

▷   What perspectives (points of view) did people hold during this time period?

▷   Did these perspectives ever change?

▷   How are these perspectives different and similar?

▷   What influences these perspectives?

▷   How did the war affect the lives of those who lived during the time?

▷   How were the experiences of these individuals similar and different?

▷   How do historians find out the answers to their questions?

▷   How do the experiences of the past affect my life?

These questions would help to facilitate the learning process, but Lydia would also encourage students to develop their own questions for future studies. She hoped that by interacting with the stories, documents, and diary and journal entries students would begin to identify other questions—questions that were meaningful to them.

Strategies for Student Grouping

By having the students work in groups based on their interests, the students would support each other, as real-world team members often do when they are grouped based on shared interest. Lydia also helped the students know the work that they were doing was meaningful. In fact, she would have the students begin to consider how their work might be shared with a wider audience. She prepared carefully, yet created an environment where dialogue was stressed, questioning was promoted, reworking plans was a common procedure of the day, and very important work would be shared and celebrated in the end. This resulted in a variety of student groups in addition to the interest-based investigations. Often, students worked alone on their contracts. At times, they met in small groups with the teacher to fine-tune research skills or to talk about formats for their culminating products. Sometimes students elected to attend these small-group coaching sessions, but sometimes they were asked by the teacher to come to one or more of the sessions. Often during the unit, students asked a peer to help them with locating resources, interpreting materials, or editing their work. Of course, there were also times when the teacher led the whole class in direct instruction, sharing information, or troubleshooting for their contract work.

Groupings had a "fluid" feel during the unit, with students reconfiguring themselves in a variety of ways to ensure success with their activities and products. In addition, Lydia varied groupings in response to her own evolving sense of student interests and readiness levels.

Gathering the Resources

Lydia began by developing a list of those whose lives would be studied in this unit and a preliminary list of resources that her students could use to gather information to answer their questions. She wanted to locate historical fiction, primary documents, art, magazines, newspapers, books, music, diaries, and journals. She wanted this unit to be of interest to the students, and she knew that she wanted to bring history alive by providing students with an opportunity to interact with the words, sounds, and images of real people from long ago (see Figure 6.9).

Determining the Teaching Methods, Identifying a Strategy for Designing the Learning Activities and Products, and Designing the Assessments

Lydia decided she would present a series of problem-based tasks to the students to guide their historical research. First, she would ask the students to each assume the role of a character from the Civil War time period, documenting the character's perspectives from the historical fiction books. They would be asked also to record the feelings, images, and words that help identify what these perspectives were and how these perspectives changed throughout the story. Second, they would be asked to gather as much information as possible about the lives of these characters

Historical Fiction Books	Description
Charley Skedaddle Patricia Beatty (William Morrow, 1987) Role: Drummer Boy, Union Army	Charley Quinn, a former member of a New York City street gang, is determined to enlist as a soldier in the Union Army to avenge the death of his brother.
Jayhawker Patricia Beatty (William Morrow, 1991) Role: Abolitionist	At age twelve, Elijah Tulley has an experience that he will never forget. Radical abolitionist John Brown visits his home and blesses him and his sisters. Elijah is forever committed to abolishing slavery, and he becomes even more passionate about the cause when his father is killed while attempting to free some slaves from a Missouri plantation. He becomes a spy for the Union Army, reporting their activities to his fellow abolitionists, or Jayhawkers.
Turn Homeward, Hannalee Patricia Beatty (William Morrow, 1984) Role: Confederate	This story is based on a story of the displacement of Georgia mill workers during the Civil War. Twelve-year-old Hannalee Reed works in a Georgia textile mill. When General Sherman's troops pass through her town, they burn the mill, round up all the mill workers, and send them to work in the North. Hannalee is separated from her younger brother and her friend, but she is determined to find them and return home. She escapes from the Kentucky household where she is forced to work as a servant and sets off on a daring adventure that brings her face to face with the horrors of war.
With Every Drop of Blood James Lincoln Collier and Christopher Collier (Delacorte Press, 1994) Role: Confederate	Johnny hopes for a chance to avenge his father's death at the hands of the Yankees. When he hears about a supply convoy leaving for the Confederate capital of Richmond, Virginia, he decides to join in the effort. Before the wagons get very far, Yankee soldiers attack it, and Johnny is shocked to find himself taking orders from a young African American soldier who takes him prisoner. The friendship that forms between them makes Johnny question the point of the war as well as his own beliefs about African Americans.
Lincoln: A Photobiography Russell Freedman (Clarion Books, 1987) Role: President	This is a detailed and balanced account of the life and career of Abraham Lincoln. Illustrated with a wealth of photographs and prints, the biography gives readers a close look at the complex and fascinating man who led the nation through one of its darkest hours.
Across Five Aprils Irene Hunt (Follett Press, 1964) Role: Both Perspectives	Nine-year-old Jethro, who lives in southern Illinois, has an idealized view of war based on stories from history books about dramatic battles and their glorious heroes. When the Civil War breaks out, however, painfully dividing his family as it divides North and South, Jeth must confront the many confusing and horrifying realities of war. At age 10, his father ill and his older brothers off fighting in the war, Jeth becomes the man of the household. *Across Five Aprils* spans the four long years of the war, during which Jethro is transformed from a boy into a young man.
Escape from Slavery: The Boyhood of Frederick Douglass in His Own Words Michael McCurdy, Editor, (Alfred A. Knopf, 1994) Role: Abolitionist	Skillfully selected excerpts from Frederick Douglass's autobiography paint a vivid portrait of the great abolitionist. The story of Douglass's childhood provides a close look at slavery from the perspective of the enslaved, and the account of his escape and subsequent career is both dramatic and inspirational.
The Story of Booker T. Washington Patricia and Fred McKissack (Children's Press, 1991) Role: Slave	This book provides a brief overview of the life of Booker T. Washington, with many photographs and other illustrations.

Figure 6.9 *(Continued)*

(Continued)

The Boys' War Jim Murphy (Clarion Books, 1990) Role: Confederate and Union Soldiers	Many of the soldiers who fought on both sides of the war were not men but children. Jim Murphy's book is an account of the war from the perspective of these young soldiers. It contains many quotations from the boys' journals and letters as well as photographs of the soldiers and the battlegrounds where they fought and died. The book captures their firsthand experiences of war, from the thrill of enlistment through the horrible reality of combat.
Shades of Gray Carolyn Reeder (Macmillan, 1989) Role: Both Perspectives	The war has left 12-year-old Will Page without any immediate family: his father and brother were killed by the Yankees; his sisters died of an epidemic spread from a Union encampment near his Virginia home; and his mother died of grief over these losses. Will reluctantly goes to live with his Uncle Jed and his family, who refuse to fight for the Confederate Army. With his anger directed toward the Union Army, Will comes to understand that the moral issues involved in the decision to fight were not as clear-cut as he thought and that good people can have honest disagreements.
Harriet Tubman M.W. Taylor (Chelsea House Publishers,1991) Role: Abolitionists	Part of the Black Americans of Achievement series, this biography tells the incredible life story of the architect of the Underground Railroad, which helped hundreds of slaves make their way to freedom. The text is augmented with many photographs and drawings that bring the text to life.
Up From Slavery Booker T. Washington (Doubleday, 1963) Role: Slave and Political Activist	The great political activist and educator tells the story of his life in his own words. Washington was born into slavery and freed under the Emancipation Proclamation, after which he devoted his life to helping African Americans make a place for themselves in the economy and society of the United States. The full text of *Up From Slavery* is also available online.
Till Victory Is Won: Black Soldiers in the Civil War Zak Mettger (E. P. Dutton, 1984) Role: African American Soldiers	The story of African Americans and their involvement in the Civil War. Initially, in 1861, they were not allowed to fight. Eventually, they would gain the right to fight, and this book tells of their struggles and the stunning contributions they made on the battlefields as soldiers and on the waters as sailors. The book is based on firsthand accounts, with photographs and drawings that illustrate how blacks influenced the outcome of the war and the decades that followed.
Soldier's Heart Gary Paulsen (Bantam Books, 1998) Role: Union	A story of a 15-year-old boy who enlists in the Minnesota Volunteers not as a flag bearer or drummer, as many young boys did; Charley lied about his age and took on the combat role. Charley isn't concerned with freeing the slaves, he just wants to teach those Rebels a lesson for daring to break up the Union.
For Home and Country: A Civil War Scrapbook Norman and Angel Bolotin (Lodestar Books, 1994) Role: All	Visual information that concentrates on the social effects of war.
Historical Documents	
The American Civil War Homepage	Images of war time, biographies, music, women in the Civil War, newspapers, and some images of war time.
National Archives and Records Administration (NARA)	This site contains reproducible copies of primary documents from the holdings of the National Archives of the United States.
Library of Congress: American Memory http://memory.loc.gov/amme m/cwphtml/cwphome.html	This site contains photographs and historical documents that can be used by the students to locate information about the Civil War and other time periods.

Figure 6.9 References for Lydia's Civil War Research Project in the Curriculum of Practice

or individuals like them by using historical references, such as photographs, diary entries, journals, music, and any other resources they could find in the library or on the Internet. These references would be used to provide evidence of these perspectives and to document changes to support their original findings gathered from their text.

Third, Lydia identified the types of skills and methodologies required to assist the students in analyzing these documents, recording notes, and drawing conclusions about these data. These skills and methodologies would be the focus of some of her lessons. These included explaining the steps of historical research, generating research questions, taking notes, distinguishing between primary and secondary sources, establishing the validity and reliability of sources, analyzing print and nonprint sources, and drawing conclusions from data. She would also help them work through the steps of research, modifying assignments for students who needed more support or who needed more challenge. Lydia created a chart to help her students work through the research process (see Figure 6.10). They often referred to this chart to keep them on track during the research process.

Then Lydia decided to create a contract (see Figure 6.11) that would outline the procedures for student investigations during their study. She found this contract useful—all the students could refer to it throughout the study. Lydia would encourage students working at a high level of knowledge and independence to develop their own work plans rather than following the one prescribed in the contract.

The nature of Lydia's learning contract for the students actually addressed several key curricular components. The contract not only included a number of learning activities (e.g., reading the historical novel and gathering data on the character they are developing) but also included short-term products that gave evidence of student understanding (e.g., the double-sided notebook entries and completed data sheets). These short-term products also served as assessment vehicles for Lydia as she tracked student understanding and growth throughout the contract period. In addition, the rubric in the contract guided both students and Lydia in assessing progress during the contract period and assessing the quality of the students' culminating products. In fact, completion of Items 8 and 9 on the contract resulted in culminating products that illustrated students' grasp of essential understandings in the unit as well as their skill in working like historians. This latter emphasis is, of course, a central goal for the Curriculum of Practice Parallel.

Developing Extension Activities

Lydia knew it would take the students from three to four weeks to complete this unit of study. She would build some of the teaching and learning activities into her reading and writing classes so that she could address two sets of standards simultaneously. This would provide the necessary time to explore this unit in depth.

To extend the lessons, numerous people were identified to assist in helping the students become better researchers. With the help of a parent volunteer, Lydia was able to locate a Civil War buff in the community who helped her teach the students how to analyze historical documents. She also found a museum director who taught the students how to analyze historical photographs. Numerous parent volunteers

---

Research Steps

Define the Research Problem

Begin with a problem that is puzzling. A puzzle is not just a lack of information but a gap in our understanding. You need to ask: What is the problem that we are investigating?

Review the Evidence

Review the available evidence in the field. Researchers need to sift through whatever related research exists to see how useful it is for their purpose. You need to ask, What have others found out about this problem or topic that might help me understand what I need to study?

Make the Problem Precise
Researchers try to clarify the problem they are studying. Sometimes, they ask questions in order to reach a better understanding of the thing that they are studying. At other times, they develop hypotheses or educated guesses that can be written in such a way that the material gathered will provide evidence either supporting or disproving it. You need to ask, What new questions or hunches do I have that need to be investigated?

Work Out a Design

As researchers, we need to decide how we are going to collect data. In some cases, we will use surveys, interviews, questionnaires, document analysis, and observations. At other times, we will set up experimental research studies. You need to ask, What methods can I use to investigate my questions or to test my hypotheses?

Carry Out the Research

At this point, we will be collecting and recording data, contacting people to help us with our research, and solving some of the unforeseen difficulties that can easily come up as we conduct our study. You need to ask, What do I need to do first? How am I doing on my research? Have I planned accordingly? Do I need to gather other information?

Analyze the Results
Based on the evidence you have gathered, you will identify patterns and themes in your research. You need to ask, What have I found out in my research?

Report the Findings

You will need to decide how to report your data. You will need to choose a product to help you share this information with an audience and to share with them the new questions that you have about this topic. You need to ask, What is the significance of my work? How do these findings relate to my questions?

Figure 6.10   Research Steps for Lydia's Students

agreed to assist her students in their work, and Lydia welcomed them into the learning community. The most exciting individual she found was Jon Botter, the graphic artist at her local newspaper. He was glad to help the students study political cartoons. Since Lydia had found many of these cartoons on the Internet, Jon was able to use some of them to help the students take some of the cartoonists' ideas and create cartoons that depicted the time period.

Lydia also found out that some of her students had generated other interesting questions to explore during this unit. These questions were integrated into the unit so that the students could conduct follow-up research based on their new inquiries.

Civil War Contract

Have you ever wondered what it would be like to have lived during the Civil War? In the next few weeks, you and your teammates will be trying to portray what this time period was like by becoming historical researchers. With your partners, you will assume the role of an individual who lived during this time. You will read a historical fiction book to understand how it must have felt to be alive during this time period. In order to complete this project, you will need to ask yourself some questions, read the text to answer the questions that we will generate together, and document the feelings, perspectives, and changes that occur for your characters over time. If you want to know how it felt to be part of those events, you will also need to read the diaries, letters, and other artifacts that people who are like them left behind.

1. **Determine Your Role:**
   Abolitionist
   Slave
   Confederate Soldier
   Union Soldier
   Black Soldier
   Woman in the War
   Child in the War
   President

2. **Generate Questions to Guide Your Research**

You might consider questions like these:
   - What was life like for those who lived during the Civil War?
   - What perspectives (points of view) did people hold during this time period?
   - Did these perspectives (points of view) ever change?
   - How are these perspectives different and similar?
   - What influenced these perspectives (points of view)?
   - How did the war affect the lives of those who lived during the time?
   - How were the experiences of these individuals similar and different?
   - How do historians find out the answers to their questions?
   - How do the experiences of the past affect my life?

3. **Read a Historical Fiction Book**

You can select from some of the books that I have gathered for you or use others after we visit the library. Remember to select one that is appropriate for you as a reader. The important thing is that you feel comfortable reading it and that it provides you with a way to study the type of individual you are investigating.

4. **Record the Data**

You will use your notebook to record the answers to your questions. You can list your questions on the left-hand side of the notebook, and on the right-hand side of the notebook, you can record the answers to your questions that you find in your book. You will want to record pictures, images, your thoughts, and evidence from your book to support these answers. Good historians record what they are thinking, too, so feel free to capture your own thoughts and questions as you read.

Figure 6.11 *(Continued)*

(Continued)

Your research notebook will look like this:

| Left-Hand Side | Right-Hand Side |
| When was life for my character? | Will lived on a farm in Illinois. It looked like .... |

5. Gather Evidence From Historical Documents

You will need to locate historical documents to analyze to see if your perceptions of this time period are accurate. Use the Internet and any other sources to answer your questions. You will need to use many data sheets to help you record your findings.

Data Recording Sheet Questions	What You Found Out
Who wrote this document?	
Who speaks in this document?	
What is the source?	
When was the information recorded?	
What kind of document is this? (diary, journal, poetry, government document, photograph)	
What is the document about?	
What did this document help you to find out?	

6. Analyze the Results of Your Findings

Now it is time to analyze your findings. Using the information that you have gathered, look for some patterns in your data. Ask yourself some tough questions about your data and record these ideas in your journal. Do you see any patterns with respect to what your character's life was like? What were your character's viewpoints of the war? Did these viewpoints change over time? What influenced these changes?

7. Compare Your Findings to Other Findings

Sit with another group of students who studied other individuals during the Civil War. Compare your findings with their findings. Use a Venn diagram to compare the similarities and differences between your two groups.

8. Report Your Findings

Decide how to report these findings to other people. The results of your hard work need to be shared with an audience so that they can learn from you. Will you write an article for publication? Will you share this information by creating a play or perhaps orally presenting it in the form of a documentary? Use the list of products to guide your creation.

9. Apply What You Have Learned to Your Life

It is often said that events in the past change future generations and the lives they lead. What does this mean? You will work with other students in the class to decide what this means. Your group will be made up of students in all the roles that were investigated during this study. Look in magazines and newspapers and think about your own life, then ask yourself these questions: Is there evidence today that our lives are different because of the Civil War? Are the conditions of our lives so different from the conditions of the lives of those who came before us? Why do people change? How do people change? Did they have the same concerns? Did they worry about similar things? What changes took place in their lives that compare to changes in your lives?

You will need to think about these questions and any others that our class generates. Your group is responsible for investigating this idea. Your group will determine how best to show the meaning behind this statement.

10. Assess Your Learning Rubric for Conducting the Historical Research Study

During your study, we will use a rubric to modify or make changes to your research study so that you can continue to improve it along the way. At times, I will ask you to complete a self-evaluation of the work you are doing, and at other times, we will use the rubric below to guide the quality of your work.

*Student Researcher:*_____

Attributes	*The Distinguished*	*Apprentices*	*Novices*
Research Questions	Use all of the questions to guide their research; develop new questions to guide the research	Use most of the questions that they found interesting and testable; don't develop any new questions to research	Use a few questions to guide the study; don't develop any new questions to explore
Gathering the Data	Use a variety of resources; developed an accurate and extensive bibliography; use sophisticated data-gathering methods to further explore their ideas	Use many resources; developed an adequate bibliography; try to revise their study but experienced difficulty in carrying out the research	Use a few resources; used sources to find information more than to shape thinking
Recording the Data	Keep complete and accurate records, including supplementary data, in their notebooks and on data sheets	Keep complete and accurate records in their notebooks	Some records are complete and some partially complete in notebooks and on data sheets
Analyzing the Data	Are skilled at using descriptive research methods to identify themes and make inferences	Are developing a use of descriptive research methods to find themes and make inferences	Show early attempts at using descriptive research to find themes and make inferences
Interpreting Findings	Explain data; accurate, logical explanations	Explain data; accurate, logical explanations	Make some explanations of data

Figure 6.11 *(Continued)*

(Continued)

Attributes	The Distinguished	Apprentices	Novices
	Sophisticated and thorough interpretation of events through perspective of those living in that setting. Interpretations and explanations are supported by the data	In-depth interpretation of events through perspective of those living in that setting	Show basic interpretation of historical events through perspective of those living in that setting
Reporting the Findings	Address most of the questions explored. Inferences are explained using the data found. Use skills of evaluation as well as synthesis and analysis. Support claims with clear research evidence from valid sources.	Address some of the questions explored. Some inferences made, although minor errors may exist. Comprehension on an inferential level, and the key skills are analysis and synthesis. Support some claims with research evidence.	Address a few questions explored. A few inferences are made. Answers deal with material on a concrete, literal level
Significance of the Findings	Make full meaning of the information and incorporate it into their own life by generating examples	Make partial meaning of the information and incorporate it into their own life by generating examples	Make some meaning of the information but do not incorporate it into their own life by generating examples
Conceptual Understanding	Identify relationships between the concepts of change and perspective that are sophisticated. Could identify causal relationships between the two concepts by providing examples. Move beyond answering the main question(s) identified for the research study.	Identify relationships that mostly focus on the answers to the main question(s) identified for the research study. Relationships that are explained are descriptive only.	Identify a few relationships that have some connection to the questions.
Products	The performance or product is highly effective. The ideas are presented in an engaging, polished, clear, and thorough manner. The performance or product is developed with an audience in mind.	The performance or product is effective. The ideas are presented in a clear and thorough manner, showing awareness of the audience.	The performance or product is complete, providing some evidence of planning, practice, and consideration of audience.

Figure 6.11   Civil War Contract

Differentiation Based on Learner Need (Including AID)

There were many considerations that Lydia thought through before she started this unit. She decided that the format of designing the contract would assist her in providing an environment where she could attend to the differences of her students. To start, she could use multiple texts to support the varying reading levels of the students. Also, the contract was purposefully designed to allow some students to be guided step-by-step through the process while more confident learners, who loved the complexity of working on many tasks at once, could move at their own pace and in a sequence they found comfortable.

Lydia knew there were some students for whom the research project needed to be modified to provide a greater level of challenge. Depending on student familiarity with research, it was possible to enable these students to complete this project differently. She brainstormed a list of options that would allow some students to move into more complex types of research that would help them escalate their learning. She considered several options for her students, knowing that her ultimate goal was to teach students how to work much like professionals in the field and to function as scholars. Opportunities for increased intellectual demand for these advanced students include the following.

1. Interview someone who is an expert in history or sociology to identify problems or questions that need to be explored in these disciplines. After you have met with them, identify a new research topic that might be of interest to you. You will need to complete a management plan that articulates your idea, develop a set of research questions, gather the resources, and begin to identify how to analyze the data. (Students could then plan their own studies and, with the assistance of a mentor, develop projects that more approximate their readiness level.) (Identifying relevant and original research, problem finding, developing their own standards of quality, and assessing their work according to those standards)

2. Learn how to use surveys, conduct oral histories and interviews, and develop questionnaires to assist you in your research. Use these methods of research to research a question that you find thought provoking. (Learning advanced research skills; distinguishing between more relevant and less relevant approaches to addressing problems)

3. Submit your research findings to experts in the field so that you can receive some feedback. Use this feedback to make improvements in your research. You can also submit your research for publication. (Seeking feedback from experts to refine their research)

4. Locate experts who are willing to have you become part of a study in an area of mutual interest. (Escalating their involvement in the field)

5. Network with community businesses to conduct original research for them. Perhaps the museum needs someone to collect oral histories, interview older people, or even develop exhibits for their displays. (Identifying problems; planning research; identifying solutions)

6. Compare your findings with others in the field. Collaborate on ways to work together on a project. Design a collaborative teleproject. (Persistent and ongoing reflection about their own work as compared to others; identifying other issues that need to be explored)

7. Locate and use advanced research documents, books, and articles in your research. (Advancing the complexity of the research process)

8. Read original research written by experts to advance your knowledge of a particular field. (Learning the standards of quality in the field; understanding how research is critiqued)

9. Manage your own research study, determine a schedule for your work, and plan accordingly. (Guiding their own research agenda; learning how to self-regulate; setting priorities)

10. Identify student-relevant problems that need to be solved. Use these problems to design a research project that you find interesting. (Problem finding; relevance of research to self)

Looking Back and Ahead

The Curriculum of Practice Parallel is derived from and extends the Core Curriculum. Its main purpose is to help students function with increasing skill and confidence as professionals in a field would function. It exists for the purpose of promoting students' expertise as practitioners of the discipline. Therefore, its goals focus on the teaching of those specific research skills that will assist learners in identifying problems; generating questions; using methods and techniques to gather, document, and analyze data; reaching conclusions; creating meaningful products that are like those produced in the field; and sharing the findings with authentic audiences.

More important, the Curriculum of Practice assists students in moving core knowledge into a new level of abstraction and application. It deepens understanding by asking students to test ideas in new situations, identify patterns or relationships that exist between and among concepts, and elaborate on these experiences by comparing old ideas with new ones. The type of understanding developed in the Curriculum of Practice is one that enables students to use knowledge flexibly or in new ways. By using the skills and methods of the practitioner, a student should be able to demonstrate new levels of understanding, because it is through the use of these skills that new understanding will emerge.

In its relation to the Curriculum of Connections, the Curriculum of Practice assists students in making connections in a scholarly manner. The tools and techniques that are used by the students can assist them in accurately testing the strength of these connections in real life. Many connections can be further developed by using data analysis techniques to identify the validity of these connections, the limit to these connections, and the likelihood that the same connections can be applied to all situations.

The relationship between the Curriculum of Practice and the Curriculum of Identity is apparent. As adults we want our children to have lives that are personally meaningful. Our hope is that they can fill their lives pursuing fields of study that match who they are in disposition, philosophy, character, and interest. The Curriculum of Practice creates contexts in which to practice and/or study these roles in order to find out if certain disciplines match who the student is as an individual.

The relationship between and among all the parallels in the Parallel Curriculum Model facilitates an integrated and multidimensional approach to understanding a discipline. One approach is not more important than the other. Each may serve a different purpose, but in combination they provide learners with a more comprehensive understanding of how a discipline relates to their lives. In fact, the Curriculum of Identity explored in Chapter 7 has a particular and unique focus on helping young learners use the disciplines they study to learn not only about those disciplines but about themselves as well.

7

The Curriculum
of Identity Parallel

Lydia Janis was struck by the knowledge of a particular student in her fifth grade class. His name was Jacob, and whenever she talked about wars in class, Jacob displayed an unusual storehouse of information about battles, weapons and arms, people involved with the war effort, and its historical context. She was surprised when, during the unit on the American Revolution, he said that guerilla tactics were used by the Colonists, that the tactics had been used and refined by Native Americans, and that the Colonists' adopted warfare tactics that helped them to win the Revolutionary War. She recalled vividly Jacob's comments about this early American war. "The Battle of Lexington was particularly deadly for the redcoats because Minutemen ambushed them on Lexington Road. The Minutemen hid behind walls, hedges, and trees and picked off the redcoats with their muskets," he said, in a matter-of-fact tone, one day in class during a discussion of Paul Revere's ride.

Lydia wondered about Jacob and his flourishing interest in war and history. She wondered where it came from, who nurtured it, and what he would grow up to be. She envisioned him as a professor of history or perhaps an author. She found herself wondering, too, about what other experiences this young boy would have in school that might lead him to become a history scholar or an avid amateur historian. In fact, she wondered how school-related experiences contributed to the development of all children's abilities and talents.

Equally important, she realized that none of her previous standards and objectives dealt with the issues of student identity. Where, she wondered, did these important pieces fit into her curriculum? She knew that there must be more layers of possibility in her curriculum than even the facts, concepts, principles, and skills highlighted in the other parallels. "Could the knowledge objectives alone trigger the development of children's abilities and talents?" she pondered to herself.

It was at this moment that Lydia began another journey. In some ways, it was similar to the journeys that she had traveled while remodeling her Civil War unit: spotlighting the key concepts and principles about the Civil War for the Core

Curriculum Parallel; taking time to help her students see how concepts and princi-ples lead to connections across disciplines, cultures, and time in the Curriculum of Connections Parallel; and planning for her students to use the key concepts and principles as well as to incorporate the skills and methodologies of the historian into her unit in the Curriculum of Practice Parallel.

Yet, Lydia knew this new journey would take her down a different road because she was thinking about her students' likes and dislikes, interests, abilities, attitudes, values, and ways of working. She remembered a graduate course she had taken many years ago that addressed Bloom's taxonomy. David Krathwohl and colleagues (1964), including Bloom, worked to create an accompanying volume to the well-known *Taxonomy of Educational Objectives: Cognitive Domain* (Bloom et al., 1956). This second volume, *Taxonomy of Educational Goals, Handbook II: Affective Domain*, considered an affective taxonomy (Krathwohl, Bloom, & Masia, 1964). She also remembered that Connecticut's Common Core of Teaching (Connecticut State Department of Education, 1999) spoke directly to the critical need for teachers to get to know their students and how they learn. Most recently, Lydia recalled reading *Understanding by Design* (Wiggins & McTighe, 1998), in which the authors point to the importance of self-knowledge.

"What an intriguing way to think about curriculum," Lydia mused to herself. "This is one of the first times that I have started to think about my curriculum by thinking about the strengths my students bring to the classroom . . . their learning strengths: interests, abilities, how they like to learn, how they like to express them-selves." She thought back to Jacob, her history buff. "Maybe this journey will help me understand how I can help him and others understand themselves better by looking at the work of historians."

This chapter is arranged in a format similar to those preceding it. It contains: (1) a definition of the Curriculum of Identity, (2) a rationale for using this approach for curriculum development, (3) a description of characteristics for each of the cur-riculum components within the Curriculum of Identity Parallel, (4) an example of developing a Curriculum of Practice, (5) techniques for modifying the components of the Curriculum of Identity based on learner need—including provisions for Ascending Intellectual Demand, and (6) an explanation of the relationship of this framework to the other three curriculum parallels described in prior chapters.

What Does Identity Mean in the Curriculum of Identity?

Of all the curriculum approaches described in this book, the Curriculum of Identity Parallel is likely the one least familiar to readers. Like the other parallels in the Parallel Curriculum Model, the Curriculum of Identity Parallel is a lens through which educators can view the curriculum design process. Like the other parallels, the Identity Parallel hinges on the key concepts and principles of the discipline. As in the other parallels, educators use curriculum components to focus students on the "deep intent," or purpose, of the parallel. The focus for this parallel, however, is different because students are at the heart of this curriculum design process. They are at the center because the intent of this parallel is to help students sharpen their sense of themselves—their identity—in and through curriculum.

It is helpful to think about the Curriculum of Identity as a three-way mirror that continually provides different kinds of "reflective" feedback to the student (see Figure 7.1). Of course, the mirror is a metaphor for the feedback provided by teachers, teaching and learning activities, and experts in the targeted field, as well as the student him- or herself. One side of the mirror, titled Knowledge of the Discipline, provides the student with feedback about his or her knowledge in a targeted field of study. The other side panel of the mirror, called Knowledge About Myself as a Learner and Worker, provides the student with a different perspective: reflection and feedback about his or her abilities, preferred ways to communicate, learning and working preferences, and goals as they relate to those required of practicing professionals in the field.

The center panel of the three-way mirror, the front or forward-facing panel, is the Visioning Field. It is the mirror through which the student assesses the "degree of fit" between her- or himself and the discipline, both now and in the future. Using the composite image reflected in the center panel—derived from both side panels—the student perceives possibilities in the center panel and uses the Reflections of Possible Self or Selves in the center section of the mirror to make continual adjustments in his or her life course. The student modifies his or her course according to answers to many questions such as, for example, "Do I like what I am learning? Who are the professionals who use this information in their daily lives? Would I want to become like these professionals? How do people benefit from the work of these professionals? Do people like me work in this field?" Depending on the answers to these questions and many others like them, a student will be either satisfied and continue with his or her original orientation, or unsatisfied with the fit and make modifications to his or her life course. Naturally, the depth of students' insights will

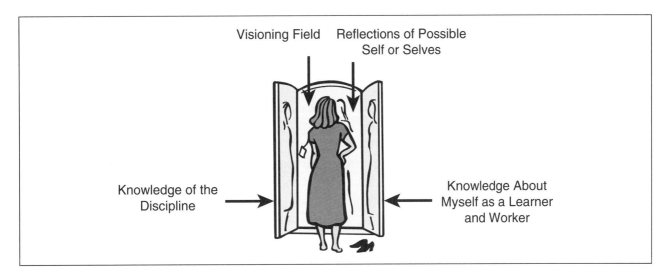

Figure 7.1 A Metaphor for the Curriculum of Identity

vary by developmental stages, as will any accompanying changes in career paths. Yet, even young children express facets of their identity. They have unmistakable interests, express likes and dislikes, and, when left to their own devices, engage visibly in goal-oriented activities.

Certainly not every student will be captivated by the study of history—or of science, math, literature, and so on. Even in the study of a content area that is not currently a match for a student's strengths, interests, and proclivities, that student can learn about him- or herself by studying "negative space." "If I don't really love history, why is that the case, and what does that help me understand about why I like what I do like?" "If I don't find the methods of a historian a match for how I work, what does that tell me about the kinds of methods that do seem to match my ways of working and connecting to the world?" "If this isn't something I can see myself working with for the rest of my life, what does seem attractive enough to think about investing my career in?"

There is room in every discipline for every student to reflect on and come to understand more fully his or her own identity as a person, worker, and potential contributor to society. The "deep intent" of the Curriculum of Identity is to guide students in such understanding, while also helping them more fully understand and grapple with the important information, concepts, principles, and skills of a topic and discipline.

Why Should We Be Concerned About a Student's Identity?

Ever since the human race began, its members have been trying to answer the questions "Who am I? What is my purpose? How do I come to understand myself and my role in the world?" (Phenix, 1964). Research and theories put forth in the past century are testimony to the importance of identity as a factor in the learning process. Maslow (1970) suggests that the highest human need is self-actualization. Self-actualization, he proposes, is based on the intrinsic motivation that is derived from learning. Csikszentmihalyi (1990) describes the trancelike quality of those deeply involved in optimal learning. Such experiences, he reports, provide a sense of discovery and a sense that the person involved is transported to a new reality. It pushes the person to higher levels of performance and consciousness. In fact, such experiences transform the self by making it more complex. The growth of self, he says, is the key to this sort of absorption in learning (Csikszentmihalyi, 1990). Thus both Maslow and Csikszentmihalyi see a direct link between the quality of learning experiences and the transformational power they hold for the learner.

Recent knowledge about the brain gives convincing evidence for the need to connect learning with an individual's emotions, a facet of identity. According to work by Jensen (1998), we learn more effectively and efficiently when learning is associated with personal feelings: "Emotions drive the threesome of attention, meaning, and memory. The things that we orchestrate to engage emotions in a productive way will do 'triple duty' to capture all three" (p. 94). In order to understand who we are, we need to understand critical components of ourselves as learners and workers—our likes and dislikes for particular phenomena, for example, as well as our values.

Finally, the literature on learning-style differences is replete with recommendations to provide students with opportunities to learn in their preferred modes of learning. This literature suggests that students learn more effectively and perform more capably when they are allowed to learn and demonstrate their learning in preferred modes.

Thus, a large body of literature and research exists about identity and how it is formed across the life span. Scholars and researchers continue to find critical links between identity, identity formation, and learning (see Figure 7.2). Specifically, learning is enhanced when it takes into consideration aspects of a student's identity: interests, values, preferred way of communicating, personal goals or life mission, envisioned contribution made to a field or discipline, culture and gender, and so forth. Enhanced learning may lead to increasing levels of intrinsic motivation, the forerunner of self-actualization. In turn, intrinsic motivation fuels learning, and the cycle continues. Put simply, the Curriculum of Identity holds promise for society at large. With proper attention to nurturing students' identities through curriculum and instruction, teachers may be able to assist more students to lead creatively productive and satisfying lives while they learn and find meaning in the fundamental information, ideas, and skills of a discipline.

Beyond the clear benefit that the Curriculum of Identity Parallel holds for society at large, it also directly benefits teachers and students. It benefits teachers because it

1. reminds us that the focus of our work is students who share with us space and opportunity to learn during critical, formative periods of time in their lives

2. makes teaching more enjoyable as we get to know students personally and in greater depth

3. provides specific techniques for learning about the identity of individual students

4. illuminates critical learning differences among students

5. pinpoints where teachers need to make adjustments in the curriculum and instruction to accommodate those learning differences

6. lessens the likelihood of the one-size-fits-all curriculum

7. helps make student learning more efficient and effective

The Curriculum of Identity benefits students because it

1. encourages exploration and mastery of required content in a highly motivating context

2. decreases anonymity

3. reduces student alienation

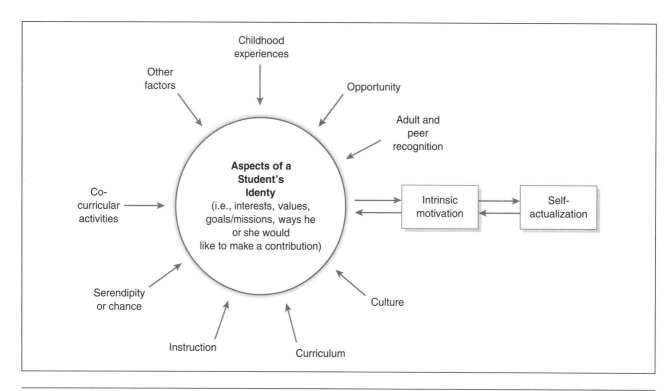

Figure 7.2 Identity and Learning

4. encourages a student's systematic examination of and reflection on his or her learning strengths (e.g., abilities, interests, learning-style preferences, expression style preferences)

5. helps students identify with the field and see possibilities for themselves by encountering experts in and beneficiaries of the discipline whose gender, race, culture, economic status, perspectives, etc. are familiar to the student

6. engenders opportunities for a student to think about the fit between his or her learning strengths and all aspects of a discipline, including cognitive aspects as well as the day-to-day life of practicing professionals, their long-term goals, and the sacrifices, commitments, responsibilities, and contributions that are required

7. illuminates student progress and development in both the affective and the cognitive realm

8. highlights student growth areas; targets possible "next steps" in the journey toward creative productivity in a field

9. clarifies for a student, over time and at increasing levels of specificity, the degree of "fit" between his or her learning and work profile and the targeted field or domain

10. informs decision making

11. increases the likelihood of creative productivity across the life span

Figure 7.3 lists some of the focusing questions that guide both teacher and student work in the Curriculum of Identity. It is through pursuit of answers to these questions that curriculum helps students come to understand themselves as they study a particular discipline.

What Are Key Features and Characteristics of Curriculum Components Within the Curriculum of Identity?

The components of the Curriculum of Identity are the same that underlie each of the other curricula in the Parallel Curriculum Model. The Curriculum of Identity has a different look, however, because in the design process, the teacher emphasizes some components more than others and modifies aspects of components in order to accomplish the goals and purposes of this particular parallel. Each of the components is discussed on the following pages. Readers may wish to use Figure 7.4 to support their learning about the components of the Curriculum of Identity. This visual representation can be used as a graphic organizer for this next section of the chapter.

- What do practitioners and contributors in this discipline think about?
- To what degree is this familiar, surprising, and/or intriguing to me?
- When I am intrigued by an idea, what do I gain from that, give as a result of that, and what difference does it make?
- How do people in this discipline think and work?
- In what ways do those processes seem familiar, surprising, and/or intriguing to me?
- What are the problems and issues on which practitioners and contributors in this discipline spend their lives?
- To what degree are those intriguing to me?
- What is the range of vocational and avocational possibilities in this discipline?
- In which ones can I see myself working?
- What difficulties do practitioners and contributors in this discipline encounter?
- How have they coped with the difficulties?
- How do I think I would cope with them?
- What are the ethical principles at the core of the discipline?
- How are those like and unlike my ethics?
- Who have been the "heroes" of the evolving discipline?
- What are the attributes of the "heroes"?
- What do I learn about myself by studying them?
- Who have been the "villains" of the evolving discipline?
- What are the attributes of the "villains"?
- What do I learn about myself by studying about them?
- How do people in this discipline handle ambiguity, uncertainty, persistence, failure, success, collaboration, compromise?
- How do I handle those things?
- What is the wisdom this discipline has contributed to the world?
- How has that affected me?
- To what degree can I see myself contributing to that wisdom?
- How might I shape the discipline over time?
- How might it shape me?

Figure 7.3 Some Focusing Questions of the Curriculum of Identity

Component	Modification Techniques
Content (Including Standards)	• Determine the concepts, principles, skills, methodologies, and dispositions (e.g., interests, attitudes, beliefs, and expression style preferences) of practicing professionals in the discipline you will teach. • Consider objectives from the Secretary's Commission on Achieving Necessary Skills (SCANS) Report, which address essential workplace skills. • Target the concepts, principles, skills, methodologies, and dispositions from the world of the practicing professionals that best match the goals and purposes of the curriculum unit. • Work with students to gather and analyze data from their learning and work profiles. Create charts that display the students' learning and work profiles. Identify patterns and trends in the class profile. Make note of individual profiles as well. • Make appropriate accommodations in the unit to address patterns in students' learning and work profiles (e.g., address students' interests, encourage students' opportunities to work in their preferred learning or expression style) and to reflect consistently on what they learn about themselves through their work.
Assessments	• Create longitudinal rubrics to identify the stages of talent development in students in a variety of content areas. Use the rubric to note the evolution of student abilities in the classroom, determine where each student is on the novice to expert continuum, and decide on strategies that can be used to guide the student to the next level of proficiency. • Utilize assessment formats that require student reflection (e.g., goal statements, reflective essays, longitudinal portfolios, journals, and personal discoveries). • Provide for choice in assessment tasks. • Provide students with time to document and analyze their own learning and work profile over time and identify emerging patterns and trends. • Ensure systematic opportunities for students to reflect upon their past, present, and future selves. • Share with parents or a significant adult where each child is in his or her development. Explore with them the ways that they can contribute to development of student interests and abilities at home.
Introductory Activities	• Provide students with a graphic organizer of the all fields within a discipline so that they can visualize the range of work done by practitioners within a discipline. • Share with students an array of products that professionals in the discipline produce (e.g., in history: fiction and nonfiction books, newspaper articles, photographs, timelines, maps, videos, charts, journals, letters, and telegrams). • Read aloud to students about famous and infamous people who have contributed to the field (e.g., *The Lighthouse Keeper's Daughter* by Arielle North Olsen (1987); *Eleanor* by Barbara Cooney (1996). Books that portray the famous people at the approximate age of the students are especially powerful. • Introduce a timeline of important turning points in the discipline that includes the names and contributions of eminent people of both genders and a variety of cultures within the field. Seek students' answers to questions such as: What did it take to become this person? What might he or she have been like as a fifth grader? In what ways am I like this famous person when he or she was my age? In what ways am I different? What parts of this person's work would interest me? What parts would I not enjoy? • Brainstorm personal characteristics of practicing professionals within the field both now and at earlier ages. Call upon students to compare their own interests and abilities to those of practicing professionals. • Share revealing audio-clips, segments of documentaries, and newspaper articles about important moments and the people who shaped those moments.

Component	Modification Techniques
Teaching Methods	• Generate questions for students' written reflection and discussion throughout the unit to assist students in thinking about the knowledge that practitioners in the field use, problems they address, ways they work, personality traits, career development, personal and work goals, and so forth and what students can learn about themselves through examining these elements. • Use independent investigations to provide students opportunity to study research on, contributions of, and working modes in the discipline. • Use shadowing experiences and mentorships to provide students with firsthand opportunities to learn about the day-to-day routines, values, and beliefs of professionals in the field. • Use problem-based learning to enhance students' awareness of problem-solving abilities employed in the field. • Use simulations to engage students in reflecting on the issues and problems of the discipline. • Use visualization techniques to assist students in reflecting on past, current, and future selves.
Learning Activities	• Have students use a multiple-step process to identify, research, and plan to solve a problem that requires a novel solution. • Help students formulate questions that they want to answer. • Ask students to use appropriate criteria to select the best possible alternative in making decisions. • Ask students to rank, prioritize, and sequence the steps involved in an independent investigation. • Help students develop or refine the ability to set appropriate goals for their work, use those goals to guide their work, modify the goals as work progresses, and assess their work according to their goals. • Help students develop the skills of introspection and the ability to compare and contrast their own personal characteristics and goals with those of the practicing professional.
Grouping Strategies	• Use individual conferences to discuss student interests, reflection, growth in learning, and work profiles and to forward student learning related to competencies in both content and personal reflection. • Use small groups for (1) interest-based explorations related to the curriculum content, (2) analysis of the class learning and work profile, (3) debriefing activities, and (4) extension activities. • Use pairs for Think Alouds that support students' reflection and self-assessment, students' analyses of their learning and work profiles for emerging themes and patterns, and students' editing. • Work with large groups of students to provide an overview of the unit, introduce the learning and work profile, hear guest speakers, and participate in field experiences.
Resources	• Locate school and community members who are practicing professionals in careers related to the unit of study. Invite them to be guest speakers and mentors for students. • Locate biographies, at appropriate reading levels, of historical and contemporary practicing professionals. • Provide students with segments of audiotapes, documentaries, or newspaper articles that chronicle significant events in the lives of people who have contributed to a field. • Provide students with a wide variety of products created by practicing professionals in the discipline. Provide time for students to examine the collection and ask questions.
Products	• Provide students with regular opportunities to analyze and reflect on products that reflect the work of practicing professionals. • Encourage students to create portfolios of their best work samples. Provide opportunities for students to assess the growth reflected in the chronology of their portfolio pieces.

Figure 7.4 *(Continued)*

(Continued)

Component	Modification Techniques
	• Ensure that students have the opportunity for self-assessment using rubrics that have been designed for products and performances. • Provide students with systematic opportunities to reflect on who they are becoming as learners and workers. Call on them to put their thoughts in journal entries, reflective essays, collages, tape-recorded reflections, and so on.
Extension Activities	• Provide opportunities for students to be involved with simulations related to the curriculum unit and their interests. • Make available supplementary videotapes on related topics. • Provide opportunities for students to visit with local experts and other professionals in related areas. • Ask the gifted education specialist to assist in locating a speaker to talk about cutting-edge research questions and state-of-the-art research techniques in their work and the discipline. • Ask the library media specialist for assistance to locate Web quests related to the curriculum topic. • Find students a shadowing experience, internship, or mentorship when appropriate. • Help students find community-based opportunities to investigate the work of practitioners in the discipline.
Differentiation Based on Learner Need (Including AID)	• Be aware that students are at different levels of development with respect to the content goals of the unit, interest in the discipline, and ability to be introspective. • Provide support for students who may have potential in the field, but who have not yet displayed interest in the topic and/or discipline. • Provide different levels of support to scaffold students' acquisition of content and skills related to their emerging sense of identity. • Provide an array of materials to accommodate students' interests, prior experiences, reading abilities, and ability to draw inferences (for example, in a mapping unit: copies of historical maps, star charts, maps of the ocean floor, town maps, road maps, topographical maps, relief maps, political maps, population maps, floor plans, treasure maps). • Support increasing levels of student independence in self-assessment regarding goals. • Assess students' current level of awareness of generic working skills such as time management, ability to work in a team, leadership skills, responsibility, sociability, and so forth as they relate to practitioners in the discipline and to self.
Lesson and Unit Closure	• Use the focusing questions for the Identity Parallel to guide closure activities. • Ask students to summarize, explain, and provide supporting evidence for key concepts and principles in the content they are studying. • Guide students in reflecting on the range of contributors and contributions to the field. • Have students, over time, analyze the work of experts in the discipline according to ways of working, work settings and conditions, habits of mind, issues and problems dealt with, methods used, ethical issues, and contributions to society. • Have students compare attributes of individuals who have had positive or negative impacts on the field (or on society through the field) and reflect on personal insights about the similarities and differences. • Provide two-column journals, comparison/contrast organizers, classroom data charts, and similar data-gathering and analysis tools, and invite students to reflect on what their study of the discipline, its methods, and its disciplinarians is teaching them about themselves individually and as a group.

Figure 7.4 Curriculum Components of the Curriculum of Identity

Content (Including Standards) in the Curriculum of Identity

While most states now have standards for students in the disciplines, we do not have the same kind of well-designed and coherent documents to set forth expectations for identity formation among young people. We do, however, have some guidance from documents such as the Secretary's Commission on Achieving Necessary Skills report, *What Work Requires of Schools: A SCANS Report for America 2000.* (U.S. Department of Labor, 1992), emerging documents from state departments of education that focus on character education, and state Codes of Professional Responsibility. The following are goals for students from selected documents that support the intent of the Curriculum of Identity.

Self-Esteem

The student believes in own self-worth and maintains a positive view of self, demonstrates knowledge of own skills and abilities, is aware of impact on others, and knows own emotional capacity and needs and how to address them.

Sociability

The student demonstrates understanding, friendliness, adaptability, empathy, and politeness in new and ongoing group settings. Asserts self in familiar and unfamiliar social situations, relates well to others, responds appropriately as the situation requires, and takes an interest in what others say and do.

Self-Management

[The student] assesses own knowledge, skills, and abilities accurately; sets well-defined and realistic personal goals; monitors progress toward goal attainment and motivates self through goal achievement; exhibits self-control and responds to feedback unemotionally and nondefensively; is a "self-starter." (U.S. Department of Labor, 1992)

Students will assume primary responsibility for learning, including identifying their needs and setting reasonable goals. (Connecticut State Department of Education, 1998a)

The following quotation addresses the professional responsibilities of teachers with respect to the development of the characters of their students:

The professional teacher, in full recognition of his or her obligation to the student, shall (a) recognize, respect and uphold the dignity and worth of students as individual human beings . . . (f) assist students in the formulation of value systems and worthy, positive goals. (Connecticut State Department of Education, 1998b, 1999)

Based on the intent of these and other documents, we can develop a short, beginning list of standards to serve as the underpinnings for the Curriculum of Identity.

Students will be able to

1. understand the components of a learning and work profile (i.e., abilities, interests, learning-style preferences, skills, goals or mission statements, and extracurricular activities) and document their learning and work profile over time

2. reflect upon their learning and working profiles, identify significant themes in their learning and work, note changes over time in these profiles, and make predictions about how their profiles might change in the future

3. develop an accurate sense of what the daily lives of practicing professionals are like (e.g., the work hours, the extent of collaboration among peers, the extent of field work, the nature of lab work, the extent to which one is required to interact with the public, the common problems and issues, the nature of ambiguity, the persistence necessary, the failures, and the successes)

4. assess the degree of fit between their own conceptions of day-to-day living with the actual day-to-day life of the practicing professional

5. identify how components of their learning profiles align with those of the practicing professional in one or more discipline(s)

Assessments in the Curriculum of Identity

Exemplary assessment tasks for any of the curriculum parallels discussed in this book are varied, closely aligned with learning goals, and diagnostic in nature. In order for assessment tasks to be effective for teachers and students working within the context of the Core Curriculum, the Curriculum of Connections, the Curriculum of Practice, and/or the Curriculum of Identity, the assessment tasks need to be adapted to address the goals and purposes of each curriculum parallel.

To align assessment tasks with the goals and purposes of the Curriculum of Identity, we can remodel our assessments in four different ways. First, we select and generate a list of assessment formats that require student reflection. Second, we address the need for student choice with respect to assessments and products, as it is choice that accommodates students' emerging and developing interests. Third, we look at the role of self-assessment within this curriculum parallel and propose two ways that practitioners can incorporate this practice. Finally, we look at longitudinal rubrics that address the talent development process and help us visualize student growth over time.

Now, review the assessment formats included in Figures 4.4 and 4.5 in Chapter 4. Close examination reveals that some of the formats are more likely than others to require student reflection (e.g., conversations, essays, concept maps, and performances). Each of these formats may require students to think about who and where they are as learners and workers. For example, a twelfth-grade English teacher who is incorporating author study within a poetry unit might ask his students to write an essay about personal sacrifices that famous authors have made using a prompt such as this:

Identify the personal sacrifices Robert Frost made in his evolution as a poet and why he was willing to make them. Then, explain the personal sacrifices you would be willing to make in order to achieve a similar level of accomplishment in your selected field. In what ways are your goals and willingness to sacrifice to reach them like and unlike Robert Frost's?

Other assessment formats that align with the introspective nature of the Curriculum of Identity include goal statements; reflective essays; photographic essays that chronicle a student's passage from novice toward expert; a journal, a log of insights, discoveries, and/or thinking; and longitudinal portfolios. These assessment formats call upon students to reflect on their work and their role in that work. Used purposefully and systematically, these reflective assessment tasks provide students with insights that will help them make appropriate adjustments in their learning, work, and/or career orientation.

Besides reflection opportunities that can clarify students' emerging sense of self, students also need recurring opportunities to explore their developing interests. Teachers can structure opportunities for interest exploration when they provide students with multiple assessment formats.

Let's look at a third grade example. Mrs. Greene is toward the end of her unit on number sense and is working on the concept of place value. She has read aloud to her students *How Much Is a Million?* written by David Schwartz and illustrated by Steven Kellogg (1985). To assess her students' understanding of the immensity of a million, she calls upon her students to complete the following task either individually or in small groups:

Think about a favorite object, like a toy or a piece of sports equipment, a favorite food, like M&Ms or gum drops, or a favorite activity, like shooting baskets or jumping rope. Using a calculator to help you, tell me:

How much 1,000,000 of your objects might weigh, or

How long 1,000,000 of your objects would be lined up side by side, or

How tall 1,000,000 of your objects might be when stacked one on top of the other, or

How long it might take you to complete your favorite activity 1,000,000 times.

Write about your findings or draw a picture to illustrate your answer.

Students naturally focused their work around their interests. One small group of students focused their solutions around a basketball and another around a soccer ball. Lots of students were interested in the candy. One student's favorite candy bar was Snickers, and he figured out how tall 1,000,000 of them would be when stacked together, one on top of another. Mrs. Greene was especially pleased when Ben and Tanesha, who invariably disliked math, showed some enthusiasm for the task. They tried to figure out how much a million buckets of water would weigh, which was the amount of water they thought it might take to fill up the community swimming pool.

Choice with respect to assessment tasks serves two important purposes. First, choice provides students with the opportunity to gravitate to an interest area and deepen their understanding of the subject as well as their role within it. Equally important, choice provides reluctant students with a pleasurable way to engage in a discipline that has been less than satisfying. The choice may even provide reluctant students with a new way to connect with a discipline.

Another way we can align our assessment practices with the Curriculum of Identity is to incorporate opportunities for students to assess their own work and learning. Self-assessment is a powerful tool. It is the ability to be reflective, to understand one's role as a learner, and where one is developmentally with respect to a set of learning objectives.

How can students become astute assessors of the nature and quality of their work? The following features should be part of every classroom in order to help students develop the capacity to reflect meaningfully on their work.

▸ Students are familiar with the performance standards.

▸ Students have the opportunity to participate in developing the criteria by which work/performances will be assessed.

▸ Students have the opportunity to understand what the criteria mean and how they will be applied to their work.

▸ Students are provided with time to reflect on their work and draw conclusions about themselves as learners.

▸ Students are provided with time to talk about their conclusions with a peer or adult.

▸ Students are provided with thoughtful feedback about their conclusions, from peers and the teacher, to enhance the accuracy of their reflection and quality of their work.

One strategy teachers can use to promote reflection is called "Think Aloud." To use this strategy, students work in pairs, with one student playing the role of a thinker and the other of a listener. The teacher poses self-assessment questions (see Figure 7.5). Thinkers then verbalize what goes through their minds as they answer the question. Listeners pay full attention and may ask clarifying questions in order to understand the thinker's thoughts. Next, the teacher conducts a debriefing period in which responses are shared and considered. Think Alouds conducted in this fashion reveal an array of important data: what students learned, what was easy about a task or performance (their strengths), what was difficult (their weaknesses), remaining misconceptions, how students feel about themselves as learners in this content area, and how well they can reflect upon their own work and themselves as learners. The strategy allows focus on both key content and student awareness of their roles as learners.

In addition to the opportunity for self-assessment on single products and performances, all students need periodic opportunities to reflect and "take stock" of themselves as learners and workers. This kind of reflective activity serves to forward a student's vision of possible selves discussed earlier in this chapter. Extending this, reflection about three different selves is required from a student to clarify his or her possible self. Students need opportunities to think about their "past self" or "past identity." The past self is the person the student perceives that he or she was last month, last summer, or last year, for example. It is a reference point by which a student measures change, as is noted in the two examples that follow.

Carmen: I used to like dinosaurs. Now, I think I like wild animals better.

Rosa: When I was little, I always wanted to be a doctor. But now I realize that I really don't like being around sick people. I want to help people, but I don't think I'd be very happy as a doctor.

Reflection can also concern the "current self," or the vision the student has of her- or himself at the current time.

Sherita: I think I learn best when I talk to others. I know for sure that I don't like learning from my social studies textbook!

Hazel: I am not a good silent reader. Every time my teacher tells us to read in class, I nearly fall asleep.

Finally, reflection can also be about a "future self," or the vision that the student has of him- or herself in a time that has yet to come.

Lia: I have always had an interest in astronomy. I know that some day I will be involved with space exploration, but I am still not sure of the area. I won't be an astronaut, but I might like to be an engineer.

Bruce: I want to be in medical research and be the one to make a breakthrough in cancer research. I have always thought about the kind of contribution I can make to the world, and this one seems a good fit for me.

- What did I learn?
- What was easy for me?
- How might I describe my strengths?
- What was still confusing for me?
- What questions do I have that might clear up my confusion?
- Who might help me?
- Did I like being involved with this work?
- What aspects were particularly interesting?
- Would I like to continue doing this kind of work in _____ (content area)? Why or why not?

Figure 7.5   Examples of Self-Assessment Questions for the Curriculum of Identity

Students need regular opportunities to reflect on all their past, present, and future selves throughout their K–12 experience. With regularly scheduled opportunities to reflect on who they are and who they are becoming, students will find both the academic content through which they see themselves and the emergence of their own self-awareness give school a new dimension of meaning. Reflection puts students in an active role and engages each of them as the "vision maker."

The last technique that we will use to remodel our assessments for the Curriculum of Identity involves the creation of longitudinal rubrics. This curriculum parallel, which stresses development of individual capacity, requires teachers to be talent trackers. They need to be able to identify the behaviors that characterize a young mathematician, a budding scientist, a young artist, or the next Gwendolyn Brooks. Furthermore, teachers need to be able to assist students' growth in their emerging strength areas. For these reasons, teachers benefit from longitudinal rubrics that not only help them spot emerging abilities in their classroom, but also provide concrete ideas for helping a student move to the next level on the continuum of development.

Figure 7.6 provides an example of a longitudinal rubric that teachers can use to spot and nurture talent in one content area, history. It is representative of rubrics teachers can create for the various content areas.

The figure contains three columns. The first column, "Stage," does not represent the age or grade level of the student. Instead, the numbers represent the escalating stages toward expertise in history. The second column contains descriptors of likely student behaviors at each level of talent development. The descriptors are by no means comprehensive but have been selected because they are representative. The final column includes actions that a teacher or parent can initiate to support advancement of the student's growth process in the area of strength. The actions merely sample and serve to "jump-start" our thinking about the varied ways we can support the advancement of abilities in young people.

This instrument and similar forms in other content areas are effective tools for teachers who are serious about developing their students' identity. The continuum supports teachers in their efforts to identify emerging preferences and abilities in their classrooms and helps them support students' learning assets (e.g., interests, abilities, and goals) with activities that will lead, step-by-step, to satisfying and productive lives.

Teachers can support development of student preferences and abilities when they use assessment tasks that require students to reflect on their role in a discipline; provide choice with respect to assessments and products; call on students to evaluate their own work; provide students with opportunities to reflect on their past, current, and future selves; and use longitudinal rubrics to keep track of students' developing talents. In this way, teachers work dually with the content for which they and their students are responsible and with the emergence of self-identity in learners through the vehicle of that content.

Introductory Activities in the Curriculum of Identity

The purpose of each element in an introduction (for example, focusing question, needs assessment, teaser or hook, rationale, objectives, and students' interests) remains the same across all of the four curriculum parallels. What changes in the

Stage	Student Behavior	Possible Action to Support Growth to the Next Stage
1	José asks numerous questions about people and events from the past.	Read books to José about famous historical people; share historical book titles with his family so they can read to him, too.
2	As a seven-year-old, José spent much longer than any of his Grade 1 classmates looking at a diorama depicting the Battle of Lexington and Concord.	Investigate local and regional historical sites; provide names of some sites he and his family can visit.
3	When offered the opportunity, José enjoys visiting historical sites, touching historical artifacts, and reading nonfiction and fiction texts about historical topics.	Help José gather information about historical sites and artifacts; enlist the support of the library media specialist and technology specialist to get additional resources for him.
4	When given options about projects, José generally chooses alternatives that address some aspect of history.	Provide extension activities for José on topics that he enjoys; suggest other related explorations he may find equally, or even more, appealing.
5	As a young adolescent, José is beginning to make a conscious effort to attend classes, read books, and, in general, increase his knowledge of and skills regarding historical topics and methods.	Discuss the discipline of history with José; talk about the methodology of the field; explore course offerings; encourage his parents to work with the guidance counselor to select appropriate history courses.
6	José prefers and seeks out the company of peers who also enjoy history. He likes working with these students on class projects. He uses free time in scouting and community projects that address historical issues or needs.	Use community resources to determine local projects and issues related to history; use the Internet to locate other resources and projects.
7	José begins to think he might be a future historian. While he enjoys every aspect of his studies and work in history, he knows he has much to learn to become a practitioner.	Locate internships for José that will provide an in-depth look at the skills and methodologies required of the practicing professional.
8	José begins to make short-term and long-term plans for professional growth. Often, he forgoes leisure activities in order to advance his personal and professional expertise.	Locate a mentorship for José. Look for regionally or nationally based organizations that have members like José, such as historical societies; encourage José to become an active member.
9	José is thinking and working like a practitioner in the field; he is developing a knack for finding interesting questions, unexplored topics, discrepant information, and controversies in history.	Encourage and support José's frequently intense work on topics that compel him. Assist with resource acquisition. Enlist professionals to advise him and provide feedback on the nature and quality of his work.
10	José enjoys his association with colleagues who like to discuss abstract ideas, who enjoy unearthing unanswered questions, and who derive satisfaction from exploring possible answers to unanswered questions.	Help José apply for grants and fellowships; encourage his attendance and participation in local, regional, and national-level conferences and reading of professional-level materials.
11	José works with colleagues, a mentor, and alone to investigate, research, and problem solve in history.	Encourage and nurture José's research, writing, and presentation skills.
12	José realizes that history fulfills him and that history must be the focus of his life's work. His behaviors, life plans, and career will revolve around this discipline. He feels actualized by the knowledge and skills he uses; he sees his life in and through history.	Encourage José to publish his own work in journals and other related publications.

Figure 7.6   Longitudinal Rubric for Spotting and Nurturing Talent in History

Curriculum of Identity is the focus of each element based on the particular goals of this parallel. These changes are discussed below.

In a high-quality curriculum, focusing questions highlight or underscore essential concepts or principles. Focusing questions, when referred to throughout the curriculum, remind teachers and students about the major purposes of the lessons and help students reflect on, gauge, and quantify their growth. In a unit about explorers, for example, focusing questions might include these: Why do people explore? What impact does exploration have on humankind? Does exploration strengthen or weaken a society?

To incorporate aspects of the Curriculum of Identity into a curriculum, a teacher may add one or two additional focusing questions for students. These questions would be cast differently than those in the other parallels because they address the role of the student within the discipline and elicit a personal response. Within the context of the explorers unit, above, they might include any of the following.

1. Who are contemporary explorers?

2. What were they like as students? How did they spend their time? What were their interests? How did they first become interested in geography, maps, and navigation?

3. How do they spend their time at work? On what sorts of questions and issues do they spend their time?

4. In what ways do the interests and values of the contemporary explorers reflect or differ from your own?

5. In what other ways are you like the contemporary explorers?

6. In what other ways are you different from them?

In a high-quality, comprehensive curriculum unit about explorers, a teaser or "hook" might include a videotape of a blast-off into space; a copy of a personal correspondence from Marie Curie; segments of an interview with Robert Ballard, famous underwater explorer; writings and recordings from the Freedom Riders in the 1960s and 1970s and again at the turn of the new millennium; pioneers in computer technology; or pictures of frontiers over the course of history. Any one of these teasers could serve to engage and motivate the students in a general way about explorers across time.

Within the context of the Curriculum of Identity, the hook or teaser will take on an introspective or personal focus. In the same Curriculum of Identity unit on explorers, a teacher may elect to play a recording of Neil Armstrong's words as he walked on the surface of the moon: "That's one small step for man, one giant leap for mankind." As a follow-up, the teacher might ask students to engage in a small group discussion around the following prompt: "What personal characteristics did Neil Armstrong possess that enabled him to take the first steps on the lunar surface in 1969? What similarities are there between Armstrong's characteristics and your own?" Within a few minutes, students would have the opportunity to create a personal connection with the unit and be drawn into the discipline.

The rationale is another element of high-quality introductions. The rationale makes clear to students the importance of the topic. Keeping the focus on identity, a teacher might engage students in small group discussions around the following introspective questions.

1. What are the "frontiers" for your generation in the 21st century?

2. If you became an explorer in the 21st century, what might your contribution or legacy be?

3. In what ways are explorers important to you? To humankind?

A fourth element in an introduction concerns the performance standards. Within the framework of the Curriculum of Identity, teachers will share with students the performance standards that relate to self-knowledge, including, for example, the following.

1. Students will develop an appreciation for the personal characteristics of explorers across time.

2. Students will be able to compare their own personal qualities with those of explorers, past and present.

It is important to point out that not all elements in an introductory set of activities have to be replaced to align Curriculum of Identity. Teachers may elect to infuse reflective opportunities into just one or two of the elements. Teachers need to assess their students' needs, the nature of the curriculum unit, and their time frame and then make reasonable decisions regarding which introductory components to remodel in order to invite students' reflective thinking.

Teaching Methods in the Curriculum of Identity

Earlier in the book, we described teaching activities as existing along dual continua: direct to indirect methods with high to low levels of teacher or peer support. Teachers have an important task in matching teaching methods to learning goals and students' learning needs. While all types of teaching methods may be employed in the Curriculum of Identity, those that readily lend themselves to the acquisition of self-knowledge include methods that provide students with the opportunity to

1. take on or otherwise closely examine the role of the practicing professional

2. reflect on and construct self-knowledge. Coaching, demonstration/modeling, visualization, role-playing, cooperative learning, jurisprudence, simulations, inquiry-based instruction, problem-based learning, shadowing experiences, mentorships, independent study, and independent investigations are teaching strategies that effectively and efficiently promote the goals and purposes of this curriculum parallel (see Figure 3.7 in Chapter 3)

Readers will note that the teaching strategies most appropriate for the Curriculum of Identity cluster toward the indirect end of the teaching strategies continuum. Within this cluster of teaching strategies, however, a wide range still exists. Visualization, one of the more direct methods, might be employed frequently by teachers in this curriculum parallel to help students move back and forth across their past selves, present selves, and future selves.

Other strategies especially appropriate to the Curriculum of Identity include simulations, shadowing experiences, and mentorships. These methods hold great promise for students seeking insights into personally meaningful future paths. As students explore day-to-day activities of professionals, the problems and dilemmas of experts, and the texture of professional interactions that characterize a professional's role, these latter inductive teaching strategies efficiently and effectively forward student self-awareness.

Learning Activities in the Curriculum of Identity

High-quality Curriculum of Identity learning activities foster cognitive engagement: analytic, critical, and synthetic thinking. They require students to perceive, process, rehearse, store, and transfer new knowledge and skills that have been introduced in the teaching activities. While all thinking skills are important, those learning activities that draw on executive processing skills and creative thinking are especially important for the goals and purposes of the Curriculum of Identity because of their capacity to promote student reflection and analysis (see Figure 3.8 in Chapter 3).

The executive processing skills are essential. To understand the day-to-day life of the professional, the student needs to develop processing skills required in any field or discipline. These include goal setting, formulating questions, developing hypotheses, generalizing, problem solving, decision making, and planning. When students are afforded these kinds of thinking opportunities, they can actually "feel" what it is like to be the practicing professional and have a much clearer sense about what it means to be a historian, an anthropologist, a musician, a mathematician, an artist, or an environmental scientist, for example.

In a similar fashion, creative thinking skills are important. In today's workplaces, people function in diverse teams on complex problems that require creative thinking. Practicing professionals must use their imaginations freely, combine ideas or information in new ways, and make connections between seemingly unrelated ideas. It is not surprising that the SCANS report (U.S. Department of Labor, 1992) lists creative thinking, decision making, and problem solving, in that order, as the most needed skills in our country's workforce. Figure 7.7 suggests other process skills of particular relevance to goals of the Curriculum of Identity.

Grouping Strategies in the Curriculum of Identity

Teachers who work with a Curriculum of Identity will use many grouping patterns. Teachers will employ one-on-one conversations with learners to help each

- Relating self to others
- Introspection
- Balancing self-acceptance and self-critique
- Developing perspective on events
- Establishing a personal compass for decision making
- Determining significance
- Prediction
- Deducing and inducing logically
- Seeing self in varied contexts
- Self-affirmation
- Developing courage
- Reading and using contextual cues
- Learning from experience
- Pursuit of wisdom

Figure 7.7 Some Additional Process Skills Key to the Curriculum of Identity

one with a variety of skills, questions, and issues related to students' work. Certainly, it is necessary for students in the Curriculum of Identity to work alone in order to reflect on evolving insights about self in relation to the discipline. On the other hand, there will be times when discussions in a pair or small group provide a useful sounding board for insights. In some instances, it will be helpful for students to work in small groups where students share interests, preferences, goals, and ideas in order to confirm, extend, or question a particular line of thought. In other instances, it should be more instructive to work with peers whose interests and perspectives differ as a means of expanding thought. Peer editing can be especially helpful when students are involved in writing reflective essays or preparing letters of introduction, for example. Further, small group instruction will play a role, too, in managing interest-based activities, debriefing sessions, differentiation, and extension activities. Finally, teachers will use large group instruction to give directions, introduce and host guest speakers to "jump-start" students' thinking, or provide an overview of the unit, a lesson, or the students' learning and work profiles. Whole-class discussions can also help build a sense of a shared journey toward understanding what it means to find one's place in a complex world.

Resources in the Curriculum of Identity

Exemplary resources for the Curriculum of Identity are those that provide students with revealing glimpses into the personal lives and daily activities of practicing professionals. They afford students the opportunity to learn the obvious, such as the career paths and the major contributions of selected individuals. At the same time, they afford students the opportunity to learn the little known, but critical, facets about an individual's life, such as the events and colleagues that provided support during crucial episodes, the personal challenges famous people faced, and how they resolved the challenges. When students are able to visualize the human side of older, more accomplished people, it is easier for them to draw parallels between those people's lives and their own. For that reason, it is critical for students from all ethnic, language, and economic groups and from both genders to see themselves in materials and human resources used throughout the unit.

Examples of resources that can offer students these kinds of unique perspectives include human resources and nonhuman resources (see Figure 7.8). These kinds of revealing resources are readily available in museums and newspapers and on Web sites.

The critical task that teachers face is to ensure alignment among the learning goals, the learning tasks, the resources, and students' unique learning needs (e.g., reading level, learning preference, and interest areas). The following example illustrates the issue of alignment. History of Science is a science content standard category in many states' curriculum framework documents. A common performance standard, Grades 9–12, might be this: "The student will recognize that changes in science usually occur as small modifications and result in incremental understandings of the world." To accomplish this learning goal, a high school teacher might assign the following learning task.

Select a person from the accompanying list of men and women in science. In a presentation format of your choice, describe the contribution of your scientist and the impact of his or her legacy on the field. Highlight the challenges, setbacks, and successes that he or she faced in order to leave a legacy to the scientific world. Use

Resources		
Human	*Nonhuman*	
	Print	*Nonprint*
Older students	Biographies	Artifacts
Younger students	Diaries/Journals/Logs	Photographs
Other students in the classroom	E-mails	Videotaped interviews
Parents	Personal letters	Personal belongings
Other teachers	Personal correspondence	News clips
Community members	Unpublished manuscripts	Audiotaped conversations
Content area experts	Notes	Documentaries
Other school personnel	Personal scrapbooks	
University personnel	Memoirs	
Business personnel	Data sets	
Service organization personnel	Web sites	
Professional groups		
Avocational groups		

Figure 7.8   Resources That Support Student Learning in the Curriculum of Identity

at least five references, at least three of which must be primary source material (e.g., letters, photographs, personal correspondence, and audio or videotapes).

To ensure appropriate learning materials for the wide range of learner interests in the classroom, the teacher needs a variety of primary and secondary source materials on the targeted scientists. Additionally, the teacher would have to ensure a range of reading levels among the print resources to accommodate students' diverse reading needs within each interest area.

Products in the Curriculum of Identity

Teachers can draw on a variety of authentic product formats in order to help students understand the nature of products required for practicing professionals and what goes into the creation of those products (see Figure 3.9, Chapter 3). It goes without saying that products or performances should be chosen with care to (1) align with the targeted learning goals, (2) have the capacity to reveal the targeted knowledge or skill, (3) reflect the work of the practicing professional, and (4) invite student reflection in ways that produce insights about personal traits, goals, preferences, values, and ways of working compared with those same traits in those who work in or are reflected in the discipline.

Students should be afforded regular opportunities to select the format for their products. A critical component of a student's identity is his or her expression style preference. For example, some students prefer to express themselves visually; others prefer to express themselves in writing. Still others prefer to express themselves through a multimedia format. When students are provided with the opportunity to choose the way they want to express themselves, they naturally gravitate to their favored format, thereby strengthening both their capabilities within a medium and a sense of their particular strengths and interests.

Self-assessment is also a powerful facet of product assignments. When products are accompanied by quality rubrics and thoughtful teacher feedback and guidance, the self-measuring process becomes an integral part of products and performances and can "trigger" students' awareness of their place on the novice-expert growth continuum and the next steps required to move ahead in the discipline.

Extension Activities in the Curriculum of Identity

Teachers can effectively use extension activities to forward a student's self-knowledge through exploration of key content. Extension activities in the Curriculum of Identity would include individual and small group investigations derived from the curriculum unit and students' interests. They might be designed to provide participating students with opportunities to interact with practicing professionals who would share not only their work with students but also their day-to-day activities and philosophies. Extension activities could enable students to learn about the lives and work of practitioners by reading journals or diaries, using the Internet, interviewing, viewing related videos, and so on. Students might also be interested in simply reading biographies or autobiographies or examining work samples or critiques of the work of experts in fields related to the unit's content goals and student interests. Extension activities might also include introspective writings in which authors representing a wide variety of backgrounds and perspectives reflect on the same sorts of questions about themselves that the young learners will encounter in the Curriculum of Identity. Such writings are available for all ages and reading levels and can be helpful to students in understanding how it sounds when others carry on a sort of interior monologue about their interests, goals, likes and dislikes, abilities, learning patterns, and so on. Put simply, extension activities in this parallel provide students with compelling glimpses of who they are and who they might become.

At some point in a final reflection about a student's extension activity, a teacher needs to ask the student what new questions the student now has related to his or her interests, skills, values, goals, and so forth. A student's answer to this question is a "tip off" to where he or she might need to go next in thinking and exploration. When teachers take the student's questions seriously and act upon them to ensure follow-up, they once again forward a student's emerging sense of identity.

Differentiation in Response to Learner Need (Including AID) in the Curriculum of Identity

By its very nature, the Curriculum of Identity is responsive to learner variance. In this parallel, students may prepare personal profile inventories and watch the profiles change over the years. This provides a unique opportunity for students to identify emerging patterns and themes and develop individual learning goals around a deepening awareness of fit within one or more disciplines. Even within this flexible framework, however, there is a need for teachers to provide students with varying opportunities for continuous movement toward expertise within a field or discipline.

At the heart of the Curriculum of Identity is a desire to help students think about themselves and their goals in the context of the disciplines that organize human knowledge. Certainly, in all grades there are students who are already passionate about science, art, literature, mathematics, history, or music. In those same classrooms are students who have never thought of themselves as mathematicians or artists, for example, but who would do so with appropriately focused, supported, and inviting learning experiences. There are also in those classes, however, students whose struggle with school will make it difficult for them to relate to the notion of self as a geologist, biographer, cartographer, and so on. To open the window of opportunity for self-reflection a bit wider, teachers may respond to learner variance by having students reflect on themselves in relation to the topic they are studying rather than the discipline in which it is housed. One such example, given earlier in this chapter, is the teacher asking her students to reflect on themselves as explorers rather than as the historians who study and write about the explorers. It is our belief that, appropriately supported, many students would benefit from seeing themselves as early scholars or practitioners in a discipline and reflecting on what those experiences reveal to them about themselves. An approach to modifying the Curriculum of Identity in response to learner need, however, is "opening up" the window through which students are invited to view themselves so that the teacher uses both the disciplines and appropriate objects of study within the discipline to help students think about themselves. Thus one student might find it more interesting and challenging, for example, to reflect on oneself as a biographer, whereas another would find it more interesting and challenging to reflect on oneself as a soldier, hero, or pioneer about whom the biography is written.

Similarly, because students' interests and capacities develop differently, learning opportunities tailored to individuals or small groups of students will, as in the other parallels, require attention to student reading levels as well as their depth of knowledge and interest in a topic or discipline. Some additional basic approaches to Ascending Intellectual Demand are the following.

▶ Use longitudinal rubrics to help student and teacher locate and respond to a student's level of proficiency on a novice to expert continuum within a topic or discipline.

▶ Vary the resources (i.e., nonhuman and human) that students use. Nonhuman resources vary in reading difficulty, complexity, and/or the degree of inference required. Human resources vary as well because individuals have different levels of expertise within a field or domain.

▶ Increase the complexity of questions or problems with which students work and on which students reflect. Within each discipline are cutting edge problems, questions, and issues. Students can begin their search for themselves in a curricular area by being involved at a "junior level." As they demonstrate increased interest and commitment to selected fields, they can take on increasingly more complex problems.

▶ Ask students to develop their own rubrics or scales to assess the proficiency of products in a topic or discipline that holds a special interest for them (e.g., a watercolor, a dance, an essay, a debate, a professional article, a science experiment, a map).

Other more complex approaches to Ascending Intellectual Demand for advanced learners are listed in Figure 7.9, and additional ideas for supporting all learners from different content areas are expanded in Chapter 8.

Lesson and Unit Closure

Lesson and unit closure activities in the Parallel of Identity, as is the case with the other PCM parallels, allow the teacher to focus student attention on the purpose or "deep intent" of the parallel. In this case, that means the teacher uses brief closure strategies to ensure that students reflect on important concepts and principles of the discipline, as well as what students are coming to understand about themselves as learners and people with contributions to make to their world as they study a topic, discipline, and practitioners in the discipline.

Also as with the other parallels, the focusing questions of the parallel are helpful in framing brief closure activities that ensure fidelity to the parallel and stretch students' thinking about their work. Closure strategies that are in keeping with the

- Looking for and reflecting on "truths," beliefs, ways of working, styles, and so on that typify the field
- Looking for "roots" of theories, beliefs, and principles in a field and relating those theories, beliefs, and principles to the time when they "took root" in one's own life
- Looking for and reflecting on the meaning of paradoxes and contradictions in the discipline or field
- Conducting an ethnography of a facet of the discipline and reflecting on both findings and personal revelations
- Engaging in long-term problem solving on an intractable problem in the discipline that causes the student to encounter and mediate multiple points of view and reflecting systematically on the experience
- Researching and establishing standards of quality work as defined by the discipline, applying those standards to the student's own work in the discipline over an extended time period, and reflecting systematically on the experience
- Collaborating with a high-level professional or practitioner in the field in shared problem solving and reflection
- Challenging or looking for limitations of the ideas, models, ways of working, or belief systems of the discipline
- Looking for parallels (or contrasts) in personal prejudices, blind spots, assumptions, and habits and those evident in the field
- Studying and reflecting on one discipline by using the concepts, principles, and modes of working of another discipline, reflecting on the interactions and insights gained

Figure 7.9   Some Paths to Achieving Ascending Intellectual Demand for Advanced Learners in the Curriculum of Identity

intent of the Parallel of Identity include class discussion of teacher observations about students; personal journals; building a classroom matrix of strengths, preferences, and insights about class members; developing concepts and principles about motivation, contribution, diverse perspectives, ethics, persistence, creativity, and other concepts related to finding one's own identity; and using excerpts from biography, autobiography, literature, or the news help students reflect on their own needs and strengths.

An Example of the Curriculum of Identity Using Lydia's Civil War Unit

Lydia has noted Jacob's developing interest in history. She is wondering who Jacob will become over the course of the next twenty years, what her role is in helping Jacob develop his interests, whether Jacob is unusual, or whether each student has a unique set of interests and abilities she can help nurture. She wonders also how a teacher blends a need to ensure student mastery of designated content and awareness of an evolving self.

Content (Including Standards)

Lydia wasn't quite sure where to start. She looked over her content standards. They helped her achieve clarity about the knowledge, concepts, principles, and skills of her curriculum. There was nothing in the standards, however, related to students' interests, abilities, or values.

Lydia's thoughts returned to her students. She sensed that the Curriculum of Identity had to incorporate students' development as people as well as content development. How would she know enough about her students to begin to intelligently take them into account in her planning?

Assessments

That afternoon, after the close of school, Lydia walked down the hall to talk with Ed Lester, a colleague who could help her with some student profile surveys.

"There are many advantages to using surveys like these," Ed shared. "First, they help me collect important information about students' learning strengths. Second, I use the information contained in the profile to analyze how I can optimize the 'fit' between the students and instruction. For example, I always provide opportunities for students to pursue an area of interest. Often, I encourage students to work in a preferred learning style (for example, by talking with others, listening to a speaker, reading) or in a preferred grouping (for example, working alone, with a partner, or with a group). I also use the document in a conference with each student. Together we review the profile, analyze how it has changed over time, and discuss ways we can further the student's interests, abilities, goals, or questions."

Ed continued, "I combine what is on the learner profile with what I have come to know about each student firsthand. Then, using a longitudinal rubric to help me, I try to figure out where the student might 'fit' on the novice-expert continuum in his or her preferred content area, like math or science." Ed pulled out a folder and took out the longitudinal rubric for history (see Figure 7.6). "Jacob, you see, is someplace around Stage 4 or 5 on this history continuum. Once I locate his approximate place on the scale, it is much easier for me to determine possible next steps that will advance him toward expertise."

Lydia decided she'd begin with the learner profile surveys. She'd tally what she learned from the surveys to get a rough sense of the distribution of characteristics across her students as well. Figure 7.10 notes the categories in Ed's student profile surveys.

Lydia was compelled by the power the profiles held for her students and her instruction. First, she thought, the learning and work profile would help her gather important baseline information about her students. She would certainly know her students better after she collected this kind of information. In turn, she could better help her students reflect on themselves as learners. Second, if she could capitalize on her students' abilities and interests, she knew that she would be able to increase their motivation for learning. She always found teaching more rewarding when students were engaged with the lessons she taught. She thought, too, that if her students were really engaged, their academic achievement should increase as well.

When she got home, Lydia laid Ed's profile survey on her dining room table. She didn't feel confident enough to collect or use all the information that Ed described. She looked at the document and said to herself, "I think I'll begin by asking students about their interests, their abilities, and how they like to learn best."

1. **Abilities/Subject Area Preference** (i.e., reading, writing, spelling, mathematics, social studies, science, art, or music)
2. **Product Preferences/Expression Style Preference** (i.e., reports, talking, projects, art work, pictures or charts, displays, acting, or helping others)
3. **Learning Preference** (i.e., talking with others, listening to a speaker, reading, watching or viewing, games, computers, pretending, or making something)
4. **Grouping Preference** (i.e., working alone, working with a partner, working in a group, or working with an adult)
5. **General Interest** (i.e., performing arts, creative writing or journalism, mathematics, business or management, athletics, history, social action, fine arts and crafts, or science, and technology)
6. **Specific Interest** (i.e., a special section where students can list high-interest topics they already have)
7. **Cocurricular Activity** (i.e., lessons and activities outside school)
8. **My Goal for the Year** (i.e., a personally meaningful objective)

Figure 7.10   Categories in Ed's Student Profile Survey

Lydia decided to create a much simpler one-page profile that she felt comfortable using with her students. She planned to talk with students first before they completed any information on the profile. She wanted to explain the importance of the document and how she planned to use the information that they provided to alter some of the components of her instruction in the upcoming unit on the Civil War. Figure 7.11 illustrates Lydia's survey.

She liked her format where everything fit on one page. She included the most essential learning characteristics she could think of: student interests, their abilities, their preferred ways to learn, and their expression style preferences. She was especially pleased with the two-column format that encouraged students to think about themselves now and in the future. Lydia knew her fifth graders did not often think of their "future selves." This learning and work profile should begin to prompt their thinking about who they might like to become, a key goal of the Curriculum of Identity.

Introductory Activities

After the fifth graders completed the survey, Lydia tallied the results for the class (see Figure 7.12). While there was quite a bit of diversity among her students, she was excited about the new information she had. After some reflection about her students and content goals, she decided to make five adjustments in her upcoming Civil War unit compared with the unit she created earlier using the Core Curriculum Parallel. First, she would change her introduction to orient students to many ways people can be historians. Second, she would invite two guest speakers to talk about their work as historians. Third, she would focus on students' specific interests and abilities through interest-based groups and extension activities. Fourth, she would have the students work as historians at some points in the unit.

Subject Areas	I Like This	I Want to Become Good at This
Reading		
Writing		
Spelling		
Mathematics		
Social Studies		
Science		
Art		
Music		
PE		
Other		

Preferred Ways to Learn	I Like This	I Want to Become Good at This
Talking With Others		
Reading		
Viewing		
Games		
Computers		
Pretending		
Making/Doing		
Working Alone		
Working With a Partner		
Working With a Group		
Working With an Adult		
Choices and Options		
Detailed Directions		

Showing How I Learn	I Like This	I Want to Become Good at This
Reports		
Talking		
Projects		
Artwork		
Pictures/ Charts		
Displays		
Acting		
Helping Others		
Media		
Other _____		

My Interests	I Like This	I Might Like This
Performing Arts		
Creative Writing/ Reading		
Mathematics		
Business		
Athletics		
History		
Social Action		
Fine Arts		
Science		
Technology/Video Games		
Other _____		

Figure 7.11 Lydia's Learning and Work Profile Survey

Subject Areas	I Like This	I Want to Become Good at This
Reading	|||	
Writing	||||	
Spelling	|||	
Mathematics	||	
Social Studies	||||	
Science	LHT	
Art	LHT		
Music	|||	
PE	LHT |||	
Other		

Preferred Ways to Learn	I Like This	I Want to Become Good at This
Talking With Others	LHT	
Reading	LHT ||	
Viewing		
Games	LHT |||	
Computers	||||	
Pretending		
Making/Doing	||	
Working Alone	||	
Working With a Partner	LHT		
Working With a Group	LHT |||	
Working With an Adult	|||	
Choices and Options	LHT LHT	
Detailed Directions	||||	

Showing How I Learn	I Like This	I Want to Become Good at This
Reports			
Talking	|||	
Projects	LHT ||||	
Artwork	||||	
Pictures/ Charts	LHT ||	
Displays	LHT	
Acting			
Helping Others	||||	
Media	|||	
Other ___		

My Interests	I Like This	I Might Like This
Performing Arts	|||	|||
Creative Writing/ Reading	|||	|||
Mathematics		
Business		
Athletics	LHT		LHT ||
History	||	||
Social Action		
Fine Arts	||||	
Science		||
Technology/Video Games	||||	LHT
Other _____		

Figure 7.12 Lydia's Class Tally of Student Profile Surveys

Finally, she would have the students reflect systematically on how their study teaches them about themselves. These changes would allow her to continue the unit's focus on her required content goals while also making an opportunity for students to use the work of historians to learn more about themselves.

Products and Resources

In addition, Lydia thought about the power that authentic products might hold for her students. She decided to bring in products designed by historians to invite her students into the study of history. She found copies of some photographs taken at the time of the Civil War, copies of political cartoons from the time period, pictures of museum exhibits about the Civil War, copies of newspaper articles written about Civil War battles, a film and video about the Civil War, and grade-level fiction and nonfiction books about this time in history. During her unit introduction and throughout the unit she would share these products with her students. She would talk with them about historians and make clear that historians share their knowledge about the past in different ways, all of which contribute to our understanding of people and events. She hoped this approach to introducing the unit would help her students begin the process of considering the work and lives of historians.

Lydia added some new resources to her unit to direct the unit toward the goals of the Curriculum of Identity. She planned to invite two practicing professionals in areas related to the Civil War to speak to her class. The work of Willis Taylor, a local historian, and Sam Gelston, a newspaper reporter, centered on history. Mr. Taylor was known for his long-standing interest in the stories from local homeowners who had convincing evidence that their homes were used as stations on the Underground Railroad. She wanted Mr. Taylor to be able to share with students (1) his stories about homes in town that had been part of the Underground Railroad Network, (2) how he had collected his stories—his methodology as a historian, (3) how students could work as historians to learn about their families, school, or community, (4) his day-to-day life as a historian, and (5) how his work as a historian has changed both him and their town. Mr. Gelston, a reporter for the local paper, had covered the war in Vietnam. She wanted him to (1) describe for students what wars are like, (2) tell them about the job of a war correspondent, (3) explain how he became interested in his job, and (4) say why he believes being a journalist and historian is a good match for him.

Grouping Strategies, Learning Activities, and Teaching Methods

Lydia's third adjustment in the Core Curriculum to change its focus to a Curriculum of Identity involved use of interest-based small group work and extension activities. She began immediately to plan these elements of her curriculum. To get started, she reviewed the learner profiles—specifically the section on students' interests. "How can I accommodate all these interests in a Civil War unit?" she wondered.

She thought about the different ways historians share their knowledge. She drew a diagram like the one in Figure 7.13. Down the left side of the page, she placed the interests of her students as reflected on their profile surveys, as well as

Students interests and co-curricular activities	What aspect of this unit on the Civil War might align with students' interests?
Music 3 students	African American spirituals, Fife and Drum Corps music
Reading 3 students	Historical fiction and nonfiction
Sports 6 students	Battle strategies, war tactics
History 2 students	Primary source documents, multiple viewpoints, videos and films, letters
Art 4 students	Political cartoons, pen and ink drawings, daguerreotypes, engravings, paintings
Video Games 4 students	Simulations, Civil War reenactments

Figure 7.13 Lydia's Chart to Align Civil War Content With Students' Interests

the number of students with the interest. In the top of the right area of the chart, she wrote her question about addressing student interest. In the rest of the chart, she wrote down aspects in the unit that matched her students' interests. She knew that students' interests were a powerful indicator of their emerging sense of self.

Lydia thought about the elements she should consider in her planning. What she needed to do was construct learning tasks for students that focused clearly on the major information, concepts, principles, and skills she needed to teach while also using students' interests as a context for learning the content or a format for products through which students expressed what they learned. For example, some of Lydia's students were interested in art. To tap into that interest, she might ask students to observe paintings from the Civil War period to see how they depicted events and conditions students were learning about and also to reflect on ways in which artists can play the role of historian. To address the interest of students who particularly enjoy video games and sports, Lydia could have students use appropriate Web sites to learn about military strategies in a key battle they would study in class and to examine ways contemporary historians are using Internet technology to preserve history. She would plan some of these interest-based activities as small group tasks through which all learners would work toward the same learning goals but do so in a variety of formats. Other interest-based options would become part of the extension activities Lydia would offer to her fifth graders.

Extension Activities

Another modification Lydia made to her unit to accommodate the Curriculum of Identity was extension activities. She planned these activities for students with a special desire to learn more about a topic that interested them. The extension activities, she knew, would arise from activities in the unit that prompted interesting student questions. In all these areas, Lydia made sure to include topics, authors, experts, mentors, and beneficiaries of contributions from the field that reflected both genders and a broad range of cultural and economic backgrounds.

Lydia continued with her plans for the Civil War unit and completed the arrangements for her two guest speakers. She asked Willis Taylor to visit the class near the beginning of the unit to pique her students' interest in the Civil War. She asked Sam Gelston to come about halfway through the unit because she wanted her students to have a basic understanding about the two different perspectives during the war that would pave the way for his talk about potential bias in newspaper accounts.

She was not surprised at the close attention her students provided both guest speakers. Although shy at first, the students warmed quickly to both Mr. Taylor and Mr. Gelston.

Lydia took time after each speaker left to talk with her students about what they heard. She used three different types of questions to help her students connect the content of the presentation with the Civil War and the attitudes, values, and skills of each presenter. She made a point to introduce her students to the visualization process in this debriefing. If students were to see themselves as future historians or war correspondents, they needed to be able to imagine these experienced adults as youngsters who were once very much like themselves. Figure 7.14 lists some of Lydia's questions for follow-up discussions.

To ensure that her students reflected on their own interests, goals, values, backgrounds, and preferences in comparison with those of the speakers, Lydia gave her students a brief reflective assignment at the conclusion of the last speaker's presentation. They used the following prompt.

Category	*Question*
Thinking Back	1. In two or three sentences, summarize what you just heard about the Underground Railroad, the Civil War, the job of the historian/journalist.
	2. What information did you already know?
	3. What was new to you?
	4. What kinds of skills and personality traits does the historian/war correspondent need to develop to be "good" at what he/she does?
	5. What other things does it take to be a good historian? A good war correspondent?
Thinking About Similarities	1. Visualize Mr. Taylor and Mr. Gelston when they were fifth graders. What interests, goals, and skills might they have had?
	2. In what ways are your interests, personality traits, goals, and skills like Mr. Taylor's? Mr. Gelston's?
	3. What do these similarities tell you about yourself?
Thinking About Differences	1. Visualize Mr. Taylor and Mr. Gelston again when they were in fifth grade.
	2. How are your interests, personality traits, goals, and skills different from theirs?
	3. What do these differences tell you about yourself?

Figure 7.14 Questions for Student Reflection in the Curriculum of Identity

Look over the learning profile that you completed recently. Based on what you know about yourself, explain what kind of a war correspondent or historian you might become. Write about yourself first as a historian then as a war correspondent. In what ways would each of these roles be interesting to you? Not interesting? How well would each role cause you to use your interests, goals, and strengths? In what ways is each role a poor fit for your interests, goals, and strengths?

Lydia was not surprised by Jacob's paragraphs. He stated up front that he was sure he wanted to be a historian. She was a bit surprised, however, by William's paper. He was a young man who remained an enigma to her. He was so quiet that Lydia often wondered what he was thinking about in class. His paper was serious in tone. William said he thought war correspondents were heroic because they risked so much to bring back important stories for people to read. Lydia made a mental note to follow up with William.

Lydia didn't have to wait long for her opportunity to speak with William. Later that week, she explained to the class what an extension activity was and made a few suggestions of options that could help them learn more about the life and work of historians. She also encouraged the students to develop their own ideas for extension activities based on questions they had or ideas that were interesting to them in their study of the Civil War to this point. Later, she asked who wanted to pursue an extension activity related to the Civil War. Four students raised their hands, and one was William. She asked to see the small group of students just before recess that afternoon.

Lydia worked with Jacob first. In talking with him, she learned of his particular interest in weapons. They decided he would try to find a historian to interview whose work related to weaponry in the Civil War. An Internet interview was one option.

Shauna and Beth wanted to read more about young women who fought as soldiers during the war. They had heard Lydia talk about the book *Girl in Blue* by Ann Rinaldi (2001), a story about Sarah Wheelock, who disguised herself as a boy and worked as a male nurse in the Civil War. They would read some additional historical fiction about women in the Civil War and also learn about how the authors of the books did their research to write historical fiction. William wanted to read more diary entries and newspaper accounts written by or about Union and Confederate soldiers. He didn't know yet quite what he wanted to do with what he learned but thought he might like to write some original poems. Lydia suggested he could look at poems based on history and see how those writers used the subject matter of history to write poetry. She now had a clearer sense that William's thoughts were more intense and deeper than those of many students his age.

Lydia shared the students' ideas for extension activities with Ed. He volunteered to help both Lydia and the students. He recommended that Lydia send the students to his room once a week during social studies so he could help them plan their investigations. Lydia felt relieved. She was glad to work with the students on their ideas but knew Ed had materials and experiences that would help them as well.

For example, Lydia was delighted when Ed shared a project self-evaluation form with her (see Figure 7.15). In particular, she liked the way it required students to reflect on their new learning, as well as the prompt that asked them to think about new questions they might have.

ASSESSING MY LEARNING

Please fill in the information about your project. Then read each question below. Rate yourself on a scale from 1 to 5, with 1 being the lowest and 5 being the highest. Explain your answers.

Name: _____

Project Title: _____

Goal 1: _____

Goal 2: _____

Goal 3: _____

1. How well did you achieve your goals?   1 2 3 4 5

2. How well did you learn new information and ideas? (Please explain below.)   1 2 3 4 5

3. How well did you learn new skills? (Please explain below.)   1 2 3 4 5

4. How well did you use new tools or methods? (Please explain below.)   1 2 3 4 5

5. How well did you learn new things about yourself? (Please explain below.)   1 2 3 4 5

6. What part of your work makes you the most proud?

7. If you had to do your project over again, what would you change and why?

8. How does your work show that you have grown or improved in some way?

9. What new question do you have? How can I help you begin to find your answer?

Figure 7.15 Ed's Student Self-Assessment Form

An additional adaptation Lydia included in her revised unit was a whole-class product that would allow students to work as historians on a common product. Based on the presentation by Willis Taylor about local involvement in the Underground Railroad, Lydia would lead her students to research that portion of their community history through the use of a variety of primary and secondary resources.

Mr. Taylor agreed to provide suggestions for their work and give them feedback as they progressed. Ultimately, students would develop a brochure on houses in their town that once served as stations on the Underground Railroad. The brochure would be targeted at young visitors to the historic houses and would include a section on students as historians. Even though this product would not require exhaustive research, it would give students a shared experience with doing historical research, drawing and supporting conclusions based on what they learned, and communicating accurate and informative data in an interesting way. This shared experience would also provide a great laboratory for group reflection on the methods and contributions of historians, the traits and interests required to be a historian, and how these elements helped them understand their own strengths and interests.

The final adaptation Lydia made in the Curriculum of Identity unit on the Civil War was taking care to ensure that students regularly considered the roles of varied kinds of historians and their products and contributions, and to link those learning experiences with student reflection on what they learned about the Civil War, the work and contributions of historians, and their own profiles. She had already built some of these reflections into introductory activities, student profile surveys, particular learning activities including visits with the guest speakers, the interest and extension activities, and the community history product. She would take care to use brief class discussions, student journal entries, and small group sharing to focus consistently on this aspect of the unit.

Lydia looked back at her work on the Curriculum of Identity. She was proud of her progress and of the emphasis on student identity that she had incorporated in the Civil War unit. The five major changes she had made to her unit—the introduction, two guest speakers, interest-based groups and extension activities, the shared community history project, and continual reflection on students' thinking about their own profiles as learners and workers through the lens of the historian—aligned her curriculum with the goals of the Curriculum of Identity.

Differentiation in the Components of the Curriculum of Identity Based on Learner Need, Including (AID)

Lydia knew the Curriculum of Identity unit was abstract and entered new territory for most of her students. In reflecting on students' differences in readiness to learn and degree of sophistication as a learner, she knew she needed to consider three questions. First, how would she support the success of students for whom introspection and abstract thinking were difficult? Second, how would she help her students come to understand that people from varied cultures, genders, and economic groups impact and are impacted by the field? Third, what would she do to ensure challenge for those students who found even the level of complexity and ambiguity in this unit to be insufficiently challenging?

For students needing extra help and support, she would certainly make sure to have a variety of media available in resource materials and to make certain there were plenty of materials in a range of readability suited to her students for whom reading continued to be difficult. She would also model and provide sample responses to abstract questions to give students images of the sorts of thinking called for in activities requiring reflection. Lydia could also lead small group discussions in which students could formulate their responses with teacher guidance and peer input. Further, she could begin with these students by emphasizing questions with more concrete answers, such as ways historians express themselves and descriptions of their working environments. She would also be attentive to indications of student interest in and comfort with topics in the unit. It might be, for example, that some students would find it more comfortable to think about themselves in relation to soldiers, farmers, merchants, or conductors in the Underground Railroad than in relation to the work of the historian. If this proved to be the case, she would encourage the students to make comparisons that worked for them. After all, the goal of the Curriculum of Identity is self-discovery. If that happens through one lens better than another, so be it.

For students whose thinking "pushed against the edges" of her unit's requirements, Lydia would provide more complex resources, emphasize the use of primary documents, and present resources that reflected widely divergent perspectives on the content or on what it means to work as a historian. She might also take a lead from the Curriculum of Connections and have the students study similarities and differences among historians, their methods, and their contributions in several time periods or in countries with differing cultures or types of government. Certainly, she would meet with these students to set criteria for their products and personal reflections that genuinely tested their skills. Two related goals she would use for these students were (a) being certain students saw truly expert-level criteria for historical writing and products and (b) having students articulate some of their own goals for personal excellence in research, writing, and production. The gifted education specialist and the two guest speakers could also help with this advanced level of standards setting. Finally, she might introduce these students to critiques of historians and famous people who were important in the unit. It could be useful to very deep thinkers to confront the reality of criticism as a part of life—even the lives of those whom we think of largely in terms of success and praise.

Through all of these approaches—and the unit as a whole—Lydia would ensure that her students encountered a wide range of people who contributed to and benefited from the study of history in general and of the Civil War in particular. She wanted each of her students to recognize himself or herself in the work and biography of historians. In selecting guest presenters, mentors, writers, video and audio resources, and consumers of history, she would be conscious of demonstrating the broad range of contributors to the history of the Civil War and the broad range of people who benefited from carefully developed and maintained histories of the Civil War.

Lydia reflected back on her work with the Curriculum of Identity and was convinced her time had been well spent. First, she felt she knew her students personally much more than in past years of her teaching. Now, when she looked at the faces in front of her, the students were much better defined in her thinking. She had a better sense of the abilities and dreams of her students. She also had a clearer sense of how she could help nurture those abilities and dreams. She truly felt that she had reached a turning point in her career. Until recently, she envisioned herself simply as a teacher. Now, she also saw herself as a steward entrusted with the evolving identities of twenty-six remarkable young people.

Lydia also saw clear evidence that students were more cognizant of their own interests, abilities, and working preferences. She was still amazed at conversations among her students in which they shared interests and insights with one another. Provided with consistent opportunities to reflect on their interests, abilities, values, and goals in relationship to practicing professionals, she felt confident that the students would make more confident and informed decisions in their lives.

It was also evident that student motivation in her class was very high. Students were highly engaged with the guest speakers, small group tasks, personal reflections, and community history project. Somehow, the combination of personal relevance in the subject matter and the expectation to work and think like professionals gave the class a new sense of dignity.

Lydia knew she was not yet through learning about the possibilities of curriculum. In fact, she was eager for the next challenge. It occurred to her that, like her students, she was moving along a continuum toward expertise, and she liked the feel of it.

Unit and Lesson Closure

While Lydia designed a portion of her Curriculum of Identity closure activities to ensure student clarity on essential information, skills, concepts, and principles from the Civil War unit, she made sure that the closure activities served as a catalyst for student reflection on what they were learning about themselves through their study of the Civil War, history, and historians.

Lydia used the Curriculum of Identity focus questions as she developed closure activities to ensure that she and her students considered multiple aspects of their evolving self-awareness. Two closure activities she found to be particularly interesting to her students involved a bulletin board gallery of student photos and information and a class blog. The bulletin board was called "Tomorrow's Experts," and contained a photo of each student, a data card for each student, and a set of columns on which the teacher or students could check attributes of contributors in history that they believed were important about themselves. Lydia made notes as she observed her students working. During lesson closure, she would often ask students whether a particular characteristic of contributors to history or actors in history pertained to them. After a brief explanation, she or the students would check attributes on the columns by their photo or add a statement to their data cards that seemed significant in thinking about themselves in relation to history. All of the work was done in pencil, and students could modify the cards and columns at any point.

The second popular closure activity resulted in a class blog. As students developed principles related to the work of historians or to their own work, Lydia or a student would add the principle to the blog with the day's date and a brief explanation of their thinking. She could review the blog with students during subsequent classes and closure activities. In addition, parents and students enjoyed reviewing the blog as well. Over time, Lydia and a number of her students added materials, reflections, and other representations of their work with the Identity study of the Civil War as well. The blog not only encouraged students to reflect on what they were learning about history and themselves, but also proved to be useful in understanding how students can learn about themselves by studying history and historians and achieve a deeper understanding about history and historians by reflecting on themselves.

Looking Back and Ahead

The Curriculum of Identity Parallel is unique among the other parallels in the Parallel Curriculum Model. Whereas the other parallels focus on facts, concepts, principles, skills, and connections, the Curriculum of Identity Parallel extends the focus to include affective components: interests, appreciations, values, attitudes, and, eventually, a life outlook.

In spite of the different focal points of the four parallels, they are all tightly entwined. Understanding the essential framework and meaning of a discipline is key to making meaning across disciplines, to practicing in a discipline in an authentic way, and to examining the goals and practices of a discipline as it relates to one's own development. Likewise, to practice in a discipline is to understand it better. To connect the discipline with self strengthens connections one might make within and across disciplines in varied times, places, cultures, and so on.

In fact, the interconnectedness of the four parallels in the Parallel Curriculum Model points to their potential flexibility for teachers designing curricula for individuals and groups to address a range of purposes. The final chapter in the book explores the concept of Ascending Intellectual Demand in the context of four core content areas.

Ascending Intellectual Demand in the Parallel Curriculum Model

By Kelly Hedrick & Jenny Sue Flannagan

Recently, a teacher colleague commented on her most daunting challenge as a K–12 educator: designing curriculum and instruction that "cover" the standards, challenge all children to maximize their potential, honor the academic and socioemotional needs of all students, and stay within the limitations imposed by mandated testing and local pacing guidelines. In her frustration was a sincere desire to do all of this and more. In truth, covering all of the bases seems impossible to many teachers, especially the most talented and dedicated of our field because they want it to be the best for all students. Unfortunately, many teachers find that the too numerous to count "tools" they are given (e.g., pacing charts, state and local standards, textbooks and related resources) rarely serve as tools at all. Instead, teachers often randomly select various elements of curriculum design and instructional delivery in the hopes that they will somehow find the combination that leads to units and lesson plans in which all children learn. This is due, in part, to the lack of a coherent, comprehensive curriculum framework.

The Parallel Curriculum Model (PCM) introduces a model for curriculum design that embeds the tenets of high-quality curriculum with attention to instructional delivery. In the PCM, teachers find a thoughtful blend of the best of what we know about high-quality curriculum and instruction: conceptually based, rigorous, meaningful to the learner, engaging, and authentic to the discipline. The PCM serves as a framework for thoughtful curriculum design and provides a context for the numerous tools teachers often misuse or dismiss out of frustration.

At the heart of the PCM is the notion that each learner should be challenged with incremental sophistication. Each learning experience is just above the easy reach of the learner who remains challenged and engaged because the curriculum and instruction are designed to move the learner from present ground toward expertise in the subject matter.

Ascending Intellectual Demand: The Path to Expertise

Expertise is developed over time, with careful attention to the tender balance of challenge and support. In order to effectively guide the process of developing expertise in any discipline, the authors propose a heuristic for thinking about this progression through the lens of Ascending Intellectual Demand (AID) (Tomlinson, Kaplan, Purcell, Leppien, Burns, & Strickland, 2006). AID is intended to serve as a guide in curriculum design and instructional delivery because it articulates the changes that characterize the learner at incremental stages from novice to expert. Teachers who draw from the heuristics recognize that as the student's optimal level of challenge shifts from one stage of readiness to the next, the curriculum must increase in sophistication, depth, and complexity to respond to the emerging optimal level of challenge in every learner. AID also serves as a bridge between curriculum design and instructional delivery as it focuses the teachers on what students are learning, how they are changing as learners en route to expertise, and what the learners need at each stage along the continuum from novice to expert. In order to effectively plan with AID in mind, the teacher must recognize the characteristics of a learner at each stage en route to expertise and respond to the needs of the learner through appropriate scaffolds, models, and strategies.

The heuristic is designed to be a planning tool for K–12 teachers. With a clear understanding of the characteristics and needs of each emergent learner en route to expertise, teachers are more likely to purposefully select assessment tools, interpret assessment data with accuracy, and use assessment data to create responsive curriculum and instruction. In order to create appropriate experiences for all learners along the AID continuum, it is equally important to understand which scaffolding techniques, curriculum models, and instructional strategies are the most appropriate for each stage along the continuum. Using AID, teachers plan with the pacing charts, state and local standards, textbooks, and related resources as they align the most appropriate models, strategies, and scaffolds for learners at each stage of the continuum. Regardless of the discipline of study, the goals for knowledge, understanding, and skills for each unit and each course in a K–12 scope and sequence are thoughtfully articulated and serve as the basis for curriculum design and instructional delivery.

Planning Backwards From Expertise

Two friends recently planned a white water rafting expedition. One friend has been taking these trips for years and has considerable knowledge and skill in this area, while the other does not. In preparation for the trip, they looked through the experienced rafter's picture album that detailed the many white water rafting trips she has taken over the years. In the early pictures, there seemed to be very few riffles in the water. The waves were small and as she explained, there were few if any obstructions that required maneuvering the raft. As the more experienced rafter described these easy trips, which were mostly floating down the river, it was clear that little to no knowledge or skill were required, perfect for a beginner. The next few trips moved beyond the easy beginning ones. In the photos were fairly frequent and visible rapids, and the veteran rafter explained that on these medium level trips, the courses were generally obvious, but some maneuvering was required. Tough at first, she explained that the more of these trips she went on, the more skillful she became with the support and specific feedback of her expert guide. Next, she shared what were described as "difficult" and "very difficult" expeditions. In the difficult rafting trips, there were numerous rapids and the narrow passages required several complex maneuvers. She explained that these trips were the ones where she initially felt very unsure of herself, but by the end of several of these difficult-level adventures, she was stronger and more confident with her skills. She said that she had to be patient with herself and persistent because she didn't master the maneuvers quite as easily as in the earlier levels of difficulty.

The newcomer to rafting was particularly intrigued as her friend described the skill level of very difficult. These trips involved long rapids with high, irregular waves and boulders as well as swift currents. Different from the early stages, the course in the very difficult level was not obvious and the rafters needed to scout from the banks. She explained that she had really mastered this level and what seemed tough at first, now seemed easy. To the novice, the water in the pictures seemed anything but easy. The experienced rafter then shared a few pictures taken more recently when she began rafting at the exceedingly difficult level. On these trips, she was faced with continuously rocky rapids with irregular broken water that could not be avoided, as well as a fast flow, abrupt bends in the course, and strong cross currents. The knowledge, skill, and strength required at this level were clearly well above the levels that precede it. Half jokingly, the novice asked her friend if there were any levels beyond exceedingly difficult. She responded that yes, there were, and rafters call it limit of navigability. In this level, the upper limits of skill and equipment are required. She explained that this upper level calls for risk taking only for experts.

The levels of challenge from novice to expert are found in all disciplines and fields. In every area, people begin as novices and move along the continuum toward expertise as knowledge, understanding, skills, and habits of mind are developed. It requires that at each stage along the continuum, the expert-in-the-making is provided with a level of challenge just above easy mastery, support in the form of scaffolds, and appropriate experiences that are matched to the individual's needs at the current stage. As a learner progresses through a level, challenges become incrementally greater, scaffolds are slowly removed and often replaced with new ones, and learning experiences are modified to match the needs of the learner as progress is made toward expertise. For the teacher or coach who supports the learner on the continuum from novice to expert, it is critically important that work at every stage on the continuum mirrors expertise.

In reflecting on the degrees of difficulty in white water rafting, finding a trip that would be at an appropriate level of challenge for both friends would be impossible.

To go on a trip at her level would clearly prove dangerous for a novice, while a trip at the easy level would not be enjoyable for the expert rafter who was ready for near expert-level conditions and challenges. The experienced rafter's knowledge, understanding, and skills far surpassed the novice's. For her to join her friend on a trip at the easy level would not likely be enjoyable since she is clearly ready for near-expert level conditions and challenges. Their disparate levels of experience, knowledge, understanding, and skills are similar to the variance in many classrooms.

This dilemma mirrors several challenges that teachers face on a regular basis: How do I develop expertise in all students? How do I help students with varied backgrounds and experiences and a range of knowledge, understanding, and skills? How do I maximize potential and develop expertise while covering content and following pacing guides? What combination of resources should I use in order to accomplish these goals?

AID offers a starting point: begin with the goal of all students becoming experts and work backwards from this goal while planning curriculum and instruction. Keep in mind that K–12 classrooms are filled with experts-in-the-making and that every choice a teacher makes in curriculum design and instructional delivery is intended to mirror the knowledge, understanding, skills, and habits of mind of the experts in each discipline and in each field associated with the disciplines. How do we judge whether or not we are mirroring expertise? Put simply, if an expert in any discipline or field were to examine the lessons, activities, tasks, and products in which we have our students involved and comment, "That has nothing to do with the way I work" then we have missed the goal entirely. Recently, a second grade teacher who was trained in AID and the PCM was preparing her students for conducting observations in a science lesson. As she distributed the plastic hand lenses she told her budding scientists, "Boys and girls, in the real world if scientists were going to make observations of plant parts, they would use sophisticated magnifying glasses and microscopes. We don't have that type of equipment in our school, but we do have these hand lenses. They are as close as we can get to the tools of a scientist, but I'm sure we can see the plant parts close enough to make our observations and create our diagrams in our science journals. So even though we don't have the fancy equipment, we can still use these tools to make our observations like scientists would do. How does that sound to you?" This teacher is clear on what matters in the organization of her curriculum and instruction: all students are entitled to work that mirrors expertise; all students are capable; and her job is to provide authentic experiences for students in order to develop the knowledge, understanding, skills, and dispositions that form the foundation of expertise.

Understanding the AID Continuum

The AID continuum was developed as a tool for thinking about the development of expertise in learners. Figure 8.1 outlines the characteristics of each level of the continuum. This visual representation of the progression toward expertise can be used by teachers in planning appropriate learning experiences for students across a range of readiness levels in knowledge, understanding, skills, and disposition. Effective use of AID is built upon five key assumptions:

▸ The primary goal of high quality curriculum and instruction is the development of knowledge, understanding, skills, and dispositions associated with expertise in all learners.

▸ The foundation for expertise is developed in K–12 classrooms with careful alignment of content, models, strategies, scaffolds, and learner needs.

▸ Expertise is developed over time with careful attention to balancing appropriate levels of challenge and support.

▸ The process of expertise development is highly personalized to the learner.

▸ The teacher continuously assesses the learner at each stage of the continuum to determine learner characteristics, learner needs, and the most efficient and effective instructional responses.

As teachers use the AID continuum, it is important to understand the end goal: the development of expertise in all learners. Understanding the stages of the progression toward expertise is the first step in using the heuristic to plan high-quality curriculum and instruction. With the learner characteristics of the each stage of the continuum in mind, the responsive teacher plans curriculum and instruction by aligning models and strategies with the needs of the learner. Figure 8.2 highlights the needs of learners for each level of the continuum. Effective teachers understand that time at each stage on the AID continuum is not a fixed entity. Some learners will advance quickly developing the knowledge, skills, and dispositions necessary for work beyond their current stage. Other learners will make slow and steady progress through each stage over a longer period of time. Responsive teachers acknowledge this variance and plan for a range of learners across each stage, keeping in mind that the end goal is the development of expertise in all learners. Planning teaching and learning for this range of learners within and across the stages requires flexibility in teacher practice and the use of a variety of scaffolds to support learners. It is important to remember that the intent of using a scaffold is to provide support for the learner so that he may master challenging content and skills. As this occurs, ongoing assessment of learner needs provides the information necessary to determine when a scaffold may be modified, added, or removed. And understanding the needs of the learner in order to design appropriate levels of challenge, balanced with support structures, necessitates teacher clarity on the characteristics of the learner at each stage on the AID continuum.

In using the AID continuums, it is also very important to remember that movement toward expertise in any endeavor is neither entirely linear nor single-faceted. It typifies a growth progression that learners build increasing competence in a given area of study, but "regress" in movement toward expertise when they encounter new content and other variables. For that reason, the arrows near the bottom of the

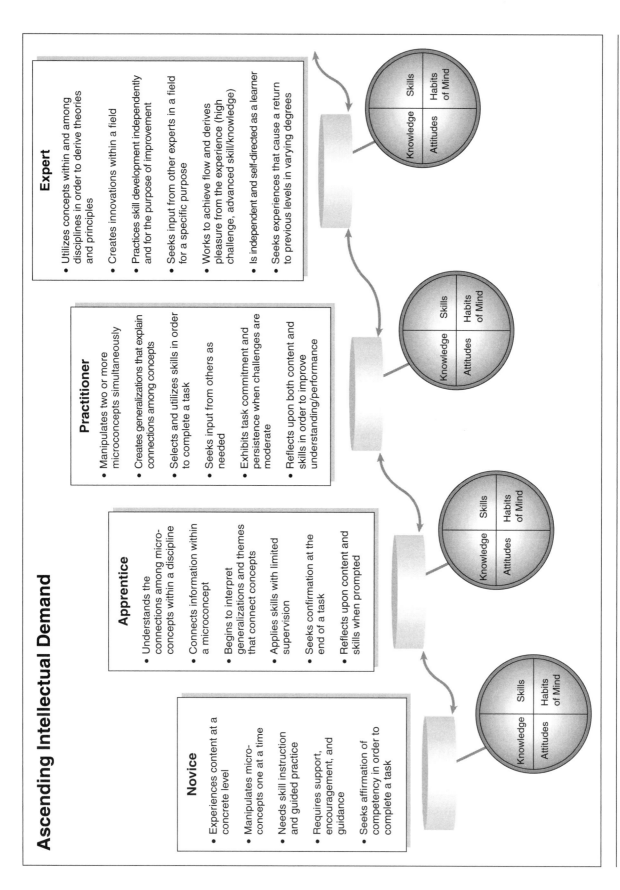

Figure 8.1 Novice to Expert Continuum

graphics in Figures 8.2, 8.3, 8.15, 8.27, and 8.39 indicate movement both forward and backward. Teachers should help students understand that substantially new learning inevitably causes periods of uncertainly and clumsiness while the learner masters the unfamiliar. In addition, learning is not just about content acquisition. Key to learning is also development of skills, attitudes, and habits of mind that characterize strong thinkers and contributors to scholarship and society. It is not only possible, but likely, that there will be learners who function, for example, at a practitioner level in terms of content and skills but display the characteristics of a novice in terms of attitudes or habits of mind that support learning. Teachers who accept this part of their role are helping students encounter consistent and appropriate challenge and should monitor and respond to the development of a learner's knowledge, skills, attitudes, and habits of mind. This should also occur with full understanding that peaks and plateaus, forward and regressive movement are an inevitable part of the fabric of learning.

On the Continuum: Novice

Everyone begins the journey toward expertise as novice. No matter the subject matter, the entry stage on the AID continuum is the novice. It is at the novice stage that the learner is introduced to the discipline or subfield. Here, the learner can only interact with the content at a concrete level experiencing discipline-based facts initially, and then concepts, one at a time. The novice makes sense of the discipline through these initial experiences, and for this reason, the introductory experiences must be concrete, requiring little to no abstraction on the part of the learner. Like the content, skills at the novice level are basic and introduced one at a time with guided, purposeful practice and specific feedback. There are few combinations of basic skills in application and only at the end of the novice stage. On the novice's first white water rafting trip, for instance, she will need the guide to introduce her to one maneuver at a time, explain it, model it, and help her through guided practice while providing specific feedback.

Working with a novice requires careful consideration to the development of learner attitudes toward the discipline. To this end, learner engagement must be a priority in the development of learning experiences for the novice. The teacher needs to focus on the learner's affective development because the novice requires support, encouragement, and guidance. The novice seeks affirmation of competency in order to complete even the most basic task. The novice faces learning experiences with little to no persistence, limited flexibility in thinking and skills application, and the absence of a variety of past experiences.

At the novice stage, the teacher plans for the introduction of information and skills incrementally. For the novice, vocabulary can be confusing as the learner tries to make sense of the new facts and skills that are introduced. Because the novice lacks proficiency with the terms that form the foundation of the discipline, it is critical that the teacher uses the nomenclature of the discipline accurately and that

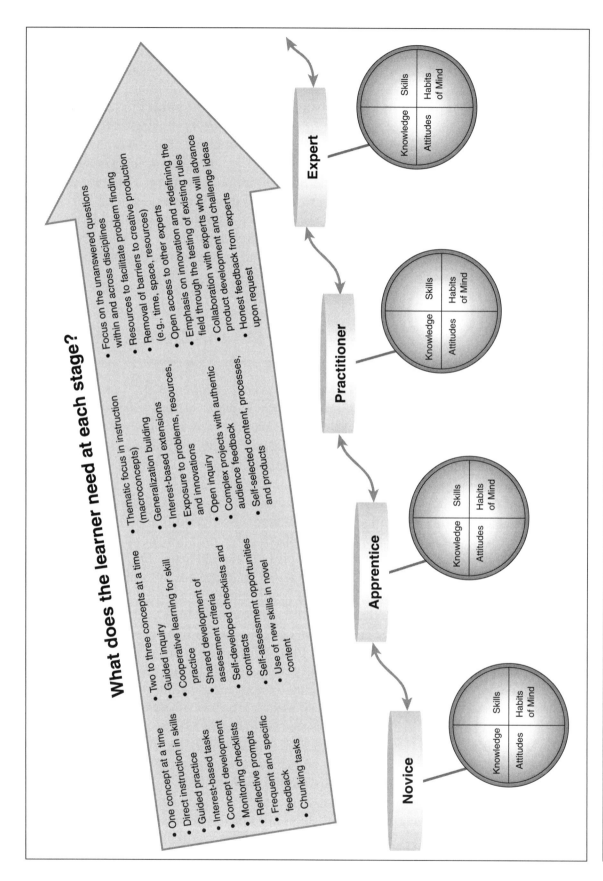

What does the learner need at each stage?

- One concept at a time
- Direct instruction in skills
- Guided practice
- Interest-based tasks
- Concept development
- Monitoring checklists
- Reflective prompts
- Frequent and specific feedback
- Chunking tasks

- Two to three concepts at a time
- Guided inquiry
- Cooperative learning for skill practice
- Shared development of assessment criteria
- Self-developed checklists and contracts
- Self-assessment opportunities
- Use of new skills in novel content

- Thematic focus in instruction (macroconcepts)
- Generalization building
- Interest-based extensions
- Exposure to problems, resources, and innovations
- Open inquiry
- Complex projects with authentic audience feedback
- Self-selected content, processes, and products

- Focus on the unanswered questions within and across disciplines
- Resources to facilitate creative production
- Removal of barriers to creative production (e.g., time, space, resources)
- Open access to other experts
- Emphasis on innovation and redefining the field through the testing of existing rules
- Collaboration with experts who will advance and challenge ideas
- Honest feedback from experts upon request

Novice

Apprentice

Practitioner

Expert

Knowledge | Skills
Attitudes | Habits of Mind

Figure 8.2 Teacher Response to Student Development of Expertise

isolated facts are organized into big ideas or concepts. Concepts are introduced one at a time through instruction and guided practice with frequent and specific feedback on student performance. Oftentimes, the novice needs concept development in order to make connections among discrete facts. Through concept development, the discipline begins to take shape in the mind of the novice. As the learner moves through the introduction of concepts with appropriate instruction, practice, and feedback, beginning connections are made among multiple concepts. This is one indication that the conceptual framework of the discipline is forming in the mind of the novice.

Direct instruction in basic skills followed by guided practice characterizes appropriate response to learner needs when working with a novice. Organization of learning experiences for the novice often includes the chunking of tasks. It is important to remember that the novice has little to no confidence in knowledge, understanding, and skills in the discipline; therefore, tasks should be designed in small increments. By chunking large tasks that require the manipulation of facts and skills, the novice makes sense of the discipline, applies basic skills, and develops confidence in abilities. While chunking tasks and using checklists are helpful to the development of expertise in the novice, the most important elements at the novice stage are frequent and specific feedback, as well as opportunities to reflect on the learning process. Learner checklists to help monitor the processes in a task may also assist the novice and instill a sense of reflection about the work. The novice has no sense of quality work and no understanding of personal success or shortcoming in the discipline, therefore, the teacher needs to be sure that while tasks are designed to challenge the novice, they also incorporate numerous structures to support the learner.

On the Continuum: Apprentice

With appropriate experiences at the novice stage, the learner progresses to the next level on the AID continuum: apprentice. The apprentice has mastered the basic elements, or key concepts and skills, that frame the discipline. At this stage, the learner makes numerous connections among discrete facts within the discipline and even utilizes numerous basic skills with ease and with limited supervision. The apprentice understands some of the connections among concepts within the discipline and can combine basic skills to attend to some advanced applications. The apprentice is beginning to construct knowledge within the discipline as he or she begins to interpret generalizations and themes that connect concepts that frame the discipline. This work requires some prompting and guidance.

While the novice needs affirmation to complete a task, the apprentice seeks confirmation of success at the end of the task. This variance is due to the development of some persistence, limited flexibility of thought and skills application, and the emergence of risk taking in the apprentice. The accumulated experiences—both successes and failures as a novice along with the frequent and specific feedback provided to the novice—leads to some confidence in the knowledge, understanding, and skills evidenced at the apprentice stage. The dispositions inherent in the expert begin to emerge at the apprentice stage. The teacher finds the apprentice to be somewhat of a conundrum. The apprentice has enough knowledge, understanding, skills, and attitude to begin taking creative risks such as asking probing questions, proposing an application idea, and offering a connection, but does not always persist as a new idea or challenge is introduced. Work with the apprentice requires a shift in teacher support from direct instruction and consistent guidance to more opportunities for learner-centered experiences with the teacher in the role of guide or coach.

At the apprentice stage, the learner is ready to work with more than one concept at a time. Where the language associated with the discipline often interrupted the flow of learning for the novice, the apprentice has interacted with the vocabulary enough to be comfortable in using the language of the discipline. The apprentice is unlikely to ask, "Is that the right word for this?" With greater mastery of the language of the discipline and a foundational grasp of the key concepts in the field, it is realistic to design teaching and learning that calls for the apprentice to grapple with two or three concepts simultaneously. The direct instruction and guided practice that characterized learning experiences at the novice stage shifts to guided inquiry and cooperative learning for skill development and application tasks at the apprentice stage.

Ongoing assessment of learner progress is even more crucial at the apprentice stage because of the delicate balance of knowledge and skills with emerging attitudes and habits of mind. Shifting instruction from predominately teacher-directed to student-centered provides opportunity for the teacher to be in the role of assessor, monitoring student progression through the apprentice level on the continuum. This shift in instructional design and the need for ongoing attention to assessment of learner needs necessitate the inclusion of tools for student self-assessment—including self-developed checklists and contracts, frequent self-assessment tools, and shared development with the teacher of assessment criteria.

At the end of the apprentice stage, the learner is remarkably different compared to the beginning of this stage. As a result of appropriate learning experiences in the apprentice stage, the learner is now ready to shift from the shared ownership of learning which characterizes the apprentice stage to becoming a practitioner with greater ownership of the process and products necessary for ongoing growth.

On the Continuum: Practitioner

The learning experiences from the novice and apprentice stages lead to the emergence of learner autonomy as a practitioner. With increased autonomy, the practitioner becomes self-directed and independent in the teaching and learning at this stage of the AID continuum. One reason for this growth is that the learner now understands the key concepts that frame the discipline as well as the interrelationships among the big ideas. The practitioner readily manipulates two or more discipline-based concepts simultaneously without prompting by the teacher. Connections among the concepts are evidenced by the formation of generalizations that connect various concepts. While the apprentice can prove or disprove a generalization when presented, the practitioner is the originator of the generalization and can support it with specific evidence from the discipline.

The learner at this stage is far more autonomous in the application of basic and complex skills. Without prompting, the practitioner can identify the skill or cluster of basic and complex skills necessary for task completion. The practitioner can adjust use of both basic and complex skills to meet individual needs in working through a task. This flexibility in skills application is the direct result of skill development through modeling, instruction, guided practice, and specific feedback provided to the learner at the novice and apprentice stages. Skill development and refinement are equally critical at the practitioner stage of AID. Here, the learner recognizes his or her shortcomings and identifies both the skill and source of support in the development and refinement of both basic and complex skills.

Two of the key differences in the learner at the practitioner stage when compared with the learner at the apprentice stage are the attitudes and habits of mind. The practitioner exhibits greater task commitment and persistence when challenges are moderate to difficult. Where the novice quits and the apprentice struggles for a short period of time, the practitioner will persist, ask for assistance, and seek new methods for working through challenging tasks. The practitioner has an appreciation for the discipline and recognizes that there is much more to learn.

At the novice stage, there is rarely reflection on the part of the learner unless directly initiated and monitored by the teacher. When prompted, the apprentice reflects on content and skills and, then, little supervision and feedback are needed. The practitioner is reflective with regards to content and skills in order to improve understanding and performance. It is not necessary for the teacher to prompt the practitioner to be reflective because the practitioner is more autonomous as a learner and therefore reflective without prompt. New experiences are viewed as opportunities for growth and discovery for the practitioner whereas the novice fears the unknown and the apprentice struggles through and tolerates that which is new.

There is a shift in the needs of the learner at the practitioner stage as the teacher becomes the manager of time, space, and resources verses the trainer or coach. The teacher now plans for open-ended experiences where the practitioner can test current limits of knowledge, understanding, and skills. Basic information and skills of the preceding stages give way to a thematic focus in teaching and learning where the learner grapples with both discipline-based and interdisciplinary concepts. The practitioner is focused on building and proving or disproving generalizations that incorporate both micro- (discipline-based) and macroconcepts (interdisciplinary). While there is much that the practitioner has learned, the practitioner is still not an expert.

With expertise as the goal, the teacher needs to shift the learning experiences so they are open-ended, problem-based, and complex so that the primary mode of teaching and learning is open-inquiry where the work is highly student-centered. It is important to include interest-based extensions including self-selected content, processes, and products beyond the minimum course content so that the practitioner has the opportunity to explore topics of interest in depth. As an expert, the learner may specialize in a subfield and these extension experiences provide the opportunity to "test the waters" of specific fields and subfields of the discipline. Equally important for the practitioner is exposure to problems, resources, and innovations that characterize the discipline. Here, the practitioner experiences many of the unanswered questions and ethical issues that the experts in a field grapple with in their work.

Assessment becomes highly personalized to the learner and the primary mode of assessment is performance-based. Performance tasks and rubrics become the primary mode of assessment in the learner environment designed to support the practitioner moving along the AID continuum toward expertise. It is within performance-based assessment and complex projects with authentic products and audience feedback that the teacher monitors and provides specific feedback to the learner who has become a partner in the teaching and learning process. Also critical is the use of rubrics where criteria are negotiated between the teacher and the learner. Encouraging ongoing development of the learner's knowledge, understanding, skills, and dispositions necessitates this evolution in the plan for teaching and learning. With appropriate learning experiences at the practitioner stage, the learner moves closer to expertise on the AID continuum.

On the Continuum: Expert

Many learners will end their learning journey at the practitioner stage having the knowledge, understanding, skills, and dispositions needed to work comfortably within a field. However, there are those individuals who will become the scholars, researchers, and producers of knowledge within a field or subfield of a discipline, and these are the experts. When first reviewing the AID continuum it seemed as though expertise was the finish line and no "teaching and learning" were necessary at this stage. The truth, however, is that the expert must continually learn and grow in order to maintain expertise and in order for the disciplines to evolve and progress.

Experts utilize concepts within and among disciplines in order to derive theories and principles. They are constantly searching for greater clarity and increased connections among the concepts. The expert moves inductively and deductively through the inquiry process simultaneously constructing and deconstructing concepts and skills in order to test the limits of the current body of knowledge in the discipline. These connections lead to more unanswered questions and new innovations in a field or subfield of a discipline. The expert him- or herself poses far more questions than provides answers.

The expert is independent and self-directed as a learner and as such, appreciates the value of skill development and hones these skills, particularly those required for inquiry and investigation in the discipline. The expert is humbled by the vastness of the discipline and seeks opportunity to collaborate with other experts, particularly those who have a different set of experiences or viewpoint. When seeking input from other experts in the field, it is always for a particular purpose such as reviewing a body of work.

There are two qualities that are unique to the expert on the AID continuum. The first is that the expert works to achieve the state of flow and derives pleasure from the experience where there is a high degree of challenge necessitating the application of advanced knowledge and skills. Becoming completely engaged by the work is unique to the expert. The other quality not seen in any other stage is the inclination of the expert to take on new challenges, perhaps in a discipline completely unrelated to his or her area of expertise, that cause a return to previous continuum stages in varying degrees. In other words, the expert stretches the limits of individual skill and knowledge in a variety of disciplines and fields.

Support of the continuous growth of the learner involves the opportunity to focus on the unanswered questions within and across the discipline. To that end, opportunities for collaboration with other experts is critical, particularly so they can advance product development and challenge one another's thinking. This requires open access and networking with a variety of experts. For the learner at this stage, there needs to be an emphasis on innovation and redefining the field through the testing of existing rules and accepted bodies of knowledge. It is critical that barriers to creative production be removed or diminished and that resources are allocated for problem solving and solution building. Finally, the expert needs honest feedback from colleagues and other experts as requested. For the expert, the journey has truly begun and it is likely there is some stage beyond that of expert that belongs on the AID continuum, but it has not been determined yet. What goes beyond expert?

Transitions on the AID Continuum

Be sure to notice that the arrows that connect each stage on the AID continuum go back and forth (see Figure 8.1). This indicates that growth along the stages on the continuum is not completely linear. In fact, it is possible for a learner to have one foot in an upper stage and one foot in a lower stage. This is due primarily to the fact that as the learner progresses through the stages, there will be new levels of challenge to face. When initially faced with a challenge, most of us return to what we know and that which makes us feel comfortable and confident. The dissonance associated with genuine challenge shakes our confidence and highlights our knowledge and skill deficits. For this reason, ongoing assessment and adjustment of content, processes, and scaffolds are critical to supporting learners along the AID continuum.

A Model for Planning Along the AID Continuum

Understanding the characteristics of each learner along the AID continuum is at the heart of using the heuristic for curricular and instructional decision making. The teacher who understands the progression of any learner from novice to expert begins to question, "What does the learner need at each stage of the continuum?" By understanding the characteristics of the learner at each stage, the needs of the learner at each stage, and appropriate instructional models, strategies, and scaffolds for the learner at each stage, the teacher begins planning with greater clarity on the necessary alignment of learner needs, curriculum content, and instructional processes.

Creating curriculum and planning instruction for varied learner needs across the AID continuum requires content knowledge and a varied teacher toolbox for assessment and instruction. Remember those curriculum guides, pacing charts, textbooks, and related resources? These materials as well as the tenets of high-quality curriculum and instruction, which form the foundation for PCM, now come into play. The responsive teacher and curriculum developer seeks to align the content, models and strategies, and scaffolds with the characteristics and needs of the learner at each stage along the continuum and will need these items to accomplish the goal of developing expertise in all students.

First, seek to understand how the learner emerges and develops in each discipline. Next, identify the appropriate curriculum content at each stage along both the AID continuum and the K–12 scope and sequence of content outlined in national, state, and local standards. Notice that the use of national standards is recommended. This is critical in most districts where state and local standards are fact-driven. National standards outline a conceptual framework needed to move students beyond the fact-oriented work of the novice to the conceptually based understandings and abstract thinking at the heart of the apprentice, practitioner, and expert stages. Pacing guides provided in many districts should provide a proposed timeline for units across a course or grade level. Consider use of these pacing recommendations as a general guide for the duration of an entire unit rather than a lock-step outline of day-to-day teaching. Curriculum guides, textbooks, and ancillary resources provided to teachers offer a plethora of tools—some will be needed and others will be tucked away from year to year, depending upon the needs of the students.

While there are general characteristics that describe learners from novice to expert with any topic of study (as illustrated in Figure 8.1 on page 238), there are discipline-specific behaviors that characterize students at each stage of development that are helpful to teachers' planning and instruction. The four major content areas—science, math, history, and English and language arts—are highlighted in this chapter along with suggestions for strategies and scaffolding that teachers can use to move all students toward expertise. Additionally, Resource A contains teaching resources for many of the strategies suggested in this chapter.

The Novice in Science

A student who is a novice in science is one who sees science as a body of isolated facts and skills. Experiments are viewed as activities and are rarely driven by a question. Students at this level often feel that an experiment is a failure when the results they collect do not come out as they planned. A clear indicator of this is when students want to go back and change their original hypothesis once an experiment is completed. Novice science students see science as very much like a cookbook with each recipe specifically outlined instead of a fluid and flexible process.

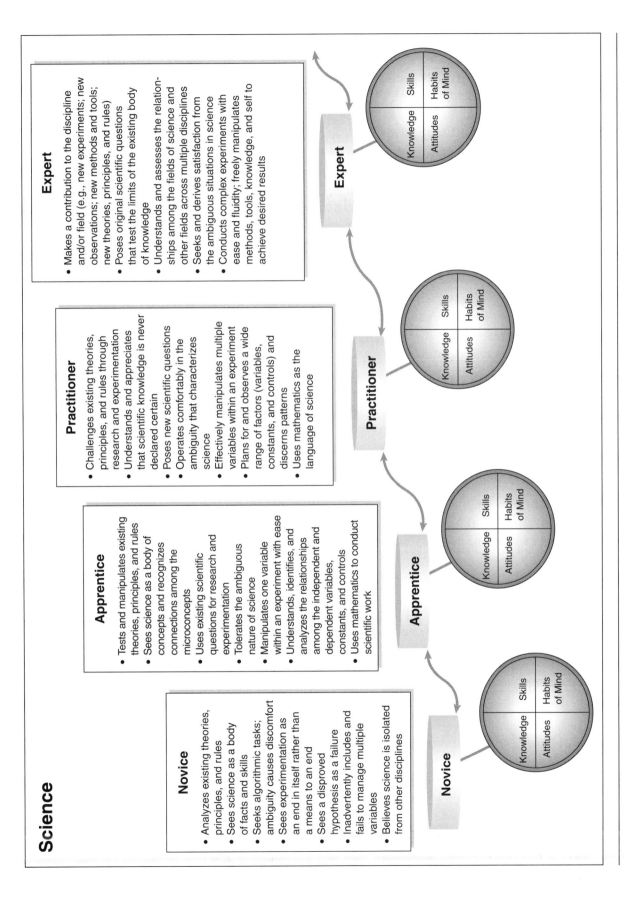

Figure 8.3 Novice to Expert Continuum in Science

247

Scientific process skills are fundamental to the work of a scientist. These skills should not be developed in isolation, but rather should be developed within experiences that are tied to content. To avoid students seeing these process skills as isolated from the field of science, it is important for the teacher to provide a context for the demonstration or modeling and guided practice, which is necessary in working with a novice. Otherwise, students are likely to question the relevance of learning the process skills. Figure 8.3 describes the novice-to-expert continuum in science.

Models and Strategies for the Novice in Science

Models and strategies that have been identified as appropriate for the novice in science provide concrete experiences for students. For instance, students who are novices should begin with highly structured inquiry experiences. Structured inquiry experiences are those that provide students with the testable question and the procedural steps. Teachers should use structured inquiry experiences as an opportunity to conduct a Think-Aloud in order to model the thinking that goes into planning an experiment. Demonstrations would also be appropriate for novices and again provide a great opportunity to conduct a Think-Aloud so students see the development of questions, observations, and inferences.

Another model that is effective to use with novices is the Wasserman's (1988) Play-Debrief-Replay. This model is most effective to use when planning an instructional sequence. Some students may come to science with very limited exposure to scientific concepts. Wasserman's Play-Debrief-Replay model of instruction provides students with a concrete experience before any content or vocabulary is introduced. Connecting structured inquiry with this model would be very effective for novices in science as they need the support and structure of being given the steps to follow in order to conduct an experiment. Figure 8.5 provides additional strategy ideas that teachers may select to address the learning needs of the novice learner of science.

Scaffolding for the Novice in Science

Scaffolds are intended to support the learner at each stage of development on the continuum toward expertise. The selection of a scaffold is critical in creating a balance between challenging and supporting the learner. Too great a scaffold and the teacher will diminish the challenge creating "easy" access to successful completion of a task. Too small a scaffold and the student will struggle to the point of frustration and give up on the task because it is too far beyond his readiness. Scaffolds are intended to be temporary ladders to assist students in their dissonance as they make sense of content and skills en route to expertise. Teachers use ongoing assessment of student progress on the continuum to determine the appropriate point at which a scaffold is no longer necessary in its current form. Figure 8.6 provides teachers with a variety of ideas they might use to support novice students in their science understanding.

The most critical scaffolds for the novice scientist are the ones associated with the scientific process skills. These techniques are intended to be used in conjunction with the models and strategies that are appropriate for use with the novice. Using the scaffolds hand-in-hand with the models and strategies, the teacher challenges and supports the learner.

Novice

- Analyzes existing theories and rules
- Sees science as a body of facts and skills
- Seeks algorithmic tasks because ambiguity causes discomfort
- Believes experimentation is an end in itself rather than a means to an end
- Sees a disproved hypothesis as a failure
- Inadvertently includes and fails to manage multiple variables
- Sees science as isolated from other disciplines
- Perceives investigations as algorithmic instead of fluid and dynamic

PROCESS SKILLS

- *Observing:* lacks an understanding of the importance of details, jumps to inference before observing.
- *Communicating:* lacks the language of the discipline, may not have the communication skills in writing, drawing, and/or speaking to effectively describe scientific phenomena.
- *Classifying:* cannot identify similarities and differences, gets lost in the sequence of logical thinking processes necessary for classifying (i.e., compare and contrast, find common characteristics, organize objects and events, identify groups, label groups).
- *Estimating:* does not recognize the value in estimating before measuring; the ability to estimate and define reasonable parameters is yet to be mastered; does not possess confidence in personal estimations because the perception of a "right answer" in science still dominates perspective.
- *Measuring:* skills in measuring (e.g., reading a ruler, careful use of tools, reading a graduated cylinder, using a protractor, reading a thermometer, using a stopwatch) are not yet developed; lacks persistence and patience in using the tools of measuring and applying measurement skills with precision.
- *Inferring:* careful observations that precede inferring are not done (may not have relevant past experiences that allow for inferring); logical thinking skills are underdeveloped.
- *Defining Concepts and Variables:* content knowledge is riddled with holes and misperceptions; accurate content is a prerequisite to clearly and accurately defining concepts and variables; does not recognize the misperceptions or inaccuracies in content knowledge.
- *Making Models:* sees scientific knowledge at the most concrete levels, cannot abstract to interpret or develop accurate models of scientific knowledge.
- *Investigating:*
- *Asking Questions:* sees questions as something that can be answered through text-based research; asks questions for which he or she has a predetermined response, does not see that a true scientific question necessitates data gathering and analysis; does not understand the difference among historical, descriptive, and experimental questions.
- *Hypothesizing:* lacks an understanding of the relationship between the manipulating variable and the responding variable, struggles with the format of a hypothesis, makes wild guesses instead of basing the educated guess on the best information available.
- *Controlling Variables:* inadvertently includes multiple variables, and does not maintain constancy among the variables being tested and therefore does not set up a fair test; fails to see the distinctions among the types of variables (i.e., manipulating, responding, control).
- *Collecting Data:* unsure of the appropriate tool to use, may have trouble constructing data tables without assistance, fails to accurately describe the conditions under which observations or measurements were made.
- *Making a Graph:* does not know the appropriate graph for the data, graphs lack appropriate labels; the x axis (showing the manipulated variable) may be confused with the y axis (shows the dependent variable), fails to accurately interpret the graph.
- *Interpreting Data:* simply reads the data, failing to examine pattern; becomes bogged down in the data and often confused by them.
- *Developing Conclusions:* sees the conclusion as separate from the rest of the experimentation and work with data; rarely connects the conclusion with the research question or hypothesis; conclusions are nebulous and vague due to limited connections and relevant use of data.

Figure 8.4 Learning Characteristics of the Novice in Science

Models and Strategies for the Novice in Science

- *Kaplan's Depth and Complexity Dimensions:* in order to help students think in deep and complex ways about science content they are required to know, the elements of depth (i.e., language of the discipline, details, patterns, trends, unanswered questions, rules, ethics, and big ideas) and complexity (i.e., points of view, over time, and interdisciplinary) guide students to think about content information, apply inquiry skills, and make connections among all they are learning in science and other disciplines.

- *Exit Tickets:* ongoing assessment information is critical in order to differentiate both content and inquiry for students. An exit ticket asks the students one-two questions about the day's lesson and/or their grasp of the science content and processes. Teachers use the information from the exit tickets to determine who is ready for more advanced work, who is at grade level with the work, and who needs more scaffolding in order to be successful.

- *Question Stems:* one of the most challenging aspects of inquiry is the formulation of a testable scientific question; question stems are the beginning part of a question that assist students in forming their own question by completing the stem. Another form of the question stem is the question cube. There are two cubes with words such as who, what, how, why, when/where, and which. The other cube has words such as is, can, will, might, would, and did. Students roll both cubes and create a question using both words. While question stems and question cubes assist students in formulating scientific questions, the novice scientist needs help in selecting the most appropriate question for the topic, concepts, materials, and experimentation goals.

- *Mind Mapping:* students put their scientific topic or concept in the center of the page and draw lines, pictures, and add words and/or numbers to represent those ideas that come to mind when they think about the topic or concept they are studying. Students are encouraged to make connections among their ideas and illustrate them.

- *Concept Mapping:* students create a map of ideas based upon the big ideas in their study. A concept map focuses on major and subconcepts rather than topics. Connections are a critical element of a concept map and these often lead to formation of a generalization. Mind maps are an excellent precursor to concept mapping.

- *It Says, I Say, And So:* It Says is where students list their observations they collected. I Say is where students add any prior knowledge or information they have on their observations, and the And So column is where students make sense of their observations plus what they already have experience with in order to make an inference.

Figure 8.5 Models and Strategies for the Novice in Science

The Apprentice in Science

Apprentice students in science are able to tolerate the ambiguity of science and are not as concerned with the fact their hypothesis does not match the data collected. These students are the ones that you will see asking, "What went wrong? How could I do this differently?" They may still need more practice with the various process skills used in science; but, they understand how to develop scientific questions when guidance is provided.

At this stage on the science AID continuum, the learner is demonstrating some persistence when challenged and greater confidence in the application of process skills. The apprentice in science is beginning to make connections among scientific knowledge and to formulate understandings as the conceptual framework of the field emerges in his or her mind. The apprentice demonstrates an understanding of the role of mathematics in conducting experiments and reporting scientific findings. It is important that curriculum and instruction design honors these emerging understandings and skills to foster continued growth in the learner. Figure 8.7 highlights characteristics of learners of science content who are at the apprentice stage of understanding.

Scaffolding for the Novice in Science

- Provide specific feedback targeted at helping the learner grow. Feedback should be focused and specific enough to correct misperceptions about content knowledge and facilitate growth with process skills.
- Model all process skills for the developing scientist. Modeling can be done in a variety of formats, but the goal must be to use modeling for the purpose of demonstrating scientific content, processes, attitudes, and habits of mind present in expert scientists.
- Provide students with direct and targeted teaching on the types of research (historical, experimental, and descriptive) and the questions associated with each type.

PROCESS SKILLS

- *Observation:* prompting students during their observations helps the novice slow down and use all appropriate senses for taking in information about scientific phenomena; pose questions such as "Describe what you see, feel, and hear in this situation."
- *Communication:* develop the critical language arts skills (i.e., reading, writing, speaking, and researching); scientific and general vocabulary development are necessary for all learners who may not be able to communicate their understanding because they simply lack the terminology; use the language of the scientist, not a modified version of the language of the discipline, in developing communication skills among developing scientists.
- *Classifying:* teaching, modeling, and having student scientists practice each of the stages of classifying (i.e., compare and contrast, find common characteristics, organize objects and events, identify groups, label groups) with specific feedback on their work are critical for developing novice learners.
- *Estimating:* guide practice to develop student skills in estimating; use estimation throughout the scientific process so students develop an understanding of the importance of good estimation skills; seek opportunities for students to use their own estimates as a reference point throughout the scientific process; in debriefing, share examples of when good estimate would save time, effort, and energy.
- *Measuring:* guide practice with each of the tools of the scientist to develop student skills related to measuring; as students develop proficiency with the tools, begin to have them select the appropriate tools and unit of measure for a specific task.
- *Inferring:* encourage developing scientists to see the connection between observations and their own past experiences (including accurate content knowledge is essential) to the development of an inference; helping students distinguish between a wild guess and an educated guess is dependent upon learning experiences that build bridges among observations, past experiences, and conclusions (inference); direct questioning at helping students use careful observations and reflection on past experiences in order to develop an inference; calling upon students to explain how they developed their inference based upon observations and past experiences; allowing opportunity to clarify student misperceptions.
- *Predicting:* helping students develop predictions based upon patterns and trends in observations, knowledge, and inferences is necessary; specifically distinguish between wild guesses and valid predictions.
- *Defining Concepts and Variables:* allow hands-on experiences combined with content mini-lessons to help developing scientists define concepts and variables; differentiate content according to learner readiness in order for all student scientists to grow in this area.
- *Making Models:* use of concept-based curriculum and higher-level thinking in conjunction with clusters of lower-level thinking skills is key for developing scientists as they move from concrete to abstract representations; organize science curriculum using big ideas (e.g., change, patterns, systems).
- *Investigation:* incorporate structured inquiry at the heart of the novice scientist's work; include limited ambiguity in the task.

Figure 8.6   Scaffolding for the Novice in Science

Apprentice

- Uses and/or develops scientific questions and protocols with guidance
- Frequently moves from one process skill to another without fully applying any one skill (e.g., skips estimating before measuring); this is due to a lack of patience, but results in limited scientific findings and limited increase in proficiency from the applications of process skills
- Still developing in the use of process skills, and this results in fragmented results (e.g., knows how to measure, but is still not precise)
- Beginning to understand that accuracy is dependent upon the measurement tool selected and the effectiveness of its use
- Beginning to connect the purpose of observations and inferences in making predictions about future events; there is a shift from wild guesses to valid predictions
- Tolerates the ambiguous nature of science
- Understands, identifies, and analyzes the relationship among the independent and dependent variables, constants, controls
- Uses mathematics to conduct scientific work
- Conducts limited research with guidance

Figure 8.7   Learning Characteristics of the Apprentice in Science

Models and Strategies for the Apprentice in Science

The novice in science needs structured inquiry experiences, but the apprentice needs guided inquiry because knowledge, understanding, skills, habits of mind, and attitudes have progressed. A strategy that is most effective to move students away from structured inquiry into guided inquiry is the "Four Question Strategy." While this strategy might be known best for use with science fairs, it can effectively be used in the science classroom with content examples. The purpose of the strategy is to guide students to a testable question. Once teachers have modeled this process with students, most apprentice science students will be able to work independently or with other apprentices and then reconvene as a class to debrief.

When working with an apprentice in science, teachers should use an experimental design diagram so students can see how a scientist plans experiments by identifying variables, constants, and procedures; creating data tables; and writing conclusions. This is helpful in making the shift from structured to guided inquiry.

Learners at the apprentice stage can more appropriately use the tools of the scientists, and they should be given access to increasingly sophisticated tools and process throughout the apprentice stage. The use of computer probes or software such as Excel are ideal for the apprentice, as the emphasis should be placed on analyzing data, not manual calculations. Additional ideas for teachers to use with students who are at the apprentice stage of work may be found in Figure. 8.8.

Scaffolding for the Apprentice in Science

Scaffolds for apprentices in science provide students with assistance for the various process skills because it is through the well-planned application of these skills

Models and Strategies for the Apprentice

- *Task Cards:* teacher-made information cards with procedures and/or prompts to provide a focus for the activity (differentiated according to student readiness).

- *Four Question Strategy:* (initial stages of apprentice) technique to assist learners in designing an original experiment. Questions about materials and procedure are posed, brainstorming as many possibilities that can be asked.

- *Experimental Inquiry Model:* (later stages of apprentice) a cycle of steps that can help learners organize their thoughts and ideas while remaining focused on a specific problem. The steps are Problem Statement (initial inquiry),Hypothesis (predicting), Experimental Design (materials and procedure), Data Collection (observations/measurements), Analysis/Interpretation of Data (inferring), Drawing Conclusions (answering the question /problem), and Extension (further inquiry—pose new questions that are related to the original question that can lead to new investigations).

- *Modeling:* the teacher shows students through a variety of sources the types of data and scientific questions that real-world scientists collect and pose.

- *Questioning:* the teacher uses a variety of question strategies to assist scientific questions.

- *Concept Mapping:* a technique that visually shows how a topic is connected to subtopics, problems, disciplines, etc. and can be used inductively and deductively.

- *Tiered Levels of Experimental Designs:* the teacher shows students a variety of experimental designs that are at different levels of complexity with regard to content, materials and procedures, and time.

- *Student-Centered Labs:* the teacher provides several opportunities for students to design and conduct their own experiments rather than always following teacher-led activities/demo/labs.

- *Student Publications:* the results of student-designed investigations are written following the format of a scholarly journal and published in a variety of outlets.

- *Expert Feedback:* students submit their work (including publications) to "experts" for feedback (e.g., high school students in upper level science courses, middle and high school teachers for elementary and middle school; doctoral students and college professors for middle and high school).

- *Science Fair Competitions:* competitions that are held at the local, state, regional, national, and international levels that involve original research from students at various ages and grade levels.

- *Case Study Analysis:* students review case studies that describe science explorations to identify the strengths and weaknesses in the research design.

- *Statistics:* teachers introduce basic statistical analysis (mean, mode, standard deviation, standard error, and population sampling).

- *Performance-Based Assessments:* students are evaluated through projects (individual, partners, or small groups) that show their knowledge, understanding, and skill with regard to specific science content.

- *Computer Technology:* students use Microsoft Excel to organize and analyze data, as well as other software that may aid in data collection and analysis.

Figure 8.8 Models and Strategies for the Apprentice in Science

that scientific knowledge, understanding, skill, habits of mind, and attitudes are developed. Figure 8.9 provides a number of ideas that may be useful for teachers to assist various apprentice learners. The use of scaffolds at this stage on the science continuum is focused on balancing the need for greater student ownership of the process skills and content with attention to increasing the sophistication of both content knowledge and skills application. While experimentation and the application of process skills should increase content knowledge and lead students to new

---

Scaffolding for the Apprentice in Science

- Provide specific feedback and an opportunity for self-assessment targeted at helping the learner grow. Feedback should be focused and specific enough to correct misperceptions about content knowledge and facilitate growth with process skills.

- Continue to provide support for students in the development of their understanding of the role of testable questions in experimental research. Assist students in aligning the testable question with the inquiry processes.

- Provide support in determining when it is most appropriate to gather information from primary or secondary sources.

- Model process skills as needed for the developing scientist. Use assessment data to differentiate process skills.

PROCESS SKILLS

- *Observing:* teacher prompting during student observations helps the novice slow down and use all appropriate senses for taking in information about scientific phenomena; teacher poses questions such as "Describe what you see, feel , and hear in this situation." Emphasis should be placed on the observable physical properties of objects or materials.

- *Communicating:* development of the language arts skills (i.e., reading, writing, speaking, and researching) is critical for success in this area; scientific and general vocabulary development are necessary for all learners who may not be able to communicate their understanding because they simply lack the terminology; teachers should use the language of the scientist, not a modified version of discipline language, in developing communication skills among developing scientists.

- *Classifying:* teaching, modeling, and having student scientists practice each of the stages of classifying (i.e., compare and contrast, find common characteristics, organize objects and events, identify groups, label groups) with specific feedback on their work are crucial for developing skills at this stage.

- *Estimating:* guided practice is a critical component of developing student skills in estimating; use the estimate throughout the scientific process so students develop an understanding of the importance of good estimation skills; seek opportunities for students to use their own estimates as a reference point throughout the scientific process; and share examples of when a good estimate would have saved time, effort, and energy.

- *Measuring:* guided practice with each of the tools of the scientist will develop student skills related to measuring; as students develop proficiency with the tools, introduce the practice of selecting the appropriate tool and unit of measure for a specific task.

- *Inferring:* developing scientists need to see the connection between observations and their own past experiences (including accurate content knowledge) and the development of an inference; helping students distinguish between a wild guess and an educated guess is dependent upon learning experiences that build bridges among observations, past experiences, and conclusions (inference); teacher questioning should be directed at helping students use careful observations and reflection on past experiences in order to develop an inference; calling upon students to explain how they developed their inference based upon observations and past experiences is an opportunity to clarify student misperceptions.

- *Predicting:* help students develop predictions based upon patterns and trends in observations, knowledge, and inferences; specifically distinguish between wild guesses and valid predictions.

- *Defining Concepts and Variables:* allow hands-on experiences combined with content mini-lessons to help developing scientists define concepts and variables; differentiate content according to learner readiness in order for all student scientists to grow in this area.

- *Making Models:* use concept-based curriculum and higher-level thinking in conjunction with lower-level thinking skills in order to scaffold for developing scientists as they move from concrete to abstract representations; organize content using big ideas (e.g., change, patterns, systems).

- *Investigating:* structured inquiry is at the heart of the apprentice scientist's work; include limited ambiguity in the task.

Figure 8.9 Scaffolding for the Apprentice in Science

understandings, teachers of science must recognize that the instructional plan including scaffolds are in two distinct areas: declarative knowledge (i.e., content) and procedural knowledge (i.e., process skills). The two areas should be planned explicitly and separately. This avoids the inclination of some science teachers to teach students the scientific method as a checklist rather than inquiry as a fluid and flexible process. Failure to appropriately plan for both areas often leads to cookbook teaching. Ongoing assessment of student readiness in both content knowledge and process skills is critical in order to plan appropriate scaffolds, including the timing of introducing and slowly removing the scaffolds.

The Practitioner in Science

Practitioners in science are those students who are fluid in the application of process skills during scientific research. They are able to develop their own testable questions and also plan, conduct, and evaluate their own experiments. They are comfortable with the ambiguity in scientific research and can manipulate multiple variables within an experiment. They understand that mathematics is an integral part of science but they may need more work with various research models. These are the students that constantly share their work with other science students and teachers. See Figure 8.10 for behaviors that characterize learners who are at the practitioner stage of understanding in science.

To extend the work of the practitioner, these students should be introduced to a variety of research methods in the specific fields of science and time to work through many of them over time. To increase the level of sophistication in data analysis and the presentation of findings, statistics should be part of the instructional process, not as a separate field of study but as an integral part of scientific research. The feedback should help the practitioner understand how descriptive and inferential statistics need to be reported in order to ensure effective communication of findings.

Models and Strategies for the Practitioner in Science

Models and strategies that are effective in continuing the growth for practitioners extend learning experiences beyond the classroom and science department to the larger scientific community. Figure 8.11 suggests many ideas that teachers can use with learners at this stage of development. Teachers working with the practitioner scientist must use models and strategies that allow for open inquiry, placing the teacher in the role of guide or facilitator. In this role, the teacher selects models and strategies to create a student-centered learning environment driven by the scientific questions posed by the practitioner. The teacher is primarily an organizer of time, space, and resources.

Mentorships, internships, and apprenticeships can be used to expose the practitioner to fields of science and current research in those fields not studied in K–12 settings as well as to careers. Practitioners need an opportunity to share their data and

---

Practitioner

- Effectively applies a range of process skills during scientific investigation
- Fluid in the application of multiple process skills during scientific research and investigation:
  - Sees the process skills of observation, communication, and classification as interrelated and interdependent. Understands the need for accuracy and care in observation with accuracy.
  - Understands the connections among the process skills of estimating and measuring. Sees the critical need for accuracy and sound reasoning in the selection and use of tools.
  - Inferring and predicting are identified as important process skills at this stage.
    The shift from wild guesses to educated guesses is based upon the learner's understanding of inference and prediction.
    The inherent connection among the process skills of estimating, measuring, inferring, and predicting emerges at the middle stage of practitioner.
  - The most sophisticated process skills of defining concepts and variables, making models, and investigating are evident at the early state of practitioner and more refined at the later stages.
- Understands that the nature of scientific questions drives the selection and application of process skills
- Problem-solves during scientific research and investigation using a range of process skills independently and in conjunction with one another
- Consistently demonstrates precision and accuracy in measuring
- Clearly explains predictions based upon observations, prior knowledge, personal experiences, and inferences
- Poses new scientific questions based on research and/or prior experimentation
- Identifies the appropriate evidence (data) in order to sufficiently answer the question
- Determines the protocol for gathering data, organizing the data, and reporting the data
- Attempts to link evidence to the body of literature/research in the field
- Understands the needs of constructive criticism for growth, but feels uncomfortable with the process of review because they see their work as their contribution, not a contribution to a particular field
- Operates comfortably in the ambiguity that characterizes science
- Effectively manipulates multiple variables within an experiment
- Develops a clear line of logic for organizing research and experimentation
- Demonstrates facility with the tools and process skills in scientific research and investigation
- Collaborates with fellow scientists in order to support common goals, validate approaches, share ideas and theories, assist with error analysis (i.e., help one another identify strengths and weaknesses)

Figure 8.10 Learning Characteristics of the Apprentice in Science

receive feedback from an expert, so conference presentations and scientific competitions are essential for the learner at the practitioner stage on the AID continuum. The intent in participating in competitions is to receive expert feedback and interact with other scientists.

Scaffolding for the Practitioner in Science

Just as the models and strategies for the practitioner focus on learner autonomy, the scaffolds utilized with the practitioner are highly individualized and likely to be applied to a specific area, such as a process skill, where the practitioner needs to hone skills. For example, the practitioner who needs to refine reporting of findings may need to work with a librarian with advanced training in research and research reporting in

---

Models and Strategies for the Practitioner

- *Orbitals*: students participate in interest-based enrichment opportunities that inform the unit of study at hand. Orbitals tend to be short adventures for students in areas of personal interest. Process and product are determined by the learner.

- *Independent Research*: students investigate topics of interest with expert advisors.

- *Mentorships, Internships, and Apprenticeships*: students work with individuals and organizations conducting scientific experiments to learn the methods, procedures, and tools used by professionals.

- *Technology*: students use scientific software and electronic probeware to collect, organize, and analyze data that professionals use in scientific explorations.

- *Science Fair Competitions*: students prepare and present original research in competition with others at the local, state, regional, and national levels.

- *Poster Presentations*: students prepare professional poster presentations for local, state, and national conferences (e.g., American Association for the Advancement of Science, AAAS; American Junior Academy of Sciences, AJAS).

- *Volunteering*: students volunteer as assistants in plenary lectures at conferences, assisting expert scientists.

- *Research Grants*: students apply for research grants to defray the costs of materials and/or travel to professional meetings in connection with research projects.

- *Coauthorships*: students partner with mentors to write for peer-reviewed scientific journals; this may include writing for science education journals with teachers at the middle school and high school levels.

- *Mentoring*: students act as mentors for novice and apprentice level scientists.

- *Science Fair Judging*: students act as judges for science fairs at the elementary and middle school levels.

Figure 8.11 Models and Strategies for the Practitioner in Science

order to find examples of high-quality research to use as models. Scaffolds for the practitioner are likely to be used on a more limited basis and ongoing assessment continues to be critical in monitoring the need for specific scaffolds. Because the practitioner has a good sense of individual strengths and weaknesses in content knowledge and process skills, it is most appropriate to use self-assessment and learner reflection to determine the type, format, and use of a particular scaffolding technique. Figure 8.12 contains additional scaffolding ideas for the practitioner in science.

The Expert in Science

While it may be assumed that expert scientists have nothing else to learn, this is not the case. Opportunities should be focused around developing collaborations with experts in the fields and across other fields of study in order to continually develop new questions, ideas, and theories. Experts need opportunities to be challenged, to defend their ideas, and to apply their own understandings within their field as well as to other disciplines. Figure 8.13 highlights behaviors that describe experts in science. Experts need to work to continue to contribute to the field by conducting authentic research studies and to share the results of their work with colleagues. Additional ideas for supporting growth for experts may be found in Figure 8.14.

Scaffolding for the Practitioner in Science

- Provide specific feedback (from teacher and outside experts) on various design elements in the experiments.
- Incorporate library and technology support to enhance expertise in advanced research methods and organization of information.
- Include student-centered critiques based on evidence.
- Emphasize research ethics.
- Ensure the understanding of research design and the role of research design in the process.
- Encourage understanding and work with a variety of research models (posttest only, pretest only).
- Emphasize the role of reliability and validity (control for threats to validity).
- Allow for participation in science fairs, conferences, and symposiums where students get feedback from scientists and experts in a variety of scientific fields.
- Use descriptive and inferential statistics in data analysis.
- Allow for experience with more than one variable in an experiment and with identifying the main effects in the data analysis.
- Expose students to developmental and correlational research with some opportunity to analyze existing studies, plan future studies, and conduct even modified studies.
- Analyze published research to design an appropriate experimental design diagram.
- Complete performance-based assessments with specific feedback aimed at growth.
- Provide experience in conducting a literature review as part of the research process.
- Allow for interest-based opportunities that support learner inquiry into topics of personal interest.

Figure 8.12   Scaffolding for the Practitioner in Science

Expert

- Demonstrates automaticity with the tools and process skills in scientific research and investigation
- Clearly links explanation to current scientific knowledge, pushing the field forward by extending the body of knowledge
- Poses original scientific questions that test the limits of the existing body of knowledge in a field
- Seeks and derives satisfaction from the ambiguous situations in science
- Demonstrates persistence despite personal and professional obstacles
- Has a sense of needing to know the answer as a driving force to engage in continuous research
- Seeks to make a contribution to the discipline and/or field (e.g., new experiments, new observations, new methods and tools, new theories, principles, and rules)
- Conducts complex experiments with ease and fluidity, freely manipulates methods, tools, knowledge, and self to achieve desired results
- Seeks interaction with other experts for purposes of ideas clarification, new ideas, and research
- Identifies error in their own research and problem-solves to minimize error
- Invites constructive criticism by publishing findings from research studies in scientific journals, participation in symposium, conferences, and seminars
- Proposes theories open to review once sufficient evidence is gathered, organized, and analyzed
- Collaborates with fellow scientists for the purposes of critical analysis and refinement of ideas and to push the existing body of knowledge in field forward

Figure 8.13   Characteristics of the Expert in Science

Opportunities to Support Growth in Science

- Collaborating with experts within their field of scientific expertise
- Collaborating with experts in other fields (e.g., science, economics, politics, ethics, research, education)
- Writing for peer-reviewed journals
- Presenting at local, state, national, and international conferences both individually and collaboratively with colleagues
- Attending and participating in seminars and symposiums
- Serving as mentors for science practitioners
- Developing and submitting grant proposals for new research in the field
- Reviewing research proposals submitted for grant funding
- Field-testing equipment and processes introduced to the field and providing feedback
- Judging scientific competitions at the high school and college/university levels
- Developing courses for student scientists at the high school and college/university levels
- Teaching courses for practitioner scientists at the undergraduate and graduate levels
- Reviewing K–12 and college-level textbooks for content accuracy

---

Figure 8.14 Supporting Growth for Experts in Science

Planning the Path Toward Expertise in Science

The National Science Education Standards (National Academy Press, 1996) outline a very different picture of how science should be taught today than when we took science many years ago. The standards emphasize students should be engaged in scientific inquiry, which is at the heart of what real scientists do in their work. In essence, students should not only develop their understanding and knowledge of science content, but should be able to study the world as scientists. This entails being able to make observations, ask questions, make predictions, plan investigations, use tools, design data-collection methods, analyze and interpret data, draw conclusions, and compare those conclusions to other information.

Developing student expertise with the knowledge, understanding, skills, habits of mind, and attitudes necessary to conduct complete inquiries is not an easy process. Too often teachers and students view inquiry in science as conducted through a series of steps known as "the scientific method." Further still, cookbook lab activities, while appropriate at the beginning stages of inquiry, do not accurately reflect how scientists work. Moving students from novices to apprentices in science, particularly related to experimental design, requires guided practice and the use of strategies that students can internalize.

Identify Desired Results

Beth, a second grade teacher, is working on developing a curriculum unit around the concept of change, specifically changes in weather. Before she begins developing or identifying any activities for the unit, she starts the design process by identifying what students need to know, understand, and be able to do. Her state standards and local curriculum objectives state that students need to know (1) the types of clouds, (2) that changes in weather patterns are characterized by daily differences in wind, temperature, and precipitation, (3) that weather data are collected and recorded using instruments, and (4) how weather impacts human activity. They also need to know the water cycle is an example of matter changing phase, and they should accurately use terms like evaporation and condensation that are used by scientists to describe the process.

Beth makes a note that by the end of the unit, students should be able to observe and chart daily weather conditions and types of clouds and identify the stages of the water cycle. In addition, they should be able to discuss how weather changes impact our lives. Beth also identifies that a key goal set forth by the state is that students should be conducting investigations related to the science topics found in the standards.

Determine Acceptable Evidence

In a conversation about her unit, Beth discussed how this unit would be an appropriate time for students to begin to plan out experiments. Beth shared that one thing she had noticed over the last few weeks was that most of her students got frustrated when their predictions were not supported by the data collected. In fact, she shared that she had resorted to having the students write their predictions in pen because so many of them wanted to erase their predictions. On the other hand, she had a small group of students that seemed to be becoming bored with the structured approach to the labs. During one lab in particular, these five students began to test things on their own when they were finished with the experiment. When asked her if she gave a preassessment for the process skills of science, she explained that these same five students were already thinking along the lines of manipulating variables.

Plan the Instructional Sequence Using Appropriate Models and Strategies

As the planning process continued, Beth went through and developed her instructional sequence. She purposefully chose to use strategies listed under the novice level identified in the AID for science. Based on her observational data and the inquiry pretest, she felt her students still resembled novices, but she also knew she needed to think about the five students who would benefit from a more challenging learning plan, particularly experiments. In response to the data she collected, Beth decided to use Kaplan's (1974) Frame of the Discipline with all students when she introduced the unit. She felt this model would help her students see the language and process skills of the disciplinarian as well as allow them to create authentic products like weather symbols and maps. She also wanted to allow students to see that as they study the various topics in science like weather or plants, there are common words, skills, and products that all scientists use. Beth also saw the model as a great opportunity to introduce students to experimental design templates. She wanted her students to understand that writing is a skill that scientists use, and by using a template, she had now given her students a tool they could use when they were asked to design their own experiment.

With regard to lab experiences, Beth elected to continue using structured inquiry experiences for a majority of the class. She planned to begin during this unit to conduct Think Alouds so students could hear how she was thinking through the design phase. Midway through the unit, Beth planned on using the four-question strategy with the students who had begun to show evidence of their readiness to design their own experiments. This strategy would give those students a framework for developing a testable question. In time, all students would learn how to use the strategy, but in this unit, Beth saw an opportunity to use flexible grouping to challenge those who were ready.

The AID continuum in science was helpful to Beth because she used it to first identify the characteristics of the expert scientist-in-the-making and subsequently use those characteristics to assess the readiness of her own students. With the needs of her students in focus, she was able to identify the most appropriate models and strategies for use with both her novices and those students a little farther along the continuum, but still novices overall. Her scaffolds were selected to support her students at all points along the AID continuum in science. Beth's goal was clear—develop scientific expertise in all students and support them on their journey from novice to expert.

The Novice in Mathematics

Just as there were distinct stages of progression that learners pass through on their way to becoming experts in science, there are specific behaviors that identify students moving toward expertise in mathematics. Figure 8.15 illustrates common characteristics that are often found in learners at each stage of the developmental continuum in math. Similarly, there are suggested characteristics—strategies and supports that can guide teachers of mathematics in moving students from one level of growth to the next. More details of those ideas follow.

A student who is a novice in mathematics sees the discipline as computation and lacks a context for understanding how the discipline is connected to other fields. The novice in mathematic solves problems in isolation, seeing each problem as merely the application of the basic operations of addition, subtraction, multiplication, and division. At the novice stage, the student struggles with a new mathematical situation if it is not a replica of problems solved previously. Figure 8.16 reveals other behaviors teachers might observe in their novice math students.

For the novice in mathematics, computation is efficient but is derived from rote memorization rather than an understanding of mathematical concepts and how they are applied and connected to one another. As a result, the novice is unlikely to take creative risks in mathematics and needs frequent feedback in order to accomplish multistep problems, particularly when multiple concepts and operations are applied. This feedback, then, must focus on modeling connections and conceptual understanding in order to help the novice develop deep understanding of mathematic principles and promote self-efficacy in the learner.

Mathematics

Novice

- Applies the skills of discrete mathematics, but lacks a conceptual understanding
- Identifies the principles, but cannot apply them unless prompted
- Computes efficiently, but lacks fluency
- Sees limited relationships among numbers and number systems
- Identifies only the most basic patterns
- Needs frequent feedback and assurance during problem solving
- Sees the "right answer" as the goal

Apprentice

- Connects the relationships among mathematical facts and skills through concepts
- Computes fluently and makes reasonable estimates
- Applies skills with confidence and develops greater understanding beyond number and operations
- Makes connections across mathematical ideas
- Understands the principles that frame a field (i.e., measurement, algebra, geometry, statistics)
- Develops skills and understanding through complex problem solving
- Sets goals that extend beyond computational accuracy

Practitioner

- Uses the principles of mathematics to make connections among concepts across multiple fields within mathematics
- Makes appropriate selections about which tools and methods to use
- Understands patterns, relations, and functions
- Applies skills with automaticity
- Understands change in a variety of contexts
- Uses a variety of tools and methods with efficiency in the analysis of mathematical situations
- Appreciates the role of mathematics in other disciplines
- Formulates questions for research that can be addressed through one or more fields of mathematics

Expert

- Uses computation as merely a means to an end
- Questions existing mathematical principles
- Moves easily among the fields of mathematics through the use of macroconcepts
- Links mathematical principles to other fields through real-world problems
- Seeks the challenge of unresolved problems and the testing of existing theories
- Seeks flow through the manipulation of tools and methods in complex problem solving
- Views unanswered questions in other disciplines through the concepts of mathematics
- Uses reflection and practice as tools for self-improvement

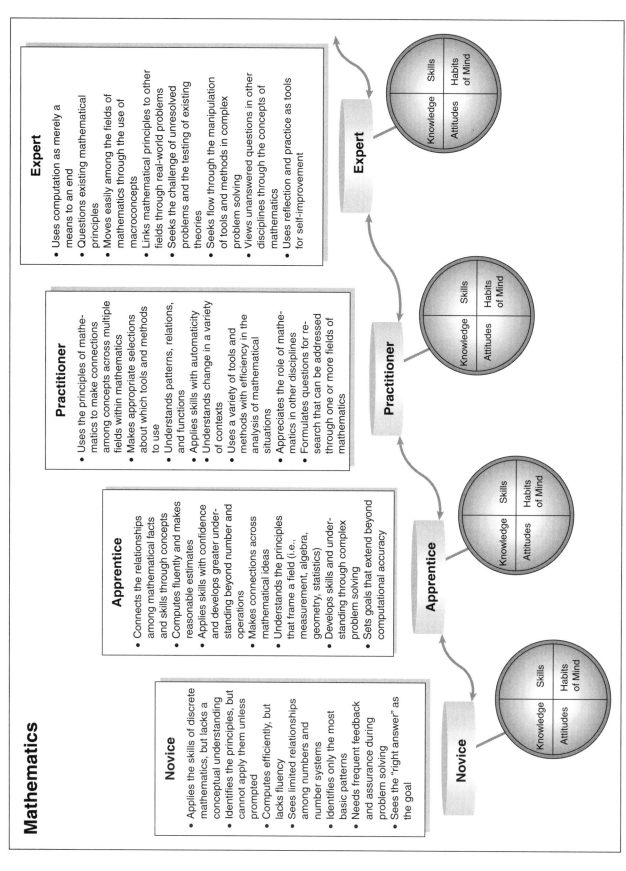

Figure 8.15 Novice to Expert Continuum in Mathematics

Novice

- Applies the skills of discrete mathematics, but lacks a conceptual understanding
- Identifies the principles, but cannot apply them unless prompted
- Computes efficiently, but lacks fluency
- Sees limited relationships among numbers and number systems
- Identifies only the most basic patterns
- Needs frequent feedback and assurance during problem solving
- Sees the "right answer" as the goal

Figure 8.16 Learning Characteristics of the Novice in Mathematics

Models and Strategies for the Novice in Mathematics

While direct instruction and teacher-centered experiences have their place at times in all classrooms, the novice in mathematics needs curriculum and instruction designed to provide experiential opportunities to discover concepts and principles and to make connections across mathematical ideas. It is difficult for many teachers of mathematics to avoid front-loading student problem solving with direct instruction and telling and instead begin with student experimentation and playing with ideas. Just like the novice in science, the mathematical novice lacks both a context for meaning making and any confidence in her own abilities. Beginning the learning plan with student-centered, cooperative activities that involve the manipulation of materials and ideas and then moving to direct instruction in the form of mini-lessons promote learner independence and the development of a desire to know on the part of the student.

Ongoing assessment, including self-assessment, is critical in the instructional plan for the novice in mathematics. Process logs and exit tickets are tools highly recommended for instruction planned for the novice. Process logs provide opportunity for the novice to explain thought processes, record ideas, note patterns, and reflect on struggles as well as accomplishments. It is understood that the teacher will review the process log regularly and make notes, pose questions, and redirect students thinking, but the log will not be graded. Exit tickets are likely to be needed when students are working with a new concept or algorithm and the teacher needs to check in on how students are feeling about their grasp of the concepts and processes. Like the process log, information from the exit ticket is for assessment and not for evaluation. Figure 8.17 reveals several models and strategies that may be helpful to novice learners in mathematics.

Scaffolding for the Novice in Mathematics

Scaffolds for the novice in mathematics are designed with two primary goals in mind: develop student understanding of the major concepts in mathematics as they

---

Models and Strategies for the Novice in Mathematics

- *Kaplan's Frame of the Discipline:* students "frame" their work through the lens of an expert in a particular field of mathematics.

- *Cooperative Learning:* working collaboratively is an important part of any mathematics environment as student work mirrors that of expert scientists; providing students with a variety of partners in multiple configurations serves as a scaffold because they share ideas and resources, verbalize their theories, and formulate conclusions. Information gathering with a partner or team assists those students who become overwhelmed by the organization of data.

- *Concept-Based Curriculum (Erikson's Model):* students focus on the explanatory themes and concepts in order to make connections.

- *Wasserman's Play-Debrief-Replay:* students are given materials and instructed to "play" with them to see how they work or act; direct instruction follows in the form of a mini-lesson where the focus is on content knowledge; students return to the materials with more specific instructions (e.g., activity or structured inquiry).

- *Kaplan's Depth and Complexity Dimensions:* in order to help students think in deep and complex ways about the science content they are required to know, the elements of depth (i.e., language of the discipline, details, and patterns) students are guided to think about content information, apply inquiry skills, and make connections among all they are learning in science and other disciplines.

- *Exit Tickets:* ongoing assessment information is critical in order to differentiate both content and inquiry for students. An exit ticket asks the students one-two questions about the day's lesson and/or their grasp of the science content and processes. Teachers use the information from the exit tickets to determine who is ready for more advanced work, who is at grade level with the work, and who needs more scaffolding in order to be successful.

- *Centers for Hands-On Exploration:* centers or stations with manipulatives, task cards, and real-world practice problems for students to spend time "playing" around with mathematical ideas provide opportunity for experience in discipline.

- *Process Logs:* students record the process of their work including notes, ideas, frustrations, and success. This reflective tool is helpful in assessment, but should not be used for evaluation.

- *Think Alouds:* the teacher (or student) walks through their process of working and/or problem solving explaining each step along the way; it is almost as though the participants are listening to the teacher or student Think Aloud throughout the work process.

- *Mind Mapping:* students put their scientific topic or concept in the center of the page and draw lines, pictures, and add words and/or numbers to represent those ideas that come to mind when they think about the topic or concept they are studying. Students are encouraged to make connections among their ideas and illustrate them.

- *Concept Mapping:* students create a map of ideas based upon the big ideas in their study. A concept map focuses on major and subconcepts rather than topics. Connections are a critical element of a concept map and these often lead to the formation of a generalization. Mind maps are an excellent precursor to concept mapping.

- *Mini-Lessons:* brief lessons of no more than fifteen minutes are focused on a particular concept, idea, or skill. The lesson is a precursor to guided practice or independent application.

Figure 8.17   Models and Strategies for the Novice in Mathematics

are applied in the real world and develop student self-efficacy in working with mathematical concepts and processes. With these goals in mind, the teacher should select scaffolds that help the student develop a sense of autonomy in working with mathematics. Too often, support in mathematics reverts to telling instead of supporting students in challenging experiences. Several ideas that may be effective for teachers to use with their novice math students are described in Figure 8.18. Teachers must see that the end goal is not the right answer and the process of

---

Scaffolding for the Novice in Mathematics

- Model processes, including models for problem solving.
- Use manipulatives.
- Use visualization of equations.
- Practice application of math concept-explanation of real world.
- Use children's literature to engage and spark student interest in mathematics.
- Introduce students to real experts in mathematics from a variety of cultural and ethnic groups.
- Develop metacognitive reflection through prompts in order to focus students on the efficiency and effectiveness of their problem solving rather than on computation and getting the "right answer."
- Identify real-world problems where mathematics is the root to all or part of the problem to provide a context of the introduction and practice of basic skills.
- Construct models to communicate understanding (e.g., visual/spatialization, pattern, equation, volume).

Figure 8.18 Scaffolding for the Novice in Mathematics

student inquiry is more important when designing learning experiences and when selecting support structures. Ongoing assessments such as process log entries and exit tickets should be used to help determine when a particular scaffold is no longer needed or needs adjustment.

The Apprentice in Mathematics

Where the novice in mathematics focuses on computation as the end goal, the apprentice in mathematics sees the computation as the tool and set of processes for problem solving. The apprentice handles computation with fluency and flexibility as he or she is comfortable with the manipulation of mathematical ideas and has greater confidence than the novice in applying facts and ideas in a variety of situations. The apprentice makes connections across mathematical concepts and sees both basic and some advanced concepts. Figure 8.19 highlights characteristics that are commonly observed in students who are working at an apprentice level of understanding in mathematics.

The apprentice in mathematics does not yet see the more advanced concepts and struggles with the application of new ideas if the patterns and connections to existing knowledge are not readily identified. The apprentice is beginning to see how mathematics is applied in other disciplines, but still compartmentalizes most of mathematics within its own discipline, failing to see its application in other fields.

Models and Strategies for the Apprentice in Mathematics

When planning for instruction with the apprentice in mathematics, teachers must focus on extending learning experiences to real-world investigations and the use of performance-based assessment. It is important that the apprentice is engaged in problems that will encourage risk taking and application of multiple concepts and processes without clearly defined models to imitate. Several strategies that teachers can use for apprentice math students are found in Figure 8.20. Direct instruction is on an as-needed basis and is organized within the problem-solving process. At the later stages of the apprentice stage, mathematical projects should be introduced as a natural progression in challenge once students are becoming comfortable with performance-based tasks and rubrics.

Apprentice

- Connects the relationships among mathematical facts and skills through concepts
- Computes fluently and makes reasonable estimates
- Applies skills with confidence and develops greater understanding beyond number and operations
- Makes connections across mathematical ideas
- Understands the principles that frame a field (i.e., measurement, algebra, geometry, statistics)
- Develops skills and understanding through complex problem solving
- Sets goals that extend beyond computational accuracy

Figure 8.19   Learning Characteristics of the Apprentice in Mathematics

---

Models and Strategies for the Apprentice in Mathematics

- *Real-World Investigations*: students are immersed in the problem first and then given direct instruction as needed in solving the problems.
- *Wasserman's Play-Debrief-Replay:* students are given materials and instructed to "play" with them to see how they work or act; direct instruction follows in the form of a mini-lesson where the focus is on content knowledge; students return to the materials with more specific instructions (e.g., activity or structured inquiry).
- *Rubrics:* students receive clearly articulated expectations for quality work and levels of performance.
- *Process Logs:* students generate ongoing reflection and analysis of work.
- *Orbitals*: students participate in interest-based enrichment opportunities that inform the unit of study at hand. Orbitals tend to be short adventures for students in areas of personal interest. Process and product are determined by the learner.
- *Performance Tasks:* teachers assess understanding through complex problems.
- *Kaplan's Frame of the Discipline:* students "frame" their work through the lens of scholars and practitioners who use mathematics.
- *Group Investigation:* students organize data, discuss data, and create ways to represent data.
- *Mini-Lessons:* students focus on specific knowledge and skills.
- *Think Alouds:* students employ reflective analysis of a process in a step-by-step manner.

Figure 8.20 Models and Strategies for the Apprentice in Mathematics

Scaffolding for the Apprentice in Mathematics

The models and strategies recommended for the apprentice (see Figure 8.21) are directed at increasing sophistication of learner content knowledge and skills application. Scaffolds at this stage on the AID continuum should be selected with this goal in mind and are designed to support the learner in reaching the challenge, but not diminishing it. This is particularly challenging as student dissonance is going to increase throughout the apprentice stage. Teachers working with the apprentice in mathematics must use appropriate interpretation of formative assessments to discern between productive struggle and frustration in order to effectively scaffold for the learner.

The Practitioner in Mathematics

The practitioner in mathematics seeks challenges and is bored with routine problems that merely require computation. The practitioner understands mathematical patterns, relations, and functions and seeks opportunities to identify new patterns, develop unfamiliar algorithms, and manipulate mathematical ideas. Computation, for the practitioner, is the most basic tool and one that is applied with automaticity.

The learner at the practitioner stage has become a questioner pressing existing theories in mathematics and searching for something new. At this stage on the AID continuum, the learner sees the bigger picture of the discipline and its role in other disciplines. The mathematical practitioner sees geometric lines in every room, algorithms in new ideas, and mathematical patterns in the written word and in speech. Figure 8.22 describes behaviors common to practitioners in mathematics.

Scaffolding for the Apprentice in Mathematics

- Use whole group, small group, and individual problem solving and application of skills and concepts.
- Model and provide specific feedback on the use of technology tools for data collection, analysis, and representation (graphing calculators, probes, spreadsheets, data basis).
- Provide specific feedback and an opportunity for self-assessment targeted at helping the learner grow. Feedback should be focused and specific enough to correct misperceptions about content knowledge and facilitate growth with process skills.
- Provide support in determining the most appropriate way.
- Provide guided practice and specific feedback in a variety of problem-solving methods.
- Guided practice in solving "fuzzy" problems where information is incomplete or misleading.
- Continue using manipulatives but shift to student directed use of tools.
- Model mathematical concepts as they are applied in other disciplines (music, science, architecture, landscaping).

Figure 8.21 Scaffolding for the Apprentice in Mathematics

Practitioner

- Uses the principles of mathematics to make connections among concepts across multiple fields within mathematics
- Makes appropriate selections about which tools and methods to use
- Understands patterns, relations, and functions
- Applies skills with automaticity
- Understands change in a variety of contexts
- Uses a variety of tools and methods with efficiency in the analysis of mathematical situations
- Appreciates the role of mathematics in other disciplines
- Formulates questions for research that can be addressed through one or more fields of mathematics

---

Figure 8.22   Learning Characteristics of the Practitioner in Mathematics

Models and Strategies for the Practitioner in Mathematics

Open-ended, student-centered, interest-based learning experiences are essential in curriculum and instruction for the practitioner in mathematics. It is important for the teacher working with practitioners to expose them to those who work with mathematics through mentorships, job shadowing, and apprenticeships. The use of independent study allows the apprentice to identify a topic, formulate questions, select processes, identify resources, and work through the study to develop a product. These recommended experiences (see Figure 8.23) for the practitioner are designed to focus the learning on authentic content, processes, and products that are learner driven in design.

Scaffolding for the Practitioner in Mathematics

Curriculum models and strategies for the practitioner focus on learner engagement in interest-based, authentic problems, processes, and products. The teacher's role is that of facilitator. Scaffolds for the practitioner in mathematics are designed to provide access to a variety of resources and situations and to support student work. Figure 8.24 provides suggested practices for teachers to use to support practitioners in mathematics.

The Expert in Mathematics

The expert in mathematics (see Figure 8.25) appreciates beauty in numbers and seeks opportunity to work on complicated problems in a variety of disciplines. The expert on the AID continuum for mathematics questions existing principles in mathematics and formulates questions more than he or she seeks answers. The expert can grapple for years on a single problem or theory. Exposure to other expert practitioners is critical for the expert in any discipline, and this is particularly true for the mathematician. Figure 8.26 offers suggestions for pushing the expert to grow in his or her understanding of mathematics.

Models and Strategies for the Practitioner in Mathematics

- *Independent Study*: student selects topic, processes, products, and resources; feedback focuses on alignment of research purpose, process, products, and results.
- *Kaplan's Frame of the Discipline*: students study rules over time, rules from different perspectives, and unanswered questions in mathematics in other disciplines (science, sociology, economics).
- *Simulations*: immersion in real-life situations to solve problems and apply mathematical ideas and processes.
- *Internships and Apprenticeships*: students work in fields that rely heavily on mathematics knowledge and understanding (e.g., forensics lab, doctor's office, computer fields).
- *Partnerships With Mentors*: students write for peer-reviewed mathematical journals; this may include writing for mathematics education journals with teachers at the middle school and high school levels.
- *Socratic Seminar or Paidea*: students explore unanswered questions within the field of mathematics.

Figure 8.23 Models and Strategies for the Practitioner in Mathematics

Scaffolding for the Practitioner in Mathematics

- Have students analyze qualitative and quantitative research in order to identify the role of mathematics in different types of studies.
- Use analysis of research to determine the effectiveness of methodology.
- Apply familiar models to new problems.
- Expose students to the unanswered questions in the field of mathematics including models for addressing them.
- Collaborate with other practitioners and experts in theoretical and practical applications in structured learning and working environments.
- Allow opportunities and resources to test mathematical rules, theories, and applications.

Figure 8.24 Scaffolding for the Practitioner in Mathematics

Expert

- Uses computation as merely a means to an end
- Questions existing mathematical principles
- Moves easily among the fields of mathematics through the use of macroconcepts
- Links mathematical principles to other fields through real-world problems
- Seeks the challenge of unresolved problems and the testing of existing theories
- Seeks flow through the manipulation of tools and methods in complex problem solving
- Views unanswered questions in other disciplines through the concepts of mathematics
- Uses reflection and practice as tools for self-improvement

Figure 8.25 Characteristics of the Expert in Mathematics

Opportunitites for Continued Growth for the Expert

- Teaching graduate or undergraduate courses in mathematics
- Publishing work for the purpose of feedback and sharing of ideas
- Working collaboratively with experts in a variety of fields in pursuit of resolution to unanswered questions
- Designing and conducting studies to test existing theories
- Developing new theories in supportive environments
- Developing mathematical models and explanations for situations and phenomena found in the real world
- Using mathematical patterns and trends to predict future conditions (e.g., spread of disease, homelessness, economic trend, natural trends, e.g., bird migration)
- Seeking grants to fund research

Figure 8.26 Supporting Growth for Experts in Mathematics

Planning the Path Toward Expertise in Mathematics

One of the goals in mathematics instruction is to move students towards the ability to link mathematical principles to other fields through real-world problems. A clear example of this expertise in action can be found in the CBS drama series *Numb3rs*. One of the characters, a math professor, each week applies various mathematical formulas to real-world crime cases in an effort to solve them. In essence, this is what an expert in mathematics is able to do. Developing student expertise, particularly when they are at the apprentice stage on the AID continuum, requires increasing challenge and providing frequent and specific feedback.

Bill, a middle school math teacher, is working on planning a unit that is focused on the concepts of geometry, specifically engaging students with the use of the Pythagorean Theorem. Several big ideas that Bill wants his students to understand are (1) that functions are a fundamental mathematical concept that express a special kind of relationship between two quantities and (2) that understanding a function, such as the Pythagorean Theorem, is a tool that can be used to solve problems when specific criteria exist. In addition to these two ideas, he wants his students to see that problem solving in mathematics is a lot like doing experiments in science. There is a process to thinking about problem solving.

Identify Desired Results

Just as Beth did with her science unit, Bill begins planning by identifying what students need to know and do by the end of the unit. Using his state and local standards, Bill writes down that his students will need to know that in a right triangle, the square of the length of the hypotenuse equals the sum of the squares of the legs (altitude and base), that this relationship is known as Pythagorean Theorem ($a^2 + b^2 = c^2$), and it can be used to find the measure of any one of the three sides of a right triangle if the measures of the other two sides are known. By the end of the unit, students should be able to identify the parts of a right triangle, find the measure of a side of a right triangle when two other sides are given, verify the Pythagorean Theorem using pictures or models, and solve real-world problems using it.

Determine Acceptable Evidence

From preassessment data, Bill has identified that his students are well versed in the principles of mathematics, but he notices many of his students were not able to make connections between the mathematical principles and the real-world problems presented on the preassessment. He has noticed that some students lack confidence in their problem-solving abilities. When he examines the AID for mathematics, he makes the determination that his students are not novices and not yet fully apprentices, but somewhere in the middle of the two stages. He recognizes some students are further along the continuum towards apprentices than others. With this in mind, Bill examines the models and strategies as well as the scaffolds that have been identified for use with the apprentice in mathematics.

Plan the Instructional Sequence Using Appropriate Models and Strategies

In developing the instructional sequence, Bill purposefully chooses to use the Wasserman's (1988) Play-Debrief-Replay model of instruction to develop his lesson sequence. In Play-Debrief-Replay, students are given materials and instructed to "play" with them to see how they work or act; direct instruction follows in the form of a mini-lesson where the focus is on content knowledge. Students then return to the materials with more specific instructions. Although the Play-Debrief-Replay model of instructional development is also a model designed for use with novices, it is appropriate for students who are in the apprentice stage along the continuum. When used with apprentices, however, the sequence of learning experiences should be developed to provide the learner with less direction and more autonomy in the learning process.

The first activity Bill designs allows students to use an online interactive Web site called "Squaring the Triangle." Using this interactive program, students manipulate moving sides of triangles. Bill has students keep track of what happens as the length of the sides changes in relation to the measures of the angles and the area of the triangle. They record their findings in a process log. Specifically, he wants to know what patterns they observe. Bill forms a temporary group made up of his students who exhibit some of the qualities of a novice in his preassessments. He debriefs with these students several times during the squaring the triangle activity to ensure they are developing conceptual understanding and not struggling too much with the computation.

Once all students have had time to make observations, Bill introduces the concept of the Pythagorean Theorem. He specifically states that the theorem is a mathematical equation that is used for work in architecture, construction, and measurement. He points out to his students that the equation is a tool to address real-world problems. Students are then given an opportunity to try solving a few equations working in cooperative learning teams. Bill has decided to use cooperative learning groups organized homogenously by readiness as a scaffold for students as they work with the new concept. Again, he works with one of the groups made up of emerging apprentices. This time, his learning group is smaller because he noticed significant growth in several students during his work with students in the squaring the triangle activity. When exit cards show that some students are still struggling, he uses flexible grouping to provide more assistance to those students who need practice with the formula. Hint cards are also used when students are working in small groups. For students who understood the problems, fuzzy problems are given and they are asked to solve them. In whole group discussions, Bill asks all students to explain how they arrived at their answers.

Bill recognizes that he will have some students later in the year who will not need to play first and then have direct instruction. The beauty of the Play-Debrief-Replay instructional model is that any part of it can be used depending on the readiness of the students. Continuing to provide students with teacher-directed instruction when they are ready to work independently will only make students dependent upon the teacher. In order to continue students towards expertise, students must be allowed to fly solo.

The Novice in History

Students of history who are moving toward expertise pass through the same stages of development as do the students in science and mathematics. The behaviors teachers might see in their students at each stage of growth are provided in Figure 8.27. Again, each level is further described along with the strategies and supports teachers might use to assist learners who are at a specific stage of development.

The novice in history does not see the context for historical events, people, and places, nor does the novice understand their relationship to the patterns, trends, and concepts and principles that shape the discipline. The novice instead sees each historical event or period of history as a collection of isolated facts. Because the novice is functioning primarily at the topical and factual levels of knowledge and understanding, the novice does not understand the larger concepts that frame the study of history including change; patterns; interaction among social, political, geographic, economic, and historical concepts; and cause and effect. The novice studies history primarily through rote memorization, often committing the information to short-term memory and therefore fails to deepen understanding in any significant ways. Figure 8.28 details the characteristics of the novice in understanding history.

Models and Strategies for the Novice in History

Planning curriculum for the novice in history should begin with a conceptual framework and be taught through experiential and inductive processes. Concept-based curriculum organizes the facts and topics that characterize history for the novice into big ideas that will be reoccurring throughout the K–12 study of history. As students begin to understand macroconcepts (universal, overarching) and

History

Novice

- Defines history as isolated people, places, and events
- Sees the facts and skills, but not the concepts that link them
- Studies history through rote memorization
- Needs experiences with sequencing to establish a sense of chronology
- Identifies causes and effects as isolated events
- Lacks an appreciation for history and its relevance to self and the world in the present and the future

Apprentice

- Understands history at the conceptual level
- Seeks connections among microconcepts in order to make sense of historical patterns and trends
- Poses historical research questions
- Has a clearly defined sense of chronology
- Understands the complexity of causes and effects
- Recognizes the importance of perspective in historical events, human perspectives, and consequences

Practitioner

- Analyzes contemporary events through a historical lens with automaticity
- Understands chronology, but has the ability to follow themes across events and time periods regardless of the direction (present to past, past to present)
- Identifies unanswered questions and crafts researchable questions to investigate them
- Understands the social, political, economic, and technological influences on patterns and trends
- Understands and appreciates the influence of individual experiences, societal values, and traditions on historical perspectives

Expert

- Moves easily from the theoretical to the practical and vice versa in response to a situation
- Challenges accepted bodies of knowledge, methods, and research findings
- Develops themes and connections across historical events, periods, and fields without reliance on but with acknowledgment of chronology
- Uses the knowledge and skills of the discipline across diverse fields and disciplines
- Displays curiosity and seeks challenge through unanswered questions in the field
- Marvels at the richness of history and its importance in shaping the present and future
- Systematically and with automaticity utilizes the knowledge, skills, and processes of the discipline to investigate

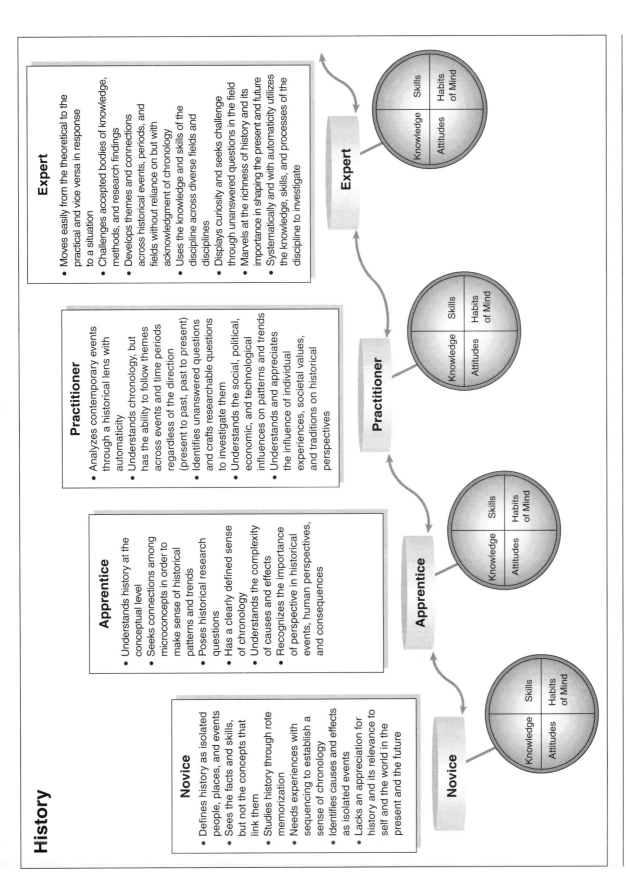

Figure 8.27 Novice to Expert Continuum in History

273

Novice

- Defines history as isolated people, places, and events
- Sees the facts and skills, but not the concepts that link them
- Studies history through rote memorization
- Needs experiences with sequencing to establish a sense of chronology
- Identifies causes and effects as isolated events
- Lacks an appreciation for history and its relevance to self and the world in the present and the future

---

Figure 8.28 Learning Characteristics of the Novice in History

microconcepts (subject-specific, discipline-based), they can begin to recognize these same ideas in the other disciplines of social science so closely related to history: culture, sociology, politics, geography, anthropology, archeology, and economics.

Engaging with the content and processes of historical study is important for all learners on the AID continuum, but the novice must focus on hands-on interaction with the concepts and processes of history. Programs such as History Alive! and Interact® simulations are excellent resources for creating engaging and interactive learning experiences. It is important that the novice has opportunity to engage in cooperative learning situations that encourage an exchange of ideas, discussion of new concepts, and practice with new process skills such as those associated with research.

Historians gather information and form generalizations on the information. To give students an authentic understanding of the discipline, instruction for novices in history should require them to gather information, organize a line of logic, and present their findings. In the early stages, this may be through forming a generalization or creating a theory. It is important that these processes are modeled frequently and practiced with specific feedback throughout the novice stage so that by the end of the novice period on the AID continuum, the learner understands the processes of inductive thinking as they are applied in history. Other strategies suggested for teachers to use with their novice history students may be found in Figure 8.29. It is important to note that while these strategies are listed here for students of history, many of the strategies were recommended earlier for other fields of study.

Scaffolding for the Novice in History

The primary foci in scaffolding for the novice in history are to help the shift from a topical and factual study of history to a conceptually based understanding, and also to support the inquiry process in history. Thinking conceptually will be

---

Models and Strategies for the Novice in History

- *Context*: students learn history as a story to establish a context for dates and events.

- *Kaplan's Frame of the Discipline*: students "frame" their work through the lens of an expert in a particular field of history. The study of the American Revolution is more meaningful for students as they look at the language, process skills, and products used by the historian to interpret the causes, events, and effects of the American Revolution.

- *Cooperative Learning*: working collaboratively is an important part of any social studies environment as student work mirrors that of expert scientists; providing students with a variety of partners in multiple configurations serves as a scaffold because they share ideas, resources, verbalize their theories, and formulate conclusions. Information gathering with a partner or team assists those students who become overwhelmed by the organization of data.

- *Concept-Based Curriculum (Erikson's Model)*: students focus on the explanatory themes and concepts in order to make connections. For example many historical events are shaped by political, economic, and social themes.

- *Kaplan's Depth and Complexity Dimensions*: students think in deep and complex ways about the science content they are required to know, the elements of depth (i.e., language of the discipline, details, patterns, trends, unanswered questions, rules, ethics, and big ideas) and complexity (i.e., points of view, over time, and interdisciplinary) as they are guided to think about content information, apply inquiry skills, and make connections among all they are learning in science and other disciplines.

- *Exit Tickets*: students receive ongoing assessment, which is critical in order to differentiate both content and inquiry. An exit ticket asks the students one or two questions about the day's lesson and/or their grasp of the science content and processes. Teachers use the information from the exit tickets to determine who is ready for more advanced work, who is at grade level with the work, and who needs more scaffolding in order to be successful.

- *Question Stems*: one of the most challenging aspects of inquiry is the formulation of a testable scientific question; question stems are the beginning part of a question that assists students in forming their own question by completing the stem. Another form of the question stem is the question cube. There are two cubes with words such as who, what, how, why, and when. Students roll both cubes and create a question using both words. While Question stems and question cubes assist students in formulating scientific questions, the novice scientist needs help in selecting the most appropriate question for the topic, concepts, materials, and experimentation goals.

- *Mind Mapping*: students put their scientific topic or concept in the center of the page and draw lines and pictures and add words and/or numbers to represent those ideas that come to mind when they think about the topic or concept they are studying. Students are encouraged to make connections among their ideas and illustrate them.

- *Concept Mapping*: students create a map of ideas based upon the big ideas in their study. A concept map focuses on major and subconcepts rather than topics. Connections are a critical element of a concept map, and these often lead to the formation of a generalization. Mind maps are an excellent precursor to concept mapping.

- *Webquests*: students explore topics of interest and interact with content information.

- *Visualization*: students use pictures to remember the sequence of events.

- *History Alive!*: students interact and are engaged with content and skills.

Figure 8.29 Models and Strategies for the Novice in History

the biggest challenge for the novice. Tools such as mind mapping, concept mapping, video streaming, and developing multidimensional timelines are helpful for the novice in seeing the larger picture of historical studies beyond isolated people, places, and events. Timelines are also helpful in assisting the novice in the development of a sense of chronology, which is extremely difficult, especially in the primary to upper elementary grades.

Scaffolding for the Novice in History

- In teaching history as a story, develop the use of graphic organizers to tell the story including concept maps
- Focus on inductive reasoning in the collection of facts and topics in order to form a generalization
- Teach the difference between descriptive research versus historical research
- Use video streaming in presentations and student presentations
- Use whole group and small group and analysis and interpretation of primary and secondary source documents
- Use role play and interview "historical character" to enable students to "experience" their story
- Use timelines with students to establish a sequence of events
- Develop multidimensional timelines that show corresponding social, political, economic, and geographic topics simultaneously with historical events
- Use mind mapping
- Use concept mapping

Figure 8.30 Scaffolding for the Practitioner in Mathematics

The Apprentice in History

The greatest transformation from the novice to the apprentice stage on the AID continuum in history is that the learner now understands the key concepts that frame the study of history. As an apprentice, the learner grapples with both the discipline-based concepts as well as the macroconcepts that link multiple disciplines to the study of history. The concept of perspective now takes shape for the novice who is also able to judge the credibility of sources by recognizing bias. The concepts of cause and effect are firmly established in the mind of the apprentice. Characteristics of the apprentice in history may be found in Figure 8.31.

Models and Strategies for the Apprentice in History

Many of the models and strategies that are recommended for the novice remain of value in planning curriculum and instruction for the apprentice. The difference in implementing these tools is in the intended purpose and the role of the teacher. Figure 8.32 lists several ideas that teachers might benefit from using with their history students. For the apprentice in history, it is important to develop curricula and organize instruction so that the learner is engaged in the content at a deeper level with the teacher in the role of guide and facilitator. The modeling and guided inquiry so necessary at the novice stage now shifts to increased learner engagement with the content. The teacher is more of a guide supporting the apprentice as new sources of information are sought and new concepts are introduced.

Apprentice

- Understands history at the conceptual level
- Seeks connections among microconcepts in order to make sense of historical patterns and trends
- Poses historical research questions
- Has a clearly defined sense of chronology
- Understands the complexity of causes and effects
- Recognizes the importance of perspective in historical events, human perspectives, and consequences
- Recognizes bias
- Understands cause and effect

Figure 8.31 Learning Characteristics of the Apprentice in History

---

Models and Strategies for the Apprentice in History

- *Kaplan's Frame of the Discipline:* students "frame" their work through the lens of an expert in a particular field of history. Expand students' use of the frames of the discipline frame within the field of social science (such as anthropologist, historian, political scientist, sociologist, psychologist, and economist). Encourage student use of multiple frames (perspectives on a single event).
- *Debates:* students are encouraged to apply information in the construction and defense of an argument.
- *Socratic Seminar:* students discuss information, generalize formation, and support generalizations with facts and reasoning.
- *Kaplan's Depth and Complexity Dimensions:* students think in deep and complex ways about the science content they are required to know, the elements of depth (i.e., language of the discipline, details, patterns, trends, unanswered questions, rules, ethics, and big ideas) and complexity (i.e., points of view, over time, and interdisciplinary). Focus should center on patterns and trends.
- *Webquests:* students explore topics of interest and interact with content information.
- *Dimensions of Learning:* students apply emphasis on error analysis, constructing support, and decision making.
- *Synectics:* students are encouraged to make connections among abstract thinking.
- *Marzano's Error Analysis:* students analyze historical fiction.

Figure 8.32 Models and Strategies for the Apprentice in History

Scaffolding for the Apprentice in History

To support the apprentice in history as expectations for conceptual thinking and learner autonomy increase, scaffolds should be selected to increase learner access to novel ideas, new tools for conducting research, and a wide range of materials beyond the textbook. Historical research and all scaffolds for students to conduct investigations in the discipline are vital at the apprentice stage on the AID continuum. Figure 8.33 provides ideas for teachers to support learners at this stage of growth.

Scaffolding for the Apprentice in History

- Model the development of historical research questions.
- Train in historical inquiry.
- Provide interest-based differentiation in order to explore personal areas of interest.
- Provide specific feedback and an opportunity for self-assessment targeted at helping the learner grow. Feedback should be focused and specific enough to correct misperceptions about content knowledge.
- Provide support in determining when it is most appropriate to gather information from primary or secondary sources.
- Use photographs, movies, and paintings (prints) to assist students in seeing historical events.
- Use simulations to enable students to experience historical events, conditions, and perspectives.

Figure 8.33 Scaffolding for the Apprentice in History

The Practitioner in History

At the practitioner stage in history, the learner has an accurate understanding of how the historian works, how to conduct inquiry in the discipline, and how the discipline is shaped and influenced by the major concepts in history as well as the other social sciences. The practitioner in history needs to be challenged to identify and to investigate the unanswered questions in the discipline. This will require more sophisticated inquiry and investigation tools and skills. Characteristics of the practitioner student of history are detailed in Figure 8.34.

The practitioner understands that history is more than just past events, but is a discipline of the past, present, and future. The practitioner studies current events with an understanding of the social, political, cultural, economic, and geographic influences on the events of today, understanding the patterns of past events, their repetition in the events of the present, and how these events will shape the future.

Models and Strategies for the Practitioner in History

When selecting models and strategies for working with the practitioner, it is most important to focus on increased depth and complexity along with interest-based opportunities for investigation. Several strategies that teachers might find effective to use are suggested in Figure 8.35. Kaplan's (1974) Frame of the Discipline "depth and complexity" prompts as well as the "frames of the disciplinarian" can be used at the practitioner stage as self-directed tools. The practitioner understands both the discipline of history and how the historian conducts work, so the next level of challenge should be to put the information and the tools in the control of the learner with monitoring, feedback, and guidance from the teacher.

Practitioner

- Analyzes contemporary events through a historical lens with automaticity
- Understands chronology, but has the ability to follow themes across events and time periods regardless of the direction (present to past, past to present)
- Identifies unanswered questions and crafts researchable questions to investigate them
- Understands the social, political, economic, and technological influences on patterns and trends
- Understands and appreciates the influence of individual experiences, societal values, and traditions on historical perspectives

Figure 8.34 Learning Characteristics of the Practitioner in History

---

Models and Strategies for the Practitioner in History

- *Kaplan's Frame of the Discipline*: extend use to encourage students to move in and out of multiple vantage points and see the interconnectedness of the various fields of social science (geography, history, political science, psychology, anthropology, sociology, and economics).

- *Kaplan's Depth and Complexity Dimensions*: students are helped with thinking in deep and complex ways about the science content they are required to know, the elements of depth (i.e., language of the discipline, details, patterns, trends, unanswered questions, rules, ethics, and big ideas) and complexity (i.e., points of view, over time, and interdisciplinary). Focus should center on unanswered questions and ethical issues.

- *Marzano's Historical Investigation*: students identify a situation in history with conflicting viewpoints. Students develop a hypothetical scenario with one or more viewpoints. Students then research and analyze information in order to determine the plausibility of the hypothetical scenario.

- *Orbitals:* students participate in interest-based enrichment opportunities that inform the unit of study at hand. Orbitals tend to be short adventures for students in areas of personal interest. Process and product are determined by the learner.

- *Performance Tasks:* teachers assess understanding through complex problems.

- *Internship or Mentorship*: students work with experts in an area of interest (e.g., civil war battleground, college/university, historical museum, library).

Figure 8.35 Models and Strategies for the Practitioner in History

---

Scaffolding for the Practitioner in History

The practitioner works like a historian and therefore will need more tools and greater access to the resources of the discipline. It is likely that technology, library media, and outside experts will be needed to support the work of the practitioner. Mini-lessons on skills will be necessary and should be planned as they are needed by the learner. See Figure 8.36 for scaffolding ideas to use with the practitioner in history.

Scaffolding for the Practitioner in History

- Expose students to a variety of research models that can be applied to historical research.
- Encourage analysis and interpretation of varied viewpoints on a topic.
- Emphasize research ethics.
- Provide specific feedback (from the teacher and outside "experts") on various design elements in the experiment.
- Incorporate library and technology support to enhance expertise in advanced research methods and organization of information.
- Use student-centered critiques based on evidence.
- Encourage analysis of historical patterns and trends over time (making connection past, present, future).
- Use simulations to enable students to experience historical events, conditions, and perspectives.

Figure 8.36 Scaffolding for the Practitioner in History

The Expert in History

The expert in history has applied the knowledge and tools of the discipline in a variety of situations as a practitioner and is now ready to add to the existing body of knowledge in the field. Where the practitioner tests existing beliefs in the field and attempts to answer the unanswered questions in the discipline, the expert is ready to add to the bodies of knowledge, methods, and research in the discipline. This may mean challenging accepted theories and principles. A list of specific behaviors that describe an expert in history may be found in Figure 8.37.

The expert in history displays an intense curiosity about history, and this is usually in a specific topic or period. Unlike the novice who saw only facts related to a topic, the expert understands the topic within the full framework of history and all of its complexities. The facts serve as the details within the big ideas of the discipline. The expert appreciates the patterns, trends, ethics, and unanswered questions within the big ideas that frame the topic or period and seeks to add to the body of knowledge and understanding about the topic or period. The expert needs access to other experts within and beyond the discipline and also needs support in accessing avenues for sharing findings. Figure 8.38 provides additional ideas for supporting the expert in history in continuing to learn and grow.

Planning the Path Toward Expertise in History

As students move along the AID continuum, challenges become greater and the support structures must be modified in order to allow for access to increased challenge. Overreliance on support structures develops dependence in the learner. The selection of models, strategies, and scaffolds shifts from the apprentice to the practitioner

---

Expert

- Moves easily from the theoretical to the practical and vice versa in response to a situation
- Challenges accepted bodies of knowledge, methods, and research findings
- Develops themes and connections across historical events, periods, and fields without reliance, but with acknowledgement of chronology
- Uses the knowledge and skills of the discipline across diverse fields and disciplines
- Displays curiosity and seeks challenge through unanswered questions in the field
- Marvels at the richness of history and its importance in shaping the present and future
- Systematically and with automaticity utilizes the knowledge, skills, and processes of the discipline to investigate

---

Figure 8.37 Characteristics of the Expert in History

Opportunities to Support Continued Growth for the Expert

- Teaching graduate or undergraduate courses in the field of history
- Publishing
- Field studies (civil war historian traveling to different libraries)
- Collaborating with experts in the field that share the same perspective
- Development of documentaries

Figure 8.38 Supporting Growth for Experts in History

stages. At the initial stages of novice and apprentice, the teacher is focused on developing an accurate understanding of the discipline and guiding practice in the development of the process skills in the discipline. Modeling, specific feedback, and structured to guided practice characterize much of the work with the novice and the apprentice. At the practitioner stage, the focus shifts to increased learner autonomy, models, and strategies that increase challenge, along with greater flexibility and personalization of the scaffolds. An ill-placed scaffold or one that is left in place too long can impede the learner's independence and self-direction, so ongoing assessment remains important for the teacher.

Students who are working at the practitioner level on the AID continuum should have the opportunity to self-select content, processes, and products. They also are ready for interest-based extensions. This next example illustrates how a high school social studies teacher used interest coupled with investigation in history.

Identify Desired Results

Melody teaches eleventh grade history. For the past few years, she has wanted to do something different with her unit on the Roaring 20s and the Great Depression. In the unit, students are expected to know the causes and impact of the depression.

They also have to know how the New Deal addressed the government's response to solving problems. By the end of the unit, students had to be able to formulate historical questions and defend findings based on inquiry and interpretation.

Determine Acceptable Evidence

In the past few years, Melody has had one activity during this unit specifically developed for students who were ready to analyze the Great Depression through a historical lens. Most of the students in previous years exhibited the characteristics of an apprentice. They understood history at a conceptual level and certainly, by the end of the year, could pose historical questions. This year, however, Melody has a few students who began the school year by posing their own historical questions.

Plan the Instructional Sequence Using Appropriate Models and Strategies

In the learning sequence, Melody changes the beginning of one of the lessons to allow her to work with those students in small groups. She introduces students to Marzano's (1992) Historical Investigation. In the application of Marzano's Historical Investigation, students identify a situation in history with conflicting viewpoints. With this, students develop a hypothetical scenario with one or more viewpoints. They research and analyze information in order to determine the plausibility of the hypothetical scenario.

It is important to understand that this strategy should not be used simply because students are confused about an idea. Rather, this strategy should be used as a tool to help students take charge of the learning process in order to clear up confusions or contradictions found in information on a topic. Melody recognizes that Historical Investigations is an appropriate strategy for the student who has reached the level of a practitioner because it is a complex process in which students construct a hypothetical scenario and find evidence to either support or refute it.

To prepare the students to conduct a historical investigation, Melody begins by allowing the students to work as a group and provides the group with a template to use as she models the process with a noncontent example found in the newspaper. While modeling, Melody asks the students to work collaboratively to describe the newspaper story. She asks them to discuss what they already knew about the story and what was confusing to them. The process continues until, together, they create a hypothesis with Melody working from outside the group only prompting and redirecting the group when necessary. Last, Melody asks the students to work together to analyze historical evidence that they had collected in order to determine if the hypothetical scenario was possible. To continue to support the practitioners, she provides students with a variety of structured graphic organizers and encourages them to use them or to construct their own organizer if needed.

As the students work through their analysis, Melody meets with them periodically to determine the stage of their readiness and to provide them with additional resources as needed. The students determine an audience for their findings—a university professor of history. In preparation for them to invite the professor to review their work, Melody conducts a mini-lesson with the students.

The Novice in English and Language Arts

English and language arts is the last content area in this chapter to illustrate the stages of growth that learners progress through as they move toward expertise. Like the other content areas, specific behaviors related to each stage help teachers identify where their learners are in order to make appropriate decisions for supporting learners' growth. These characteristics of learners at each stage of growth may be found in Figure 8.39. Student behaviors, strategies, and supports for teachers to use with their students at the various stages of growth are described in the sections that follow.

At the novice level on the AID continuum in English and language arts, the learner sees the processes of reading, writing, speaking, and researching as separate from one another and not applicable in other disciplines. The novice may focus on writing with attention to grammar, mechanics, and style in English class when instructed to do so, but does not proofread or edit when writing a paragraph in social studies. Other behaviors that teachers might see in their students who are at the novice stage of understanding in this content area may be found in Figure 8.40.

The novice does not recognize the interconnectedness of all of the communication strands. The irony is that the novice in English and language arts often struggles with multiple strands (i.e., reading, writing, speaking, researching) as a result of a deficit in one area due to the interconnected nature of this discipline. For example, the learner who has difficulty with reading comprehension may have difficulty with writing and researching. When working with a novice, it is important to understand the disconnected view of the discipline.

Models and Strategies for the Novice in English and Language Arts

The models and strategies recommended for the novice in English and language arts are intended to accomplish several goals: (1) to help the learner connect the process skills within the field of English and language arts; (2) to help the learner connect with literature, and as result, connect personally with the other strands of written communication, oral communication, and research; (3) to help the learner become a producer in the field of English and language arts. Several ideas that teachers might use with their novice students are found in Figure 8.41.

Models and strategies should be used that create a balanced approach to literacy through which students are reading, writing, speaking, and researching to learn the skills for transfer—not merely practice and application for the sake of practice and application. In order for the novice to connect the skills of literacy with one another and appreciate their interconnectedness, he or she must learn and apply them in concert with one another. Disjointed and decontextualized practice frustrates the novice and fails to move students along the continuum toward apprentice.

Reading can be a productive avenue for engaging the novice and prompting further reading, writing, oral communication, and research. Reading selections for the novice are critically important because they must be designed to provide an appropriate level of challenge with careful consideration to what will engage the individual student.

English and Language Arts

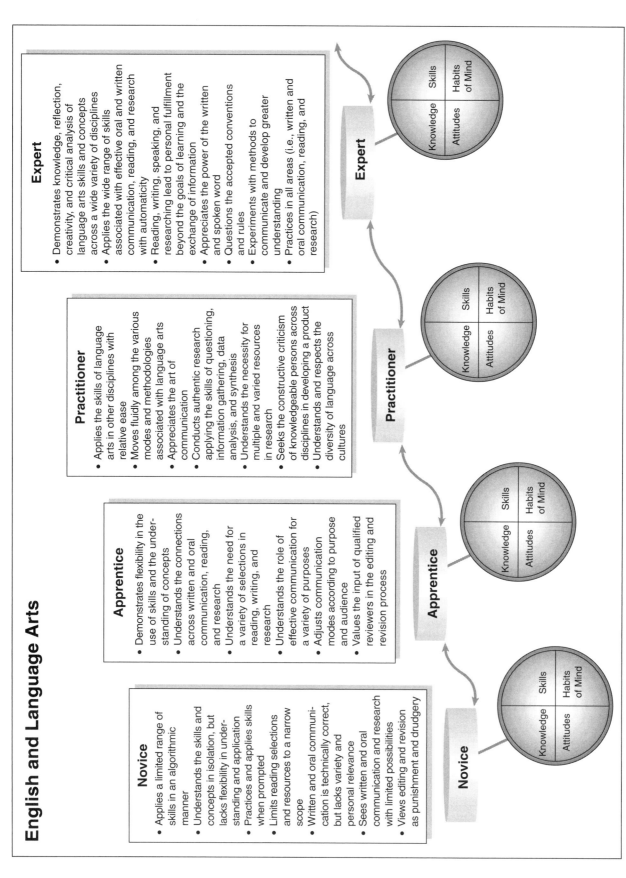

Novice

- Applies a limited range of skills in an algorithmic manner
- Understands the skills and concepts in isolation, but lacks flexibility in understanding and application
- Practices and applies skills when prompted
- Limits reading selections and resources to a narrow scope
- Written and oral communication is technically correct, but lacks variety and personal relevance
- Sees written and oral communication and research with limited possibilities
- Views editing and revision as punishment and drudgery

Apprentice

- Demonstrates flexibility in the use of skills and the understanding of concepts
- Understands the connections across written and oral communication, reading, and research
- Understands the need for a variety of selections in reading, writing, and research
- Understands the role of effective communication for a variety of purposes
- Adjusts communication modes according to purpose and audience
- Values the input of qualified reviewers in the editing and revision process

Practitioner

- Applies the skills of language arts in other disciplines with relative ease
- Moves fluidly among the various modes and methodologies associated with language arts
- Appreciates the art of communication
- Conducts authentic research applying the skills of questioning, information gathering, data analysis, and synthesis
- Understands the necessity for multiple and varied resources in research
- Seeks the constructive criticism of knowledgeable persons across disciplines in developing a product
- Understands and respects the diversity of language across cultures

Expert

- Demonstrates knowledge, reflection, creativity, and critical analysis of language arts skills and concepts across a wide variety of disciplines
- Applies the wide range of skills associated with effective oral and written communication, reading, and research with automaticity
- Reading, writing, speaking, and researching lead to personal fulfillment beyond the goals of learning and the exchange of information
- Appreciates the power of the written and spoken word
- Questions the accepted conventions and rules
- Experiments with methods to communicate and develop greater understanding
- Practices in all areas (i.e., written and oral communication, reading, and research)

Novice → Apprentice → Practitioner → Expert

Knowledge | Skills | Attitudes | Habits of Mind

Figure 8.39 Novice to Expert Continuum in English and Language Arts

---

Novice

- Applies a limited range of skills in an algorithmic manner
- Understands the skills and concepts in isolation, but lacks flexibility in understanding and application
- Practices and applies skills when prompted
- Limits reading selections and resources to a narrow scope
- Written and oral communication is technically correct, but lacks variety and personal relevance
- Sees written and oral communication and research with limited possibilities
- Views editing and revision as punitive and drudgery

Figure 8.40 Learning Characteristics of the Novice in English and Language Arts

Since the goal for the novice is developing transferable skills, the learner must be a producer focused on skill development and not simply on the end product. Metacognitive reflection through journals (paper or computer) and portfolios is quite helpful in promoting this goal. Models and strategies selected for the novice must provide students with the opportunity to create through the application of the process skills in English and language arts and then reflect on their work and personal growth.

Scaffolding for the Novice in English and Language Arts

Scaffolds for the novice in the English and language arts are intended to provide support in the specific areas of the discipline where students struggle beyond an acceptable level. The scaffolds in this discipline are constantly changing for novices because when the scaffolds are used in partnership with appropriate models and strategies, the readiness levels associated with the discipline's strands are likely to change routinely. The novice needs frequent assessment and specific feedback. This serves to develop autonomy, but also provides guidance for the teacher in selection, modification, and removal of scaffolds. Suggested support strategies for teachers to use with their novice learners may be found in Figure 8.42.

The Apprentice in English and Language Arts

Apprentices on the AID continuum in English and language arts now see the interconnectedness of the strands of the discipline. While they may not have equal development in all of the areas, they recognize their strengths and weaknesses. Several characteristics that are commonly found in the apprentice stage of growth are highlighted in Figure 8.43. As a novice, the learner tackled reading that was challenging at the time and created a writing piece following edits and revision. Now, the learner is more persistent in working through a challenging reading selection and appreciates the importance of revising before publishing writing. The

Models and Strategies for the Novice in English and Language Arts

- *Read Alouds:* emergent readers need to hear books read aloud; book selection should be based on topics of high interest to the learner.
- *Think Alouds:* teachers should model strategies and how to solve problems out loud so students can hear and see a teacher's thinking process.
- *Guided Practice:* teachers and students work together where more of the ownership for the task is on the student. Teachers provide concrete and specific feedback.
- *Interactive Practice:* teachers should work with students to complete a task or solve a problem.
- *Questioning:* teachers should model the use of questions prior to reading and how those questions can be used to self-monitor; avoid posing questions that require a "right" answer, but instead use questions that prompt student interaction with text.
- *Interactive Notation System for Effective Reading and Thinking:* students make mark notations in the passage as they are reading (i.e., students use symbols to indicate each comment for I agree, I disagree, that is new, I don't understand, wow, that is interesting, that is important).
- *Making Connections:* students make connections: text-to-text, text-to-self, and text-to-world.
- *Entry Points:* students role play character actions and dialogue prior to writing.
- *Scribing:* another student, classroom volunteer, or teacher scribes for students.
- *Anticipation Guides, KWHL, Brainstorm, and Categorize:* students use specific strategies for prior assessment.
- *Variety:* teacher incorporates a variety of genres and topics in reading selections.
- *Grouping by Readiness With Regard to Phonemic Awareness:* students who have already mastered phonics can go ahead and read with a group of students who are at the same readiness while those who need more instruction should work directly with the teacher.
- *Low-Risk Environment for Reading:* teachers can plan lessons that provide students the opportunity to make inferences, check conclusions against the text, and be wrong.
- *Read/Pause/Retell/Reread or Read On:* students receive strategies in retaining details.
- *Portfolios:* collection and revision of written work with a focus on student reflection and monitoring over time.
- *Exit Tickets:* ongoing assessment information is critical in order to differentiate both content and inquiry for students. An exit ticket asks the students one or two questions about the day's lesson and/or their grasp of the English and language arts content and processes. Teachers use the information from the exit tickets to determine who is ready for more advanced work, who is at grade level with the work, and who needs more scaffolding in order to be successful.
- *Technology:* students use a computer, laptop, or Alpha Smarts for writing in lieu of paper and pen.
- *Mind Mapping:* students put their English and language arts topic or concept in the center of the page and draw lines, pictures, and add words and/or numbers to represent those ideas that come to mind when they think about the topic or concept they are studying. Students are encouraged to make connections among their ideas and illustrate them.
- *Concept Mapping:* students create a map of ideas based upon the big ideas in their study. A concept map focuses on major and subconcepts rather than topics. Connections are a critical element of a concept map and these often lead to the formation of a generalization. Mind maps are an excellent precursor to concept mapping.
- *Socratic Seminar:* students explore answers and share ideas at the end of the novice stage.
- *Literature Circles:* students can be introduced to discussion groups at the end of the novice stage.

Figure 8.41 Models and Strategies for the Novice in English and Language Arts

Scaffolding for the Novice in English and Language Arts

- Expose the novice to materials for reading and writing; books, paper, and pens are essential; interaction with print is imperative for beginning readers and writers.
- Use preassessments to guide instruction; instruction should build from what students already know about language.
- Preassess prior knowledge of topics and readings in order to make connections.
- Model the development and use of questions for self-monitoring. Similar to metacognition, self-monitor encourages students to think about whether they understand what they are reading and learning.
- Introduce new vocabulary prior to reading.
- Model the use of context clues through Think Alouds and then give guided practice.
- Move from Think Alouds to guided practice, to interactive practice as students progress in skill development in all areas of language arts (i.e., reading, writing, and speaking).
- Use direct teaching of strategies for reading and writing; instruction in the strategy should help students understand how, when, and why to use the strategy.
- Embed the use of reading and writing strategies in all content areas.
- Introduce a variety of graphic organizers to summarize information from text and organize information for writing.

Figure 8.42 Scaffolding for the Novice in English and Language Arts

Apprentice

- Demonstrates flexibility in the use of skills and the understanding of concepts
- Understands the connections across written and oral communication, reading, and research
- Understands the need for a variety of selections in reading, writing, and research
- Understands the role of effective communication for a variety of purposes
- Adjusts communication modes according to purpose and audience
- Values the input of qualified reviewers in the editing and revision process

Figure 8.43 Learning Characteristics of the Apprentice in English and Language Arts

apprentice understands the richness in reading and writing in a variety of genres, although he or she may have a clear preference for one or more genres.

Models and Strategies for the Apprentice in English and Language Arts

The apprentice needs models and strategies that encourage self-direction and increased sophistication in materials—in all strands. The apprentice also needs to conduct research at a more sophisticated level beginning with a self-formulated question. While the novice needs to see the application of the strands of English and language arts, the apprentice needs greater integration of these strands in all learning experiences. Wherever possible, an integrated approach to teaching and learning should be emphasized so that the process skills in all strands of English and language arts are embedded in other disciplines. Reading instruction is likely to give way to literature studies at later times in the apprentice stage. Additional strategy ideas for teachers to use with learners at this stage of growth in English and language arts are found in Figure 8.44.

Scaffolding for the Apprentice in English and Language Arts

Scaffolding for the apprentice includes the scaffolds needed at the novice stage, but individualized to the learner. For the apprentice, the scaffolds added are critically important in the development of the process skills related to research. The challenge for teachers of English and language arts is to clearly understand how research is conducted in the various disciplines so that instruction and scaffolds planned for the apprentice provide an accurate picture of research including both processes and products. The focus remains on the transferable skills and not the product. Several suggestions for assisting the apprentice may be found in Figure 8.45.

Models and Strategies for the Apprentice in English and Language Arts

- *Research:* students can be guided in various elements and processes of research.

- *Primary and Secondary Sources*: students can be provided support in determining when it is most appropriate to gather information from each.

- *It Says, I Say, And So:* students list their projections or predictions in the "I Say" column. After reading, they indicate what the test says in the "It Says" column. Finally, in the "And So" column, students reconcile their initial ideas with what they learned from the text.

- *Preview/Analyze/Connect:* students should be encouraged to use throughout process.

- *Visualizing*: students can use as a strategy for help with recall of a sequence of information.

- *Rubrics for Writing:* students receive specific criteria introduced at the beginning and throughout process.

- *Paired Reading:* students work together to self-monitor and construct meaning.

- *Shared Inquiry:* teachers can introduce this activity through the use of Junior Great Books.

- *Portfolios:* teachers can use for collection and revision of written work with a focus of taking written work from draft through revision to publication.

- *Socratic Seminar:* students can practice listening and response skills throughout process.

- *Literature Circles:* student discussions can be practiced throughout process.

Figure 8.44 Models and Strategies for the Apprentice in English and Language Arts

Scaffolding for the Apprentice in English and Language Arts

- Move Think Alouds to one-on-one among children.
- Introduce the processes of research (e.g., summarizing, paraphrasing, citing sources at early stages of apprentice with the goal of students' practicing the process skills of research with specific feedback).
- Focus on students' applying the process skills associated with research at later stages of apprentice.
- Provide specific feedback and an opportunity for self-assessment targeted at helping the learner grow. Feedback should be focused and specific enough to correct misconceptions about the use of reading strategies.

Figure 8.45 Scaffolding for the Apprentice in English and Language Arts

The Practitioner in English and Language Arts

With appropriate experiences at the novice and apprentice stages, the practitioner no longer sees English and language arts as a separate discipline from the others. Behaviors that describe practitioners in this content area are highlighted in Figure 8.46. Beyond the rich study of literature, the discipline has been transformed into the process skills that the practitioner applies in all disciplines. As they are applied, the practitioner is keenly aware of personal strengths and weaknesses. The earlier focus on self-assessment and the work of the teachers in providing specific feedback leads to self-direction in the practitioner. At this stage on the AID continuum, the learner appreciates the art of communication in all of its forms and applies the process skills in all strands with automaticity.

Models and Strategies for the Practitioner in Language Arts

At the practitioner level, the models and strategies increase in sophistication and should be applied in all disciplines outside the English and language arts classroom

Practitioner

- Applies the skills of language arts in other disciplines with relative ease
- Moves fluidly among the various modes and methodologies associated with language arts
- Appreciates the art of communication
- Conducts authentic research applying the skills of questioning, information gathering, data analysis, and synthesis
- Understands the necessity for multiple and varied resources in research
- Seeks the constructive criticism of knowledgeable persons across disciplines in developing a product
- Understands and respects the diversity of language across cultures

Figure 8.46 Learning Characteristics of the Practitioner in English and Language Arts

(see Figure 8.47 for recommendations). Access to experts, particularly from varied disciplines, is significant in the development of the practitioner en route to expertise. Integrated curricula will provide the best avenues for the models and strategies recommended for the practitioner in English and language arts.

Scaffolding for the Practitioner in Language Arts

As a practitioner works through more sophisticated and integrated processes, the teacher serves as a resource and scaffolds are highly individualized. Because there are a variety of process skills within each strand of English and language arts, the learner may be a practitioner overall, but may require support in specific areas. Ideas that teachers might use to support practitioners are listed in Figure 8.48.

Models and Strategies for the Practitioner in English and Language Arts

- *Writing Rubrics*: students are aware of criteria throughout process.
- *Socratic Seminar:* listening and response tactics can be practiced along with other forms of student-directed discussion.
- *Literature Circles:* discussions can be organized throughout process.
- *Orbitals:* students participate in interest-based enrichment opportunities that inform the unit of study at hand. Orbitals tend to be short adventures for students in areas of personal interest. Process and product are determined by the learner.
- *Independent Studies/Research Projects:* students are matched with expert advisors.
- *Expert Writers and Expert Researchers:* students are encouraged to work with those immersed in the practice and profession.
- *Publication and Sharing:* students can submit work through participation in literary and/or book clubs to encourage the refinement of knowledge, understanding, and skills.

Figure 8.47 Models and Strategies for the Practitioner in English and Language Arts

---

Scaffolding for the Practitioner in English/Language Arts

- Provide specific feedback (from the teacher and outside "experts") on various design elements in the experiment.
- Incorporate library and technology support to enhance expertise in advanced research methods and organization of information.
- Use student-centered critiques based on evidence.
- Emphasize research ethics.
- Encourage understanding of research design and the role of research design in the process.
- Use performance-based assessments with specific feedback aimed at growth.
- Allow for experience in conducting a literature review as part of the research process.
- Provide interest-based opportunities to support learner inquiry into topics of personal interest.

Figure 8.48 Scaffolding for the Practitioner in English and Language Arts

The practitioner does need support and sometimes direct instruction or modeling in new areas. One example is research ethics. It isn't until the practitioner stage that the sophistication of research and the audience for reporting is so advanced that the learner will likely grapple with this topic, but it is critical in the development of the practitioner when expertise is the goal.

The Expert in English and Language Arts

Experts on the English and language arts continuum appreciate the richness of the written and spoken word and seek opportunities to experience new works and to create their own contributions to bodies of research and literary works. The expert applies the process skills associated with English and language arts with a focus on continual refinement to the most specific of skills, but all the time understanding the role of the skill in the bigger picture of communication. Figures 8.49 and 8.50 outline the characteristics of experts and the opportunities needed for their continued growth.

Expert

- Demonstrates knowledge, reflection, creativity, and critical analysis of language arts skills and concepts across a wide variety of disciplines
- Applies the wide range of skills associated with effective oral and written communication, reading, and research with automaticity
- Reading, writing, speaking, and researching lead to personal fulfillment beyond the goals of learning and the exchange of information
- Appreciates the power of the written and spoken word
- Questions the accepted conventions and rules
- Experiments with methods to communicate and develop greater understanding
- Practices in all areas (i.e., written and oral communication, reading, and research)

Figure 8.49 Characteristics of the Expert in English and Language Arts

---

Opportunities to Support Continued Growth for the Expert

- Publishing in literary magazines
- Collaborating with practitioners and other experts
- Acting as a reviewer for peer-reviewed journals and publishing companies
- Teaching graduate and undergraduate courses

Figure 8.50 Supporting Growth for Experts in English and Language Arts

Planning the Path Toward Expertise in English and Language Arts

The target for all students on the AID continuum is expertise. But expertise is not the end point. Experts still need to be challenged and afforded opportunities to grow. The following glimpse into an Advanced Placement composition course illustrates the importance of continued challenge for students that are working at the expert level on the continuum.

Identify Desired Results

Mrs. Smith's Advanced Placement Composition/Journalistic Writing is a writing course built upon journalistic techniques while employing critical thinking and reading. Newspapers, news magazines, current fiction and nonfiction, as well as many of the traditional British authors are read by the students. The students discuss and analyze the texts through writing. Students do not have to be gifted to take the course, but they do have to have an interest, strong parental support, a teacher recommendation, and a firm commitment to writing. At the end of the year, students take the Advanced Placement Language and Composition test. If students earn a sufficient score on the test, they can earn freshman English composition credits. The objective of the course is for students to become skilled readers of prose written in a variety of periods, disciplines, and rhetorical contexts, and become skilled writers who compose for a variety of purposes. In order to do this, students should be able to apply effective strategies and techniques in their own writing. They should be able to move effectively through the stages of the writing process, with flexibility and application of the skills inquiry through research. They should also be able to produce expository, analytical, and argumentative compositions that focus on a complex central idea. The students should also be able to develop ideas with appropriate evidence drawn from primary and/or secondary sources determining the credibility of the sources.

Determine Acceptable Evidence

Mrs. Smith has a variety of students enrolled in the course. Most of the students plan on attending college, and all of them love to write. Preassessment data indicate that most students need to develop a more stylistic maturity in their prose as well as the development of interpretive skills. Most students also need to be able to have more opportunities to use writing as the vehicle to analyze text in a thoughtful manner. The assessment does indicate that a few students have expertise with writing. Analysis of these writing samples indicates a clear stylistic maturity not shown by the other students. The writing from these students shows they have the ability to create and sustain an argument, and they understand that their writing is an important tool to convey their opinions and ideas. The writings have coherent explanations, clear transitions, and use evidence from primary sources they read over the summer.

Plan the Instructional Sequence Using Appropriate Models and Strategies

Mrs. Smith recognizes from the assessment that she needs to provide some mentorship opportunities for those students who did well on the assessment. As she works through her units for the year, she identifies points in every unit where those students can work with identified mentors in journalism and in the publishing industry. She works on developing activities in the various units that will allow them to also publish for the newspaper and for literary magazines. All students, by the end of the course, will be responsible for publishing, but in order for the students who are already quite skilled at writing, she cannot leave her instructional plans as they were written. Mrs. Smith also includes ongoing assessments for all of the students in the class in preparation for involving more students in the mentorship and independent studies.

With this responsive instructional plan designed, Mrs. Smith gives careful consideration to her role as teacher. While she has seen the emergence of expertise in some students by the end of this course in the past, she has never recognized such advanced skills in a group of students. With a new plan for their work, she also realizes that her facilitative skills are going to have to be honed as this plan is going to challenge her students in ways she has not seen before. And, while somewhat intimidating, it is exciting to anticipate their production of new works. Mrs. Smith also decides to keep an electronic journal of her teaching and reflection throughout the course. As she explains to the students, "I'm taking a creative, professional risk here and I need to regularly reflect on what is working and not working for everyone, including me."

Using the AID Continuum

There is something quite artful in the Parallel Curriculum Model (PCM) when the AID continuum is applied. The solid foundation for curriculum design in the PCM—partnered with attention to the development of knowledge, understanding, skills, habits of mind, and attitudes of the learner through AID—transcends the flat expectations of a learning experience focused on minimum competency. The focus on the development of expertise in the PCM and the AID continuum is so much richer than the empty promise of learner growth as defined by success on state mandated testing and No Child Left Behind (NCLB). If students are to be successful in the 21st century, transferrable skills defined by expertise in the discipline must be the focus, not isolated facts and topical understandings, both of which are readily forgotten. We encourage teachers who are searching for a more focused and purposeful avenue for designing curriculum and instruction to give consideration to the use of the AID continuum and its alignment of student characteristics and needs with appropriate curriculum, instruction, and scaffolds. The AID applied in the context of the PCM assists teachers and curriculum designers in honoring all students as experts-in-the-making.

Resource A

Teaching Resources for Chapter 8

Science Resources

Play-Debrief-Replay

Wassermann, S., & Ivany, J. W. (1996). *The new teaching elementary science: Who's afraid of spiders?* (2nd ed.). New York: Teachers College Press.

Experiments

Fantastic Online Science Experiments!: http://www.questacon.edu.au/html/activities.html
Exploratorium: The Museum of Art, Science, and Human Perception: http://www.exploratorium.edu/index.html

Cooperative Learning

"How Long Does Trash Last?" A Cooperative Learning Activity: http://www.education-world.com/a_lesson/03/lp308-04.shtml

Kaplan's Frame of the Discipline

Kaplan, S. (1974). *Providing programs for the gifted and talented: A handbook.* Camarillo, CA: Ventura County Schools.

Exit Tickets

Tomlinson, C. A. (2003). *Fulfilling the promise of the differentiated classroom.* Alexandria, VA: Association for Supervision and Curriculum Development.
Differentiation (sample exit cards): http://www.riley.ccsd21.org/Resources/tech_differentiation.html

Question Stems

Meier, L. N., Hand, B., Hockenberry, L., & Wise, K. (2008). *Questions, claims, and evidence: The important place of argument in children's science writing.* Portsmouth, NH: Heinemann.

Mind Mapping

Inspiration (software that facilitates mind mapping and concept mapping): http://www.inspiration.com

Freemind (software that facilitates mind mapping and concept mapping): http://freemind.sourceforge.net

Four Question Strategy

Teaching With Inquiry: http://www.science-house.org/workshops/web/4question.html

Exploratorium: The Museum of Art, Science, and Human Perception (science fair competitions): http://www.exploratorium.edu/lc/pathfinders/scifairs/

The WWW Science Fair Library (link to science fairs accessible through the Internet): http://physics.usc.edu/ScienceFairs/

Case Studies

Cothron, J. H., Giese, R. N., & Rezba, R. J. (2000). *Students and research.* Kendall/Hunt: Dubuque, IA.

Center for Gifted Education. (2008). *What's the matter? A physical science unit for high-ability learners in grades 2-3.* Waco, TX: Prufrock Press.

Scientific Software and Probeware

Mindstorms (system created by Lego equipped with a variety of sensory probes) http://mindstorms.lego.com

Access Excellence: The National Health Museum (information on using probeware in the classroom): http://www.accessexcellence.org/LC/TE/PW/

Math Resources

Play-Debrief-Replay

Wasserman, S. (2000). *Serious players in the primary classroom: Empowering children through active learning experiences.* New York: Teachers College Press.

Kaplan's Frame of the Discipline

Kaplan, S. (1974). *Providing programs for the gifted and talented: A handbook.* Camarillo, CA: Ventura County Schools.

Exit Tickets

Tomlinson, C. A. (2003). *Fulfilling the promise of the differentiated classroom.* Alexandria, VA: Association for Supervision and Curriculum Development.

Popham, W. J. (2008). *Transformative assessment.* Alexandria, VA: Association for Supervision and Curriculum Development.

Concept Mapping

Inspiration (software that facilitates mind mapping and concept mapping): http://www .inspiration.com

Freemind (software that facilitates mind mapping and concept mapping): http://freemind.source forge.net

Rubrics

teAchnology (one of many places to start with rubrics): http://www.teach-nology.com/ web_tools/rubrics/math

Arter, J., & McTighe, J. (2000). *Scoring rubrics in the classroom.* Thousand Oaks, CA: Corwin Press.

Process Logs

Sperry Smith, S. (2008). *Early childhood mathematics.* Upper Saddle River, NJ: Allyn & Bacon, Inc.

Simulations

The Stockmarket Game: http://www.smg2000.org

Socratic Seminar of Paideia: http://www.paideai.org

History Resources

Kaplan's Frame of the Discipline

Kaplan, S. (1974). *Providing programs for the gifted and talented: A handbook.* Camarillo, CA: Ventura County Schools.

Concept-Based Curriculum

Erickson, H. L. (2007). *Concept-based curriculum for the thinking classroom.* Thousand Oaks, CA: Corwin Press.

Exit Tickets

Tomlinson, C. A. (2003). *Fulfilling the promise of the differentiated classroom.* Alexandria, VA: Association for Supervision and Curriculum Development.

Popham, W. J. (2008). *Transformative assessment.* Alexandria, VA: Association for Supervision and Curriculum Development.

Mind Mapping

Inspiration (software that facilitates mind mapping and concept mapping): http:// www.inspiration.com

Freemind (software that facilitates mind mapping and concept mapping): http:// free mind.sourceforge.net

Webquests

Webquest.org (an extensive list of webquests ready for classroom use) http://webquest.org

History Alive!

History Alive! America's Past (a tutorial on this resource): http://tutorial.teachtci.com

Dimensions of Learning

Marzano, R. J. (1992). *A different kind of classroom: Teaching with dimensions of learning.* Alexandria, VA: Association for Supervision and Curriculum Development.

Error Analysis

Marzano, R. J., & Kendall, J. S. (2006). *The new taxonomy of educational objectives* (2nd ed.). Thousand Oaks, CA: Corwin Press.

Historical Investigation

Marzano, R. J., Brandt, R. S., Hughes, C. S., Jones, B. F., Pressisen, B. Z., Rankin, S. C., & Suhor, C. (1988). *Dimensions of thinking: A framework for curriculum and instruction.* Alexandria, VA: Association for Supervision and Curriculum Development.

Developing Documentaries

C-SPAN's Student Cam (an annual documentary contest for students) http://www.student cam.org/About.html

English and Language Arts Resources

Interactive Notation System for Effective Reading and Thinking

Vaughan, J. L., & Estes, T. H. (1986). *Reading and reasoning beyond the primary grades.* Upper Saddle River, NJ: Allyn & Bacon, Inc.

Entry Points

Gardner, H. (1993). *The unschooled mind: How children think and how schools should teach.* New York: Basic Books.

Literature Circles

Daniels, H. (2001). *Literature circles: Voice and choice in book clubs and reading groups.* Portland, ME: Stenhouse Publishers.

Rubrics

teAchnology (one of many places to start with rubrics): http://www.teach-nology.com/web_tools/rubrics/math

Arter, J., & McTighe, J. (2000). *Scoring rubrics in the classroom.* Thousand Oaks, CA: Corwin Press.

References

Amabile, T. M. (1983). *The social psychology of creativity.* New York: Springer-Verlag.

Ausubel, D. P. (1968). *Educational psychology: A cognitive view.* New York: Holt, Rinehart & Winston.

Bandura, A. (1977). Self-efficacy: Toward a unifying theory of behavioral change. *Psychological Review, 84,* 191–215.

Bateson, M. C. (1989). *Composing a life.* New York: Atlantic Monthly Press.

Beatty, P. (1984). *Turn homeward, Hannalee.* New York: Morrow.

Beatty, P. (1987). *Charley Skedaddle.* New York: Morrow.

Beatty, P. (1991). *Jayhawker.* New York: Morrow.

Binet, A., & Simon, T. (1916). *The development of intelligence in children.* Baltimore, MD: Williams & Wilkins.

Bloom, B., Englehart, M., Furst, E., Hill, W., & Krathwhol, D. (1956). *Taxonomy of educational objectives. Handbook I: Cognitive domain.* New York: Longmans Green.

Bolotin, N., & Bolotin, A. (1994). *For home and country: A Civil War scrapbook.* New York: Lodestar.

Bourman, A. (1996). *Meeting of minds.* Portland, ME: Walch.

Brandt, R. (1998). *Powerful learning.* Alexandria, VA: Association for Supervision and Curriculum Development.

Brown, M. (1949). *The important book.* New York: Harper & Row.

Bruner, J. S. (1960). *The process of education.* Cambridge, MA: Harvard University Press.

Bruner, J. S. (1966). *Toward a theory of instruction.* Cambridge, MA: Harvard University Press.

Burns, D. E. (1993). *A six-phase model for the explicit teaching of thinking skills.* Storrs, CT: University of Connecticut, National Research Center on the Gifted and Talented.

Collier, J. L., & Collier, C. (1994). *With every drop of blood.* New York: Delacorte.

Collins, M., & Amabile, T. M. (1999). Motivation and creativity. In R. J. Sternberg (Ed.), *Handbook of creativity* (pp. 297–312). New York: Cambridge University Press.

Connecticut State Department of Education. (1998a). *The Connecticut framework: K–12 curricular goals and standards.* Hartford, CT: Author.

Connecticut State Department of Education. (1998b). *Regulations concerning state education certification, permits, and authorization.* Hartford, CT: Author.

Connecticut State Department of Education. (1999). *Connecticut's common core of teaching.* Hartford, CT: Author.

Cooney, B. (1996). *Eleanor.* New York: Viking.

Costa, A., & Kallick, B. (2000). *Discovering and exploring habits of mind.* Alexandria, VA: Association for Supervision and Curriculum Development.

Csikszentmihalyi, M. (1990). *Flow: The psychology of optimal experience.* New York: Harper & Row.

Csikszentmihalyi, M., Rathunde, K., & Whalen, S. (1993). *Talented teenagers: The roots of success and failure.* New York: Cambridge University Press.

Delpit, L. (1995). *Other people's children: Cultural conflict in the classroom.* New York: New Press.

Dewey, J. (1938). *Experience and education.* New York: Macmillan.

Douglass, F. (1855). *My bondage and my freedom.* New York: Miller, Orton and Mulligan.

Dunn, R., & Griggs, S. (1995). *Multiculturalism and learning style: Teaching and counseling adolescents.* Westport, CT: Praeger.

Dweck, C. S. (1999). *Self-theories: Their role in motivation, personality and development.* Philadelphia: Taylor and Francis/Psychology Press.

Dweck, C. S. (2006). *Mindset: The new psychology of success.* New York: Random House.

Erickson, H. L. (2007). *Concept-based curriculum and instruction for the thinking classroom.* Thousand Oaks, CA: Corwin Press.

Feldman, D. (1992). Has there been a paradigm shift in gifted education? In N. Colangelo, S. G. Assouline, & D. L. Amronson (Eds.), *Talent development: Proceedings from the 1991 Henry B. and Jocelyn Wallace National Research Symposium on Talent Development* (pp. 89–94). Unionville, NY: Trillium.

Fitzhugh, G. (1857). *Cannibals all! or slaves without masters.* Richmond, VA: A. Morris.

Fleischman, P. (1996). *Dateline: Troy.* Cambridge, MA: Candlewick.

Freedman, R. (1987). *Lincoln: A photobiography.* New York: Clarion.

Gagné, R. M., & Briggs, L. J. (1979). *Principles of instructional design* (2nd ed.). New York: Holt, Rinehart & Winston.

Gardner, H. (1993). *Frames of mind: The theory of multiple intelligences.* New York: Basic Books.

Glasser, W. (1969). *Schools without failure.* New York: Harper & Row.

Grigorenko, E., & Sternberg, R. (1997). Styles of thinking, abilities, and academic performance. *Exceptional Children, 63,* 295–312.

Hoemann, G. (2001). *The American Civil War homepage.* Retrieved July 11, 2001, from http://edweb.sdsu.edu/people/bdodge/scaffold/CW/warweb.html

Howard, P. J. (1994). *An owner's manual for the brain.* Austin, TX: Leornian.

Hunt, I. (1964). *Across five Aprils.* River Grove, IL: Follett.

James, W. (1885). On the functions of cognition. *Mind, 10,* 27–44.

Jensen, E. (1998). *Teaching with the brain in mind.* Alexandria, VA: Association for Supervision and Curriculum Development.

Kaplan, S. (1974). *Providing programs for the gifted and talented: A handbook.* Camarillo, CA: Ventura County Schools.

Krathwohl, D. R., Bloom, B. S., & Masia, B. B. (1964). *Taxonomy of educational goals. Handbook II: Affective domain.* New York: Longman.

Lee, H. (1960). *To kill a mockingbird.* New York: Harper & Row.

Levy, S. (1996). *Starting from scratch.* Portsmouth, NH: Heinemann.

Library of Congress. (2000). *Selected Civil War photographs.* Retrieved July 11, 2001, from http://lcweb2.loc.gov/ammem/cwphtml/cwphome.html

Mahoney, A. S. (1998). In search of the gifted identity: From abstract concept to workable counseling constructs. *Roeper Review, 20(3),* 222–226.

Mansilla, V. B., & Gardner, H. (1998). What are the qualities of understanding? In M. S. Wiske (Ed.), *Teaching for understanding: Linking research with practice.* San Francisco: Jossey-Bass.

Marzano, R. (1992). *A different kind of classroom: Teaching with dimensions of learning.* Alexandria, VA: Association for Supervision and Curriculum Development.

Maslow, A. H. (1970). *Motivation and personality* (2nd ed.). New York: Harper & Row.

McCurdy, M. (Ed.). (1994). *Escape from slavery: The boyhood of Frederick Douglass in his own words.* New York: Alfred A. Knopf.

McKissack, P., & McKissack, F. (1991). *The story of Booker T. Washington.* Danbury, CT: Children's Press.

McQuerry, M. (2000). *Nuclear legacy: A collaborative research study with middle school students.* Columbus, OH: Battelle Press.

Mettger, Z. (1984). *Till victory is won: Black soldiers in the Civil War.* New York: E. P. Dutton.

Murphy, J. (1990). *The boys' war: Confederate and union soldiers talk about the Civil War.* New York: Clarion.

National Academy Press. (1996). *National science education standards.* Washington, DC: Author.

National Archives and Records Administration. (2001). *NARA.* Retrieved July 11, 2001, from http://www.nara.gov

National Center for History in the Schools. (1996). *National standards for history.* Los Angeles: Author.

National Research Council. (1999). *How people learn: Brain, mind, experience, and school.* Washington, DC: National Academy Press.

Olsen, A. (1987). *The Lighthouse Keeper's Daughter.* New York: Little, Brown.

Paulsen, G. (1998). *Soldier's heart.* New York: Bantam.

Phenix, P. H. (1964). *Realms of meaning.* New York: McGraw-Hill.

Piaget, J. (1928). *The child's conception of the world.* London: Routledge and Kegan Paul.

Piaget, J. (1955). *The child's construction of reality.* London: Routledge and Kegan Paul.

Reeder, C. (1989). *Shades of gray.* New York: Macmillan.

Renzulli, J. (1977). *The enrichment triad model: A guide for developing defensible programs for the gifted.* Mansfield Center, CT: Creative Learning Press.

Renzulli, J. S., Leppien, J. H., & Hayes, T. S. (2000). *The multiple menu model: A practical guide for developing differentiated curriculum.* Mansfield Center, CT: Creative Learning Press.

Rinaldi, A. (2001). *Girl in blue.* New York, NY: Scholastic.

Schlechty, P. (1997). *Inventing better schools: An action plan for educational reform.* San Francisco: Jossey-Bass.

Schwartz, D. M. (1985). *How much is a million?* New York: Lothrop, Lee & Shepard.

Sís, P. (1997). *Starry messenger: Galileo Galilei.* New York: Farrar, Straus & Giroux.

Sís, P. (1998). *Tibet: Through the red box.* New York: Farrar, Straus & Giroux.

Sternberg, R. J. (1985). *Beyond IQ: A triarchic theory of intelligence.* New York: Cambridge University Press.

Sullivan, M. (1993). *A meta-analysis of experimental research studies based on the Dunn & Dunn learning styles model and its relationship to academic achievement and performance.* Unpublished doctoral dissertation, St. John's University, Queens, NY.

Taba, H. (1962). *Curriculum and practice.* New York: Harcourt, Brace & World.

Taylor, M. (1991). *Harriet Tubman.* Broomall, PA: Chelsea House.

Tomlinson, C. (1999). *The differentiated classroom: Responding to the needs of all learners.* Alexandria, VA: Association for Supervision and Curriculum Development.

Tomlinson, C. (2001). *How to differentiate instruction in mixed-ability classrooms* (2nd ed.). Alexandria, VA: Association for Supervision and Curriculum Development.

Tomlinson, C. (2003*). Fulfilling the promise of the differentiated classroom: Strategies and tools for responsive teaching.* Alexandria, VA: Association for Supervision and Curriculum Development.

Tomlinson, C., Kaplan, S., Purcell, J. Leppien, J., Burns, D., & Strickland, C. (2006). *The parallel curriculum in the classroom: Book 1.* Thousand Oaks, CA: Corwin Press.

Tyler, R. (1949). *Basic principles of curriculum and instruction.* Chicago: University of Chicago Press.

U. S. Department of Labor. (1992). *What work requires of schools: A SCANS report for America 2000.* Washington, DC: Government Printing Office.

Vygotsky, L. S. (1962). *Thought and language.* Cambridge, MA: MIT Press.

Vygotsky, L. S. (1978). *Mind in society.* Cambridge, MA: Harvard University Press.

Washington, B. T. (1963). *Up from slavery.* New York: Doubleday.

Wassermann, S. (1988). Play-Debrief-Replay: An instructional model for science. *Childhood Education, 64,* 232–234.

Whitehead, A. N. (1929). The rhythm of education. In A. N. Whitehead (Ed.), *The aims of education.* New York: Macmillan.

Wiggins, G., & McTighe, J. (1998). *Understanding by design.* Alexandria, VA: Association for Supervision.

Index

**CORWIN
PRESS**

The Corwin Press logo—a raven striding across an open book—represents the union of courage and learning. Corwin Press is committed to improving education for all learners by publishing books and other professional development resources for those serving the field of PreK–12 education. By providing practical, hands-on materials, Corwin Press continues to carry out the promise of its motto: **"Helping Educators Do Their Work Better."**

NATIONAL ASSOCIATION FOR
Gifted Children

MISSION STATEMENT

The National Association for Gifted Children (NAGC) is an organization of parents, teachers, educators, other professionals, and community leaders who unite to address the unique needs of children and youth with demonstrated gifts and talents as well as those children who may be able to develop their talent potential with appropriate educational experiences. We support and develop policies and practices that encourage and respond to the diverse expressions of gifts and talents in children and youth from all cultures, racial and ethnic backgrounds, and socioeconomic groups. NAGC supports and engages in research and development, staff development, advocacy, communication, and collaboration with other organizations and agencies who strive to improve the quality of education for all students.